The World Trade Organization Millennium Round

The failure to launch a new round of multilateral trade negotiations at the World Trade Organization's Ministerial Conference in Seattle in December 1999 has clearly demonstrated that, at present, no clear perspective for the future course of international trade policies exists. The issues that may enter the agenda of a 'millennium round' under the auspices of the WTO therefore merit careful analysis of their likely economic, social and political impact.

The World Trade Organization Millennium Round covers these substantive issues and the broader implications of a potential trade round. The contributors argue persuasively for meaningful reforms at both national and international levels, and a clear case for freer trade emerges from their analyses. This comprehensive and up-to-date volume provides:

- a guide to the policies, interests and perspectives of the major players;
- broad coverage of the economic issues and the politics involved in the various areas of international trade policy making;
- an analysis of the necessity and the likelihood of further liberalization in both old and new sectors as well as of systematic and institutional issues; and
- recommendations for change urgently required to reform both the WTO as an organization and the international trading system in order to meet the demands of a global economy.

This book is a significant resource that will be indispensable to students, professionals and all people seeking to increase their understanding of this highly topical subject.

Klaus Günter Deutsch and **Bernhard Speyer** are Senior Economists at Deutsche Bank Research.

Routledge Studies in International Business and the World Economy

The World Trade Organization Millennium Round

Freer Trade in the Twenty-first Century

Edited by Klaus Günter Deutsch and Bernhard Speyer

London and New York

First published 2001
by Routledge
11 New Fetter Lane, London EC4P 4EE

Simultaneously published in the USA and Canada
by Routledge
29 West 35th Street, New York, NY 10001

Routledge is an imprint of the Taylor & Francis Group

Distributed exclusively in India by Oxford University Press

Typeset in Goudy by Taylor & Francis Books Ltd
Printed and bound in Great Britain by Biddles Ltd, Guildford and
King's Lynn

British Library Cataloguing in Publication Data
A catalogue record for this book is available from the British Library

Library of Congress Cataloging-in-Publication Data
The World Trade Organization Millennium Round :
freer trade in the twenty-first century /
Klaus Günter Deutsch and Bernhard Speyer.
p. cm.
Includes bibliographical references and index.
1. Free trade. 2. Foreign trade regulation.
3. Commercial policy. 4. International trade.
5. World Trade Organization. I. Speyer, Bernhard.
HF1713 .W67 2001
382'.71–dc21 00-059259

ISBN 0–415–23815–3 ✓

Contents

Illustrations

Figures

Tables

ERRATUM

The World Trade Organization Millennium Round   0-415-23815-3
Klaus Günter Deutsch and Bernhard Speyer

The Publishers and editors would like to apologise for the omission of the Notes on Contributors:

Stefan Bach, German Institute for Economic Research, Economic Structures and Public Sector Department, Königin-Luise-Straße 5, 14195 Berlin, Germany.

Dietrich Barth, European Commission, DG Trade – M 1, Rue de la Loi 200, Brussels, Belgium.

Richard Blackhurst, former Director of Economic Research, GATT/WTO Secretariat (1985-1997), Adjunct Professor of Economics, Graduate Institute of International studies, 1211 Geneva 21, Switzerland.

Klaus Günter Deutsch, Senior Economist, Deutsche Bank Research, Unter den Linden 13-15, D-10117 Berlin, Germany.

Wendy Dobson, Professor and Director, Institute for International Business, Rotman School of Management, University of Toronto, 105 St. George Street, Toronto, Ontario, M5S 3EG6, Canada.

Georg Erber, German Institute for Economic Research, Industry and Technology, Königin-Luise-Straße 5, 14195 Berlin, Germany.

Andreas Falke, Lecturer in International Politics, Georg-August-Universität, Göttingen and Principle Economic Specialist, American Embassy, Neustädtische Kirchstr. 4-5, 10117 Berlin, Germany.

J. Michael Finger, Lead Economist, Development Research Group, The World Bank, 1818 H Street N.W., Washington D.C 20433, USA.

Christopher Findlay, Professor, Asia Pacific School of Economics and Management, The Australian National University, Canberra, ACT 0200, Australia.

Carsten Fink, Economist, International Trade, Development Research Group, The World Bank, 1818 H Street N.W., Washington D.C 20433, USA.

Gerhard Fisch, SPD Parliamentarian Group, Platz der Republik 1, 11011 Berlin, Germany.

Hiroya Ichikawa, Professor of Economics, Sophia University, 7-1 Kioi - Cho, Chiyoda – Ku, Tokyo 102-8554, Japan.

Cord Jakobeit, Director, Institute for African Affairs, Neuer Jungfernstieg 21, 20354 Hamburg, Germany.

Rolf J. Langhammer, Professor and Head of Research Department "Development Economics and Global Integration", Kiel Institute of World Economics POB 4309, 24100 Kiel, Germany.

Matthias Lücke, Head of Research Team "Industrialisation and International Trade", Kiel Institute of World Economics POB 4309, 24100 Kiel, Germany.

Maki Kunimatsu, Keidanren Kaikan, 1-9-4, Otemachi, Chiyoda-ku, Tokyo 100-8188.

Bernhard May, Senior Research Fellow, German Society for Foreign Affairs, Rauchstr. 18, 10787 Berlin, Germany.

Patrick A. Messerlin, Professor of Economics, Institut d'Etudes Politique, 187 Boulevard St. Germain, 75007 Paris, France.

Henry R. Nau, Professor of Political Science and International Affairs, Elliott School of International Affairs, The George Washington University, Stuart Hall 202C, 20113 G. Street, Washington D.C. 20052, USA.

Phedon Nicolaides, Professor and Head of Unit on EC Policies and the Internal Market, European Institute of Public Administration, P.O. Box 1229, 6201 BE Maastricht, The Netherlands.

Sylvia Ostry, Distinguished Research Fellow, Centre for International Studies, University of Toronto, Munk Centre for International Studies, 1 Devonshire Place, Toronto, Ontario, M5S 3K7, Canada.

Carlos A. Primo Braga, Manager, Information for Development Program, The World Bank, 1818 H Street N.W., Washington D.C 20433, USA.

Philip von Schöppenthau, EPPA European Public Policy Advisors, 2 Place du Luxembourg, 1150 Brussels, Belgium.

Philip Schuler, Doctoral Candidate, Department of Economics, University of Maryland, College Park, MD 20742, USA.

Bernhard Speyer, Senior Economist, Deutsche Bank Research, Grosse Gallusstr. 10-14, 60272 Frankfurt/M, Germany.

Stefan Tangermann, Professor, University Göttingen, Institut für Agrarökonomie, Platz der Göttinger Sieben 5, 37073 Göttingen, Germany.

Tony Warren, Professor, Asia Pacific School of Economics and Management, The Australian National University, Canberra, ACT 0200, Australia.

Stephen Woolcock, Lecturer in International Relations, London School of Economics & Political Science, Houghton Street, London WC2A 2AE, UK.

Preface

The multilateral trading system has not developed along a smooth path since the early 1980s. On the contrary, trade policy has experienced long periods of only minimal progress, occasional full stops and sudden leaps forward. In December 1999, trade policy ground to a halt again at the Ministerial Conference of the World Trade Organization, which was held in Seattle in the United States of America. Hopes for a new round of multilateral trade negotiations, a 'Millennium Round', did not materialise.

The Uruguay Round, whose long and winding road stretched from Punta del Este in 1986 to Marrakech in 1994, took place around the time we were studying at the Free University of Berlin, while the early years of the WTO roughly coincided with our PhD dissertations. Trade policy again leapt forward in the late 1990s, when several sector liberalisation agreements were reached. All seemed to develop pretty well.

When, in the summer of 1999, our lunchtime talk again reverted to the prospects for a new round of multilateral trade negotiations in the WTO, we wondered what kind of economic benefits a new round might yield and how the politics might evolve. We concluded that we, on our own, did not have a clear picture of several complex issues that would be of importance. We therefore decided to launch a book project on the 'Millennium Round'.

We gratefully acknowledge the commitments that the authors have made. All were asked to explain the issues in a non-technical way, to discuss the interests of the main players in their respective fields, to offer recommendations and to give judgements on the likely course of action. We are particularly thankful that all authors upheld their commitments after the 'Battle in Seattle', occasional pessimism (realism?) notwithstanding.

Many thanks are due to Robert Langham at Routledge, whose work has made a speedy processing and production of this volume possible. We also gratefully acknowledge the help of Victor Bright and Gareth Jones, who substantially improved the English of several contributions, including our own.

Klaus Günter Deutsch and Bernhard Speyer
Berlin
May 2000

Part I
International trade policies

1 The Millennium Round

Prospects for trade liberalisation in the twenty-first century

Bernhard Speyer and Klaus Günter Deutsch

Introduction

In the 1990s, the internationalisation[1] of economic activity made a great leap forward. The long boom in the US economy, the transition to the European Single Market and European Economic and Monetary Union, and economic growth in Asia and Latin America created an environment that enabled international trade to prosper. The internationalisation of economic activity also extended to foreign direct investment and global capital flows. The pursuit of economic growth using sound macroeconomic policies, market economics at the microeconomic level, trade liberalisation and international financial integration became the mantra almost everywhere around the globe.

Even though several 'emerging market economies' suffered severe financial and economic crises in the late 1990s, the world economy did not lapse into a recession. Despite this shock, the international trading system proved surprisingly stable. The regime based on the World Trade Organization came to be widely regarded as the cornerstone of a market-oriented world economy. The People's Republic of China, one of the trading nations that is not yet a member of the WTO, is on the verge of joining the institution. There is no longer any rival power to oppose the system – a situation unthinkable fifteen years ago. There is a virtually global intellectual consensus – among governments at least – that liberal, rules-based trade is a desirable policy objective. The unprecedented rise of democratic governance and economic openness should also bode well for free trade.

Despite these breathtaking developments, the international trading system has entered a phase of great policy uncertainty. There is less threat of a sudden bubbling up of protectionism, which then leads to a collapse of the world economy, as in the aftermath of the Great Depression of the 1930s. The real threat is that the structures of international governance established in successive rounds of multilateral trade negotiations fail to be adapted to a changing world economy and gradually become less relevant to traders and governments. The symptoms of crisis are easy to recognise: policy squabbles abound between powerful players; the US Congress discusses whether the USA should leave the WTO; the EU often finds itself at odds with rules established with its consent and shows no readiness to correct its behaviour; the least developed countries cannot afford the implementation of elaborate rules; and large and small traders (firms, farmers, electronic service providers) increasingly take trade policy into the private realm of single-handed talks with governments about changing this or that rule. Finally, the 1999 meeting of trade ministers of WTO member states in Seattle, USA, brought into the open a certain amount of disagreement on the very usefulness of multilateral trading rules, the desirability of a new round of trade negotiations, the potential agenda, the benefits and the risks.

As in previous phases of pre-negotiating a new round of trade talks, confusion reigns and controversies abound (see Winham 1986 on the Tokyo Round; Croome 1995 and Preeg 1995 on the Uruguay Round). New ideas about what to tackle at the multilateral level have to match the policy preferences of the powerful players and also, increasingly, of the developing countries. A balance has to be sought between market liberalisation, making rules and institutional reform. Whereas member states used the Tokyo Round as the first round encompassing far more than just tariff cuts to focus on rule making, they turned the Uruguay Round into an even larger venture covering new sectors and issues (on the results, see also Whalley and Hamilton 1996; Ostry 1997). This included making rules in areas such as services, intellectual property rights, anti-dumping and investment; opening up markets in agriculture, textiles and clothing, as well as tariff cuts and reductions in non-tariff barriers; and institutional reform, which culminated in the establishment of the WTO itself and the creation of a binding mechanism of conflict resolution, the dispute settlement mechanism (DSM), one of the most supranational of legal arrangements.

The trade debate has not stopped since then (Krueger 1998; Schott 1998). A multitude of issues have been raised worldwide that could or should be dealt with in the WTO. The number of parties to the debate has increased. Apart from traders and governments themselves, unions, non-governmental organisations (NGOs) embracing social or environmental purposes, and others are putting forward their demands. Almost every conceivable international economic problem has been linked to trade policy by some important player on the globe.

This implies that it is no longer possible to strike trade deals without public scrutiny. Even disregarding the riots, the media attention devoted to the Seattle ministerial conference was certainly far more intense than anything that Punta del Este saw almost fifteen years ago.

However, not everything is new. The fundamental mechanics of trade negotiations remain unchanged. Trade politics is still a 'two-level game', where governments bargain with each other at the international level and have to sell the results of those bargains at home (Putnam 1988; Evans *et al.* 1993). The stance and the room for manoeuvre of each government is therefore circumscribed by its influence in international trade diplomacy as well as by the demands and the influence of domestic interest groups favouring or opposing liberalisation and rule making in the multilateral trading system.

Governments also still face the perennial dilemma of being torn between strengthening international rules and preserving national autonomy. Governments know only too well that the stability of the international trade regime, indeed of the global economic system, is in their own interests, given that international trade accounts for a higher share of GDP than ten years ago in most countries and given the interdependencies stemming from the international flows of capital, investment and knowledge. It is fairly obvious that international trade will flourish if governments pledge to accept some basic rules. Of course, this constrains national autonomy. As trade increasingly affects public policies pursued for entirely different reasons inside the borders of the nation-state and not only covers tariffs and other border restrictions, multilateral trade rules have to extend to the realm of domestic affairs. National autonomy has to be rebalanced with the cross-border effects of economic internationalisation.

Trade policy has moved firmly into the area of deeper integration. Trade negotiations are no longer just, or even primarily, about telling governments what not to do at the border but are instead about prescribing what to do inside. Almost all border measures (e.g. tariffs, quotas) indisputably had a protectionist motivation; consequently, trade liberalisation was all about shifting rents between different groups of society and sharing the efficiency gains to be reaped from trade liberalisation. By contrast, rules and regulations within borders have a multitude of motivations, making it more difficult for governments to find acceptance at the domestic level.

At the same time, at the international level, trade negotiations are no longer just about swapping market-access concessions but are about dealing with the intricacies of deeper integration issues. This implies that new forms of bargains must be struck between WTO member states, bargains that take into account different stages of development and different economic and social orders.

The players are also changing. Deeper integration has brought into the game representatives of 'civil society' that often have little knowledge of, or little interest in, the purely economic side of international rule making or trade and investment liberalisation. Neither the institutions – first and foremost the WTO – nor the processes of international trade negotiation are designed to accommodate these groups. At the same time, another trend can be observed: multinational companies, which had hitherto been vocal supporters of the multilateral trade rounds and in doing so had often tilted the domestic balance in favour of liberalisation, have remained rather silent. There are a number of possible explanations for this: either they are content with the market access available; or they use technology to circumvent barriers; or they are increasingly in a position to pursue trade policy privately.

While new players enter the scene, the mature players seem to have forgotten their script. For almost fifty years, the USA took the lead. Trade policy was a presidential matter, and Congress delegated its powers to the president. US President Bill Clinton concluded the Uruguay Round, which his predecessors Ronald Reagan and George Bush had launched and negotiated to a large extent. In Seattle in December 1999, President Clinton could not persuade WTO member states to agree to start a new round of trade talks. Many observers noticed a lack of interest in a new comprehensive trade round on the part of the US government. This can partly be explained by the fact that after ten consecutive years of strong economic growth the USA may not perceive any urgent need for the extra economic boost that would flow from trade liberalisa- tion. In addition, a strong and vibrant USA was undoubtedly in no mood to grant substantial concessions to bring other nations to the negotiating table. But the stance taken by the USA reflects a more fundamental change in attitude. Ever since the ratifications of the North American Free Trade Agreement in 1993 and of the Uruguay Round results in 1994, it has been impossible to forge a coalition and provide the intellectual leadership for further liberalisation. US trade policy thus has become tangled in domestic disputes. This leaves the WTO ship without a captain – just at a time when the growing heterogeneity of WTO membership means that more leadership is required rather than less.

However, there is no easy substitute for US leadership. The prime contender is the European Union, which certainly made a strong pitch to position itself as the heir to the American throne; it surprised everyone by presenting a wide-ranging, substantial negotiating position that even laid an extensive groundwork for some of the more difficult deeper integration issues, such as competition and investment policy. However, few, and possibly not even the EU itself, would seriously claim that it is yet capable of carrying the world with it.

Uncertainty therefore abounds about the politics of global trade talks and the desirable objectives of trade policy. At present, there is a serious possibility that Seattle may prove to have been the end of multilateral trade negotiations. This is not a victory for the protesters but rather a reflection of the above- mentioned structural changes in the world economy since the end of the Uruguay Round. This is not to say that the world will return to outright protec- tionism and economic isolationism beyond the usual measure of restrictive practices (anti-dumping actions, special safeguards, and so on). The multilateral trading system is very robust; the rules are by and large intact, dispute settle- ment is used widely and observed in most cases; and there is little sign of large trading nations resorting to full-blown protectionist instruments. Noticeably, even at the height of the financial crises of 1997/98 countries did not shy away from their commitments. Also, technological progress in general and electronic commerce in particular make it more difficult to impose trade barriers, although this should not be exaggerated, as governments retain substantial tools at their disposal to hinder trade.

However, avoiding a relapse into protectionism is not the same as moving forward with the multilateral trading system. It will certainly require much stronger political leadership, both domestically and internationally, than in previous rounds to bring together the widely diverging interests of WTO member states, business interests and 'civil society', and of governments and their citizens. It will also take a lot of effort to finally open up those industries that have escaped liberalisation for fifty years. Thus, at the start of the millen- nium, the world trading system is clearly at the crossroads: on the one hand, between maintaining a workable if somewhat precarious *status quo*, which may be complemented by a few sectoral and/or plurilateral liberalisation agreements; and on the other hand, a serious if arduous effort to lay the foundations for a global, rules-based international trade regime that, while paying due respect to the interests of all countries and all groups in society, provides the appropriate framework for a global economy.

Summary of the book

The contributions to this book discuss the interests and policies of major trading nations, most of the topics that have been on the agenda for the pre-negotiations of a new round for some years now, and some of the systemic issues that trade policy makers around the globe will have to tackle in one way or another. The stakes are high, and the issues require serious study.

All our contributors pledged to provide easy-to-understand explanations of the issues, to describe the positions of key players in the respective games and to specu-late on the prospects for action. They also agreed to provide some simple and balanced recommendations on how a particular policy problem could possibly be approached in a potentially up-coming new round of trade negotiations.

International trade policies

Andreas Falke gives an introduction to US trade policy making for a new round. He argues that domestic politics in the USA has changed in the 1990s. Despite the long period of economic growth, the traditional champions of free trade in the US business and farming community could not maintain their policy dominance. Instead, other interest groups have gained in prominence, and the US Congress did not provide President Clinton with the wherewithal of international trade leadership: 'fast-track' authority. However, the USA launched some important market-access initiatives in the WTO, produced tangible results for export-oriented groups and also used the DSM quite actively. The US stance regarding a new round has been shaped by a multitude of domestic considerations. Apart from exporters, NGOs have become an influen-tial constituency, which the Clinton administration has courted publicly. At least until Seattle, the USA was unable to square the circle. The need to handle the very diverse domestic constituencies conflicted with the requirements of seeking international consensus on an agenda for a new round of talks. Falke argues that once the domestic political storms over the potential risks and costs of 'globalisation' are gone, the USA may well return to multilateral trade policy leadership. For the USA, other avenues do not seem to be attractive after all.

The position of the EU regarding the new round has developed rapidly in the late 1990s. Despite the considerable odds against handling itself and its diverse constituencies successfully, the EU managed to produce a rather comprehensive blueprint for progress. It deserves credit for doing so. However, Klaus Deutsch argues that the EU agreed to an overly ambitious set of objectives regarding rule making and put too little emphasis on market-access issues. Also, the EU failed to reach a position that would be sufficiently attractive to other key players, in particular the USA and influential developing countries. This reflected strategic shortcomings such as the lack of a huge and credible incentive of market opening or a credible threat. Contending for leadership is not really a near-term prospect for the EU at the start of the new millennium, Deutsch concludes. However, the outlook is not that bleak after all, as greater willingness to grant market access at home (agriculture, anti-dumping, cars, services) and greater effort to pry open foreign markets (in service industries in particular), a less ambitious approach to rule making, and redoubled efforts at transatlantic and North–South cooperation seem as feasible as they are desirable.

The traditional process of trade policy making in Japan will have to change if Japan is to play a major role in a new trade round, argue Hiroya Ichikawa and Maki Kunimatsu. The business community no longer feels adequately represented by the government, and coordination both between ministries and between the government and the private sector is insufficient. It therefore comes as no surprise that there is no grand strategy for a new round in Japan at present. There is some consensus in Japan for a comprehensive round, which may in any case be the only way to reach solutions for the agricultural sector that would be acceptable on the level of domestic politics. The interest of Japanese business in further liberalisation of services trade might become a domestic counterweight to agricultural protectionism. In contrast to the farming lobby (against) and business (generally in favour), trade unions and NGOs do not play a major role in influencing Japan's stance on a possible Millennium Round – yet. While being cautious on the inclusion of social and environmental issues into the WTO, the authors nevertheless take the view that mechanisms and institutions should be established to ensure that a dialogue is established with civil society to ensure political acceptance of liberalisation.

Turning to developing countries, Michael Finger and Philip Schuler are very critical about the treatment their interests received during and after the Uruguay Round as well as in the run-up to a possible Millennium Round. They point out that there was a severe imbalance in the results of the Uruguay Round, with developing countries giving more than they received. Despite their concessions on the 'new issues' (GATS, TRIPs, TRIMs), developing countries have been short-changed as rich countries have not opened their markets in the ways they had promised. Consequently, a number of developing nations ask why there should be a new round when some members have not even implemented promises made in the last one. In addition, the costs of implementing the obligations undertaken have been substantial, raising the question of whether this is a wise way for a poor nation to spend its scarce resources. Correcting the unbalanced outcome of the Uruguay Round in the areas of agriculture, services and industrial tariffs are at the top of the agenda for developing country members. In contrast, the prospective new topics of another round (labour, environment, investment, competition and, again, intellectual property) should be more properly approached as development issues with a trade dimension rather than as trade issues with a development dimension. Unlike in the area of tariffs and quotas, a one-size-fits-all approach is not appropriate here.

Bernhard May observes that globalisation poses a challenge to democracy as it creates both winners and losers, erodes the boundaries of the nation-state and weakens the authority of the state without replacing it by some democratically legitimised international institution. As trade liberalisation is rightly seen as being inextricably linked to globalisation, it is not surprising to find that it faces growing opposition, which coincides with a general trend among the inhabitants in rich countries of calling for more participation. As May notes, there are two aspects to the democratisation of trade policy: the first issue is whether WTO member countries are democracies; if so, national trade policy is sufficiently legitimised. The second issue is whether there is a role for democratic structures at the international level of the WTO itself. May concludes that establishing a parliamentary assembly at the WTO would probably not solve the problem of squaring the circle of effective governance and democratic accountability. However, the transparency of WTO proceedings could be enhanced, and rules governing the participation of NGOs in deliberations, but not in decisions, could be established. Also, the effective participation of developing countries should be improved through institutional reforms, a matter also taken up by Sylvia Ostry and Richard Blackhurst.

Major policy issues

Dietrich Barth points out that although trade in services has grown faster than trade in goods since the early 1990s, levels of protection still remain extremely high. This is mainly due to an extensive web of regulations governing services. While in most instances protection is not the intention of those regulations, they often have this effect. Since regulations often reflect a host of social, environmental and other concerns of governments and their constituencies, they cannot and should not simply be removed with the stroke of a pen. Rather, the protectionist aspects of regulations that do not fulfil those functions in public policy need to be tackled. Thanks to the 'built-in agenda', negotiations on further market opening in the services sector started on 1 January 2000. However, disagreement on whether there should be sector agreements (the US position) or an integrated effort (the EU position) will probably hamper progress. The success of negotiations will also depend on developing countries' interests receiving sufficient consideration. Barth, among others, recommends that negotiations focus on reducing the current imbalance in commitments across countries and sectors, that negotiations should be comprehensive, and that a horizontal method of liberalisation should be applied to speed up the process.

Considering the future course of financial services liberalisation, Wendy Dobson notes that the focus of analysis must be different to the analysis of other sectors: since financial market development is a central factor in a country's long-term growth and development, liberalisation must take into account not only aspects of efficiency but also of development. Dobson argues that progress in financial services liberalisation will be slow because of the asymmetry of interests between the two main groups of players, the mature industrialised countries and advanced developing countries. While OECD governments seek improved market access to advanced developing countries for their large financial firms, governments of these member states are more concerned about the potentially disruptive effect that financial liberalisation can have on development and macroeconomic stability. The answer to this conflict of interest is not to halt reform and liberalisation. Rather, liberalisation must proceed while placing the emphasis on financial stability. This suggests an innovative form of *do ut des* as the basis for liberalisation. Rather than both partners swapping market-access 'concessions', industrial countries should offer technical assistance to build stronger financial systems, while developing countries pledge to open their financial markets in a deliberate sequence tuned to the specific circumstances of their respective economies. Dobson also notes that market opening may well follow from unilateral and regional initiatives. Therefore, the potential role of multilateral liberalisation is still open to discussion.

While financial services may require innovative approaches, further liberalisation in the areas of telecommunications and transportation services can proceed within the normal GATS framework, Christopher Findlay and Tony Warren write. The only aspect that does require particular attention is access to essential facilities to ensure that markets are fully contestable. According to the authors, in telecommunications, current schedules do not reflect the actual policy environment. Negotiators therefore have the opportunity to expand the scope of the agreement dramatically without engaging in significant domestic reform. Still, binding current policy would be valuable in itself, as future liberalisation negotiations could then start from a more advanced stage. As far as maritime transport is concerned, GATS has emerged as the most important force pushing this sector towards freer trade. WTO members are obliged to start negotiations on a further liberalisation of maritime transport services in 2000, and there is a fairly good chance of significant market opening. With respect to air transport, the hard rights currently excluded from GATS are under pressure for reform from forces largely outside GATS. The authors argue that there are two reform options: either to remove the current GATS Annex on air transport, subjecting air transport fully to the usual disciplines of the GATS, or to reform the structure of bilateral agreements from within, which would create huge advantages for those who moved first and further, in particular US carriers.

The rapidly growing area of e-commerce is currently largely unregulated. Stefan Bach and Georg Erber depict two competing approaches to the creation of an appropriate institutional and regulatory framework: one, advocated by the EU, is to rely an *ex ante* regulation; the other, similar to the US position, is to trust in the emergence of self-regulatory mechanisms. Notwithstanding the power of the USA, time is also on the side of the USA as rapid technological developments create realities that cannot easily be reversed. Four additional areas need to be addressed: the protection of intellectual property rights, data protection, legal issues and taxation. On all four, positions still differ widely. On taxation, there is a general consensus that the Internet should remain a free trade area; however, an agreement is also evolving that existing tax regulations should apply to e-commerce as well. Finally, Bach and Erber argue that there is an urgent need to ensure that developing countries benefit from the opportunities that e-commerce offers. Otherwise, a digital divide between and within countries could emerge.

In recent years, the classic distinctions between national competition and international trade policies have become blurred in some highly politicised cases. The obvious question arises of whether and, if so, how these policies can be better linked both in a substantive and a formal sense so as to avoid bitter conflicts in future. The matter was discussed in Seattle, but no consensus emerged. The EU is at loggerheads with the USA over the issue, and developing countries baulk at both players. Phedon Nicolaides explores the 'art of the possible' in his paper. He argues that not much is possible. There is no consensus on whether and how to proceed. He explores all possible avenues, only to conclude that none of the multilateral approaches under deliberation will deliver tangible results in the near future. When ideas cannot be reconciled, power reigns. He envisages unilateral power politics by the two main players, the EU and the USA, some bilateral cooperation between them, and 'policy taking' by everybody else. Developing countries in particular have argued that the key objective should be to constrain the use of anti-dumping measures by applying multilateral competition rules. Nicolaides considers this the least likely outcome given the interests in the North.

The use of anti-dumping restrictions has reached proportions that represent a systemic threat to world trade. However, a mere reform of anti-dumping procedures alone will not do the trick. Rather, Patrick Messerlin argues, an integration of all trade remedies is necessary. It should be accepted that there is always the possibility that countries will perceive a need to temporarily opt out of their commitments by citing the necessity of using safeguards. The international trade regime is robust enough to accommodate this need, but strict conditions must be attached to it, in particular a time limit and, at the end of the transition period, the choice between rescinding or renegotiating the corresponding commitment. Messerlin proposes a minimal and a more ambitious programme. The former would improve existing safeguard procedures, discipline anti-dumping reviews and reduce the current bias in favour of dumping determination. The latter would reflect that anti-dumping measures are actually a response to different issues – price discrimination, cyclical dumping, predatory and strategic pricing; the starting of anti-dumping procedures in the first two cases should be made difficult, if not impossible; the latter two cases should be handled under competition laws. If the matter were to be put on the agenda of a new round, trade negotiators would find a ready-made 'blueprint' for reform in this article. It is hard to envisage a single reform from which developing countries stand to derive greater benefit.

Whether investment will be included in the agenda of the next trade round will depend on there being a comprehensive agenda, Stephen Woolcock writes. Contrary to the general perception, there is a long history of international agreements on rules for cross-border investment. OECD countries reached a broad consensus. Beyond this basic consensus, however, there are differences, particularly between the USA and the EU, over what the regime should cover and in which forum it should be negotiated, the USA favouring the OECD and the EU multilateral negotiations within the WTO. Woolcock clearly sees a need for a multilateral framework for investment within the WTO, because the existing patchwork of plurilateral, regional and bilateral investment rules cannot, in the long run, provide the predictability and confidence that is needed for FDI flows to continue. However, there is no consensus in favour of a WTO framework for investment at present, not least because governments are wary of risking political capital on the issue bearing in mind the vociferous opposition of NGOs to the Multilateral Agreement on Investment. In the short to medium term, the GATS and the TRIPs Agreement may serve as substitutes, but this is unlikely to be a viable solution.

While being difficult to assess rigorously, experience with the TRIPs Agreement, Carsten Fink and Carlos A. Primo Braga note, has been encouraging. This is all the more satisfying as the TRIPs Agreement requires governments to take positive action on IPRs, which usually implies changing legislation. For further negotiations, two kinds of matter arise. One is the issues that are raised by the built-in agenda of the agreement and by the expiry of deadlines embedded in the TRIPs Agreement. Here, it is possible that developing countries will call for an extension of deadlines. Other issues stemming from the built-in agenda concern the patentability of biotechnology inventions and the establishment of a multilateral system of notification and registration of geographical indications for wines and spirits. The others are revisions and extensions that might be sought by some members. Here, surprisingly, industrial countries have submitted hardly any demands to expand the TRIPs framework. Fink and Primo Braga argue that industrial countries would like to see existing agreements implemented by all WTO members first and that opposition from NGOs made governments cautious about presenting further demands. The authors conclude that the TRIPs Agreement represents an important component of the multilateral trading system, providing ground rules for international commerce in knowledge and information-intensive goods. Nevertheless, there remain significant institutional and financial challenges for developing countries in implementing effective IPRs regimes.

The rival contender in that regard is agriculture. Farm trade has a serious impact on the interests of developing countries. Stefan Tangermann reviews the state of play in that field. In fact, due to the 'built-in agenda', new multilateral talks on agriculture have already started in March 2000. As Tangermann points out, the Uruguay Round agreement brought agriculture back into the orbit of a rules-based trading system but made only modest inroads into the established systems of domestic support, import protection and export subsidies. Hence, a lot of work still lies ahead for the negotiators. Whereas progress on import liber-alisation and further reductions in export assistance seem within reach, a reduction in trade-affecting forms of domestic support requires a deepening of reforms, in particular in the EU, which will be difficult in the short term yet unavoidable in the long run. The prospects are less clear in those issues that touch upon consumer demands, health and so on. Tangermann concludes that negotiations will probably move beyond a minimal adjustment package and target more substantial trade-related reforms of farming. The risk of deadlock over farm trade developing appears to be much lower than at the Uruguay Round.

Gerhard Fisch addresses the complex relationship between regional and multilateral trade policies. Obviously, the future of the international trading system will continue to be shaped by both approaches, with the emphasis shifting over time. When multilateralism stalled in the 1980s several nations, most notably the USA, contemplated (or even threatened) to resort to region-alism and bilateralism as alternative roads towards liberalisation. After the failure of Seattle, is there a danger that, once again, we are at the beginning of a new wave of regionalism? Presumably not. As Fisch argues, although WTO member states are clearly aware of the difficulties of reaching multilateral consensus, there is no general sentiment that multilateralism should be dispensed with altogether. This view is supported by the fact that the new regionalism is marked by outward-looking characteristics, i.e. a drive to open up markets and a willingness to broaden membership. Even more importantly, Fisch points out, the traditional view on regionalism disregards the important positive contribution that regionalism can make to further liberalisation: regionalism is the superior way of dealing with the challenges of deeper integra-tion, which require policy coordination rather than just the removal of border measures. It is also the natural result of economic geography and the best way to deal with North–South conflicts. Thus regionalism clearly is a complement to rather than a substitute for multilateral liberalisation.

Philip von Schöppenthau takes a fresh look at the heated but rarely illumi-nating debate about 'trade and social standards'. He states that the issue of labour standards will not disappear from the trade scene by itself and that both sides would gain from engaging in a constructive dialogue. He recommends that industrialised countries offer substantially better market access to countries that respect labour standards, with the EU being particularly well positioned to take the lead. Commercial reality has moved far beyond policy struggles already, he argues, because developing countries that oppose the linking of trade and labour standards turn a blind eye to the commercial reality at home. Exporters in the South have to comply with EU or US importers' demands that labour standards be observed in the production of the goods they import. This new trend should be addressed by policy makers in both the North and the South, von Schöppenthau recommends.

Cord Jakobeit argues that concerns for the environment do not necessarily have to be at odds with the WTO. Since the issue came up in the early 1990s, the WTO has adopted a cautious approach, assigning a Committee on Trade and Environment (CTE) to examine the relationship. The report produced by the CTE for the first ministerial conference in Singapore in December 1996 merely summarised the differing views of the CTE's members and contained no recommendations for modifications to WTO rules. This mainly reflects the substantial resistance against any such modification from developing countries. The latter see the issue as yet another protective barrier and infringement on their sovereignty, whereas internationally operating NGOs have brought the issue to the international agenda, lobbying hard with OECD governments and increasingly with the WTO itself. Jakobeit argues that the suggested solution to the potential trade and environment conflict lies mainly in the content of future multilateral environmental agreements, whose design will have to become more sophisticated to accommodate the conflicting views.

Systemic issues

A third set of papers is devoted to a sytemic view of the world trading system. Any consideration of systemic issues confronting those who manage, for better or worse, the international trading system still has to start in Washington, not in Geneva. Notwithstanding fifty years of multilateral trade diplomacy, the rise of new trading powers in Europe and Asia and the significant economic development of the South, the USA is still the pivotal player in world trade. It seems that Seattle proved the point in a negative respect. Henry R. Nau tries to solve the riddle of why the USA, despite enjoying the best economic conditions it has seen for several decades, has failed to provide the necessary leadership since the conclusion of the Uruguay Round. Nau does not find systemic reasons for the failure to do so. He asserts that US President Clinton pursued the wrong strategy even at the Seattle meeting, given his desire to take the lead in multilateral trade policy. Clinton's ill-founded geo-economic foreign policy approach, Nau argues, subjected US trade policy to protectionist forces at home and alienated former free trade allies abroad. Nau also dismisses the notion that 'globalisation' has gone out of control. Rather, it is Western values that are in the driver's seat. The next US president, Nau argues, should get back to basics, work with the USA's allies, first and foremost within the Group of Seven democracies, and get trade policy started again. There are no systemic constraints, and plenty of opportunities to spread the gospel and make globalisation work for non-US citizens as well.

However, not everybody is yet aboard the multilateral trade ship. Noting that countries accounting for 10 per cent of world trade and 5 per cent of world GDP still remain outside the WTO, even though most have applied for membership, Rolf Langhammer and Matthias Lücke advocate a strategy for streamlining and, hence, speeding up accession negotiations. They note that the most common stumbling blocks on the way to accession are, first, new members are increasingly expected to implement essentially the entire, wide-ranging body of WTO rules; and, second, current WTO members use their leverage in the negotiations to achieve substantial market access in the acceding countries. To overcome these problems, Langhammer and Lücke suggest that some rules of thumb be obeyed: first, applicants should not be required to grant market access to a greater extent than current members at a similar stage of development. Based on this, the authors are critical of the deal negotiated between the USA and China. Second, applicant countries should fully accept the need for transparency in their trade-related policies. Third, clear priorities should be set for the necessary changes in national legislation: while important changes need to be made early on, extended implementation periods for non-essential items could be tolerated.

Dispute settlement is widely regarded as the very heart of the WTO. However, as Bernhard Speyer warns, there is a danger that WTO member states will increasingly regard the institution as little more than a courthouse to settle their trade disputes. The Uruguay Round certainly gave teeth to the DSM, which had long been needed to bolster members' confidence in the institution. The fact that the new DSM is widely used shows that this aim has been achieved. However, while strengthening the judicial elements of the DSM has certainly made it more effective, there is an urgent need to preserve the diplomatic elements of dispute settlement. Fortunately, both member states and the WTO itself (in particular the appellate body) seem to understand this and act accordingly. Clearly there is some scope to improve DSM procedures, but this has to be done while preserving its diplomatic character. Opening the DSM to private parties beyond what is current practice is incompatible with this.

According to Sylvia Ostry, there is need for institutional reform of the WTO. In the Uruguay Round, trade liberalisation moved into the sphere of deeper integration, which meant telling governments what to do rather than what not to do, as was the GATT model of negative integration. In such a world, the protective buffers that GATT explicitly allowed effectively became protectionist tools. By moving beyond shallow integration, an imbalance opened up between the WTO's reach into member states' sovereignty on the one hand and the participation of 'civil society' on the other. Moreover, the organisation has become a magnet for dissent, in particular voiced by NGOs. Greater transparency is one way of countering the charge of a democratic deficit, but Ostry is sceptical of giving private parties more access to the WTO, given the questionable democratic legitimacy of NGOs. Instead, she recommends a number of institutional changes. First, an executive committee should be established to enhance the flexibility and adaptability of the WTO. Second, given the limited resources of its secretariat, the WTO should establish a research network, which would also help to form a consensus on the future path of liberalisation. Third, the marginalisation of poor countries must be stopped, which requires more technical assistance from richer countries. Finally, to avoid policy overload and conflicting objectives, labour and environmental issues should be dealt with by the ILO and a still-to-be-founded World Environmental Organization, not at the WTO.

Richard Blackhurst analyses the WTO's experience with decision making and suggests a fundamental change in the way that member countries arrive at recommendations to be adopted by consensus. As GATT's membership increased, and as developing countries began to participate much more actively in GATT activities, the so-called 'concentric circle model' became the organisation's way of coping with the problem that while membership in virtually every GATT body was open to all GATT members, once the active participation in a meeting exceeded a certain number (say twenty-five), the group's work became increasingly cumbersome, inefficient and ultimately impossible. Under this model, an issue-specific 'inner circle' of members functions as a discussion, debate and negotiating group for the issue at hand. It either reports the results of its efforts to a larger circle of members or directly to the entire membership, which is asked to take a consensus decision on the recommendations. Carried over to the WTO, this model was heavily criticised by many countries at the first WTO ministerial conference in Singapore in December 1996, and again even more roundly – and publicly – attacked at the 1999 ministerial conference in Seattle. Blackhurst argues that in those instances in which it is impossible to constitute an inner circle without excluding one or more WTO members wishing to be included, continued reliance on the informal concentric circle model can only progressively damage the WTO's ability to function. He makes the case for creating a formal 'WTO consultative board' whose design and operating procedures would draw on the strong points of both the GATT's Consultative Group of 18 (1975–87) and the IMF/World Bank boards, while at the same time avoiding the shortcomings – from a WTO perspective – of both. The discussion includes a look at which WTO members are likely to oppose the creation of such a board initially and which members could be expected to support the proposal.

Notes

The views expressed in this article reflect only the personal views of the editors.

1   The editors prefer this term to describe the economic integration of the global economy. See Friedman (1999) for a lively discussion regarding the often-used term 'globalisation' and its social and political dimensions.

References

Croome, J. (1995) *Reshaping the World Trading System. A History of the Uruguay Round*, Geneva: WTO.

Evans, P.B., Jacobson, H.K. and Putnam, R.D. (eds) (1993) *Double-Edged Diplomacy. International Bargaining and Domestic Politics*, Berkeley, Los Angeles and London: University of California Press.

Friedman, T.L. (1999) *The Lexus and the Olive Tree*, New York: Farrar, Straus & Giroux.

Krueger, A.O. (ed.) (1998) *The WTO as an International Organization*, Chicago and London: University of Chicago Press.

Ostry, S. (1997) *The Post-Cold War Trading System. Who's on First?* Chicago and London: University of Chicago Press.

Preeg, E.H. (1995) *Traders in a Brave New World. The Uruguay Round and the Future of the International Trading System*, Chicago and London: University of Chicago Press.

Putnam, R.D. (1988): 'Diplomacy and domestic politics: the logic of two-level games', *International Organization* 42(3): 427–60.

Schott, J.J. (ed.) (1998) *Launching New Global Trade Talks. An Action Agenda*, Washington: Institute for International Economics.

Whalley, J. and Hamilton, C. (1996) *The Trading System after the Uruguay Round*, Washington: Institute for International Economics.

Winham, G.R. (1986) *International Trade and the Tokyo Round Negotiation*, Princeton, NJ: Princeton University Press.

2 The USA: why fundamentals do not always matter, or: It's politics, stupid!

Andreas Falke

Introduction

If this essay had been written ten years ago, the agenda and concerns would have been quite different. The key catchphrases of the 1980s, a turbulent decade in US trade policy, would have still resonated strongly: American unilateralism, managed trade, protectionist impulses and competitiveness (or lack thereof). Given the stalemate in the Uruguay Round, negotiations at the time and a rather unfavourable policy environment, the USA resorted to other approaches, namely unilateralism, managed trade and the pursuit of preferential regionalism (Richardson 1994: 627–58). Doubts were clearly articulated as to whether multilateralism would still be the dominant approach in US trade policy or whether it would be supplanted by unilateralism, managed trade and a plethora of minilateralism initiatives.

The trade deficit, although clearly in retreat from its pinnacle in the mid-1980s, was still a permanent reference point for US trade policy and continued to inspire the debate in less constructive ways. It was popularly interpreted as a sign of either lack of US competitiveness or of closed markets and unfair practices by America's trading partners, rather than as a consequence of macroeconomic imbalances and exchange-rate misalignments. The pursuit of fairness and narrow reciprocity became the principal objectives in strategies to 'level the playing field'. Significant was the rise of protectionist trade remedy actions under anti-dumping, countervailing duty and other sections of US trade law, although the USA was not the only country that registered such an increase (Nivola 1993; Richardson 1994: 637).

On the political level, there was a surge in trade policy activism by the US Congress, transforming the legislature into a co-equal player with the executive branch, if not the principal agenda setter. This shift was clearly demonstrated by the many, albeit unsuccessful or thwarted, attempts to legislate the deficit out of existence. It was also evident in the Omnibus Trade and Competitiveness Act of 1988, the first major piece of trade legislation initiated by the legislature since the infamous Smoot–Hawley Bill, a clear response to what Congress saw as unacceptable agent slack on the part of the executive. Congressional activism peaked with the 1988 Act, but thanks to it, the pattern of executive responsiveness to general congressional trade policy designs – beyond narrow constituency concerns – was firmly established. Agent slack on the part of the executive was much reduced, binding trade policy more closely to congressional preferences (Odell and Eichengreen 1998: 200–6; Falke 2000).

Ten years later, the trade policy landscape has changed completely. The Uruguay Round was brought to a successful conclusion. The new World Trade Organization also fulfilled a longstanding demand of American trade policy makers: a dispute settlement mechanism with real teeth, deciding cases in a calculable time-frame. Significant agreements in the new WTO on financial services, telecommunications and trade in information technology products followed. The concerns about American unilateralism subsided. Super 301 and Section 301 are words now rarely found in serious trade policy discourse. Calls for managed trade, through either voluntary export restraints or negotiated import targets, have disappeared. Rather, during the financial crisis in Asia, when a number of Asian currencies plummeted, the USA kept its markets open and acted as an importer of last resort, greatly facilitating the Asian recovery. Congress has neither started any new protectionist schemes nor pushed any market-opening initiatives upon the executive. Congress is vigilant, but is not given to the hectic legislative activism of the 1980s.

Based on a strong surge in business investment and productivity growth, the USA has enjoyed the longest economic expansion in its history, combining low inflation with unemployment rates of less than 5 per cent at the end of the millennium and wiping out an endemic budget deficit. At the same time, the integration of the USA into the world economy has continued unabated. Trade now accounts for close to 25 per cent of US GDP, compared with 11 per cent in 1970 (Council of Economic Advisers 1999: 6). With the exception of a persistent current account deficit, the setting for trade policy making, compared with the 1990s, appeared highly favourable. The structural fundamentals were pointing in the right direction. However, at the end of this period, the administration had no fast-track authority, it had to live with the failed WTO ministerial conference in Seattle, and it faced an uphill battle over normal trade relations status for China in Congress, all indicating diminished support for trade liberalisation in US society (and no other country willing or able to pick up the baton). What had gone wrong?

The answer is that in the aftermath of the NAFTA debate, the domestic political base of trade policy making has changed dramatically, putting severe constraints on policy makers to pursue liberalisation initiatives on any level if it involves serious *quid pro quos*. In the context of globalisation, trade has become part of wider societal and political discourse, linking it causally to broader socioeconomic development, concerns about sovereignty and the ability of governments to assure the well-being of citizens under national rules. Trade policy is now also seen as instrumental for achieving objectives other than market access, namely labour and environmental standards, beyond US borders. With these new themes, new actors have emerged in the interest group arena of trade policy making, changing the calculations of trade-offs between export-oriented and import-competing industries.

Trade policy has been politicised to an unprecedented degree. It has been taken out of the hands of experts and the subsystems in which it used to be insulated from non-germane political designs. This is a challenge that American trade policy makers have not been able to cope with. Even worse, foreign leaders are intent on copying it. As one aspect of 'globalisation back-lash', this 'societalisation' of trade policy is spilling over to other Western democracies and is becoming a common challenge. In fact, the USA to a large extent defined this challenge and pressured others to accept it, although it is debatable whether this was in its long-term interest. Together with other concerns, such as the relationship between food safety and trade, this has led to a much more attentive public and media attention to trade on both sides of the Atlantic. In pushing these new themes, the USA has again underscored its role as agenda setter, but as of now, with uncertain consequences for the multilateral system.

The trade deficit and economic vitality

A feeling of *déjà-vu* was generated in the 1990s by the persistence of the trade deficit. The merchandise trade deficit rose from $74 billion in 1991 to $277 billion in 1999, and the current account from $4.4 billion (artificially low due to allied Gulf War contributions) to $233.4 billion in 1998. In fact, 1998 was a watershed, with an increase of more than 25 per cent as a consequence of the Asian crisis and growth differentials between the USA and its major trading partners. These numbers conceal a healthy growth in exports, which increased from $416 billion in 1991 to $679 billion in 1997. In 1998, US exports fell for the first time since 1986, albeit by a slight 0.8 per cent.

However, the real story behind the trade deficit in the 1990s was the differ-ence in terms of its macroeconomic context and of the political response that it touched off. In relative terms, the trade deficit was smaller than its peak in the 1980s. The 1999 trade deficit was equal to 2.9 per cent of GDP, compared with 3.2 per cent in 1987. In the 1980s, the deficits were twin: the trade deficit was actually fuelled by a growing fiscal deficit combined with a tight monetary policy that led to a an appreciation of the dollar and a surge in imports. In the 1990s, this chain of causality did not work in the opposite direction as the budget deficit came down and eventually went into surplus. Because external deficits equal national savings (public plus private) minus investment in the national income and product account framework, only the public side improved. Private savings continued to shrink, only to collapse at the end of the 1990s. In this context, the composition of savings matters with regard to external deficits. Analysis has shown that the import intensity of government spending is only about 17 per cent, whereas the same measure for consumption is 58 per cent and for investment spending 50 per cent.

This implies that the increase in public saving combined with a fall in private savings could not correct external accounts but rather worked to stimulate imports. However, in contrast to the 1980s, when investment rates fell, investment expanded dramatically in the 1990s, reaching a rate of nearly 17 per cent and thus driving the economic boom. The strength of the economy and the phenomenal increase in US stock market valuation attracted foreign investment, which bid up the market value of the dollar and more than compensated for all the weakening that lower interest rates following lower budget deficits could have brought. In addition, after the Asian financial crisis, the appreciation of the dollar was helped by the flight to quality, when investors bought government securities and other US dollar-denominated assets. Ensuing lower interest rates fuelled economic activities and with the appreciation of the dollar led to a boost in imports. There is concern that the persistent decline in the trade balance and its link to an equally persistent decline in personal savings cannot continue for ever, but the general pattern of spending was certainly better balanced between consumption and investment than in the 1980s (Mann 1999).

The interesting point here is that the persistence of the external deficits elicited different political responses in the 1990s. The deficit was not seen as an object for trade policy measures but as a consequence of macroeconomic factors such as differential growth rates, savings, investment behaviour and the movement of exchange rates. Partly due to the thematic leadership of the macroeconomic team in Washington, i.e. the Treasury and the Federal Reserve Board, it was not interpreted as a sign of unfair trade practices, industrial policy machinations by foreign governments or a decline in the industrial competitiveness of the USA. However, sharply asymmetrical bilateral balances remained. The trade deficit with Japan was over $60 billion in the late 1990s, closely followed by the deficit with China, which rose from $3.5 billion in 1988 to almost $57 billion in 1998 (Nanto 1999). In its policy impact, the burgeoning trade deficit was benign. There were no attempts at forced correction through surcharges, as proposed by some members of Congress in the 1980s, or initiatives based on concepts of strategic trade policy to compensate for the perceived comparative advantages created by governments in strategic sectors.

The other factor that was highly damaging to the trade policy climate and the commitment to multilateralism in the 1980s was the debate about general US decline and its specific economic sibling. In the 1990s, the competitiveness debate was conspicuous by its absence. Due to massive restructuring and productivity increases, American industry staged an amazing comeback. The United States is in a relatively strong competitive position overall in terms of its productivity, its capacity to apply new technologies and its ability to respond to market shifts. Interestingly, the comeback was not restricted to the growth- and export-oriented high-tech sector. The USA showed renewed comparative advantage in sectors such as glassware, textiles, floor coverings and specialty fabrics, where it seemed to have lost all competitiveness. Competitive strength is increasingly shown in sub-sectors, or product niches, that are skill- and technology-intensive, while many low-productivity sub-industries have been abandoned. The Internet economy and the USA lead in its hardware and software infrastructure is the other dimension of US productivity. To this has to be added the continuing strength in agricultural and natural resources products and the competitiveness of high value-added service sectors (Richardson *et al.* 1998).

From the point of view of its regained competitiveness, the USA is in an enviable position to take advantage of market-opening initiatives in a new WTO round. Instead, however, trade policy making in Washington has been characterised by stalemate and indecision since the conclusion of the Uruguay Round (Destler 1999). Regional initiatives have been stalled, and at Seattle, the USA, together with its trading partners, failed to launch a new round. What are the reasons? The reasons evidently have little to do with basic economic factors, the established trade policy mechanisms or the positions of the traditional players in trade policy such as producer interests. They have to be found in the wider political and social context of trade policy making in the USA. Societal interests have gained a determining influence on trade policy, and trade policy is being politicised beyond its actual core, i.e. gaining market access or fending off import competition.

The NAFTA legacy: The changing political base of trade policy making

The fight over the implementation of the North American Free Trade Agreement dramatically changed the debate about and the politics of trade policy in the United States. The agreement was vehemently opposed by unions, environmental groups and a host of other NGOs, who feared that a free trade agreement with a developing country would lead to unfair competition through what critics called 'social' and 'environmental dumping', finally leading to a lowering of social and environmental standards in the USA. This criticism, which resonated particularly with Democratic congressmen, led to calls to include provisions on social and environmental regulation as a condition for liberalising trade. At the time, President Clinton tried to square the circle, i.e. reject NAFTA as negotiated by President Bush and propose a NAFTA 'enriched' by environmental and social side agreements to make congressional passage possible. Congress did pass NAFTA, but in the end the inclusion of side provisions did not persuade a majority of Democratic congressmen to support the agreement. It passed only because Republicans supported it (Nolan 1999: 81–3).

This outcome emboldened NGOs to focus on trade policy to further their own non-trade agenda. As a consequence, the politics of trade policy making changed for good. Labour unions, environmental groups and other NGOs with non-germane objectives became new players in the interest group game of trade policy and added a strong non-producer-related element. The critical point here is that these are all groups that since the Reagan administration had been marginalised in terms of their ability to influence the domestic policy process in their respective areas. This was even true of their natural allies, the Democrats in Congress and a newly elected Democratic administration. Discovering trade policy as a new priority opened up new vistas of activity and mobilisation where meeting their concerns would have no immediate and visible domestic costs. Involvement in trade policy expanded the room for manoeuvre of political mobilisation that was not available given a domestic power constellation that did not favour any expansion of social benefits or more stringent environmental regulation – witness the debate about global warming in the USA.

In the beginning, the opposition to trade agreements was confined to agreements with developing nations, where stark differentials in social and environmental agreements could much more easily be highlighted than in abstract discussions of multilateral trade principles such as MFN treatment.

Trade instruments were increasingly seen as leverage to force developing countries to comply with US domestic conceptions of what international social and environmental regulations should be. Soon, however, the new groupings began to oppose any type of trade liberalisation, claiming that it would undermine American social or environmental standards or, in the more right-wing terms of the Pat Buchanan–Ross Perot school, US sovereignty. In the process, these groups could appeal to a diffuse feeling that was the legacy of the recession of the early 1990s and the ongoing trend of corporate restructuring. Trade liberalisation could increasingly be cited as the source of social ills, from declining living standards and wage inequality to job losses. The Globalisation backlash in the USA is increasingly linked to trade liberalisation, and multinational corporations are seen as the main culprits (Frost 1998; Elwell 1998). From this perspective, trade policy, as Marcus Nolan has argued, has been transformed into a sort of social work, or a palliative for grievances that could not be dealt with domestically (Nolan 1999: 83–8). The effect of these groups was to make any type of trade liberalisation suspect, including multilateral market opening and its domestic policy mechanism such as fast-track authority.

The interesting question is why business, particularly the export-oriented multinationals, did not rise to the challenge to act as a countervailing force. The reasons are complex, but in a way the multilateral trading system is becoming the victim of its own success. Past trade liberalisation has been so successful in bringing down barriers that outright protectionism is no longer a threat (Stokes 2000). Given all the domestic opportunities created by the economic expansion and improved competitiveness, business felt less pressed to pursue trade liberalisation. Even 'behind-border' structural barriers such as restraints on competition or on foreign direct investment, or a lack of protection for intellectual property rights, while remaining important issues for US companies, do not inspire engagement. This may be due in part to the fact that the current US lead in crucial high-technology goods creates dependence on US supplies that puts market-access problems in a more benign perspective. The high market capitalisation of US companies puts them in a very strong position to expand market share by way of mergers and acquisitions. In the end, business-to-business arrangements are a more effective, better-targeted and faster means of achieving market access. From that point of view, bilateral and minilateral trade deals, should the NAFTA trauma be overcome, may be more compatible with business-to-business arrangements than drawn-out multilateral rounds, as they have the advantage of addressing very sector- and company-specific problems in direct talks with individual emerging market governments, where the USA can bring its full commercial clout to bear. This is one of the reasons why the US business community invested more political capital in China's WTO accession than in a new WTO round (*ibid.*).

Congressional attitudes and the fate of fast-track authority

One of the victims of changing societal attitudes towards trade liberalisation was the granting of fast-track authority, the mechanism by which the constitutional sovereign over trade policy making, the US Congress, ensures that it will approve the results of international negotiations through a straight up or down vote within a circumscribed period without opportunities for effective amendments. Since the last expiry of fast-track authority, all attempts at re-authorisation have failed. The inclusion of labour and environmental standards proved to be a crucial point of contention, with Republican members of Congress favouring fast-track authority being strictly limited to negotiating objectives directly related to trade with Democrats favouring their inclusion to raise standards in developing countries and equalising the competitive disadvantage of US producers. At the same time, congressional Republicans used the fast-track issue as a way of embarrassing and hurting President Clinton. It was also claimed that the fast-track delegation of authority would give the president too great a latitude without effective control by Congress and thus represent a lack of democratic control (Holliday 1999). This mechanism was maligned by the anti-trade coalition of labour unions, environmental groups and the diffuse array of anti-globalisation NGOs. Blocking fast-track authority became one of their principal goals.

After some unproductive debates with Congress and some unsuccessful Republican initiatives, President Clinton proposed fast-track legislation in 1997, severely limiting the coverage of trade and environmental issues. Since he could persuade only forty-three House of Representatives Democrats to support the Bill, he asked the House to adjourn for the year without a vote. In 1998, House Speaker Newt Gingrich, in the face of Democratic indecision, brought the issue to a vote, resulting in a defeat of 234 votes to 180 against the delegation of fast-track authority, with only twenty-nine Democrats voting 'yes' and seventy-one Republicans opposing it. In the context of rising domestic prosperity reaching all segments of the US population, the debacle reflected deep anxieties over globalisation and brought stalemate to the US trade policy agenda (Destler 1999). How this stalemate can be broken is not clear. However, it is clear that congressional passage of fast-track authority requires strong presidential leadership to give the case for trade the necessary national focus and forge a strong coalition of pro-trade moderates in both parties in Congress (Kolbe and Matsui 1998: 34). The ensuing debacle at Seattle has given another boost to the anti-trade/anti-fast-track coalition. However, strategies are available to blunt their thrust by limiting fast-track authority to multilateral and sectoral negotiations that do not quite carry the stigma attached to free trade agreements with developing countries, such as NAFTA. There is also solace in the fact that multilateral negotiations have commenced in the past without fast-track authorisation. The inference to be made from the start of such negotiations, would be that this would give enough momentum to have fast-track authority granted in the end.

The evolution of the US agenda for a new WTO round

The basic philosophical support among economic elites and trade policy makers for multilateralism remains strong in the United States. Although there is general support for a multi-track strategy combining bilateral, regional and multilateral negotiations, when all the chips are down, multilateral negotiations give the 'biggest bang for the buck'. With tariffs and trade barriers already low or non-existent, the USA can only benefit from the asymmetrical gains achieved from liberalisation by developing countries. As President Clinton said at the World Economic Forum in Davos:

> There is no substitute for the confidence and credibility the WTO lends to the process of expanding trade based on rules. There's no substitute for the temporary relief WTO offers national economy, especially against unfair trade and abrupt surges in imports. And there is no substitute for WTO's authority in resolving disputes, which commands the respect of all member nations. If we expect public support for the WTO … we've got to get out of denial of what's happening now.
>
> (Clinton 2000)

And regionalism, although currently tainted by NAFTA, is not an antidote to multilateralism. It has the potential to foster a constructive symbiosis with multilateralism. Regional and bilateral approaches would offer a form of insurance against intransigence by other big players such as the EU, India and later China. Also sectoral approaches, seen by US industries as the most effective way to improve market access, are not incompatible with multilateralism *per se*, as the Information Technology Agreement has shown. In fact, some trade analysts conceive of a multilateral round as a series of 'round-ups' rolled together consecutively into a round, allowing mini-packages and the addition of new items to the negotiating agenda (Hufbauer and Schott 1998: 126).

Further, the Clinton administration has welcomed the dispute settlement mechanism (DSM) as a useful framework for settling disputes and has found the outcome of cases favourable to the United States. Out of twenty-four cases brought up to November 1999, the USA lost only two (Council of Economic Advisers 1999: 3). What is undermining the acceptance of the DSM among US business leaders and policy makers is the continued non-compliance by the

USA's trading partners, such as the EU in the banana and beef hormone cases. US commitment to the DSM may even be undermined further by the WTO decision concerning the tax advantages accruing to US businesses with foreign sales corporations. This case, which involves a significant dollar volume, is seen by the USA and the business sector as the breach of an implicit bargain on a legitimate way to neutralise disadvantages that result from the unitary tax system used by the USA and thus implicitly puts the US tax system on trial. It is seen by policy makers and business primarily as a harassment suit (*Financial Times* 2000).

It is not surprising that the domestic stalemate as well as the new equanimity of the business community has influenced the US agenda for a new round. The impatience of internationally oriented high-tech firms, which reflects ever-shorter technology life-cycles, has been the reason for insisting on a limited time-frame of negotiations to produce results quickly. Companies with urgent needs will lose interest in a round when a conclusion is held hostage by the trickiest and thorniest issues. A short time-frame of, say, three years implies a manageable agenda that will yield immediate deliverables. Ironically, this has led to the USA abandoning its strategy of deeper integration, which attacked deep-seated regulatory and structural barriers such as investment and competition policy, which had been the thrust of US trade liberalisation since the mid-1980s. On the part of business, it represents the result of learning from failed attempts to liberalise investment regimes under the MAI and APEC. However, it should be pointed out that the push for a quick conclusion of a new round is not shared by the other export-oriented sector, agriculture, which is well aware that agricultural liberalisation is a hard nut to crack and thus can be expected to take longer than three years, making a single undertaking more difficult.

The US WTO agenda had to satisfy possibly conflicting needs: it had to include the now traditional market-access agenda for industry, high-tech service providers and agriculture, all areas where the USA enjoyed competitiveness. A Democratic administration had to be responsive to the concerns of the labour movement that lower labour standards in developing countries put American workers at a disadvantage. It also had to take note of the diffuse fears of the anti-globalisation movement (non-traditional public interest, including environmental groups) that the WTO is an undemocratic and closed institution that is not responsive to the needs of 'civil society', however vaguely that is defined. As President Clinton argued in Seattle:

> I'm glad the others showed up, because they represent millions of people who are now asking questions about whether this enterprise in fact will take us all where we want to go. And we ought to welcome their questions and be prepared to give an answer, because if we cannot create an intercon-nected global economy that is increasing prosperity and genuine opportunity for people everywhere, then all of our political initiatives are going to be less successful ... For 50 years, trade decisions were largely the

province of trade ministers, heads of government, and business interests. But now, what all those people in the street tell us is that they would also like to be heard. And they're not so sure that this deal is working for them.

(Clinton 1999a: 2495)

In picking up the concerns of 'civil society', the Clinton administration transferred a Tocquevillean concept of US politics to trade politics. Any type of policy making, including international economic policies, has to be open to the participation of voluntary civic groupings such as NGOs (Galston 2000). The populist touch that now enters trade policy making may be regrettable. It is clear that this leads to a much more complicated agenda with strong political overtones, effacing pure market-access concerns. But the USA, as the EU agenda and the debate in Germany under a red–green government have shown, is not isolated in this approach, although it clearly was the agenda setter here. While the traditional market-opening agenda, with the crucial exception of agriculture, should be compatible with the interests of the OECD world, at least in theory, it is much more difficult to square the social standards/NGO approach with the interests of the developing world. This approach actually pitted the USA against developing and emerging markets, which are those countries where the USA sees the greatest potential for improved market access. This somewhat compromised the US commitment to do more for developing countries.

A true tribute to the domestic concerns about trade, jobs and union activism, and a response to a statutory requirement to implement the legislation of the Uruguay Round, was the demand for a working group on trade and labour within the WTO with an emphasis on core labour standards and closer collaboration with the International Labour Organization. On trade and the environment, the US negotiating objectives were fairly modest or vague, calling for the elimination of environmentally damaging agricultural subsidies, the liberalisation of environmental goods and services, and environmental impact statements for trade agreements. Other issues that reflected the US commitment to the concerns of 'civil society' was the call for more transparency, openness and accountability of the WTO to allow more involvement by NGOs and enhance consultation with them. The USA well knew that the inclusion of labour standards would be opposed by the developing world. So it had another reason not to push issues such as investment and competition, which were likely to engender only resentment among developing countries and which were unlikely to yield any immediately palpable results. A discussion of investment issues in the WTO would also have provoked the opposition and resentment of NGOs, whose resistance was one of the reasons for the failure of OECD negotiations on a multilateral investment agreement (Henderson 1999). The same was true for government procurement, where the USA insisted on greater procedural transparency instead of more material market access. What the USA was not willing to concede was a review of trade remedy laws, especially anti-dumping laws. Given the import surge after the Asian crisis, any changes in the

US anti-dumping regime was off-limits. The USA was also unwilling to give anything on textiles.

The traditional market-access agenda revolved around the built-in agenda inherited from the Uruguay Round, with agriculture and services in the fore-front. For agriculture, the elimination of trade-distorting subsidies, particularly export subsidies, enjoyed priority. For industrial goods, the focus was on acceler-ated tariff liberalisation in eight sectors, including chemicals and energy equipment, an initiative that put a premium on achieving quick results and a second information technology agreement while not ruling out a larger package of tariff cuts. Consistent with the push for quick results were a reform of the dispute settlement understanding, a moratorium on tariffs on electronic commerce and transparency in government procurement initiatives.

What the USA tried to accomplish was to serve the natural market-opening interests (high-tech, agriculture, services), to placate the domestic non-trade lobbies over their concerns about the trading system, and not to burden devel-oping and emerging market countries excessively, as they had the greatest market-access potential. With the EU and Japan, the USA remained at odds over the liberalisation of agricultural markets, above all export subsidies. Here it had the support of the agricultural exporting nations, the Cairns Group, which includes a number of developing countries. With the EU, there were also tactical differences over the scope of the round and respective generosity towards developing countries.

After the fiasco in Seattle, the question is: was the US agenda to blame? It is true that the US agenda was not really visionary. It was more geared to the needs of domestic policy than a reflection of the pre-eminent position of the USA in the current world economy. In that sense it can be called timid. In the end, it was an expression of political pragmatism that with the usual compro-mises at the end would have been a basis for a new round, particularly if the tight time constraints that the EU shared were taken into account.

In the end, the failure in Seattle was overdetermined. Strategic preparation was non-existent, tactics badly flawed. None of the major players was willing to make any meaningful concessions. The proceedings were marred by the events and protests in the street, which hampered communication and negotiation. The atmosphere was not helped by remarks by President Clinton on the role of sanctions in securing labour standards,[1] although it is highly questionable whether these remarks doomed the talks. In the end, time ran out, and it was all a game of blame attribution and avoidance.

Despite all the talk of the new role of developing countries and emerging market economies and all the turmoil that the NGO protesters in Seattle created, the fact remains that the WTO ministerial conference in Seattle failed because of the inability of the established players, principally the Quad group, to agree on an agenda between themselves. This inability was the true reason for the failure. As Jeffrey Schott has argued, the key damage to the WTO was self-inflicted (Schott 2000). The protesters simply provided the background noises. The problem for the future will be that the diffuse coalition of NGOs, attributing the failure to its own actions, has claimed victory and, through media attention and support, will be emboldened to intensify its activities and finally become the public gauge for the value and merit of trade negotiations (*Foreign Policy* 2000), a perfect foil for protectionist interests to hide behind.

After Seattle: whither American trade policy

The preferred outcome would be an instant restart of talks. Although no winning formula has emerged, during the first three months of 2000 there were signs that the USA and the EU were making serious efforts to restart the WTO engine. This may defy conventional wisdom, according to which no significant moves are possible during an election year in the USA. However, the Clinton administration already defied conventional wisdom by putting the normal trade relations status for China's WTO accession on the agenda. However, Gary Hufbauer has speculated that politics is present in this move in the form of a behind-the-scenes deal between the Clinton administration and the American labour movement: 'I'll trash Seattle, and you don't trash China, as a way to rationalize the fumble at Seattle' (Hufbauer 1999). However, should the China initiative fail, the path of the Clinton administration will be characterised by a string of failures: the loss of fast-track authority in 1997, the MAI debacle in 1998, Seattle in 1999 and China in 2000. This chain of events poses the question of whether Seattle is merely a short interruption in the march towards greater liberalisation or a turning point that marks the end of the market-opening agenda in a multilateral setting.

Should the latter be true, what would be alternative routes for US trade policy? Gary Hufbauer (*ibid.*) has argued that while it is impossible to return to a purely market-opening approach, trade policy as such may be irrelevant in the face of a market-opening automatism embedded in today's economic order of globalisation:

> With dramatic cuts in transportation and communications costs, the ascendancy of multinational corporations, the rise of e-commerce, plenty of globalisation will occur even if trade ministers take a 10-year holiday. Moreover, thanks to the overwhelming success of the US economy, sensible countries will enthusiastically sign on to the Washington consensus and Anglo-Saxon capitalism without another USTR or IMF mission abroad.
>
> (*ibid.*)

The other strategy would be to align oneself with the anti-globalisation and protectionist forces, particularly labour, subscribe fully to the pursuit of social issues and try to find workable solutions with the more pragmatic wings of these groups. The question here is what the USA (or any other industrialised country) would be willing to give in terms of compensation to the developing world, which sees these issues as a drag on their competitiveness (accelerated textile liberalisation, the end of restrictions on agricultural products relevant to the developing world, etc.).

As this is not feasible, it is quite likely that the developing and developed world will resort to a purely symbolic treatment of these issues. This amounts to an exercise in organised hypocrisy, to borrow a term from Stephen Krasner, which would eventually breed only cynicism. Another way of accommodating globalisation critics would be to buy off the only real force in the anti-globalisation coalition, American labour, through palliative domestic policies, i.e. an expansion of social programmes. This would constitute a return to the 'embedded liberalism' concept promulgated by John Gerard Ruggie as the basis of success for trade liberalisation in the postwar era (Ruggie 1983). However, despite budget surpluses, no support seems to be forthcoming for such a policy shift in the American political universe. The pure empowerment approach, based on the concepts of participatory democracy, also has limits because it substitutes process for substance. No serious policy maker really subscribes to the substantive claims of NGOs (e.g. 'patents kill'), thus relegating NGOs to a procedural plane, a form of escapism. In the end, policy makers may have no other chance but to subject NGOs to a reality check and publicly scrutinise their more outlandish claims and attack the lofty legitimacy of the self-proclaimed civil society. The implicit claim of NGOs to represent a *de facto* world counter-government may turn out to be hollow, and the shallowness of the political support that these groups enjoy may be exposed, and therefore those few voices that have substantive contributions to make can be selected. But this requires courage by politicians in a world of media-driven uncertainty. The worst outcome would certainly be the degeneration of trade policy to a morality play between governments and NGOs, with disinterested business on the sidelines pursuing available market opportunities.

This begs the question of what trade strategies would be most amenable to business should no new multilateral consensus emerge. The first that comes to mind is unilateralism, but that may be too *ad hoc* and carry too many political costs in terms of collateral damage. More likely candidates are an (informal) sectoral approach, based on the built-in agenda and additional reciprocal bargains where possible, and a revival of regionalism, with eventual opportunities to fold such initiatives into a multilateral round. The problem with regionalism is that after NAFTA it is even more stigmatised as producing social and environmental ills. Only a drastic shift in attitudes can help here, which may come about if US companies feel increasingly disadvantaged by preferential agreements that benefit only its trading partners. But returning to multi-lateralism via regionalism, although pursued by American policy makers in the past, is a twisted and arduous road, where there is no good game plan (Odell and Eichengreen 1998).

What should be done? First, should the favourable economic climate continue, any administration should make a greater effort to exploit it to create support for multilateral liberalisation. With Alan Greenspan the new hero of the American public, arguments should resonate strongly that it was only the

USA's openness to trade that allowed the Federal Reserve to engineer inflation-free growth. Second, try to make multilateralism the most promising game in town and try to set it apart from regional initiatives, which are still tainted by the stigma that attaches to NAFTA. Make it clear to the American public that multilateral initiatives produce better balanced results. Third, let trade policies be less driven by politics and play down the concerns of 'civil society'. In most cases, the proponents of 'civil society' are savvy political entrepreneurs who use any type of policy to expand their room for political mobilisation. With the exception of the unions, their support among the American public is tenuous and links to established players in US politics thin. The cost of exposing the weakness of their arguments is small. Fourth, the USA, together with other industrialised countries, must make more substantial concessions to the developing countries, particularly in textiles and anti-dumping. There is no trade liberalisation without some pain, even if that is difficult for some segments of the American public to swallow.

Multilateralism may just have gone into short-term hibernation until the current political storms are over and American concerns over globalisation have subsided in the wake of the phenomenal growth of the US economy. If prosperity continues, the American people may just come to the conclusion that globalisation has indeed gone very far but that it is not such a bad thing and is of great benefit to individuals and society as a whole.

Notes

The opinions expressed in this chapter represent the personal opinions of the author and not those of the US government or any US government agency.

1   The original quote is as follows:

> so that labor unions in wealthier countries want to have certain basic, core labor standards observed in poorer countries because they think it will be better for average people, so that the trading system actually benefits them … that working group should develop these core labor standards, and then they ought to be a part of every trade agreement. And ultimately, I would favor a system in which sanctions would come for violating any provision of a trade agreement. But we've got to do this in steps.
>
> (Clinton 1999b)

References

Clinton, W. (1999a) Telephone Interview with Michael Paulson of the *Seattle Post-Intelligencer* from San Francisco, California, 30 November 1999, in *Weekly Compilation of Presidential Documents*, 6 December 1999, 2485–8.

—— (1999b) remarks at a World Trade Organization luncheon in Seattle, in *Weekly Compilation of Presidential Documents*, 6 December 1999, 2494–9.

—— (2000) 'Globalisation and world trade', address to the World Economic Forum, 29 January, available at http://usinfo.state.gov/journals/ites/0200/ijee/clinton.htm.

Council of Economic Advisers (1999) *America's Interest in the World Trade Organization: An Economic Assessment*, a report by the Council of Economic Advisers, Washington.

Destler, I.M. (1999) 'Trade policy at a crossroad', *The Brookings Review*, Winter 1999, 26–30.

Elwell, C. (1998) *Is Globalisation De-industrializing the US Economy? An Analysis*, CRS Report for Congress, Washington.

Falke, A. (2000) *Abkehr vom Multilateralismus? Politisches System und Handelspolitik in den Vereinigten Staaten von der Reagan Administration bis zum Abschluß der Uruguay-Runde*, Opladen: Leske & Budrich.

Feketekuty, G. (ed.) (1998) *Trade Strategies for a New Era. Ensuring US Leadership in a Global Economy*, New York: Council of Foreign Relations.

Financial Times (2000) 'Bananas, beef – and now export subsidies', 18 February, p.13.

Foreign Policy (2000) The FP Interview: 'Lori's War', pp. 29–30, Spring.

Frost, E. (1998) 'Gaining support for trade by the American public', in G. Feketekuty and B. Stokes (eds) *Trade Strategies for a New Era. Ensuring US Leadership in a Global Economy*, New York: Council of Foreign Relations, pp. 65–82.

Galston, W. (2000) 'Civil society and the art of association', in *Journal of Democracy* 11(1): 64–70.

Henderson, D. (1999) *The MAI Affair, a Story and its Lesson*, London: Royal Institute of International Affairs.

Holliday, G. (1999) *Fast Implementation of Trade Agreements: The Debate over Reauthorization*, CRS Report for Congress, Washington.

Hufbauer, G. (1999) 'World trade after Seattle: implications for the United States', Institute for International Economics, December, available at http:/207.238.152.36-/Newsletr/new99–10htm.

Hufbauer, G. and Schott, J. (1998) 'Strategies for Multilateral Trade Liberalisation', in G. Feketekuty and B. Stokes (eds) *Trade Strategies for a New Era. Ensuring US Leadership in a Global Economy*, New York: Council of Foreign Relations, pp. 125–41.

Kolbe, J. and Matsui, R. (1998) 'Forging a new bipartisan consensus for free trade', in G. Feketekuty and B. Stokes (eds) *Trade Strategies for a New Era. Ensuring US Leadership in a Global Economy*, New York: Council of Foreign Relations pp. 28–37.

Mann, C.L. (1999) *Is the US Trade Deficit Sustainable*, Washington: Institute for International Economics.

Nanto, D. K. and Jones V. C. (1999) *US International Trade: Data and Forecasts*, Washington D.C. : Congressional Research Service, CRS Issue Brief.

Nivola, P. (1993) *Regulating Unfair Trade*, Washington D.C.: Brookings Institution.

Nolan, M. (1999) 'Learning to Love the WTO', *Foreign Affairs* September/October, 81–3.

Odell, J. and Eichengreen, B. (1998) 'The United States, the ITO, and the WTO: exit options, agent slack, and presidential leadership', in A.O. Krueger (ed.) *The WTO as an International Organization*, Chicago: University of Chicago Press, pp. 181–209.

Richardson, J.D. (1994) 'US Trade policy in the 1980s: Turns – and Roads not Taken', in M. Feldstein (ed.) *American Economic Policy in the 1980s*, Chicago: University of Chicago Press.

Richardson, J.D., Feketekuty, G. and Zhang, Rodriguez A. E. (1998) 'US performance and trade strategy in a shifting global economy', in G. Feketekuty and B. Stokes (eds) *Trade Strategies for a New Era. Ensuring US Leadership in a Global Economy*, New York: Council of Foreign Relations pp. 39–64.

Ruggie, J.G. (1983) 'International regimes, transactions, and change: embedded liberalism in the postwar economic order', in S. Krasner (ed.) *International Regimes*, Ithaca, NY: Cornell University Press, pp.195–231.

Schott, J. (2000) 'WTO trade talks: moving beyond Seattle', *Economic Perspectives*, February, available at http://www.usia.gov/journals/ites/0200/ijee/schott.htm.

Stokes, B. (2000) 'Preparing to bypass the WTO', *Financial Times*, 29 March, p.15.

3   The EU: contending for leadership

Klaus Günter Deutsch

After more than five decades of systemic leadership of the USA in world trade diplomacy, the European Union[1] emerged as a rival contender in the late 1990s. More than any other trading entity, the EU tried to generate support for further multilateral trade liberalisation and rule making in a new round of trade talks under the auspices of the WTO. Former Trade Commissioner Sir Leon Brittan, in particular, deserves much credit for acting as a policy entrepreneur who moulded a host of unresolved technical and legal trade issues into a coherent EU policy position and a potential agenda for a new round of multilateral trade negotiations (MTN). He also coined the term 'Millennium Round', although this has not so far been officially sanctioned.

The governments of the EU member states reached a broad consensus on the objectives for and the approaches to a new trade initiative by the end of October 1999 (Council of the European Union 1999), based on much preparatory work by the European Commission up to July (European Commission 1999). The EU's position comprised a further opening of markets in manufacturing and services; free electronic commerce; rule making in new areas such as competition, investment, social standards and the environment; suggestions on how to improve practical matters such as the implementation of Uruguay Round agreements by poor countries or changes to customs procedures ('trade facilitation'); improvements in specific issues such as intellectual property rights, technical barriers to trade and public procurement; and measures aimed at strengthening the position of developing country exporters. The EU was also prepared to start new talks on farm trade, which were scheduled for 2000 as part of the 'built-in' agenda of the Uruguay Round agreement. The EU was principally ready to discuss trade defence measures in general and anti-dumping in particular. However, the EU was not prepared to accelerate the phasing out of the Multi-Fibre Agreement regulating trade in textiles and clothing, which some developing countries had demanded.

In the rather hectic run-up to the third ministerial conference of the WTO in Seattle in December 1999, the EU managed to clarify and consolidate its position internally but noticed that there remained a considerable gulf between its approach and the policy positions of the United States, the Cairns Group of agricultural exporters and several influential developing countries, such as India and Brazil. At the meeting in Seattle, EU negotiators could not reach their objective of starting a new and comprehensive round of trade talks, even though they had reacted flexibly to the demands of the USA and developing countries. After the failure in Seattle, the EU took stock. Absolving itself from responsibility, US President Clinton was held accountable for the ultimate failure of the ministerial conference. The EU continued to favour a comprehensive round based on the policy position of October.

In the following, the principal determinants of the multilateral trade policy of the EU with respect to the agenda of the planned new round of trade talks will be discussed. I will also consider the specific positions that the EU has adopted. Finally, I will reflect on the strategy and its problems and offer some broad recommendations.

The making of EU trade policy

The policy approach of the EU to the Millennium Round reflects its economic interests, the complex politics of making trade policy in Brussels itself (Deutsch 1999; Messerlin forthcoming; Schöppenthau 1999) and the recently emerged policy priorities of big member state governments and the Commission regarding standards.

Economic interests

The EU is the biggest trading region on the globe and a key player in the multilateral trading system. However, the economic power of the EU is limited, as most high-growth areas in world manufacturing and services are dominated by US corporations. Therefore, EU interest in aggressively opening foreign markets has been rather weak. As EU corporations typically have a comparative advantage in moderately growing industries of medium technological intensity, they have broadly been supportive of freer trade at the margins. However, levels of protection in the EU have remained high in farming, textiles and clothing, coal and steel, cars, and electronic goods (Messerlin forthcoming). Protectionist interests have also scored numerous small victories in imposing contingent protection on non-EU markets, but the EU has remained rather weak in multilateral trade matters.

Decision making in Brussels

The EU has a complex internal structure for making trade policy (Deutsch 1999; Hayes 1993; Schöppenthau 1999; Schuknecht 1992). It is composed not only of Community institutions such as the Commission, the European Council and the European Parliament but also of member states with very different internal structures. The EU's trade policy is therefore subject to the influence of different ideas, interests and institutions. In the end, the very diverse demands of interest groups, governments and Community institutions have to be meshed into a Community position in close cooperation with the European Council and the Commission.

In the past two decades, the multilateral, 'high-track' strand in the Common Commercial Policy (CCP) of the EU has tended to reflect the political compromises between 'open' and 'closed regionalists' among the governments of member states, the liberally inclined Commission, interest groups and trading partners. A liberal minority of 'open regionalists' among member states, usually comprising Germany, the Netherlands, the UK and Denmark (and since the latest enlargement also Finland, Sweden and potentially Austria), often had to confront a Euro-Colbertist coalition of 'closed regionalists' led by France. The liberal forces in the EU could prevail internally only if they could involve the EU in international negotiations, in which the demands of trading partners could be formally brought to bear and the external pressure on the EU kept high. In those instances, a politics of freer trade, a managed liberalisation of external trade, unfolded in quite different trade circumstances, even at the end of the Uruguay Round, in agriculture and textiles and clothing (Deutsch 1999; Schöppenthau 1999).

The need for external compromise and mutual benefit led to a complex set of three-level games of political negotiation that took place simultaneously in national political systems, in Community institutions and in international talks with trading partners. The intermingling of these different levels of political talks finally facilitated a breakthrough in trade reform. Astute political manoeuvring by key commissioners (usually the trade and agriculture portfolios) and the German and French governments as the two informal leaders of the conflicting camps of 'open' and 'closed regionalists' was required to get the EU moving forward.

However, decision making on multilateral trade matters proved to be a highly complex matter. The Uruguay Round negotiations, which were repeatedly on the verge of failure and required decisions to be taken at times by a 'Jumbo Council' consisting of thirty-six ministers of member state governments, revealed serious shortcomings in trade policy making in the Community. The political machinery was highly consensus-oriented, crisis-prone and not adequately equipped for first disentangling efficiency and distributional concerns and then solving them appropriately. This fact of EU political life implied that liberalisation agreed in the GATT would have to remain politically managed and circumscribed. This constrained EU negotiators in engaging in integrative bargaining and made them concede some politically costly measures in exchange for gains in other issue areas.

This mode of policy making and the resulting politics had both advantages and disadvantages. The advantage was that most major interests of key governments and interest groups had a fair chance of being taken into account. Also, governments of trading partners could expect the EU not to change course quickly and suddenly embrace protectionist policies beyond established patterns of sectoral closure and contingent protection. However, the drawback was a system in which the authority of key negotiators (commissioners) was only minimally delegated by the European Council and heavily circumscribed.

Also, the flexibility of negotiators to react to moves of trading partners remained severely curtailed, and the effectiveness of policy making depended on a broad internal consensus, which typically was confined to general principles and win–win situations and stopped far short of accepting the partly negative distributional implications of particular trade policy moves. This left the EU particularly ill-equipped to launch bold new initiatives towards liberalising trade (Deutsch 2000).

Changing political priorities

Since the late 1990s, new governments have been elected in all the large EU countries. Centre-left governments came to power in France, Germany, Italy and the UK. Despite some notable policy differences in the domestic affairs of the socialist or social democratic governments of Lionel Jospin, Gerhard Schröder, Massimo D'Alema and Tony Blair, they all embraced the benefits of the internationalisation of trade, investment and finance and supported freer trade. That has also been true for the conservative Spanish government of José Maria Aznar. New and outright protectionist policy stances did not emerge. Moreover, these governments shared a strong concern about the cross-cutting issues of social standards, environmental protection and trade. Here, the impact of public opinion, in which the possible negative aspects of economic internationalisation ('globalisation') received far more attention than the benefits of liberalisation actually experienced by consumers, was noticeable. Also, the pressure from non-governmental organisations (NGOs) and trade unions could be felt clearly. These governments therefore favoured establishing new rules covering these issues in the WTO.

The inclusion of new players in the trade policy process was a deliberate move by both the Commission and several of the member state governments. In retrospect, it is not clear whether the intention was to broaden support for multilateral trade rules, to balance potential protectionist interests with single-issue groups favouring rule making on essentially non-trade concerns, or to shift the whole trade debate into uncharted waters of global governance in the WTO and away from old-fashioned if meaningful notions of consumer welfare, competition and economic growth. The Seattle ministerial conference revealed clearly the down side risk of politicisation yet failed to provide evidence that new political opportunities were also created. It remains to be seen whether the EU will reconsider its approach to 'civil society'.

Other players in the EU trade policy debate, corporations and interest groups, remained passive in the run-up to the new trade round. European industry remained broadly supportive of free trade, but did not voice strong demands for further liberalisation and/or rule making in specific matters. Also, the position of the unions became increasingly ambiguous, as many of them seemed to take for granted the argument that import competition reduces the income of low-wage labour and called for the introduction of social standards in world trade rules.

EU farm groups still counted their losses stemming from the combined blows of the Uruguay Round Agreement on Agriculture and the two steps of Common Agricultural Policy (CAP) reform in 1992 and 1999. They started to adapt politically to the new reality of the heightened budgetary concerns of EU governments and the prospect of EU enlargement, which implied further adjustment of the CAP, but they remained forces of unabashed agricultural protectionism.

From the Uruguay Round to the Millennium Round

Since the conclusion of the Uruguay Round in 1994 and the establishment of the WTO, the EU has been busy not only with implementing the results of the Uruguay Round and defending highly costly disputes over bananas and beef raised using hormones but also with broadening the agenda beyond the scheduled talks on services and agriculture. In farming, the EU did not expect great benefits to be achieved in political terms. And in services, where considerable export interests exist, conflicts with both the USA and several developing countries looked likely. The EU therefore lobbied hard for a wide agenda of new trade talks in which a multitude of cross-cutting package deals with the USA and developing countries would eventually become feasible. However, the EU's quest for classic multilateralism was not met by an unequivocal response from Washington.

In the 1990s, US trade policy took a turn. Presidential attention and USTR activism shifted from a systemic leadership perspective still prevailing during the Uruguay Round to a much more clearly focused yet narrow interest-based approach towards multilateralism in general and liberalisation in particular. The USA turned to become the driving force behind sectoral advances in multilateral rule making and liberalisation. The EU, given its export interests in those sectors, had no sensible alternative to playing a constructive role in those talks. Agreements on information technology, basic telecommunications and financial services were concluded in 1996–97. In these sectoral issue areas, transatlantic cooperation worked well and the EU was ready to commit itself to keeping its market open. Many Latin American countries were also ready to liberalise. Apart from Japan, Asian cooperation was more limited, however.

The EU's policy position for the Millennium Round

In the late 1990s, the EU devoted considerable energy to convincing its trading partners that a new round of multilateral trade talks was both desirable and feasible. The USA only signalled in late 1998 that it would in principle be willing to consider a new round, whereas many developing countries remained sceptical or openly rejected the idea of a new round well into 1999.

The EU submitted a comprehensive proposal at the end of October 1999, based on a communication of the Commission of July in which the essential policy positions had already been laid down (Council of the European Union

1999; European Commission 1999). In general terms, the EU proposed to start new talks on widening the scope of multilateral trade rules, strengthening the system and broadening its political basis. There was little emphasis on improving market access abroad and on import liberalisation in the EU itself. The Commission, to broaden support for its position, engaged interest groups and NGOs in a dialogue, established a process of academic evaluation and enhanced the transparency of its policy position substantially by using the Internet.

The EU preferred a 'comprehensive' round that would take no longer than three years from start to finish. It should be negotiated as a 'single undertaking', that is without further sectoral interim agreements or an 'early harvest', as the US government initially preferred. The position of the EU comprised defensive, offensive and integrative elements. The EU pursued a clearly defensive strategy in farm trade, which was already on the agenda, in textiles and clothing, and in anti-dumping issues. Offensive, market-opening interests surfaced only in a few issue areas, such as tariff reductions in manufacturing, rules governing free trade in electronic commerce, trade in services and in a special offer to open the markets of industrial countries to exports from the least developed countries (LDCs) until 2003. The EU also proposed to make rules on competition and investment. On integrative elements, the EU favoured establishing rules balancing trade and environmental concerns. Brussels preferred a discussion in appropriate forums of social standards and development, particularly the issue of trade facilitation, i.e. customs paperwork, which puts a heavy burden on the governments of developing countries. The EU also favoured a renewal and strengthening of the TRIPs Agreement, the inclusion of public procurement in the framework of WTO rules and some modest changes to the workings of the dispute settlement mechanism. Some of these important topics are discussed in more detail below.

Farm trade[2]

The position of the EU regarding farm trade talks was straightforward. Based on Article 20 of the Agreement on Agriculture of the Uruguay Round, it was ready to continue negotiations on all aspects of farm trade. The internal reform of EU farming decided in March 1999 in Berlin as part of the Agenda 2000 package provided the platform. The EU preferred a continuation of 'blue box' measures (production-related domestic support), while the states of the Cairns Group and the USA preferred their phasing out, further reductions in trade-distorting domestic and export support and modest import liberalisation of the sky-high tariffs that had resulted from the 'tariffication' exercise of the Agreement on Agriculture. However, the EU also favoured a continuation of the right to subsidise exports, the extension of the 'peace clause', which excludes farm trade from normal DSM procedures until 2003, and of the special safeguard clause beyond the deadline. Furthermore, the EU argued that the 'multifunctionality' of farming should be included in WTO language. Finally, Brussels wanted to negotiate on export credits, food aid and state trading in farming and to improve the access of EU farmers to foreign markets.

The position of the EU was clearly less defensive than in the early 1980s (see Deutsch 1999 on the farm trade talks in the Uruguay Round). A deepening of CAP reform was for many governments a matter of time and political convenience. Politically, the French debate shifted in the direction of reform (Messerlin forthcoming), as some French farmers were the most efficient in the EU and, therefore, potential winners of a more market-oriented reform of the CAP. However, France had limited CAP reform at the Berlin European Council summit in March 1999. Also, the new German government wanted to control agricultural expenditure, deepen the reform of the CAP and slowly prepare the CAP for enlargement.

In that context, multilateral negotiations on farm trade in the framework of an MTN could certainly be expected to generate further pressure on the EU to deepen reform and deal with sky-high protection and resurgent export subsidies. The Cairns Group and the USA could reasonably expect some further reform and liberalisation. Despite some sharp and unresolved controversies on the issue of whether an elimination or a further reduction in export subsidies should be the formal objective of the negotiation, farm trade and EU agricultural protectionism seemed unlikely to become a major stumbling block to freer trade again as it almost had in the Uruguay Round. Rather, a Millennium Round could blow stronger winds into the sails of reformers at a time when change would be most needed.

Services[3]

Although it is not widely appreciated, EU corporations rank first in global trade in services, with British, French and German firms the big traders. This rapidly growing sector of the European economy generated $1.3 trillion in global trade, or 20 per cent of total world trade, in 1998. In 1995, including intra-EU trade, the share of EU firms in global trade in services was 44.5 per cent, or about 25 per cent excluding intra-EU transactions, compared with 16.1 per cent for the USA, which ranks second (Barth 1998: 25). However, most services have only recently become tradable internationally and, given dense domestic regulation, effective levels of protection are still very high. Estimates of overall levels of services protection are far above 50 per cent for all three major trading regions (Messerlin forthcoming). Multilateral rule making was initiated with the GATS in 1994, but multilateral liberalisation has only recently been started with sector agreements. In the future, substantial potential gains for EU consumers may be reaped by opening up sheltered services markets – and substantial losses of producer rental income also may be incurred!

European service firms have showed competitive strength in quite a number of fields in recent years, with telecommunications, banking, insurance, publishing, professional services and tourism the most notable areas. Telecommunications, and financial and professional services are the most rapidly growing sectors and have already been partly liberalised in the common market and in the multilateral framework. However, many service sectors are more difficult. Most transport services, for example, have a history of conflict or bilateral management and have to be considered unlikely to yield substantial multilateral liberalisation in the medium term – in particular, maritime transport and the core business of air transport. The movements of natural persons and government procurement have also proved very difficult to tackle in past attempts.

The EU was a main proponent of strengthening the GATS in a new MTN, of further market opening and liberalisation. It favoured the extension of the application of the m.f.n. rule, which in many cases is still given conditionally for up to ten years, and of commitments to domestic treatment and the opening of sectors in specific schedules by all WTO members. Asian countries in particular, apart from Japan, have kept their markets closed so far.

The EU continues to demand talks on maritime and supplementary air transport services and shows a readiness to consider a second agreement on information technology (ITA II) extending the coverage of products to be traded freely. Furthermore, the EU favours the adoption of horizontal approaches to market opening, rule making on the strengthening of GATS disciplines, on safeguards and subsidies, and on the movement of natural persons. On the defensive side, the French and Belgium movie industries and their respective governments captured the EU regarding trade in audio-visual material, which the EU did not want to liberalise, to the detriment of Hollywood and its European fans.

Social and environmental standards[4]

The EU has been a driving force in promoting multilateral discussion on the trade and labour standards issue, and it has also promoted rule making on trade-related environmental measures. Several centre-left governments seemed to like the idea of pleasing their union constituency on labour rights, and a range of concerned environmental NGOs by the standards rhetoric, which would have to be substantially watered down, or 'paid for' dearly in terms of granting much more substantial access to the EU market to exporters in developing countries.

In the extremely contentious area of linking trading rights to countries' adherence to core labour standards, as agreed in the International Labour Organization (ILO), where significant moves towards strengthening the international regime had occurred in 1998/99, the EU moderated its position substantially. It abandoned the idea of creating a working group in the WTO and instead called for a four-point programme:

- the WTO and ILO ought to enhance their cooperation;
- support for the work of the ILO and a role as observer in the WTO;
- creation of a joint standing working forum of both institutions, which would prepare for a WTO ministerial conference no later than 2001; and
- the provision of incentives and the definite renunciation of sanctions.

(Council of the European Union 1999)

The proposal proved to be so soft that delegations in Seattle noticed a narrowing of differences on the issue. However, US President Bill Clinton, in a newspaper interview during the conference, indicated an intention finally to use sanctions to enforce core labour standards, which brought the ministerial conference to a sudden stop.

The approach of the EU to rule making on environmental issues as they affect world trade was both less controversial and, from an economic point of view, less ambiguous. The EU position was not very specific – greater legal clarity of the relationship between trade rules and measures taken for environmental reasons, production and production methods, eco-labels, and the precautionary principle – and did not obviously threaten the narrow commercial interests of developing countries or heavy polluters among industrial countries. The pre-negotiations could hardly have foundered because of clean air.

Expanding the rulebook: competition and investment[5]

There could hardly be a greater contrast between on the one hand the standards approach, which proved as politically popular as it was economically unsound, and on the other hand the attempt to make rules on competition and investment, which seemed as sound as it was unpopular. It is fair to state that the principled liberal approach of the EU towards establishing rules in both issue areas within the WTO framework (and its potential for enforcement) exhibited true characteristics of conceptual leadership.

Notwithstanding the failure of OECD governments to reach consensus on the Multilateral Agreement on Investment in 1998, the EU lobbied strongly for establishing rules within the confines of the WTO, a very ambitious goal indeed. Specifically, the EU sought legal clarity regarding the definition of foreign direct investment and the coverage of the rules to be agreed. The EU wanted to strengthen the protection and non-discrimination of foreign investors and encourage members to commit themselves to enhancing market access. The EU also favoured legal clarity regarding the rights of countries to regulate investors (Council of the European Union 1999).

Similarly, the European Commission (1999) made a case for establishing core competition principles in the multilateral framework. It proposed adopting common anti-competitive practices, negotiating provisions for international cooperation between competition authorities and creating dispute settlement mechanisms, even though the potential immediate benefits of all this to the EU itself and to its trading partners were less than self-evident. The vast majority of internationally relevant competition cases have been handled by either the US or the EU authorities, or both, and so have been subject to one of two different but similar sets of strict rules. The benefits of multilateralising basic rules would have to be found in constraining and guiding developing countries in legislating competition laws in accordance with agreed multilateral principles. However, the approach of the EU smacked of hypocrisy, as Brussels was unwilling to put its essentially arbitrary anti-dumping arsenal on the competition negotiation table as favoured by several of the developing countries particularly hurt by the abuse of rich countries' contingent protectionism. Nor did anyone consider ruling export cartels to be against WTO rules. It seemed, therefore, that agreement on competition principles was not within the grasp of EU negotiators, despite its appeal in terms of *Ordnungspolitik*.

Perspectives

After the failure of Seattle, the EU took stock and agreed internally that its approach had not been to blame. The defensive strategies in farming, textiles and dumping mostly affected the export interests of developing countries and were partly compensated for by the LDC initiative and a readiness to take trade facilitation further. As the EU had moderated its demands regarding social and environmental standards, the overall approach offered neither substantial gains nor heavy costs to developing countries. The offensive and integrative strategic elements contained in the approach of Brussels were designed more to broaden a very narrow US approach, which focused on export interests. However, the enthusiasm of trading partners to engage in wide-ranging rule making on tangential matters proved limited up to Seattle and did not increase sufficiently at the meeting. Most notably, the lack of interest on the part of the US administration regarding a comprehensive widening and deepening of the multilateral trading system left the EU in a lonely position. If, eventually, Seattle is not interpreted by historians as representing the beginning of the end of multilateral commercial diplomacy but as a temporary setback on the way to rule making for global capitalism, then it may have taught the lesson that transatlantic cooperation and a shared vision as to where to lead the global trading system was still indispensable at the end of the 1990s. Without energetic US leadership, the EU could not set the agenda for multilateral trade policy alone.

Internal political constraints deprived the EU of the power to fully embrace the leadership role that the Commission at least was hoping and working for. The EU had neither a carrot nor a stick big enough to induce or force other trading nations to go along. The common market in manufacturing in Europe was already quite open in most industries. Only a significant reduction in tariff and non-tariff protection in steel, cars and integrated circuits substantially enhanced self-discipline in administered protection (anti-dumping policy, safeguards and non-tariff barriers), and great cuts in the protection of agriculture, textiles and clothing, and services could therefore have offered substantial gains to non-EU exporters and the incentives for their governments to accept wide rule making in exchange. For a variety of reasons, trade in services seemed to be the only carrot on offer, but it proved not big enough.

Nor was there a stick. There is no clear exit option for regional integration as an alternative route to multilateralism, ongoing enlargement talks notwithstanding. Further regional economic integration was on the agenda in any case, but mostly for political reasons. A credible protectionist or unilateral retaliatory threat (such as Section Super-301 in US trade law) was not available to policy makers in Brussels; most of its protection is bound in the WTO except for anti-dumping policy.

Given these structural limits to EU leadership, the third ministerial conference in Seattle demonstrated to governments on both sides of the Atlantic and those in the developing world that the hard work of finding a compromise on the agenda of future trade talks was still ahead of them. Obviously, the compromise would have to rest on both transatlantic cooperation and a suitable approach to meeting the emerging needs of developing countries, many of which had made tremendous moves towards opening up their economies and embracing the benefits of economic exchange in the past two decades.

However, the political dynamics originating from other policy developments may change the fortunes in favour of the EU in the coming years. In particular, the planned enlargement of the EU will both further increase the clout of the EU in world trade diplomacy and generate additional pressure for streamlining internal modes of decision making and for reforming protectionist policies in agriculture. Also, the admission of new members is likely to lead to traditional squabbles about trade-diverting effects and the potential compensation of trading partners in the WTO. On balance, the need for internal economic adjustment, particularly in labour- and resource-intensive economic activities, will increase further but will limit the readiness of Brussels to embrace additional doses of external liberalisation. However, it might still allow for a multilateral binding of the increasingly open European market.

It appears that there will be a window of economic opportunity in the first half of the decade during which the EU would still find the political attention and energy required to steer through a demanding MTN. The potential for further market opening in farming, textiles, trade in manufacturing (tariff reductions) and services is clearly present. As in the past, however, the EU is still devoid of a strong and focused input of export-oriented and competitive manufacturing and services firms that would generate the required support for the opening of markets abroad. Much more specific work on the possibility of using horizontal, quantitatively based measures of opening up highly protected services markets is clearly needed, in particular in the OECD, which may generate the conceptual knowledge, as proved by the work on agriculture in the past.

Some rule making in the environmental field also seems within reach. However, the prospect of extensive rule making in areas such as investment, competition and labour standards is limited. Even though developing countries could well gain from multilateral rules on investment and competition, they may feel unnecessarily constrained by binding themselves in the WTO. They will feel even more constrained regarding labour standards, on which the economics is far less clear. However, they will probably have to seek improvements in these areas for purely marketing and commercial reasons.

Recommendations

The position of the EU regarding an MTN suffered from two defects. It was not sufficiently attractive to developing countries; nor was it closely coordinated with the United States. It therefore seems that the position of the EU will need to be changed gradually, in particular becoming more focused and deeper in several issue areas.

The EU may therefore consider its approach to developing countries. It should credibly signal a deepening of agricultural reform, which will be on the agenda for budgetary and enlargement reasons in any case. In particular, the EU could indicate a willingness to phase out 'blue box' measures over a couple of years after a new agreement, reduce agricultural tariffs by a substantial across-the-board percentage and show readiness to negotiate a substantial further reduction in export subsidies by both volume and expenditure. Also, the EU should show more willingness to accelerate the much delayed process of liberalisation of trade in textiles and clothing and formally propose to put the strengthening of disciplines on anti-dumping and other trade defence measures on the agenda. The EU should uphold its LDC initiative and generate support among other industrial and advanced developed countries and continue to take 'trade facilitation' and implementation problems seriously.

It also seems appropriate for the EU to strengthen the market-access and liberalisation aspect of its position as opposed to the extensive rule-making part. The EU should redouble its efforts to specify market-opening demands in services, put more emphasis on tariff and NTB reductions in manufacturing, consider an early agreement on information technology products and e-commerce as both having economic benefits, if some negotiation drawbacks, and work closely with the USA on delineating a potential package for liberalising world trade.

In the field of rule making, the EU should definitely maintain its position of treating social standards as clearly out of the formal framework of an MTN and not strive to have it included in an agreement. Member state governments may well find a way to please domestic constituencies by debating these matters on their own merits in appropriate international forums without threatening the whole edifice of multilateral trade rules once again. Regarding environmental rules, there seems to be potential to reach a consensus on the clarification of rules concerning the interaction of environmental agreements and trade. As far as competition and investment are concerned, the EU probably needs to postpone or substantially water down its principled approach beyond a new MTN, as the international consensus does not yet seem to have evolved as far as to embrace a fully fledged rule-making role for the WTO. Also, the immediate benefits do not seem strong enough for governments to risk possible adverse consequences for domestic politics for a non-essential matter.

The EU may also consider further internal institutional and policy reforms to equip itself with a better decision-making system more suited to achieving its objectives, as recommended by the author (Deutsch 1999). Such a reform would entail:

- a much enhanced role for the trade commissioner, possibly even the creation of a separate trade authority;
- a clear constitutional delegation of negotiating authority on the basis of a broad mandate of the European Council without its micro-management during an MTN;
- a provision for formal ratification by the European Parliament of the EU's position on the start and conclusion of an MTN;
- the establishment of a policy instrument allowing for a temporary and digressive trade adjustment assistance to troubled workers, which could be financed out of the discretionary part of the structural funds;
- the establishment of a permanent trade advisory body that would comprise all relevant interest groups and consult the Trade Commission on trade strategy; and
- the establishment of a regular economic evaluation of policy options and changes, which has been started with the 'sustainability impact assessment study' (Kirckpatrick and Lee 1999).

Without substantial internal policy changes – in terms of both substance and institutions – the EU's quest for international leadership will be accepted by neither developing countries nor the United States. Further trade reform is looming down the road, and there are good reasons for trading partners to engage the EU in a new MTN to strengthen the reformers among governments, corporations and public opinion. Left to itself, the EU probably cannot lead trade diplomacy or change its ways appropriately.

Notes

This article expresses the opinions of the author only.

1   Strictly speaking, trade policy is still a matter for the European Community (or the European Community for Steel and Coal, which, again, is regulated separately). In some paragraphs, I refer to historical developments prior to the advent of the EU without changing the abbreviation. This is solely for the reason of simplicity.
2   Regarding the specifics, see Chapter 15 in this book.
3   Regarding the specifics of the issues, see Chapters 7, 8 and 9 in this book.
4   Regarding labour see Chapter 17; regarding environmental issues see Chapter 18, both in this book.
5   Regarding competition see Chapter 11; regarding investment see Chapter 13, both in this book.

References

Barth, D. (1998) *Perspektiven des internationalen Dienstleistungshandels*, Bonn: Friedrich Ebert Stiftung.

Council of the European Union (1999) *Preparation of the Third WTO Ministerial Conference – Council Conclusions*, 25 October, available on the Internet at http://www.europa.eu.int /comm/trade/2000_round.

Deutsch, K.G. (1999) *The Politics of Freer Trade in Europe. Three-level Games in the Common Commercial Policy of the EU, 1985–1997*, Hamburg, Münster and New York: LIT and St Martin's Press.

—— (2000) 'Exchange-rate policy-making in the euro area: lessons from trade?' in R. Mundell and A. Clesse (eds) *The Euro as a Stabilizer in the International Economic System*, Norwell, Mass.: Kluwer Academic, pp.111–34.

European Commission (1999) *Communication to the Council and to the European Parliament: The EU Approach to the Millennium Round*, July, available on the Internet at http://www.europa.eu.int/comm/trade/2000_round.

Hayes, J.P. (1993) *Making Trade Policy in the European Community*, New York: St Martin's Press.

Kirckpatrick, C. and Lee, N. (1999) *Sustainability Impact Assessment Study*, available on the Internet at http://www.europa.eu.int/comm/trade/2000_round.

Messerlin, P.A. (forthcoming) *Measuring the Costs of Protection in Europe*, Washington: Institute for International Economics.

Schöppenthau, P.V. (1999) *Die Europäische Union als Akteur der internationalen Handelspolitik. Die Textilverhandlungen der GATT-Uruguay-Runde*, Wiesbaden: DUV.

Schuknecht, L. (1992) *Trade Protection in the European Community*, Chur: Harwood Academic.

4 WTO trade negotiations viewed from Tokyo

Hiroya Ichikawa and Maki Kunimatsu

Introduction

The process of trade policy making in Japan will have to change if Japan is to play a major role in the forthcoming WTO negotiations. The term 'Japan Incorporated', which has often been used to characterise Japan's political economy, conjures up images of a big and ubiquitous state that is instinctively distrustful of *laissez-faire* capitalism and relies on administrative guidance for control. According to this view, the scope of state intervention is exceedingly wide, and the Ministry of International Trade and Industry (MITI) prefers vigorous intervention to the market mechanism.

But globalisation puts pressure on 'Japan Inc'. The prolonged economic recession during the 1990s, which was caused by the burst of the bubble economy and was followed by a serious systemic financial crisis, brought a strong message to the Japanese people that they no longer benefit from the old-fashioned model. Instead, an increasing number of Japanese call for further deregulation of markets in order to strengthen the competitiveness of Japanese corporations.

However, a serious problem of policy making for the next trade round exists. For example, the business community in general seems to feel that the ministries responsible for the various industries rarely listen to industry views and do not inform the industry of the state of negotiations. Even if some government agencies and ministries are informed about the demands of industries for the next round of negotiations, the complicated bureaucratic barriers between different government agencies hinder the flow of this information to other agencies. It seems that there is nobody in Japan who would be able to develop a grand strategy for the next round of negotiations.

The question arises: what will be on the agenda of the next WTO negotiations? And who will benefit? In the increasingly interdependent world, trade negotiations are not confined to trade issues at national borders but are closely linked to domestic social and economic regulations. A high degree of effective cooperation between ministries, a comprehensive analysis of the issues and timely, unrestricted exchange of information are required.

The conventional *shingikai* (advisory councils for the various ministries) approach is no longer adequate. It lacks transparency, and the participation of the public has been too limited. What is needed is a more transparent and innovative mechanism for the formulation of trade policy that is open to different groups of society. Leaving everything to trade experts and technocrats will not result in a fruitful approach to the new round.

Comprehensive round of negotiations versus narrow negotiation packages

Severe conflicts

The world's key policy makers face major challenges to the multilateral trading system. Seen in this light, the Japanese government's present position on the agricultural negotiations in particular is disappointingly passive, which is a reflection of weak leadership of the main political parties. According to the official Japanese position announced in May 1999, the 'WTO should establish a set of rules and disciplines which ensure the differences in natural conditions and historical background of agriculture in each member country'. This Japanese stance emphasises 'the importance of multi-functionality of agriculture', which refers to food security, among other concerns. This concept explicitly assumes instability of the supply of and demand for food in international agricultural markets and regards domestic agricultural production as an indispensable basis for food security. While Japan's agricultural community is content with this position, the issue of Japan's import tariffs and import quotas for rice may become an important subject in forthcoming farm trade negotiations.

Japan will not be able to play a major role in the forthcoming round if it adopts such a position. A couple of months after the Seattle ministerial conference, the General Council agreed on the framework for negotiations on services and agriculture for the year 2000. This seems to be at least one step forward. However, there is a growing consensus both in the Japanese government and in business that a comprehensive round of negotiations should be launched. Without multilateral efforts in the area of investment, a review of anti-dumping rules, further tariff reductions for trade in goods and other areas, the negotiations in agriculture and services will not make progress.

The built-in agenda should finally be integrated into a comprehensive round of negotiations. Table 4.1 illustrates the major trading partners' attitudes at this point in time: Japan and the EU are in favour of the comprehensive approach, whereas the USA and developing countries oppose it. Among developing countries, Thailand, Mexico, Chile, Argentina and Hungary have shown an interest in new trade negotiations, while countries such as India, Malaysia, Egypt and Pakistan are not interested. They maintain that they have not seen the benefits from the Uruguay Round. In past negotiations, the United States provided strong leadership for an open multilateral system and, ironically, its very success has resulted in its retreat from multilateralism. Successive rounds of multilateral tariff negotiations fostered increased competition from abroad, which in turn has increased protectionist pressures in the USA. This led Americans to see themselves more as a competitor in, rather than as a protector of, the open multilateral trading system.

It is quite clear that trade liberalisation has been in Japan's self-interest. The average tariff rates applied to minerals and manufactured goods were reduced from 3.8 to 1.5 per cent in Japan as a result of the Uruguay Round, compared with 3.5 per cent (down from 5.4 per cent) in the USA and 3.6 per cent (down from 5.7 per cent) in the EU. Japan should have provided much stronger leadership before the Seattle ministerial conference, but agricultural pressure groups did not permit the fragile Liberal Democratic Party and its alliance to exercise such a strong leadership role. In February 2000, President Clinton informed Mr Kono, Japanese minister of foreign affairs, of the US intention to start the new round of negotiations before the Okinawa summit of the Group of Seven. In Tokyo, however, no substantial progress is expected until after the US presidential election.

Substantive issues in the next round – the perspective of the Japanese business community

While farmers' groups maintain a defensive position on the next round, neither labour unions nor NGOs are yet playing a major role in public debates in Japan on the WTO. This leaves the business community as the most important group to shape a constructive Japanese position for the new round, for which it is in fact actively calling. The business community recognises that the globalisation of economies is to be facilitated through the expansion of transactions in services and information. Keidanren (Federation of Economic Organizations of Japan), the leading Japanese business organisation, actively participates in the public debate and has publicly stated its belief that the new negotiations will serve to provide a renewed infrastructure for the expansion of the world economy in the early decades of the twenty-first century.

In the era of GATT, the world trade system has gone through several rounds

Table 4.1 Attitudes to a comprehensive new round of trade negotiations

	Japan	*EU*	*USA*	*Developing countries*
Launching round	+ +	+ +	+	− / +
BIA promotion	− −	− −	+ +	− / +
Services	+	+	+ +	+
Agriculture	−	−	+ +	+
Anti-dumping	+ +	+	−	+
Investment	+	+ +	−	−
Labour standards	−	+	+ +	−

of negotiations, which started from the tariffication of quotas and tariff reductions and the elimination of so-called non-tariff barriers and then extended to the protection of intellectual property rights and to trade in services. The coverage of GATT/WTO has been expanded to such an extent that it now deals with issues that go deeply into the domestic regulations and the social and economic systems of member countries. Since the establishment of the WTO in 1995, free trade principles have been extended to information technology in the Information Technology Agreement. The Basic Telecommunications Agreement and the Financial Services Agreement, both of which go far beyond the traditional liberalisation of cross-border transactions, have also been reached. They cover the reduction of restrictions on investment in services as well as the harmonisation of domestic regulations in a pro-competition manner.

Building on this, the Japanese business community as it is represented by Keidanren, whose members depend so much on international trade rules and which has been a powerful supporter of the free trade system itself, expects progress in the following issue areas:

- rule setting on international investment, competition and electronic commerce;
- a review and strengthening of anti-dumping rules;
- intellectual property rights;
- a liberalisation of trade in services; and
- tariff reductions in the case of industrial products.

Keidanren emphasises that the next round of negotiations should cover areas of mutual interest for both developing and developed countries. This will only be possible if the negotiations cover many different issues. The increased interdependence of the world and the increased globalisation of economic activities have brought difficult and complex issues to the forefront. However, the Japanese business community regards the launching of a comprehensive round of negotiations as an inevitable and important step towards establishing the new infrastructure for the expansion of the world economy early in the next century.

Japan's preferences regarding trade in services

New talks on trade in services have been started as part of the built-in agenda of the Uruguay Round at a special meeting of the Council for Trade in Services under the chairmanship of Ambassador Marci of Canada.

It is generally understood elsewhere that the Japanese services sector is not as competitive internationally as this sector is in the USA or Europe. This perception has led observers to speculate that the Japanese services sector would naturally seek protection. It is suggested that the Japanese government and businesses do not favour a liberalisation of trade in services. It is often thought that Japan's position is similar to those of other developed countries.

However, it may be stressed that Keidanren's view is different.[1] According to internal discussions in Keidanren, which started in the summer of 1999, many members believe that they should look for new business opportunities in the services markets both domestically and in other countries.

This could be accomplished by the liberalisation of services markets in developing countries as well as by further deregulation at home. Thus there is a growing voice in favour of negotiations. Keidanren's view reflects both suppliers and users of services.

The official policy paper to be submitted to the Japanese government (seventeen ministries and agencies) may be summarised as follows:

- The negotiations on trade in services will be one of the most critical agendas in the next WTO negotiations. Japanese industry is strongly interested in the direction and possible result of these negotiations.
- At present, many Japanese firms face a number of obstacles in their services transactions with other countries. The negotiations on liberalisation in trade in services are expected to eliminate discriminatory regulations imposed on the business activities of foreign companies in developing countries and to increase the transparency of the various services-related regulations and procedures.
- At the same time, producing a successful conclusion to the negotiations will require the pro-active participation of developing countries. Negotiations should respond sensitively to the circumstances of each developing country and provide active support for institutional development such as legislation and human resources.
- To ensure the effective implementation of the above, consideration should be given to combining the traditional request-and-offer approach with a formula approach. A formula approach would be particularly effective in areas such as foreign ownership restrictions, where the extent of regulations can be gauged numerically.
- Horizontal liberalisation for specific 'modes of supply' of services trade should also be considered. For example, when a company is establishing a foreign commercial presence (mode 3), problems sometimes arise in sending executives, engineers and other key personnel (mode 4) to the country in question. It will be vital to allow the free movement of executives and engineers in services areas where the establishment of a foreign commercial presence is permitted.
- In addition, the rapid development of electronic commerce is opening the way for many services that could traditionally be provided only under a foreign commercial presence (mode 3) or the movement of natural persons (mode 4). They now can be offered under cross-border transactions (mode 1) and consumption abroad (mode 2). In many cases, no commitments have so far been made for these services in national schedules due to a lack of technical feasibility. Member countries now need to make positive commitments to liberalisation in order to promote the development of

electronic commerce. Despite the fact that m.f.n. exemptions as such are against the fundamental spirit of the GATS, many countries have exemptions registered in a range of areas. As stated in the GATS Annex II (Exemptions), m.f.n. exemptions should also be the subject of negotiations in the next round, while those countries that have registered exemptions should in principle be required to withdraw these by 2005 at the latest.

- The sound development of electronic commerce will depend on keeping government regulations to a bare minimum and developing an electronic commerce framework based on the voluntary efforts of private industry. In the WTO context, it will be important to maintain the freeze on customs duties on electronic transmissions. Where services already covered under GATS disciplines are provided through digital means, all such services should be subject to GATS rules regardless of the means of delivery.

- Japanese business also believes that negotiations should address a strengthening of discipline on domestic regulations. In this regard, (1) undeveloped and opaque legal systems subject to arbitrary operation and sudden changes (e.g. no legal precedent, oral explanations of new regulations, unfair service permission systems, etc.) and (2) opaque and unreasonable licensing requirements and procedures (e.g. licensing criteria and fees, etc.) should be reviewed and rules to improve transparency established. An 'understanding' or guidelines on the transparency provision in GATS Article III should be considered.

- With regard to pro-competition domestic regulations, as seen in the reference paper on the Basic Telecommunications Agreement, detailed consideration should be given to the specific situation in each particular sector. Although the reference paper on the Basic Telecommunications Agreement promoted liberalisation by providing guidelines to those countries seeking to liberalise, the definition of the terms of liberalisation and the allocation of responsibility for the burden of proof must be clarified to the greatest extent possible.

- Development of GATS rules in the area of government procurement, safeguards and subsidies should be considered.

- As far as sectors are concerned, Japanese business places a high priority on the financial (banking, insurance, securities), telecommunications, construction, distribution and transportation (air and maritime) services sectors.

Regarding TRIMs, the following specific commitments by member countries should be included in the negotiating schedules so that obstacles to business in services transactions can be reduced or eliminated:

- foreign ownership restrictions;
- nationality and residency requirements for company executives and staff;
- restrictions on overseas remittances;
- performance requirements (technology transfer, etc.); and
- domestic procurement requirements for materials and services.

The rise of civil society

There are nearly nine million employees of NGOs in the USA, almost six million in the EU and more than two million in Japan. The past decade has witnessed the emergence of NGOs as active participants in international policy debates. These NGOs are building global networks. New international economic agreements on trade and investment cover much broader areas than ever before, with means of enforcement that are more effective than ever before. New information and communications technologies link a large number of people in multiple locations simultaneously and allow decisions to be made and action to be taken in real time across the world.

Global economic rules on trade and investment are the result of negotiations between governments that are primarily responsible for protecting national interests. Furthermore, global trade agreements that shape national economies are still negotiated in the tradition of the GATT – narrowly defined trade agreements produced by a 'trade Mafia' of legal experts and economists who are highly specialised in the detailed provisions of trade and investment.

However, many NGOs observe that these economic agreements have major implications for human welfare that go well beyond the conventional trade agreements of the past. Japan's NGO community began to express its concerns about the implications of a new trade round for the ability of countries to implement environmental protection measures and labour standards. The voice of Citizen Forum 2000, for instance, raises a fundamental question as to the meaningfulness of the forthcoming agricultural trade negotiation on grounds of global environmental and food security.

The influence of the NGOs cannot or should not be neglected any longer. Therefore, the WTO has established constructive relationships with NGOs with a view to enhancing their understanding of trade negotiations and obtaining their support. At present, however, the dialogue between negotiators in governments and NGOs is inadequate or immature in many countries, including Japan. Furthermore, as most governments hold positions different from those of domestic NGOs, international alliances between NGOs are likely to be strengthened much further.

Recommendations

Dialogue of government, industry and NGOs

It is perhaps worth mentioning that a body for government–industry dialogue on WTO negotiations was established in September 1999, based on the proposal by Keidanren and supported by major ministries. Continuous and intensive discussions have been held between ministries, including the Ministry of Foreign Affairs, the Ministry of Finance, MITI and the Ministry of Agriculture. No ministry has been excluded *a priori* from this dialogue, and neither have experts from industries in the various sectors. The Ministry of

Foreign Affairs also holds briefing sessions for NGOs (including groups concerned with the environment, food security, consumer protection and agriculture) and often invites officials from other ministries.

Establishing a formal procedure for handling complaints

However, the establishment of a formal procedure for complaints on foreign trade policy and measures may be required. Japanese businesses should participate more actively in various forms of discussion on the WTO negotiations on rule making and liberalisation of trade. At the same time, they should pay more attention to using effectively the routine function of dispute settlement in the WTO through government channels. At present, no clear procedure is available to Japanese firms to take up issues with the Japanese government directly, even when they consider themselves to be injured by trade restrictions or actions by foreign governments. The United States and the EU have already built such procedures into law such as the US Trade Act Section 301 and the EU Trade Barrier Regulation. In order to terminate informal requests to the government from business firms, which tend to lead to somewhat arbitrary decisions, and secure a maximum degree of transparency, the establishment of a formal system for the handling of complaints in Japan would seem helpful.

A cost–benefit paper

Furthermore, the government should publish a basic negotiating position paper containing a proper analysis of the costs and benefits, and the impact on society. This would facilitate a public discussion between government agencies, industries, consumers, academics and NGOs. Without this, momentum for the new round will not be sustainable in Japan.

Towards a new round

A free multilateral world trade system sustained by the GATT and the WTO has been a common asset of existing and future members of the WTO. Member states should continue to strive for its ultimate goal – an improvement in the quality of life of all people as a result of the increasing international division of labour (despite the fact that WTO trade rules do not always reflect international trade theory). The present priorities must be, first, to accomplish a substantial liberalisation of trade in goods, services and investment, and, second, to review and strengthen rules on trade and investment, intellectual property rights, anti-dumping measures, and other matters. The agricultural policies of Japan should be reconsidered so that the Japanese initiative in the new round can be aggressively pursued. In order to achieve this, more active public discussions are required to create a consensus among government, farmers, business and citizens. However, the political leadership is still too weak.

Environment and labour standards

The trade and environment debate raises difficult issues and submits the principles of the world trade order to scrutiny from a new perspective. However, the proposal to integrate environmental concerns or labour standards, for instance, into the multilateral trade order might not lead to success in new negotiations, as evidenced by unsuccessful attempts to link trade and other issues in the past. Those who are in favour of laws furthering environmental and other public interests in a country fear that the rulings of WTO panels place existing domestic laws in jeopardy, and this threatens legitimate domestic policy objectives. They maintain that the legal constraints imposed by the WTO create obstacles to the formation of domestic political coalitions between sectoral interest groups pursuing protectionist aims and public interest groups.

Any formal linkage of trade to environmental or labour standards permits governments to depart from the basic principles of the world trade order without establishing effective new disciplines. As a consequence, governments would always be able to justify resorting to discretionary, second-best policy instruments. A fundamental lesson that can be drawn from the GATT's links with monetary, development and competition policies is that, upon entering the realm of the second-best, the realm of the rule of the law is left behind, and any such links therefore entail a move away from the legal framework governing international trade relations.

The environment, for example, is a huge issue in itself. Different countries have very different environmental measures and policies, and no clear international consensus has yet been reached on environmental damage and its causes. Given the limited knowledge at present and the lack of an international consensus, it would be wise not to link trade and environmental issues in the WTO framework. However, issues on which a reasonable international consensus already exits, such as in the case of the Montreal Protocol, the Basle Convention and the Washington Treaty, may be reviewed and discussed within the framework of the WTO with respect to their impact as trade-restricting measures. International cooperation on cross-border pollution and global environmental pollution should be left to more appropriate international forums. The WTO is not a supra-organisation towering above all other international organisations. It might collapse if too many social issues are brought into the negotiations. The WTO should be used as an organisation to provide a set of trade rules that are adequate for the needs of the time. At the same time, the WTO should strengthen its efforts to construct a positive relationship with civil society and find a way to deal effectively with social issues such as the environment, labour standards and development.

Notes

1   Concerning the basic position and specific requests, specific service sectors are trying to elaborate on them at this stage. Keidanren established a 'Japan Services Network' in October 1999 to promote information exchange between various services sectors and to enable discussion with their foreign counterparts, such as the European

Services Forum and the Coalition of Services Industries in the USA. Such attempts may demonstrate the supportive attitude of Japanese business in the success of services negotiations.

5 Developing countries and the Millennium Round

J. Michael Finger and Philip Schuler

Many voices are insisting that the next WTO round be a 'development round'. Upon taking office in September 1999, WTO Director-General Michael Moore declared that his top priority for the next three years would be to expand trading opportunities for developing countries. The centrepiece of his effort is a call to eliminate tariffs imposed by industrialised countries on imports from the world's poorest countries. Former World Bank chief economist Joseph Stiglitz argues that any future trade round will not succeed unless it reflects the interests and concerns of developing countries (Stiglitz 1999). And the developing countries themselves, at a workshop held to prepare for the Seattle ministerial conference, proposed that the next round of multilateral trade negotiations be a 'development round'.

In this paper, we will review the positions that developing countries have taken regarding another WTO round, and we will document concerns that they have expressed about the unbalanced outcome of the Uruguay Round – developing countries gave more than they got. We will also point out that the WTO has entered areas that are primarily development issues, which are more properly approached as development issues with a trade dimension than as trade issues with an add-on development dimension. There is need for a renewed development effort in these areas, but we question whether a WTO negotiating round is the best medium for such an effort.

The Uruguay Round bargain[1]

The grand North–South bargain struck at the Uruguay Round was that developing countries would take on significant commitments in 'new areas' such as intellectual property and services. In exchange, industrialised countries would open up in areas of particular export interest to developing countries: agriculture and textiles/clothing. For developing countries, the new areas included more than services, intellectual property and other areas that were new to the GATT/WTO system. Also new to most developing countries were commitments in the areas covered by the eleven Tokyo Round codes (e.g. standards, rules of origin, subsidies and anti-dumping). Few developing countries had signed these codes.

As the impact of the Uruguay Round began to be felt, developing countries have become frustrated with the imbalance in its results. The market-access 'surplus' of concessions that they thought they had negotiated is proving to be less than expected, the costs of what they took on in new areas are proving to be larger than expected, and the benefits they will receive are smaller.

Market access

When the score is totalled, a developing countries' 'surplus' on market access is not apparent (Finger and Schuknecht 1999). Looking first at tariffs (see Table 5.1), the developing countries' tariff reductions covered as large a share of their imports as did those of the developed countries. Their tariff cuts – when measured by how they will affect exporters' receipts – were deeper than those of the developed countries. The percentage of imports covered by GATT-bound rates is now almost as high for the developing countries as for the developed. The deadline set by the Uruguay Round agreement for the elimination of all quantitative restrictions (including VERs) except those sanctioned by specific WTO provisions has passed and all countries seem to have complied. The WTO has received no complaints about failure to meet this obligation, by developing countries or by industrialised countries. As for NTBs generally, the tariffication of agricultural protection meant that all countries that used NTBs in that sector had to remove them. Apart from agriculture, the best available information shows as significant a reduction of NTBs by developing countries as by industrial countries (*ibid.*: 14).

A major source of frustration for developing countries over the market-access bargain is what they have actually gained in agriculture and textiles/clothing. Many industrialised countries replaced existing agricultural

Table 5.1 Uruguay Round tariff concessions given and received

	Developed economies		Developing economies	
	% of imports	depth of cut $dT/(1+T)$	% of imports	Depth of cut $dT/(1+T)$
Concessions given:				
All merchandise	30	1.0	29	2.3
Industrial goods	32	1.0	33	2.7
Concessions received:				
All merchandise	36	1.4	28	1.0
Industrial goods	37	1.5	36	1.2

Source: Finger and Schuknecht (1999), table T-1, based on Finger *et al.* (1995).

quotas with tariff rates that minimally reduced and in some instances increased the degree of protection (Ingco 1995; Hathaway and Ingco 1996). Agricultural protection has been converted from an array of NTBs to tariffs-only, but reduction of trade barriers, domestic support measures and export subsidies are still to be negotiated.

The Agreement on Textiles and Clothing (ATC) has allowed industrialised countries to put off much of the market liberalisation until the very end of the transition period, that is until 2005. 'Liberalisation' to date under the ATC has been mostly on products that were not under restraint to begin with. Shortly after the agreement came into effect, the USA applied 'transitional safeguards' (allowed under the ATC) on a number of products, and the EU took anti-dumping action against several textiles exporters. These measures have raised suspicions that when the industrialised countries get to the stage of the agreement in which the obligation to remove MFA sanctions restrictions will actually begin to bite, they will replace this quota protection with anti-dumping actions and other traditional safeguards.

In sum, the market-access concessions that the developing countries agreed to make were significant and are all in place now – the deadline for tariff cuts and elimination of non-MFA quantitative restrictions was 1 January 2000. The most important market-access concessions that these countries received in exchange have yet to be delivered (textiles/clothing) or even have yet to be negotiated (agriculture).

New areas

The emerging view of what developing countries took on in the new areas is closely tied to positions that they are taking *vis-à-vis* further negotiations. Rather than present that outcome in a manner parallel to how we have presented the market-access outcome, we will blend it in with the following discussion of developing country positions. As in the market-access concessions, the deadline for implementation of commitments in the new areas was 1 January 2000, except that in several areas the least developed countries (LDCs) are exempt from some obligations and have an additional five years to implement several others.

Developing country positions

The Seattle meetings were preceded by lengthy (albeit ultimately inconclusive) discussions and exchanges of proposals for the agenda of the next round of trade talks. WTO members submitted over 225 working papers in preparation for the 1999 ministerial conference, just under half of which were submitted by developing countries. While there is no consensus across all developing countries, a number of positions have emerged from these proposals that have widespread support in developing countries.

- *No new round* The WTO must correct imbalances in the implementation of the Uruguay Round before initiating a new round of trade talks; and new talks should limit themselves to the built-in agenda of services and agriculture.
- *Services* Liberalisation of trade in services should focus on sectors important to developing countries.
- *Agriculture* Developing countries that export food call for the elimination of all subsidies and barriers to agricultural trade, while those developing countries that import food oppose the 'multifunctionality' of agriculture in industrialised countries but support trade rules that recognise it in developing countries.
- *Industrial tariffs* Developing countries should offer duty-free access to imports from LDCs, and developing countries need more flexibility to impose import restrictions when these serve development goals.
- *Non-trade issues* Trade rules must not be linked to labour or environmental regulations.

We take up these proposals in more detail below, but one issue that received considerable media attention during and after the Battle in Seattle – WTO 'transparency' – was not particularly prominent in the proposals submitted in advance of the meetings.

Implementation

Developing countries, most visibly India and Egypt, frequently ask why the WTO should initiate a new round of negotiations when members have not yet implemented promises made at the Uruguay Round. Meeting in late 1999, trade ministers from the G-77 group of developing countries listed implementation of past agreements as the number one priority for the next round of trade talks. There are two facets to the complaint by developing countries about implementation. One is that liberalisation by industrialised countries in agriculture and clothing/textiles has not yet been delivered. The other, perhaps even more serious, concerns the burden that the new obligations and their implementation place on developing countries, and the failure of the industrialised countries to provide the promised assistance with this implementation.

It costs money!

In the background here is the realisation that implementation in the new areas will cost money. While there may be a considerable political cost to tariff cuts, and considerable money will flow in different directions as a result, implementing them – changing the tariff rates – requires no more than the stroke of a minister's or a legislator's pen. A new customs system, on the other hand, requires more secure facilities, computers and sophisticated control systems, and staff training. To bring food safety regulations up to world standards, inspection and quarantine facilities must be built, animal vaccination programmes established, etc. In an earlier paper (Finger and Schuler 1999), we assessed the costs of implementing three of these agreements: customs valuation, sanitary and phytosanitary standards (SPS), and trade-related intellectual property rights (TRIPs) (three of the six Uruguay Round agreements that involve restructuring domestic regulations). Based on World Bank project experience, the bill for these three comes to $150 million – more than a full year's development budget for eight of the twelve LDCs for which we could find a figure for that part of the budget. Furthermore, legitimate questions can be raised about the wisdom of a poor country spending its marginal million dollars on implementing the intellectual property agreement rather than on, say, education for girls and women.

Pay? Now! Gain? Maybe later

Another dimension to the imbalance in the outcome of the Uruguay Round is that the commitments made by developing countries in the new areas are legally binding. The other side of the deal, the promise of implementation assistance by the industrialised countries, is not a legally binding commitment, and minimal assistance has been forthcoming. Compared with the $150 million cost for each country, multiplied by, say, 100 countries, the WTO technical assistance budget in 1999 was less than one million Swiss francs. The 'confidence-building package' put forward on 31 March 2000 by the Quad (Canada, the EU, Japan, the USA) suggested increased technical assistance to meet WTO obligations but offered no money to pay for it.

The complaint about developing countries taking on immediate and legally bound obligations in exchange for non-bound promises for future delivery applies quite broadly, e.g. TRIPs. The obligation to extend patent protection to pharmaceuticals and agricultural chemicals has a legal deadline and immediate costs – increased payments to exporters in industrialised countries. The benefits – (1) innovation aimed at specific needs of developing countries, perhaps by citizens of developing countries; and (2) direct foreign investment in these sectors – are more nebulous, less certain and are to come later.

Many developing countries are at present in violation of a number of their new areas commitments; they simply have not implemented them. In discussions conducted since the Seattle meetings, the EU has proposed a three-year extension on transition periods for SPS and customs valuation, a two-year extension on TRIMs, and greater flexibility on medicinal patents covered by TRIPs. The USA opposes any blanket extension of implementation deadlines, favouring instead reviews of requests to extend deadlines on a case-by-case basis. Behind the US position there seems to be a strategy to use WTO lawsuits against selected countries in defence of the market-access interests of US exporters. To date, discussions have centred on the length of time that developing countries should have to implement regulatory reforms. Industrialised countries have not considered the possible need to negotiate a revision of several of these agreements so that they make better economic sense as policy guidance for developing countries.[2]

Do it my way!

The content of the obligations imposed by the WTO new areas agreements can be characterised as the advanced countries saying to the others, 'Do it my way!' The customs valuation agreement basically imposes the US–EU system on everyone. The standards agreements and the TRIPs effectively require countries to make their domestic regulations compatible with existing international conventions (e.g. the Codex Alimentarius Commission and various international conventions on patents and copyrights). As these conventions codify the existing rules in industrialised countries as the international standard, compliance for those countries brings minimal implementation costs – it means little more than applying domestic regulations fairly at the border. For developing countries, it means replacing indigenous regulations and procedures by international ones. That will cost real money and may not contribute to development in these countries.

Agriculture

Article 20 of the Uruguay Round Agreement on Agriculture requires WTO members to start negotiations on agriculture by January 2000. The debate revolves mainly around the concept of 'multifunctionality' of agriculture – the argument advanced by the EU that agriculture has a multifunctional role in society and therefore trade rules must take into account a variety of social and environmental concerns. A developing country's position depends primarily on whether it is a net food importer or exporter.

As a rule, food-exporting developing countries oppose outright the concept of multifunctionality. The most vocal opponent is the Cairns Group of agricultural exporting countries, which includes both developed and developing countries. It calls for the elimination (or at least the substantial reduction) of production and export subsidies for agriculture, reducing import tariffs and generally placing agricultural trade under the same rules governing trade in other goods. These demands are aimed at breaking open the heavily protected markets of Europe and Japan, and many developing countries that are not members of the Cairns Group support these demands.

Food-importing developing countries advance a different position on agricultural trade. They agree with food exporters that the industrialised countries must abandon subsidies and their protection for agriculture, and the excessively restrictive use of sanitary and phytosanitary standards. But developing countries must be permitted to retain the flexibility to impose quotas, subsidies, etc. when they deem these necessary for purposes of rural development and food security. While the EU appeals to multifunctionality of agriculture in debates about biotechnology and food safety, food-importing developing countries tend to invoke multifunctionality when advocating policies to preserve rural incomes and security of food supplies. Interest in the precautionary principle versus sound science debate is limited to rich countries.

Talks are expected to proceed slowly, since at present they are being conducted in special sessions of the Agriculture Committee under the framework established by the Uruguay Round agreements, which does not specify any precise goals or timetable. These were to have been established at the Seattle ministerial conference. Ultimately, any agreement seems to depend on whether the USA and the Cairns Group on the one hand and the EU and Japan on the other can bridge the gaps between their positions. The veto of a Brazilian as chair of the WTO Agriculture Committee by the EU in April 2000 on the grounds that Brazil is a member of the Cairns Group does not suggest that the negotiations are off to a well-spirited beginning.

Services

Liberalisation of trade in services is the second part of the built-in agenda of negotiations mandated by the Uruguay Round. This has proved to be relatively non-controversial, even though no concrete progress was made in Seattle to craft a negotiating agenda. Post-Uruguay Round services negotiations have focused on sectors of interest to industrialised countries, such as financial services and telecommunications. Developing countries want talks to focus now on sectors where they have a comparative advantage, such as tourism, construction and shipping.

In addition to those sector-specific issues, many developing countries seek liberalisation of the movement of natural persons, one of the four modes of service delivery outlined in the General Agreement on Trade in Services (GATS). Some have proposed making immigration rules more transparent and less discriminatory. For example, Pakistan is calling for limits on the use of 'economic needs tests' (the requirement that the government must first find an economic need for foreign workers before granting visas). Pakistan is also seeking mutual recognition of professional licensing regulations.

Negotiations are currently taking place as a special session of the Council on Trade and Services. Developing countries will be more likely to achieve success if all sectors are on the table at once rather than pursuing liberalisation one sector at a time. In the 'benign mercantilist' logic of multilateral trade negotiations, carrying out talks on a sector-by-sector basis eliminates the scope for developing countries to gain access to sectors of interest in industrialised country markets by granting access to their own markets.

Industrial goods

Past GATT rounds have introduced substantial reductions in tariffs on manufactured goods, but more remains to be done. Rising above the low average tariffs of the developing countries there remain some significant tariff peaks, i.e. rates that are more than three times the national average. In several developing countries, more than 10 per cent of tariff lines carry rates more than three times the national average (Laird 1999). The sectors with such peaks tend to be those of greater export interest to developing countries: footwear, leather and leather goods, food products, agriculture and textiles/clothing (UNCTAD/WTO 1998). Hong Kong and Singapore are seeking to put all industrial sectors on the table, to reduce not only tariff peaks and escalations but also to end 'nuisance tariffs' – tariffs applied at rates so low that they raise very little revenue but that nevertheless constitute an administrative burden to traders.

As discussed above, developing countries criticise the limited liberalisation of textiles and clothing trade. The draft agenda for the Seattle ministerial conference included bracketed language calling for renegotiation of the timetables in the ATC and to limit importers' recourse to anti-dumping actions. The USA adamantly opposes reopening the ATC.

Credit for unilateral reforms

Credit at the WTO for unilateral liberalisation is a traditional part of the developing country position on market-access issues. The Uruguay Round effectively agreed that all bound liberalisation would be counted. This was made operational by allowing developing countries that had implemented unilateral liberalisation to measure their Uruguay Round contribution from the early 1980s rather than from the 1986–88 base used by the others. The 'credit issue' has included discussion of valuing unbound liberalisation, perhaps via some sort of 'soft' binding that would provide trading partners with a degree of assurance against unilateral reversals but at the same time be less restraining than normal GATT/WTO binding. Likewise, during the Uruguay Round there was discussion of how to equate extension of ceiling bindings with tariff reductions. A few attempts to provide concrete proposals, e.g. expanded coverage of ceiling bindings over 10 per cent of imports equals a reduction of tariffs of 1 per cent on 1 per cent of imports, served more to emphasise the arbitrary nature of any such formula and to recall the imprecise nature of the reciprocal bargaining process.[3] The impact of the credit issue is likely to continue to be as a political vehicle to pressure industrialised countries to give more, not through the negotiation of a 'rule' for valuing one sort of concession over another. 'Formulas' in GATT/WTO experience have been applied only within the confines of bound tariff cuts, and even there the negotiations have been basically over the agreed package – the formula fitted to the agreed package of concessions, not the other way around.

Restriction-free access for LDC exports

The G-77 trade ministers and WTO Director-General Michael Moore have called on industrialised countries to grant quota- and duty-free access to exports from the least developed countries. The 'confidence-building package' submitted on 31 March 2000 by the Quad (Canada, Japan, the EU, the USA) included extending duty-free access to the LDCs for 'essentially all' products, although the USA stipulated that 'essentially all' did not include textiles/clothing and the EU that it did not include agriculture. The World Bank and the IMF have complicated the issue by suggesting that the list of countries be extended to include highly indebted poor countries. GATT Part IV provides legal cover for discrimination in favour of the LDCs but not for such treatment of highly indebted poor countries that are not LDCs.

TRIPs

The Uruguay Round mandated a review of the TRIPs Agreement. Many developing countries complain that the thrust of TRIPs is towards forcing developing countries to extend patent protection to goods produced largely in the industrialised countries, particularly pharmaceuticals and agricultural chemicals. The 'default mode' of the TRIPs is to copy IPR systems in place in the industrialised countries, systems that do not provide mechanisms for protecting traditional knowledge, or generally, the sort of intellectual property that exists in poor countries. Implementation of TRIPs, developing countries allege, tends to redistribute income from consumers in poor countries to patent holders in rich ones without having the intended effect of enhancing economic welfare through increasing research and development. Another complaint is that industrialised countries have failed to implement technology transfers under the TRIPs Agreement and have failed to provide technical assistance to help developing countries to implement the necessary intellectual property rights regulations.

Developing countries have proposed several expansions of the TRIPs Agreement:

- to protect the innovations of indigenous and local farming communities;
- to protect geographical indications besides those for wine and spirits;
- to protect handicrafts; and
- to allow compulsory licensing of essential drugs so that these can be sold at low prices.

Legal analysis suggests that protecting indigenous knowledge and other forms of intellectual property that exist in poor countries could be readily squared with TRIPs (Reichman 1998). The problem is not that TRIPs would disallow such but that we lack trial-and-error experience of how to do it.

Two faces of openness: transparency of what? participation by whom?

The Seattle ministerial conference dramatically elevated calls for public participation in WTO decision making and for greater transparency of WTO procedures. These issues received relatively little attention in the official proposals submitted before the Seattle meetings, yet the debate over WTO openness was accorded more media attention than substantive issues, such as agriculture or services. As with 'implementation', the issues of 'transparency' and 'participation' mean different things in the North than in the South. There are two dimensions to this debate: one internal to the WTO, one external.

Non-governmental organisations and many governments of industrialised countries (e.g. Canada, the USA and the EU) are pushing for greater external openness of the WTO: rapid derestriction of documents, filing of friend of the court briefs in dispute resolution panels, and participation by civil society in WTO proceedings. Developing countries generally oppose these proposals, instead calling for the preservation of the traditional closed and intergovernmental nature of the WTO. India, Cuba and Mexico have been particularly vocal in opposing greater external openness of dispute settlement, citing the need to protect confidential business information.

Developing countries are calling for greater internal openness, complaining that they are effectively shut out of the decision-making process and leadership positions – even though developing countries represent a majority of the WTO membership, only three of twenty-six WTO division directors are from developing countries (*Bridges Weekly Trade News Digest*, 7 March 2000). Especially objectionable to delegations from smaller countries is the so-called 'Green Room' meeting process:[4] forging a quick consensus by limiting participation to key countries. The USA and the EU advanced proposals to link internal with external openness in informal discussions after the Seattle ministerial conference, but a large number of developing countries have rejected them.

Other issues

There is virtually unanimous agreement among developing countries that labour and environmental issues must not be linked to trade. Other chapters in this book cover these issues. Developing countries are reluctant to endorse negotiations on other non-trade issues, such as competition policy and investment.

Are WTO negotiations an effective way to deal with the new issues?

Rather than being exchanges of 'concessions', negotiations in the new areas have instead taken the form of establishing specific rules or standards that should be adopted by all. 'Concessions' are then implicitly whatever a country has to do to reach the standard.

Effective implementation and compliance with trade-related regulatory reforms involves a significant investment in development projects, but WTO negotiations have not supported examination from this perspective. In no case did the Uruguay Round negotiations deal with the costs of the investments that the agreements would mandate – not even with how much the costs would be, much less with how much the return would be in that application versus some alternative use.

Inappropriate diagnosis, inappropriate remedy

The goal of agreements on SPS, TRIPs, etc. was simply to prevent countries using domestic regulations as barriers to trade. As the Uruguay Round agreements did not intend to identify and provide solutions to the problems of developing countries, it comes as no surprise that they did not.[5] The only part of the customs process that the WTO agreements address is valuation, and the valuation process it prescribes presumes the availability of sophisticated electronic equipment and instantaneous access to extensive commercial and financial information. This valuation process complements the economic and institutional environment in most of the advanced trading nations: highly computerised procedures; a large volume of trade; little fiscal reliance on customs revenue; and minimal evasion of customs duties by shippers. Where volumes are high and tariff rates low, running the risk of a shipment being held up over valuation questions does not make business sense. This is not the environment that exists in many developing countries. The cutting edge of customs reform in many developing countries is simple codification – introducing the basic elements of transparency and accountability. Many customs houses in developing countries do not even have telephones.

Regarding intellectual property, it is becoming evident that the property to be protected in poor countries is different from that in rich countries. Imposing a rich country's intellectual property laws on a poor country may assure that exporters in the rich country get what they want – revenue from products that would otherwise be copied – but it does nothing to even identify, much less turn into a defensible, negotiable commercial asset, the sort of knowledge that exists in a poor country. TRIPs does a great job on the products that developing countries buy, but it does very little for what they produce.

The dynamic behind the WTO process has been the export interests of major enterprises in the advanced trading countries. Given the disparity in negotiating power between industrialised countries and developing countries, plus a lack of knowledge of what works in developing countries, it is no surprise that negotiated outcomes on rules reflect the agenda of high-income countries and of specific interest groups in these countries – and thus to establish as the world standard what already exists in the advanced countries. As policy advice for developing countries, these agreements provide inappropriate diagnoses of problems in developing countries – and likewise inappropriate remedies.

We do not know what works for development

There is minimal experience in developing countries in the new areas on which the negotiators could draw to devise such standards; e.g., poor countries have yet to attempt to create intellectual property regimes that make traditional knowledge a negotiable and defensible asset. Those of us who insist that a 'development dimension' be included in future trade agreements must admit that, in the new areas, we do not really know what we are talking about.

Multilateral negotiation of country-specific rules?

On tariffs and import quotas, one policy recommendation fits all – fewer are better than more, none best of all. One size fits all: fewer trade restrictions are better than more. In the new areas, the variety of problems in developing countries and differences in the resources available to overcome them suggest that one size does not fit all there.

The only concession that the Uruguay Round agreements made to differences between countries was to postpone the date on which developing countries would have to comply, generally by five years. However, if the new standard was appropriate and the implicit 'concessions' were understood, then the implementation period should be based on an engineering estimate of the time needed for construction, not offered as second prize in the negotiations. In reality, the implementation periods are as artificial for developing countries as are the standards, the artificiality of the former not mitigating the artificiality of the latter but expressing it.

Perhaps the greatest danger in adopting a 'one size fits all' approach is that it would prevent the accumulation of trial-and-error experience – the assessment of the real-world impacts of alternative policy options – which can inform the effective incorporation of the development dimension into multilateral rules.

It will be difficult for the GATT/WTO system to adjust to the reality that different developing countries need different policy advice in many of the new areas. The need conflicts with the basic GATT/WTO principle of non-discrimination. The World Bank process, essentially a collection of bilateral arrangements between the bank and each of its client countries, seems more appropriate.

Conclusions

The outcome of the Uruguay Round was an imbalance against the developing countries:

1   Market access: no developing country 'surplus':

- tariffs, NTBs: what they gave is as far-reaching as what they gained;
- agriculture, textiles/clothing; the industrialised countries have yet to deliver.

2   Implementation:

- bound commitments versus unbound promises of support with implementation;
- specific and immediate economic costs versus elusive and delayed gains;
- practices of industrialised countries set as international standard:
- lower implementation costs for industrialised countries;

- no political ownership in developing countries;
- useful in the industrialised countries, less so in the developing world.

The new WTO policy areas are more properly thought of as development issues with a significant trade dimension than as trade issues on to which a development dimension might be added. The call for a 'development round' is perhaps half correct. There is clearly a need for a development effort, including an effort to help the poorer countries to take better advantage of opportunities offered by the international trading system. It is less clear that a negotiating round would be an effective means of doing so.

Notes

1   This analysis of the Uruguay Round bargain draws on Finger and Nogues (2000).
2   The sense of these obligations as policy guidance is taken up in the sub-section entitled 'Inappropriate diagnosis, inappropriate remedy'.
3   Finger et al. (2000) demonstrate that the comparison of concessions received versus concessions given, even when restricted to explicit tariff reductions, varies enormously with different measures of scope and depth of coverage, e.g., value of imports versus percentage of imports:

   dT/T versus $dT/(1 + T)$

4   The 'Green Room' process is so called because in the old days the conference room adjacent to the GATT Director General's office was painted green. At times, to move forward on sticky matters, the DG would have in this room consultations with a limited number of delegates. In time this inner circle came to include 20 or 21 members, and the process, though not the green paint, was carried from Geneva to Seattle.

   (speech by N.K. Singh to Indian Council for Research on International Economic Relations, 13 December 1999)

5   In the study cited above (Finger and Schuler 1999) we reviewed World Bank project experience for information on how well, as development policy advice, the Uruguay Round agreements identify and provide appropriate remedies for the problems that developing countries face in the new areas.

References

Finger, J.M. and Nogues, J. (2000) 'WTO negotiations: the clash of different domestic politics of protection and reform', paper prepared for presentation at the CEPR/World Bank Institute workshop on 'The World Trading System Post-Seattle: Institutional Design, Governance and Ownership', organised by B. Hoekman, A. Sapir and L.A. Winters, Brussels, 17–18 July.

Finger, J.M., Ingco, M. and Reincke, U. (1996) The Uruguay Round: Statistics on Tariff Concessions Given and Received, Washington: World Bank.

Finger, J.M., Reincke, U. and Castro, A. (2000) 'Market access bargaining in the Uruguay Round: rigid or relaxed reciprocity?' in J. Bhagwati (ed.) Going Alone and the Case for Relaxed Reciprocity in Trade Liberalisation, Cambridge, Mass.: MIT Press.

Finger, J.M. and Schuknecht, L. (1999) 'Market advances and retreats since the Uruguay Round agreement', paper presented at the Annual World Bank conference on development economics, Washington, 29–30 April.

Finger, J.M. and Schuler, P. (1999) 'Implementation of the Uruguay Round commitments: the development challenge', Policy Research Working Paper No. 2215, Washington: The World Bank.

Hathaway, D.E. and Ingco, M.D. (1996) 'Agricultural liberalisation and the Uruguay Round', in L.A. Winters and W. Martin (eds) *The Uruguay Round and the Developing Countries*, Cambridge: Cambridge University Press, pp. 30–58.

Incgo, M.D. (1995) 'Agricultural trade liberalisation in the Uruguay Round: one step forward, one step back? Policy Research Working Paper Series No. 1500, Washington: World Bank.

Laird, S. (1999) 'Patterns of protection and approaches to liberalisation', paper presented at the CEPR Conference on New Issues in the World Trading System, London, February.

Reichman, J.H. (1998) 'Securing compliance with the TRIPs agreement after US v. India', *Journal of International Economic Law* 1(4), December: 585–601.

Stiglitz, J.E. (1999) 'Two principles for the next round: or, how to bring developing countries in from the cold', paper for presentation to the conference on the WTO 2000 negotiations, Geneva, 21 September.

United Nations Conference for Trade And Development and World Trade Organization (1998) 'Market access development since the Uruguay Round: implications, opportunities and challenges, in particular for developing countries and least developed countries, in the context of globalisation and liberalisation', Geneva, mimeo.

6 Globalisation, democracy and trade policy[1]

Bernhard May

> We've got to watch for what I call a chemically pure capitalism that would put the market's brand on every fear of society and challenge democracy.
>
> Prime Minister Lionel Jospin of France

Globalisation poses a profound challenge for democracy. However, there is no universal definition of globalisation. Instead, it means different things to different people. During the last decade, it has not only become the focus of serious research and discussion among academics, business people, bureaucrats and politicians but has also become the focus of almost daily discussions among people of different spheres of society. There is a vast literature on the subject, and almost anybody has a very strong opinion about what globalisation means and what kind of changes it will bring about. As one would expect, academics cannot agree on globalisation either. For one school of thought it is nothing new, but for another – and it would seem that this one is supported by the majority – globalisation is a 'completely new ball game'.

Globalisation is seen as a new engine for producing prosperity and higher income in many countries. But it is creating a new problem concerning income distribution both within and between countries in that it will create 'winners and losers'. It is very well known that losers will fight to stop the process that makes them losers, whereas winners will take what they can get without actively supporting globalisation. This is the fundamental challenge for democracies. Furthermore, because trade policy is seen as a major tool for pushing globalisation, groups in societies and countries opposing globalisation are also resisting a further liberalisation of world trade. Instead, these groups are demanding a democratisation of trade policies as well as a democratic WTO as the major 'agent' of free trade.

In this chapter, I will focus my discussion on three questions:

- the challenge of globalisation for democracy;
- the challenges of globalisation and the demand for a 'democratic trade policy' for international organisations like the WTO; and
- scenarios and policy options for governments to respond to the challenge of globalisation.

Globalisation and 'localisation': the challenge for democracy

The process of globalisation is a profound challenge for democracies, since it is eroding national boundaries, weakening the authority of the state and could undermine the support of the people for democratically elected governments, at least in principle. In a globalised economy, the scale of economic activity no longer corresponds to the territory of the nation-state but is global and transnational (Ohmae 1990). The whole purpose of a democratic system is to make sure that power is shifted back to the people and not left with a small elite. Therefore, the democratic principle of free elections is a very important one.

However, democracy does not necessarily involve the direct participation of the citizens in the political decision-making process. Instead, Western democratic political systems accept the principle of democratic representation and responsibility. This principle underlies the transfer of power to the winners of elections for the specific period of time for which they have been elected. As a result of that process, a competition between political elites takes place over political positions and political values.

All democratic political systems are linked to a region, a society, a state and maybe a nation-state. Democratic governments of those nation-states are elected by the people to govern the state, to protect the people and implement policies that are in the interests of the people and are supported by the people. In a globalised world, however, societies and states are more and more influenced from the outside, and governments cannot stop this negative influence (Cerny 1999).

This raises profound questions for all democratic political systems. First, if democracy is linked to the nation-state but the governments of those states are no longer powerful enough to control and manage influence from outside, could those developments lead to the 'death of democracy'? Second, if national democratic political systems are no longer the controlling force, what kind of democratic institutions outside the state could take on this responsibility? Third, if national democratic systems are becoming weaker, does it make sense to work towards a global democratic system, a democratic world government?

Globalisation and democracy

Will globalisation lead to the death of democracy? In today's world there are more liberal democratic countries than ever before. Especially in the 1980s and even more so after the end of the Cold War in the 1990s, more and more countries moved from an undemocratic to a democratic political system. But in the light of profound challenges for all democracies, some observers are afraid that the best days of democracy may already be behind us. Arthur Schlesinger, for example, argued that in the face of globalisation and the erosion of the traditional nation-state, the twenty-first century might see a decline in liberal democracy rather than a further step ahead (Schlesinger 1997; Krause 1999).

Second, is the nation-state still in the driver's seat? In the global economy, new boundaries are being drawn between countries, business and international institutions. As the saying goes: most nation-states are too big for the small problems and at the same time are too small for the big problems. Jessica Mathews (1997) put it succinctly:

> Increasingly, resources and threats that matter, including money, information, pollution and popular culture, circulate and shape lives and economies with little regard for political boundaries ... Even the most powerful states find the marketplace and international public opinion compelling them more often to follow a particular course.

Indeed, governments no longer have a monopoly on power – other powerful institutions are emerging. Governments are therefore less able to control, dominate and manage events, but they face more complex problems. Just to mention a few of the challenges to national governments posed by a globalising world: a global financial and economic crisis will lead to economic problems and to a decline in living standards. These problems cannot be solved by any national government, but at the same time, national governments will be held responsible by their electorates for the problems. And national governments are no more able to cope alone with environmental problems, drug trafficking, migration problems, nuclear issues, energy problems, regional wars, and so on. In fighting all these problems, more and more countries are realising that it is better to cooperate.

But the requirement for cooperation between countries is that the nation-states are still in control and that they are still powerful enough to work together efficiently to solve problems. All of that changes with globalisation. The natural boundaries of states are being eroded, and globalisation is creating new boundaries, most of the time not linked to the nation-state. Globalisation leads to global markets with global players, but there is no powerful referee on this global level to make sure that a level playing field is created and that the global players are playing a 'fair game'. The forces behind globalisation have uprooted the old boundaries of the nation-state. In today's world, those forces are first of all technology and telecommunications.

'Localisation' and democracy

There is a dilemma: on the one hand, the process of globalisation that is going on is weakening nation-states and with it governments' ability to care for national interests and to protect national sovereignty; on the other hand, in many democracies a process is going on that can be called 'localisation', which means that more and more people become involved in the political decision-making process on a local level. In terms of strengthening a democratic political system, this means more direct participation of citizens and as a result a more active democracy.

There is a strong incentive for politicians to listen to the people because politicians are elected and re-elected on a local level. As famous House Speaker Tip O'Neill put it: 'All politics is local' (Matthews 1988). If politicians do not listen to the people, some groups will join hands and work together as non-governmental organisations (NGOs) or street opposition or single-issue coalitions. We saw many of those groups demonstrating in Seattle in December 1999 opposing further liberalisation of world trade.

NGOs focus on special issues that are supported by people in society who think that they are not represented by politicians and political parties and that they are not heard in the political decision-making process. And the evidence so far is that those groups will grow stronger in democracies because of globalisation. The economic process of globalisation will lead to higher income and a better living standard on a global level. But this higher income is linked to the problem of how to distribute this new wealth – how to distribute it between countries and how to distribute it within societies. The losers in globalisation will naturally oppose it, and that will create a backlash against globalisation at a local level. And because politicians are elected at a local level, those groups can become more powerful in a democratic political system. The winners in globalisation will, first of all, quite often not know if and when they will be winners – and if they do know, they will take it for granted and will not work actively to support globalisation.

How to adapt democratic systems?

Globalisation in that sense poses two profound challenges to democracy. First, globalisation threatens democracy as such because democratic political systems are based on the territorial state and this state is being eroded by the process of globalisation. Second, globalisation poses a threat to the democratic political system because globalisation will lead to a profound restructuring process on a global level that will create many losers at a local level. It will create a political resistance against globalisation and possibly a challenge for the democratic systems at a national level. Both developments will result in a loss of democracy.

To respond to these problems it will be necessary to work towards strengthening the democratic political system, for example by implementing measures to strengthen parliaments and to obtain domestic support first before adapting to new global structures. Also, governments could decide to opt out if they cannot obtain the necessary domestic support. Furthermore, NGOs could become a new element of democratic control, assuming that NGOs could get the authority for such a role in a democratic political system (Kaiser 1996; Zürn 1998).

However, the basic question remains: how could democracies, which depend on the territorial state, cope with the global challenges posed by globalisation? The straightforward answer would be that globalisation requires a world government, but in reality, democracies will have to cope with the challenges of globalisation without a world government for the time being. But one could think about how to adapt the political systems and how democracy should be changed to respond to globalisation.

David Held thinks it could be done, and he argues in favour of a cosmopolitan democracy. One element of that approach would be to change the territorial boundaries of responsibility to make sure that areas like international financial markets, which are currently outside of any democratic control, are brought into a broadly defined democratic political system.

Second, regional and global institutions should be reformed to make them a more acceptable part of the political process. Third, a new international democratic process should include groups that so far are outside the decision-making process (Held 1991; 1995). However, this is just the beginning of a process that might lead in the long term towards a global government and a world parliament. As an alternative with a medium-term perspective, Wolfgang Reinicke (1998) proposes a global public policy, not a world government but a mixed approach to global management in which states, corporations, NGOs, regional and international organisations, and coalitions cooperate. Such a new approach would have the potential to improve the capacities of governments and international organisations to cope with the challenges of globalisation and its effects.

Do we need a democratic WTO?

The WTO is criticised for being an undemocratic international organisation lacking transparency and deciding behind closed doors as a 'rich man's club' without broad participation. Many of these critics of the WTO demonstrated in Seattle and made it a lively event. However, important members of the WTO are responsible for the disaster in Seattle as well (May 2000). The problem is very well known and is a profound one: should international organisations like the WTO become democratic institutions, or should the WTO just play the role of an agency implementing the policies and rules that are decided by the WTO member states?

John Jackson is one of the best-known experts on the evolution of world trade law and the WTO as an organisation. Concerning the criticism voiced against the WTO, he put it succinctly:

> Clearly, the WTO is not a 'perfect' institution. It still represents some of the older ideas of conducting 'diplomacy', which called for secrecy and elitism. Observers are critical of the WTO's lack of transparency, the lack of opportunities for broad participation by various private citizen groups and NGOs, and the (sometimes) seeming lack of 'democratic legitimacy' for some of its decisions ... [The WTO will have] to reconcile the need for international co-operative action with a respect for the constraints placed on its capacity for action.
>
> (Jackson 1998: 58)

Does globalisation demand a democratic trade policy and a democratic WTO? Globalisation creates two problems of democratic legitimacy, one on a national level and the other on an international level. On a national level, we are talking about different political systems. All twenty-nine OECD countries are democracies, and all are members of the WTO. But there are currently 135 WTO members, about half of which are considered democratic states. In democracies, the trade policy decision-making process is *per se* a democratic one. In a democracy, all groups are invited to participate in the political process. In the end, of course, the majority will decide.

It is therefore quite likely that small groups will take part in the decision-making process but will not be successful. These groups can respond in one of three ways in trying to become a more powerful force in the democratic decision-making process. First, they can try to obtain the support of more people in a society to become a more powerful group. Second, they can work together with other groups to build a coalition focusing on specific issues. Third, they can stay as a small group but nevertheless become a powerful force in the political process by playing the 'political game' more efficiently than others.

Several of these small but powerful groups are well organised, focus on specific issues and are well connected politically in such a way that they can play a much more important role in the political process than one would expect from looking at the size of the group. The agricultural lobby in many countries is a good example of that kind of powerful and efficient small group in a democratic political system.

Democratic member states or a democratic WTO?

The second problem of democratic legitimacy is the question of how to democratise international organisations like the WTO, assuming that this should be done. We are not talking about international organisations with democratic countries as members. Taking this criterion, in most international organisations democratic countries are in the minority. That is true of the WTO, UNCTAD, the World Bank and the IMF. As I have mentioned, all OECD members are democratic countries, and all these organisations were founded for a specific purpose and are controlled by the member states. These international organisations are not considered as an element of a democratic global government. They are much more special agencies with specific agendas that are set by the member states, and they are controlled by their member states.

Clearly, criticising the WTO as an undemocratic institution is meant to focus on critical democratic deficiencies, on the lack of transparency, on the lack of accountability, and on insufficient mechanisms for popular participation. This last point has been a source of strong criticism of the WTO, particularly by environmental groups, which argue that NGOs can bring important expertise and information to bear on WTO questions. Ever more NGOs are arguing along these lines. So far, however, there seem to be no explicit general rules regarding a role for NGOs in the various WTO activities. The WTO language speaks of 'appropriate arrangements'. At a minimum, there seems to be room for improvement to provide some role for NGOs within the WTO. However, the problem is the lack of democratic legitimacy of NGOs. NGOs are not democratically elected representatives of a society. They represent special interest groups.

Democratising the WTO therefore raises the question of creating a WTO parliament with elected members from the member states. Rubens Ricupero, secretary-general of UNCTAD, in a public lecture in Berlin in January 2000, called for a 'world parliament on globalisation', extending the issue of democratic deficiencies to other international organisations as well. But for the time being, a democratic world government with a world parliament of democratically elected members will not become reality. And in terms of what the WTO (and other international organisations) is supposed to do, it is questionable if in today's world a 'democratic WTO' would be desirable.

The profound challenge is the question of what is more important: efficiency or democracy? Is it better to have an efficient WTO with some democratic deficiencies, or is it more important to move towards a more democratic WTO that is most likely to be a less efficient organisation? One should keep in mind that the WTO is not a world government and is not supposed to become one. The WTO is an organisation with currently 135 member countries, all of which joined voluntarily. Another thirty countries are negotiating to become WTO members. All are interested in an efficient WTO to make sure that a 'rules-based' trade regime will work. Democratic deficiencies are, first of all, a problem of the member states. What the WTO is lacking is more a problem of transparency and opening up to citizen groups like NGOs and less a problem of creating a 'democratic WTO'.

Globalisation is a challenge for all societies

Globalisation is a fact of life. However, it is a double-edged sword, a powerful new engine of the world economy that raises economic growth, spreads new technology and increases living standards in rich and poor countries alike, but also an immensely controversial process that assaults national sovereignty, erodes local culture and tradition and threatens economic, social and political instability. Globalisation weakens the territorial state because countries are no longer seen as distinct economic entities. Companies and financial markets, for example, increasingly disregard national borders when making production, marketing and investment decisions.

What is needed is a broadly based discussion in all countries and societies about the effects of globalisation and about the challenges. Especially in democratic countries, it is important to organise an ongoing debate about all aspects of globalisation, including all relevant groups and if possible the whole society. Countries could try to stay away from a globalised world to avoid the negative effects, but then they would not gain from globalisation either.

Globalisation has already brought about profound change for many societies. But we are just at the beginning of the process. Societies will have to cope with that challenge, but they are ill-prepared for it. Many people are afraid of globalisation, and there is a growing backlash against it in important countries. What is needed is a basic understanding by the people of what globalisation is all about, what kind of positive and negative effects it will bring and how citizens and groups in societies will be affected and can respond to it. Creating this kind of understanding in a society is a difficult task that requires an ongoing process of learning how to adapt to a globalised world.

It can be done, and it has been done before. Important elements are market economies, open markets, free trade: all of that required the same kind of learning process in the societies involved. Member states of the European Union face the same problem: it is hard work to 'educate' people that taking part in the European integration process is a worthwhile effort because many citizens are against it as long as they react emotionally and are not forced to think carefully about all aspects of European integration.

Globalisation will further democracy

The second element must be democracy. Governments should support democratic developments at home and abroad. In 1999, a broad coalition of states ranging in size from Cape Verde to India came together and proclaimed at a United Nations Commission on Human Rights session that all individuals have a right to democracy. Only Cuba and China abstained (Rubin 1999). Human rights have been accepted as universal rights for all individuals for many decades. Even so, there are still different opinions among governments about how to define and protect those rights.

The third element of a modern state is a market economy. A good example for countries that are supporting all three elements is the twenty-nine OECD countries: they share the principles of the market economy, pluralist democracy and respect for human rights. There seems to be a growing worldwide consensus that freer trade must also protect human rights, the environment and decent working conditions. This growing consensus is supported by environmentalists, consumer advocates, human rights activists and trade unions (Mazur 2000). The message of these groups in Seattle was loud and clear. However, these groups depend on a democratic environment and have to compete within a democratic political system.

Supporting countries that are moving towards a democratic political system will also create a more democratic trade policy and a more stable social and political situation in those countries. It is not true that the economic crisis in some countries and regions would undermine democratic political systems. A case in point is the Asian financial crisis of 1997, which brought down the Suharto regime that had ruled Indonesia for more than thirty years. In South Korea, Thailand and the Philippines, however, democracies survived the crisis intact.

But one has to be realistic: moving to a democratic political system in developing countries does not necessarily mean that this will automatically lead to a decentralised system with a more efficient government and better service for the people; it could also lead to more corruption (Hoekman and Kostecki 1997). It is therefore important that those countries establishing a democratic system get the help they need. A democratic political system is a very difficult system. And the process towards more democratic countries should be supported. At the same time, one has to be aware of the problem that globalisation is posing a profound challenge to democracy and to all democratic political systems. It is therefore necessary to work towards solutions on a global level for tasks that the democratic state can no longer fulfil (Höffe 1999; MacGrew 1998).

Towards a 'more democratic' trade policy

Governments should support a democratic approach to trade that must take into account the views of developing country democracies. The industrialised democracies are still the driving force, but they are no longer so powerful as to dominate all others. They need support to tackle the old and new trade challenges as well as to strengthen democratic processes within the WTO. Developing democracies should play a 'different role' in the trade decision-making process according to their volume of trade and their number and population size. The WTO is an intergovernmental organisation, and most member states do not want to create a 'democratic WTO', so the challenge is now to focus on the 'democratic deficit' of the WTO without weakening the efficient member-driven WTO.

In that respect, one could learn from other Bretton Woods institutions. For example, the International Monetary Fund (IMF) has a different decision-making process, including a smaller executive board with twenty-four executive directors, most of whom represent a group of countries. The WTO should also accept the IMF proposal to create an outside body to review the work of the organisation on a regular basis. Furthermore, the WTO could hold hearings on important issues, giving NGOs an opportunity to present and discuss their demands and proposals.

Changing the WTO, the organisation governing the trade system, in such a way would, first, improve the transparency of the WTO; second, open up the WTO system for outsiders like NGOs; and, third, would strengthen the role of developing countries in the WTO. The OECD countries should work together to move towards achieving these goals.

To sum up: globalisation is indeed a profound challenge to democracy and will lead to a more democratic trade policy. This challenge will have to be dealt with on a local, regional, national and global level. On the one hand, the process of globalisation will erode the nation-state as the foundation of a democratic political system. On the other hand, enhanced participation by a broader range of players in the decision-making process on trade issues, for example, would foster consensus building. As a result, the debate about globalisation and trade issues would become more transparent and trade policy more democratic.

Governments do not really have a choice – globalisation is a fact of life and a challenge for all governments. Societies will have to cope and to adapt to a globalised world. Globalisation will lead to much tougher competition within and between countries. And if governments do not respond appropriately to the challenges of globalisation, their countries will lose in global competition and the living standards of their people could decline. Governments therefore face the task of explaining globalisation and guiding a public discussion about its effects. This will be a difficult process. However, it will lead to a more democratic trade policy and a more democratic WTO.

Note

1 I would like to thank the Otto Wolff Foundation as well as the German Marshall Fund of the United States for supporting the project 'Resistance against Globalisation'. This paper was written as part of that project.

References

Cable, V. (1999) *Globalization and Global Governance*, London: RIIA.

Cerny, P.G. (1999) 'Globalization and the erosion of democracy', *European Journal of Political Research*, August, 1–26.

Held, D. (1991) 'Democracy, the nation-state, and the global system', *Economy and Society* 20(2): 139–72.

—— (1995) *Democracy and the Global Order. From the Modern State to Cosmopolitan Governance*, Cambridge: Polity Press.

Hoekman, B.M. and Kostecki, M.M. (1997) *The Political Economy of the World Trading System*, Oxford: Oxford University Press.

Höffe, O. (1999) *Demokratie im Zeitalter der Globalisierung*, Munich: Beck.

Jackson, J.H. (1998) *The World Trade Organization. Constitution and Jurisprudence*, London: RIIA.

Kaiser, K. (1996) 'Zwischen neuer Interdependenz und altem Nationalstaat. Vorschläge zur Re-Demokratisierung', in W. Weidenfeld (ed.) *Demokratie am Wendepunkt: die demokratische Frage als Projekt des 21. Jahrhunderts*, Berlin: Siedler, 311–28.

Krause, J. (1999) 'The Western Democracies – towards Prevalence or in a State of Crisis?' in J. Krause, B. May and U. Niemann (eds) *Asia, Europe and the Challenges of Globalisation*, Berlin: DGAP, 187–203.

MacGrew, A.G. (1998) 'Demokratie ohne Grenzen? Globalisierung und die demokratische Theorie und Politik', in U. Beck (ed.) *Politik der Globalisierung*, Frankfurt-am-Main: Suhrkamp, 374–422.

Mathews, J.T. (1997) 'Power Shift', *Foreign Affairs* 76(1): 50–66.

Matthews, C. (1988) *Hardball – How Politics is Played*, New York: Harper & Row.

May, B. (2000) 'Erfolglos in Seattle. Der Fehlstart der WTO-Runde', *Internationale Politik*, January: 49–50.

Mazur, J. (2000) 'Labor's new internationalism', *Foreign Affairs*, January/February: 79–93.

Ohmae, K. (1990) *The Borderless World*, London: Collins.

Reinicke, W.H. (1998) *Global Public Policy: Governing Without Government?* Washington: Brookings Institution.

Rubin, N. (1999) 'It's Official: All of the World Is Entitled to Democracy', *International Herald Tribune*, 18 May.

Schlesinger, A. (1997) 'Has Democracy a Future?', *Foreign Affairs* 76(5): 2–12.

Zürn, M. (1998) *Regieren jenseits des Nationalstaats. Globalisierung und Denationalisierung als Chance*, Frankfurt-am-Main: Suhrkamp.

Part II
Policy issues

7 Liberalising international trade in services

The European perspective

Dietrich Barth

The 'built-in agenda' of the World Trade Organization contains two major topics: agriculture and trade in services. Article XIX of the General Agreement on Trade in Services (GATS 1994) provides that, in pursuance of the objectives of the agreement, members (i.e. WTO member states) shall enter into successive rounds of negotiations, beginning not later than five years from the date of coming into force of the WTO agreement – i.e. January 2000 – with a view to achieving a progressively higher level of liberalisation. The new round is commonly called the 'GATS 2000 Round'. I shall return later to the question of how it relates to the project of a comprehensive round of multilateral trade negotiations, the Millennium Round, which failed to be agreed on at the WTO ministerial conference in Seattle in December 1999.

The importance of trade in services

Structural change in the economies of most countries, including developing countries, over the past two or three decades has led to an ever-increasing role of services in both production and employment. This is also true for the European Community, where services now account for about two-thirds of GNP and total employment. Moreover, it is generally recognised that the service sector will provide important potential for further growth and employment.

Technological advances, e.g. in transport and telecommunications, have made many services increasingly tradable. Outsourcing of service supplies in industry, increasing international cooperation and work sharing and progressive liberalisation of services at the national and international levels are generating new markets for many kinds of services around the world. Services are also assuming a larger role as inputs to industrial production and trade.

As a result, since the early 1990s, international trade in services has featured strong growth, typically higher than for trade in goods. Recent estimates, which seek to capture commercial services trade under the four modes of supply defined in the GATS (cross-border trade, consumption abroad, commercial presence and presence of natural persons), suggest that world services trade totalled almost $2.2 trillion, or 7.6 per cent of world GDP, in 1997 (Karsenty 1999).

The European Union is the top world exporter of services and the most significant investor in service industries. In 1998, it accounted for 26 per cent of world exports in services (excluding intra-EU exports), compared with 24 per cent for the USA and 6 per cent for Japan. Services also account for half of the EU's foreign direct investment flows into third countries.

Barriers to access in services markets

In spite of their strong and persistent growth performance, world exports in services still account for only about 20 per cent of total world exports. The gap between trade in goods and trade in services is due to a number of reasons. These include natural or structural factors affecting the competitive position of different countries, e.g. the availability of natural, financial and human resources, the scope of domestic markets, geographical proximity to export markets, the technical infrastructure for transport and communication, and the relative costs of providing services.

These factors affect trade in services in much the same way as general competition factors affect trade in goods. However, trade in services is fundamentally different from trade in goods, as most service sectors are highly regulated by governments in order to achieve a variety of policy objectives. Depending on the sector, these may include public safety and consumer protection, functioning of financial markets, public health and legal systems, cultural policy, or immigration and employment objectives. In many instances, domestic regulation does not aim to restrict or distort international trade in services, but it often has that effect. Changing the regulatory framework to eliminate trade barriers means imposing international disciplines on domestic regulators and parliaments. This makes liberalisation of trade in services much more difficult than it is for trade in goods.

Regulatory barriers to trade in services and discriminatory practices are innumerable. They range from total exclusion of market access for new (domestic and foreign) service providers, e.g. public telecommunications monopolies or restrictions on domestic air or maritime transport (cabotage), to limitations on foreign capital participation and on service production and sales, untransparent and discriminatory licensing procedures to subsidisation of domestic service providers and discriminatory public procurement practices. Other types of trade barrier take the form of discriminatory taxation or employment restrictions for foreign service personnel.

The increasing importance of trade in services has led to intensive multilateral activities with a view to progressive abolition of barriers to market access and trade discrimination. Fifty years of successful liberalisation of merchandise trade in the framework of GATT have generated major growth in world trade and employment in both exporting and importing countries. The same is expected for trade in services, as is illustrated by the experience of the European Single Market (OECD 1998; European Commission 1999a).

Liberalisation achieved under GATS

The most important achievement of the Uruguay Round of trade negotiations in the process of multilateral services liberalisation was the adoption of the GATS. Trade in services is now covered by multilateral rules and disciplines for the first time.

The GATS covers all market services sectors. The established list covers about 160 sectors, ranging from business and professional services to communication, financial and transport services. It establishes a basic set of obligations, which in principle are immediately applicable to all members and across all sectors, in particular m.f.n. treatment and transparency of regulation. Finally, the GATS provides a legal and institutional framework for progressive liberalisation through negotiated 'specific commitments' by each member relating to market access and national treatment. After the conclusion of the Uruguay Round, negotiations were extended in important areas. In 1995, negotiations were concluded on movement of natural persons supplying services, with substantial contributions by the EU. Negotiations on telecommunications and financial services were successfully concluded in 1997, while negotiations on maritime transport were suspended in 1996 and will resume in the context of the GATS 2000 round.

To date, 139 members of the WTO have submitted schedules of specific commitments on services. However, these commitments reveal significant imbalances regarding the number of service sectors and the modes of supply covered by individual members, the limitations and conditions listed on market access and national treatment, and the number of m.f.n. exemptions. For instance, out of the 160 service sectors listed in the GATS system, only thirty-one members (of which the EU is one) have undertaken commitments in more than 100 sectors, whereas forty-four members – mostly developing countries – have commitments in less than twenty sectors.

Many efforts have been made to evaluate the results in macroeconomic and trade terms, but such evaluations differ (Hoekman 1995). However, one thing that is clear is that the GATS provides enormous potential for further liberalisation (Barth 1999).

The new round of GATS 2000 negotiations

The overall political context

Following the failure of the Seattle ministerial conference, the most immediate question regarding services is obviously whether and to what extent GATS 2000 negotiations will now proceed.

The legal obligation to enter into these negotiations remains unchanged. Consequently, negotiations were launched in January 2000. Another factor that remains unchanged is the economic interest of the EU and its services industries, as well as of many other countries, in further liberalisation of services trade. The EU will therefore actively engage in the negotiating process. However, there are a number of uncertainties that may affect the course of action. The EU and other members continue to be interested in a comprehensive round of trade negotiations rather than limiting negotiations to the two subjects on the 'built-in' agenda. Moreover, political linkages may be made between services negotiations and other trade areas. Other concerns relate to the appropriate timing of a possible new comprehensive trade initiative, which must take account of electoral calendars in some countries and the resulting stronger focus on domestic policy concerns. Finally, the Seattle process has revealed a number of institutional weaknesses of the WTO system, which must be addressed in order to enhance the efficiency and transparency of the multilateral decision-making process. These uncertainties may well affect the content and the timetable of GATS 2000.

GATS 2000 objectives of the EU

The EU's strength in services trade stems to a large extent from its openness to competition. The EU market for trade and investment in services is one of the freest in the world. Inevitably, this leads the EU to have a paramount interest in further liberalisation of trade in services worldwide.

Consequently, the EU aims to achieve the following objectives (European Commission 1998; 1999b):

- Comprehensive negotiations with a view to obtaining more and better commitments from all WTO members on market access and national treatment. The binding of autonomous levels of liberalisation since the GATS came into force is a priority, and commitments to further liberalisation should be secured. For the efficiency of the negotiations and in order to maximise the results while ensuring the coherence of commitments, horizontal formulas should be considered as a useful tool for the negotiations when appropriate. While aiming at achieving these overall interests, the EU should take into account the sensitivities of specific sectors.
- Further market opening, coupled where necessary with regulatory disciplines. The aim is to achieve real and meaningful liberalisation and to ensure the development of a transparent and predictable domestic regulatory environment justified on the basis of specific public policy objectives, which can provide legal certainty and confidence to service suppliers, investors, users and consumers. These objectives can be obtained through, *inter alia*, a substantial strengthening of the disciplines built on Article VI of GATS and, where appropriate, the development of more pro-competition disciplines to provide a basic international discipline for practices preventing or reducing market entry.
- Unfinished business from the Uruguay Round, which includes safeguards, subsidies and government procurement for instance, should be absorbed in the GATS 2000 negotiations. Likewise, other aspects of the functioning of

GATS, which have been the subject of inconclusive discussions on interpretation or implementation, could be reviewed.

- Facilitation of an increased participation of developing countries in world trade in services by duly taking into account national policy objectives and levels of development, both overall and in individual sectors.

Another area of great interest for Europe is electronic commerce, one of the most promising commercial developments of recent years. The 1998 WTO ministerial conference launched a work programme to resolve a number of important trade issues. It included a moratorium on the imposition of customs duties on electronic transmissions.

Controversial trade issues include the question of whether all electronic deliveries are to be classified as services – and therefore fall under GATS rules – and whether existing commitments on services are applicable to electronic commerce. The EU believes that the GATS is technologically neutral and that it applies fully to all electronic deliveries. After the failure of the Seattle ministerial conference to reach agreement on any point of substance, there is now a risk that some countries may no longer feel bound by their commitments on particular sectors, e.g. financial services, when they are delivered electronically. Moreover, some countries may now be tempted to try to impose customs duties on electronic deliveries as they do on physical deliveries of software, games, newspapers, architects' plans, books, etc. This would damage electronic commerce, even on what are long-recognised services such as telecommunications, financial services, distribution, architecture and consultancy. In that situation, the EU favours resuming the WTO work programme as soon as possible with a view to maintaining a liberal regulatory environment for electronic commerce while ensuring compliance with general policy objectives, e.g. on taxation, prevention of illegal content and data privacy.

US objectives

The United States, the second biggest exporter of services in the world and the most important trading partner of the EU, is also seeking improved commitments to expand market access and national treatment for its service providers. However, unlike the EU, which is in favour of comprehensive negotiations that do not exclude any sector *a priori*, the USA has focused on a more selective array of sectors where its service industries are most competitive. These include distribution, construction, tourism, professional services, audio-visual services, education, health, financial services, telecommunications, energy and environmental services. Maritime services are not included.

On electronic commerce, US efforts are aimed at ensuring that the WTO takes the most trade-liberalising approach, including further extension of the moratorium on customs duties. Furthermore, the USA wants to work towards agreement on clarifying the applicability of existing WTO rules and commitments to electronic commerce.

Japan

Japan, the third-biggest services exporter in the world, is also very interested in broader and deeper GATS commitments. It is in favour of eliminating all m.f.n. exemptions (it has none), while the EU is pursuing a more selective approach on this matter. Other developed countries essentially pursue similar general objectives.

Developing countries

Developing countries play an important role in services trade. Among the forty leading exporters in the world, fifteen are developing countries, and many rank ahead of developed countries. Together, these developing countries account for one-fifth of world services exports.

In the run-up to the Seattle ministerial conference, developing countries have emphasised their concern that GATS 2000 negotiations should take more account of their interests in line with the objectives set out by Article IV:1 of GATS, namely the increasing participation of developing countries in world trade through specific negotiated commitments relating to the strengthening of their domestic services capacity, *inter alia* through access to technology on a commercial basis, the improvement of their access to distribution channels and information networks and the liberalisation of market access in sectors and modes of supply of export interest to them. In this context, liberalisation of movement of natural persons providing services and the introduction of emergency safeguards into the GATS system are most frequently quoted by developing countries as matters of particular interest to them.

The benefits that developing countries can expect from the GATS have now been better analysed (Adlung 1999: 112). The GATS is particularly relevant to development as it provides a key opportunity to attract stable long-term investment and to improve the related infrastructure (e.g. transport, telecommunications, financial markets). Increasing participation in services trade will foster long-term growth and employment and the competitiveness of developing countries' economies as a whole.

Organisation of GATS 2000 negotiations

The legal obligation to enter into a new round of services negotiations does not define any details regarding the substance, procedures and institutional set-up for these negotiations.

The GATS only defines a number of general parameters to be applied in the negotiations. These include respect for national policy objectives and development concerns of individual members; emphasis on sectors and modes of supply of export interest to developing countries; taking account of the specific situations and difficulties of the least developed countries; and recognition of autonomous liberalisation. Article XIX:4 leaves open the choice between bilateral, plurilateral and multilateral negotiating approaches. This could also open the way for the introduction of 'horizontal' or 'formula-type' approaches, which have been suggested by some members, including the EU, with a view to rationalising and speeding up the negotiating process.

Moreover, the GATS system contains a number of specific provisions, e.g. on the review of current m.f.n. exemptions, negotiations on maritime transport and review of the (so far limited) GATS coverage of the air transport sector. It is also clear that 'unfinished business' from the Uruguay Round and the Singapore ministerial conference in 1998, i.e. work on safeguards, subsidies, government procurement and disciplines for domestic regulation, will form an integral part of the negotiations.

Article XIX of GATS requires the establishment of negotiating guidelines and procedures. In the preparatory process for Seattle, a number of WTO members had suggested elements for these. The draft text, which was essentially uncontroversial in Seattle, covered such matters as the basic substance and objectives of the negotiations, procedures and timetable, a technical review of the GATS, autonomous liberalisation and reviews of m.f.n. exemptions, and the air transport annex. The failure of the Seattle conference to reach an agreement on a comprehensive Millennium Round also invalidated this draft text. However, most of its elements will remain relevant for future consideration.

Critical issues

The GATS 2000 negotiations will have to address a number of politically sensitive issues.

Civil society

As a general principle, the EU will seek to reflect the views of civil society. In the preparatory process for the Seattle ministerial conference, Europe's service industries strongly backed the negotiating objectives and concepts developed by the EU. However, other voices from civil society expressed fundamental concerns about further liberalisation, including trade in services. There are fears that globalisation and trade liberalisation might erode national sovereignty, leaving no room for national policy objectives. Particular concerns were raised in the areas of cultural policy, social security, consumer protection, health, education and environmental policy. Behind many of these concerns lies the view, also held by many policy makers, that trade liberalisation and international trade rules are penetrating deeply into what have long been regarded as domestic policy concerns. Liberalisation of trade in services will certainly affect domestic regulation, but only in so far as it relates to conditions for international trade. It does not prevent member states pursuing objectives of national policy through regulation (GATS Article VI). This applies for instance to cultural policy, consumer protection and environmental policy. Regarding the more specific concerns that were raised in the public debate, it should be noted that under the GATS system of negotiated commitments, WTO members retain the sovereignty to accept or to refuse commitments in accordance with national policy objectives. As a general principle, services supplied in the exercise of governmental authority, including the activities of social security systems, are not subject to GATS liberalisation. Members are also generally free to take any measures necessary to protect human, animal or plant life or health. They can also regulate the entry of natural persons into or their temporary stay in their territory, provided that such measures are not applied in such a manner as to nullify or impair the specific commitments that they have made.

The EU will continue and enhance its dialogue with civil society, which has already begun with non-governmental organisations in the preparatory phase of GATS 2000. It will continue to explain the benefits and potential problems of the multilateral system, try to understand the concerns expressed and, where appropriate, take them into account in the formulation of its policy proposals.

Development

Another critical issue will be to address the particular concerns of developing countries mentioned above. The EU has already proposed a work programme that should accompany the comprehensive new round, providing a coordinated approach to trade-related capacity building, enhanced cooperation and transparency in support of trade liberalisation between the WTO and the Bretton Woods institutions and for more efficient complementarity of action by international organisations in support of policy coherence. It remains to be seen how these ideas can be pursued in the post-Seattle environment.

Movement of natural persons

Among the concerns expressed by developing countries, the most difficult issue will probably be further liberalisation of movement of natural persons supplying services (mode 4). Many service suppliers, e.g. in consulting and construction services, need to send key staff abroad to supply their services. Increasing levels of commercial presence of service companies in foreign countries require the ability to transfer key personnel between different countries temporarily, and between subsidiaries and associated companies abroad. Developing countries have asked that restrictions on movements of natural persons be reduced to the strict minimum, in particular that economic needs tests should be removed and that visas should be issued automatically for a number of sectors of export interest to them. In a situation of high unemployment, such requests will obviously raise concern among European labour and immigration authorities and policy makers, although it is clear that the GATS excludes domestic visa, immigration and employment regulation from its scope of liberalisation.

Transport

The transport sector, although it is the biggest services sector of all, is at present characterised by the almost complete absence of specific liberalisation commitments. On maritime transport, the suspended negotiations will resume as part of the GATS 2000 round. The EU will support multilateral liberalisation in this sector (while the USA has already expressed its reluctance). In air transport, multilateral liberalisation under GATS has so far been limited to three auxiliary services, while the core of traffic rights continues to be governed by the classical system of bilateral air transport agreements. The EU and its air transport industry are currently considering whether and to what extent other aspects of air transport services, e.g. ownership and control of carriers, air cargo services, transit flights and more auxiliary services might be brought closer under GATS discipline. Land transport, because of its regional character, did not receive much attention in the Uruguay Round, but it will have to be considered as an essential component of modern logistical chains and as an element of multimodal transport links with maritime and air transport.

Audio-visuals

Another critical issue is the potential conflict between GATS liberalisation and cultural, in particular audio-visual, policy objectives. Following the related Uruguay Round conflict between the EU and the United States, the GATS does not contain a formal cultural exemption. On the other hand, the EU, like the vast majority of other WTO members, did not make liberalisation commitments on audio-visual services. In addition, the EU took broad m.f.n. exemptions to cover European audio-visual policies *vis-à-vis* third countries. In the GATS 2000 negotiations the Union will ensure, as in the Uruguay Round, that the Community and its member states maintain the possibility to preserve and develop their capacity to define and implement their cultural and audio-visual policies for the purpose of preserving their cultural diversity.

Recommendations

Summing up, the following are recommendations for the GATS 2000 negotiations:

- The negotiations should aim at reducing the current imbalance in commitments across countries and service sectors. Therefore, the negotiations should be comprehensive.
- Negotiations should include sectors that have so far not been at the centre of GATS liberalisation, e.g. distribution, energy, environmental, postal and courier services.
- All WTO countries should participate actively and with a spirit to limit trade-restricting regulatory barriers to a minimum of indispensable, overriding policy concerns.
- Cross-sectoral or horizontal methods of liberalisation should be applied where appropriate to rationalise and speed up the process.

- Where appropriate, additional regulatory disciplines, including pro-competition principles, should be developed to underpin market access and national treatment commitments in individual sectors.
- WTO work on electronic commerce should be resumed to ensure a liberal trade environment for electronic deliveries and all relevant services.
- The particular needs and interests of developing countries, and the least developed countries in particular, must be taken into account.

Conclusions

The rapidly expanding services sector is contributing more to economic growth and employment creation worldwide than any other sector. It is the key to the future of the world economy. A successful round of GATS 2000 negotiations will benefit service providers and consumers, exporters and importers in both developed and developing countries. In view of the ever-increasing linkages between the production of goods and services, it will also promote worldwide trade in goods. It will therefore be important to maintain the efforts that have been made to prepare for the GATS 2000 round and to make it a success.

References

Adlung, R. (1999) 'Adjusting to services trade liberalisation: developed and developing country perspectives', in P. Sauvé and M. Stern (eds) *Services 2000: New Directions in Services Trade Liberalization*, Washington.

Barth, D. (1999) *The Prospects of International Trade in Services*, Bonn and Brussels: Friedrich Ebert Foundation and European Commission.

European Commission (1998) *GATS 2000: Opening Markets for Services*, Brussels.

—— (1999a) *The Millennium Round: An Economic Appraisal*, Brussels.

—— (1999b) *Communication from the Commission to the Council and to the European Parliament: The EU Approach to the Millennium Round*, Brussels.

GATT (1994) General Agreement on Trade in Services (GATS), in *The Results of the Uruguay Round of Multilateral Trade Negotiations*, Geneva.

Hoekman, B. (1995) 'Assessing the general agreement on trade in services', in W. Martin and L.A. Winters (eds) *The Uruguay Round and the Developing Economies*, World Bank Discussion Papers No. 307, Washington.

Karsenty, G. (1999) 'Assessing trade in services by mode of supply', in P. Sauvé and R.M. Stern (eds) *Services 2000: New Directions in Services Trade Liberalization*, Washington.

OECD (1998) *Open Markets Matter: The Benefits of Trade and Investment Liberalisation*, Paris: OECD.

8 Financial services liberalisation in the Millennium Round[1]

Wendy Dobson

Introduction

Predicting the future of financial services liberalisation requires an under-standing of the larger framework for negotiating services and the implications of that framework for recent negotiations in this sector. Trade policy experts provided the original rationale for including services negotiations in the WTO. They saw services as a way of rejuvenating the then GATT and criticise a proliferating variety of non-tariff measures that took the form of government regulations limiting access by consumers to modern services and limiting cross-border expansion by service providers. In essence, the negotiations were to be about domestic regulatory and institutional reform. GATS was intended to create openness in the burgeoning service industries by applying the principles of m.f.n. treatment, market access, national treatment (equal treatment of one's own and foreign firms), and limited and transparent (published) exemptions.

However, the initial framework was not particularly relevant to what was happening to business. GATS was little understood and there was little demand for it, although government commitments to a series of sectoral negotiations have been secured, and some binding liberalisation has occurred – in informa-tion technology in 1996 and financial services in 1997. No further progress was achieved at the Seattle ministerial conference in 1999.

The central focus in this chapter differs from the traditional approach. Instead of studying the contribution of financial services to the GATS and the future of the WTO, its focus is the reverse: since financial market development is a potentially central factor in an economy's long-term growth and develop-ment, how can WTO negotiations contribute to making that a reality? The central theme is that progress has, and will continue to be, slow because of the asymmetry of interests between the two main groups of players, the mature industrialised countries and the emerging market economies.

The first section provides the historical context of financial services negotia-tions in the WTO. The second section summarises the differing goals of the mature industrialised and the emerging market economies in the 1997 negotia-tions, which help to explain the modest progress towards liberalisation. The third section analyses three major factors that will influence future negotiations.

These include the limitations of the GATS framework and the impact of tech-nological change and market forces. The final section addresses the question: where do we go from here?

The issues

The Financial Services Agreement (FSA), concluded in December 1997, included market-opening commitments by 104 WTO members that took effect in 1999. Five members made commitments in this area for the first time. The agreement is a milestone for the WTO because a significant number of WTO members agreed to a legal framework for cross-border trade and market access in financial services and a mechanism for settling disputes. It extends the General Agreement on Trade in Services (GATS) to financial services, adding to existing agreements in the telecommunications and information technology industries. The FSA was concluded in spite of unprecedented turmoil in Asian financial markets, perhaps because it held out the hope that it would provide a signal of the authorities' determination to undertake reforms that would help to restore credibility and stability. The FSA replaces an interim agreement concluded in 1995 at the initiative of the European Union. In that agreement, the United States withdrew m.f.n. treatment in financial services and committed itself only to granting market access and national treatment to the existing operations of foreign service providers. The United States and other industrialised members of the Organisation for Economic Co-operation and Development, faced with the reluctance of governments in some important emerging market economies to provide reciprocal access, feared that the latter would become free riders on a global agreement. A US offer in July 1997 of unrestricted access to its market was conditional upon such reciprocal market access.

In an important sense, however, the 1997 FSA is less than meets the eye. For the most part, it formalised the *status quo*. OECD country commitments amounted to little further market opening. The United States provided recip-rocal access, which most OECD countries already have and which emerging market economies, with less mature financial institutions, found of little interest. With a few important exceptions, the latter economies offered little new access to their often underdeveloped banking sectors. Much of the forward momentum occurred in the insurance sector.

Financial market development contributes to long-term growth and develop-ment in two ways: by changing the speed at which capital accumulates; and by influencing the efficiency of production in an economy. Financial institutions are considered not only to mobilise an economy's resources and facilitate the transactions necessary to carry on economic exchange but also to play a critical role in managing risks and closing information gaps.[2] These institutions reduce the risks faced by investors by pooling their savings and distributing those savings among many users, so diversifying risk. They also collect and evaluate the information necessary to make prudent and productive investment decisions. And they participate in corporate governance by evaluating the performance of corporate borrowers and, when necessary, compelling them to act in the best interests of the firm, and therefore of its providers of funds (Levine 1996). Traditional analysis has tended to portray finance as an auxiliary factor in growth and development. More recently, however, as financial crises have occurred with increasing frequency, disrupting growth and other aspects of real economic activity, interest in financial reform has grown, and with it the realisation of the potentially central role in economic growth.

OECD governments seek market access through the FSA for their large financial firms, which are faced with maturing markets at home and possessing technologies that have reduced transaction costs to take advantage of business opportunities and higher rates of return in dynamic offshore economies.

The goals of the governments of emerging market economies differ. They are more interested in foreign capital flows (and to a lesser extent foreign institutions) to accelerate growth; access to financial markets in OECD countries is of less interest. Capital inflows take several forms: as short-term debt and equity (portfolio) flows, as commercial bank lending and as bonds. These instruments are subject to volatility if investors flee at any sign of uncertainty or trouble. Of more value is long-term foreign direct investment (FDI), which brings foreign ownership or control but also the transfer of more sophisticated technology. Financial services liberalisation in the WTO will promote a country's growth and welfare in two main ways: first, by providing a legal framework that reassures foreign institutions investing for the long term; and, second, by providing a source of external pressure for change and transparency. Domestic groups often resist such pressure in protecting their own interests, but it can promote sound financial institutions.

It should be noted that the term 'liberalisation' applied to financial services in the WTO refers to removing restrictions on market access for cross-border trade and for foreign service providers to locate in domestic markets. A country may allow foreign firms into its market yet restrict capital inflows and outflows. In other words, the WTO's concern with market access is distinct from capital account liberalisation, a responsibility of the International Monetary Fund (IMF), referring to the freedom with which capital inflows and outflows with varying terms of maturity are allowed to move across borders.[3] These two policies are also related. *De facto* capital account liberalisation has occurred in the past few decades as many countries have legalised foreign currency instruments in the face of increased trade flows, the internationalisation of production and improved communications.[4] Provided that there is adequate information, supervision and risk assessment, free capital movements can facilitate efficient international allocation of savings and channel these resources to their most productive uses. This is the purpose of what we call financial reform. Domestic residents benefit from access to foreign capital markets in several ways: through cheaper financing; a wider menu of options for diversifying risk and obtaining higher rates of return; and from a larger pool of investable funds.

Deregulation, market opening and capital account liberalisation do not have to march in lockstep. Taiwan, for example, has not fully deregulated its domestic market and still imposes some restrictions on capital accounts, but it permits foreign entrants. The ASEAN economies of Southeast Asia have not fully deregulated and still restrict foreign entry, but they have opened their capital accounts. Until its financial crisis began in late 1997, South Korea restricted both foreign entry and capital flows and had many domestic reforms to make as part of its accession agreement to the OECD. In the December 1997 IMF programme, South Korea agreed to remove many of these restrictions. China is now the only East Asian country that still has a closed capital account (FDI inflows are encouraged, however), and foreign participation in the financial sector remains heavily restricted.

The main players

The main players in financial services negotiations are emerging market economies and the mature industrial economies in the OECD (South Korea and Mexico are represented in both groups but for the purposes of this analysis are included in the former group). The widely differing objectives of these two groups suggest good reasons why so little movement beyond the *status quo* was negotiated in 1997. Developing countries must decide how quickly they will integrate their economies with the rest of the world and the role that they want foreign institutions to play in that process and in the domestic economy. They encourage foreign savings in order to accelerate growth over what it would be were they to rely exclusively on domestic savings. But as the Asian financial and economic crisis of 1997–98 (and the experiences of the southern cone countries in Latin America in the 1980s) demonstrated, mobile capital by itself can be dangerous if such flows are allowed without sufficient planning and management. Indeed, it is worth noting that an exclusive focus on attracting foreign capital could mean that a country overlooks a significant ingredient of financial system development, namely the role of foreign financial firms in improving its efficiency.

Going forward, the focus of the WTO negotiations on freer cross-border trade and foreign entry in financial services will reflect the fact that many standard policy interventions in the financial sector are untouched by commitments within the GATS. In particular, countries retain the scope for macroeconomic policy; the so-called 'carve-out provision' in the GATS protects prudential regulation. To the extent that they are compatible with broad market access, national treatment, and scheduled commitments to liberalise, other government financial policies can still be maintained, but in a more open context, under a multilateral agreement.

Still, while many emerging market economies have begun to reform their financial services sectors and to open their markets, having begun to realise these benefits, some are reluctant to deregulate fully, whereas others are reluctant to open up at all, citing several significant reasons.

First, the experience of countries that have deregulated their financial markets, opened their markets and liberalised their capital accounts have been mixed. Banking and financial crises are associated with reform and internationalisation, or the wrong sequence of such changes. One analysis of banking crises worldwide found that, in eighteen of twenty-five cases studied, financial liberalisation had occurred some time in the previous five years (Kaminsky and Reinhart 1995). Reforming the domestic financial system and internationalising it does entail risks, especially if governments continue to regulate and supervise financial systems in the same way that they operated them before. To minimise these risks, regulatory institutions and supervisory systems must be modernised and strengthened to enable those charged with overseeing the system to evaluate the risks inherent in a more complex, market-oriented system. Striking a balance between financial market efficiency and economic stability is difficult, as demonstrated by the US savings and loan crisis of the 1980s and its aftermath, and by Japan's ongoing struggle to work out the banking crisis that began there in the early 1990s. Dobson and Jacquet (1998) evaluated this trade-off, drawing on the results of a number of case studies of national experiences with reform over the past two decades. These findings emphasise the importance of multiple factors in the trade-off. The general conclusion, reinforced by lessons from the 1997–98 financial crisis, is that there is neither a universal recipe nor a standard sequence for domestic reform and internationalisation. However, the case studies agree that macroeconomic preconditions and the strength of the financial sector influence the chances of successful adjustment to these changes. Economies with stable and realistic prices (including the exchange rate regime) and prudent fiscal policies do better because the creditworthiness of potential domestic borrowers is superior. Those that have reformed and strengthened their domestic financial sectors – by freeing interest rates, reducing credit subsidies, and strengthening financial institutions and their supervision – have met the necessary preconditions for easing restrictions on the capital account and full-scale internationalisation.

Second, it is frequently argued that finance is special – some would say strategic – because of the crucially important services that the financial sector provides to a growing and developing economy. In this view, these services are therefore best owned and controlled by domestic interests. More sophisticated foreign entrants, pursuing different objectives, could come to dominate the industry to the detriment of national objectives. In the extreme, this argument has merit – few governments would tolerate 100 per cent foreign ownership of major domestic financial institutions.[5] On the other hand, foreign participation brings substantial benefits and can be managed; indeed, the Uruguay Round agreement explicitly allows for such management. Not only does foreign participation, judiciously supervised, provide access to foreign savings, technical transfer and a force for modernisation, but also the presence of foreign firms increases the competitiveness, efficiency and diversity of the financial sector. The speed of innovation and the interconnectedness of markets are raising the costs of maintaining the *status quo*. Failure to deregulate and to open markets denies households better returns and denies businesses lower financing costs.

These costs reduce growth and competitiveness. This link between real-sector activity and finance is perhaps the central issue, and one that is best addressed by practising macroeconomic prudence.

Third, it is argued that domestic financial reform and internationalisation are often politically difficult because, although users of financial services (including businesses, households and governments) stand to benefit, other powerful interests stand to lose. Introducing competition threatens significant interests in the local financial industry, just as reducing the role of government threatens the position of certain bureaucratic interests. Reluctant governments, which must manage the difficult political economy of financial reform and internationalisation, do have a point, which trade negotiators should take into account. Market opening and capital account liberalisation present real risks as well as political risks if financial supervision and financial institutions are not strengthened and if weakness in the real economy undermines borrowers' creditworthiness.

However, the answer is not to halt the process of reform and liberalisation. Rather, it is to proceed, while putting the primary emphasis on strengthening the system's ability to evaluate risk. The implication for negotiating strategies is that diplomatic pressure should be applied in a way that strengthens the process. This requires a delicate mixture of determined pressure for more opening with enough flexibility to make sure that the domestic political debate responds to rather than rejects that pressure, thus strengthening the hand of those who push for opening.

A political *quid pro quo* seems possible. On the one side, OECD governments may offer enhanced technical assistance to emerging market economies in building stable banking systems, including the establishment and/or the strengthening of banking supervision, and in developing their financial markets. On the other side, governments of emerging economies may commit to opening their markets in a safe sequence tuned to the specific circumstances of their economy.

The downside risk of complacency – of failing to insist on progress towards reform – is that nothing worthwhile gets done, but the downside risk of too rigid a position and too demanding requirements is that anti-foreign sentiment builds, eventually upsetting the domestic coalitions required to support reform. Clearly, such arguments convinced only a few governments. In the 1997 negotiations, only limited progress on market access to these economies was achieved, mostly in the insurance and securities industries (see Table 8.1).

The future of FSAs

Several factors will influence the future of multilateral financial services negotiations. The first is the GATS framework and its impact on market-access issues in the financial sector. GATS faces some significant design challenges, which also apply to financial services. Services are a heterogeneous group of products, with the common thread that most of them are subject to government

Table 8.1 WTO Financial Services Agreement: access to selected emerging markets, 1997

	Banking	*Insurance*	*Securities*
Status quo plus	Malaysia Mexico	Brazil Indonesia Japan South Korea Philippines Mexico	Brazil Indonesia South Korea Malaysia Philippines
Status quo	Argentina Brazil Chile India Indonesia Japan \ South Korea Thailand	Chile India Thailand	Argentina Thailand
Less than *status quo*	Philippines	Malaysia[a]	Chile India

Source: Dobson and Jacquet (1998: 93).

Note:

[a] This entry compares existing practice in 1998 with Malaysia's commitment in December 1997.

intervention. There is the added complication that financial services are seen by finance ministers to be in their purview, not that of trade negotiators. The other significant problem is that weaknesses in the GATS framework cast doubt on its ability to sustain further market opening. One source of weakness is the positive list approach to commitments. Positive lists identify sectors on which commitments are made rather than those on which they are not. This approach was all that could be agreed at the time the GATS was negotiated. It contrasts with the negative list approach, employed in the North American Free Trade Agreement (NAFTA) negotiations, in which countries commit to full liberalisation unless specific exclusions are negotiated. With the negative list approach, opening and market access are the central objectives; in contrast, the positive list tends to reinforce the *status quo* and makes it difficult to identify potentially significant sectors that are untouched by liberalisation. Furthermore, it implies that as new sectors emerge, they stand outside the market-opening framework until explicitly brought into it.

A related weakness of the GATS framework is problems with reciprocity. The division of the WTO negotiations along sectoral lines, that is separating services from goods and individual services from each other, makes reciprocity less credible and less effective. Reserving financial services negotiations for finance ministers makes such linkages even more difficult. Asymmetry in the interests of OECD and developing countries in services negotiations also adds to the difficulties. This asymmetry of interests was evident in the 1997 FSA, where developing countries complained that they had made most of the market-opening and other concessions. This is because it was OECD producers who sought access to their markets, not the converse. Nevertheless, the fact that the Information Technology Agreement (ITA) and the FSA were completed shows that the approach can deliver something.

The second factor affecting the future of financial services negotiations is the circumscribed nature of multilateral negotiations within the larger market-based trend towards internationalisation in this sector. The 1997 negotiations reflected GATS principles to the extent possible, but the outcome, at least in financial services, was largely to bind the *status quo* on market access and create agreed procedures for settling disputes, as Table 8.1 illustrates for financial services. Examined more closely, it becomes apparent that in these negotiations it was not so much the GATS that created sectoral openness but that liberalisation in these sectors had a life of its own for other reasons. Telecommunications and financial services are among the fastest-growing and fastest-evolving industrial sectors in the world economy. Their growth and evolution are being driven by the information and communications technology revolution and by domestic deregulation as governments scramble to catch up with the market forces that drive the rapidly changing transactions, business arrangements and cross-border flows in these services.

The third factor affecting the future of such negotiations is the increasingly significant role that financial market development is seen to play in an economy's long-term growth and development. The reciprocity dimension of the GATS weakens the case for reform: that market opening is in the interest of all countries. Some see the pre-commitments made by some countries as part of the reason why they made concessions in the FSA. This may be, but there were also several other significant factors, especially with respect to the East Asian economies. One was that the US and EU governments, instead of being adversaries, were united in their determination to make the agreement. Another was that US and EU businesses gave a big push to the negotiations. Yet another was the Asian crisis itself. The severity of the crisis and its extent by late 1997 made it clear that weak financial systems were one of a combination of significant causal factors in the crisis economies. Thus, although they saw little to gain from reciprocal access to the OECD economies, they were anxious to signal their commitment to reform as a way of restoring battered credibility.

Where do we go from here?

Where should we go from here? What should be the goals for financial services negotiations in the new round? These goals will be influenced by the weaknesses in the GATS and market factors outlined above. One implication is that, unlike earlier progress in goods negotiations in the GATT, future advances in market access in financial services may not come primarily from multilateral negotiations. Instead, there is a discernible trend towards other routes to market access: gradual unilateral opening has occurred in a number of countries as part of overall structural reforms; in others, it has been part of regional or bilateral liberalisation arrangements. Hence, while it is worthwhile to ask how the current WTO process can be improved, experience with the FSA suggests that future progress may be expected from a combination of such sources. For example, countries on IMF programmes in the Asian crisis have agreed to faster and more extensive domestic reform and foreign entry than was negotiated in the FSA. A commitment by APEC leaders at their 1996 summit in the Philippines gave the ITA a push. Japan and Singapore have unilaterally accelerated the modernisation of their financial sectors by allowing further foreign entry because they fear being bypassed for other international financial centres. The combination of non-WTO processes and market forces, plus the WTO providing the binding mechanism and dispute settlement, can contribute to an effective international trade regime.

The WTO role in providing the binding mechanism under the *status quo* can be improved upon. For example, financial services reforms, agreed as part of IMF programmes to strengthen national financial systems and increase resilience to future crises, should also be bound into the WTO. This does not mean that the IMF and the WTO should 'gang up' on a country; rather, it means that the country should be willing to bind the reforms that serve its long-term interests. One of the agenda items in the next round, therefore, should be to formalise a mechanism that allows countries to receive credit for such changes for use in future multilateral negotiations.

Another obvious goal is to improve the data on and transparency of barriers to cross-border transactions and foreign entry (Hoekman 1999). Lack of comparable cross-country data is a general problem in the services sectors. Many services originated as non-tradables; thus measures, if they were developed, tended to serve domestic purposes, making existing information on parameters of services production and trade scarce and difficult to aggregate across countries. Indices of openness in the financial services industries in key emerging market economies are included in Table 8.2. They summarise commitments on the degree of financial liberalisation at the end of 1996. As Table 8.1 has already indicated, little forward movement occurred in 1997.

The index in Table 8.2 weighs various types of barrier, including measures that limit the right of establishment and ownership, limits on business activity such as granting the ability to establish branch offices or install automatic teller machines, restrictions on lending or on permission to carry on universal banking services, and residency requirements for the officers or staff of foreign financial institutions. It also compares commitments (made in the 1995 FSA) with existing practice.

Commitments fall short of practice in some economies (such as banking in Hong Kong) and exceed practice in others (securities in Indonesia). By sector, entry to banking was more liberal than to securities or insurance. By economy, many governments carried on discriminatory practices, with the international financial centres in Hong Kong and Singapore being the most open. Hong Kong was the most open to all financial services, while South Korea was virtually

Table 8.2 An index of openness in financial services, 1997

	Banking		Securities		Insurance	
	Commitment	Practice	Commitment	Practice	Commitment	Practice
Hong Kong	4.20	4.75	4.00	4.40	4.40	4.00
Indonesia	3.15	3.20	3.50	3.00	3.10	2.60
South Korea	1.10	1.70	1.70	2.10	1.20	2.60
Malaysia	2.40	2.40	2.50	2.50	2.10	2.10
Philippines	2.80	3.35	2.40	2.40	2.90	2.80
Singapore	2.25	2.50	2.70	2.70	4.10	4.10
Thailand	2.95	2.85	2.00	2.00	2.80	2.80
India	2.70	2.25	2.50	2.10	1.00	1.00
Average	2.69	2.88	2.66	2.65	2.70	2.75

Source: Claessens and Glaessner (1998).

Note: 1 – most closed; 5 – most open.

closed to banking services, India was similarly closed to insurance services, and Thailand was the least open to securities firms. Interpretation of these indices requires fairly detailed country knowledge; for example, Malaysia appears to restrict foreign entry, but one of the reasons is that it has restricted new licences for insurance or securities firms to both domestic and foreign firms. Cross-border trade is less restricted than entry by foreign firms to the domestic markets. Before the 1997–98 crisis, several countries allowed free access to offshore banking services; in the wake of the crisis, some of these were substantially modified (to correct distortions associated with the Bangkok international banking facility, for example).

Improvements in transparency would also reduce the difficulties of considering a negative list to replace the positive list approach to negotiations. In order to put more pressure on countries for broader commitments, it is necessary to be able to evaluate and compare barriers to entry and cross-border flows in a wider variety of service sectors. This suggests that more could be made of the negative list approach as an alternative framework. While this is likely to be difficult to accomplish, the negative list approach has the potential of increasing transparency and the momentum for wider coverage and market opening. A broader coverage of binding commitments is also required. Few countries have made sweeping commitments to market access and national treatment in financial services. Thus another issue for the next round is to encourage countries to commit that all service sectors will be subject to national treatment and market-access disciplines, with target dates and transition periods. Surprising as it may seem, aiming to bind the *status quo* for only a specified share of all commitments is a moderately ambitious starting point. Complementing this with efforts on rules to increase the impact of multilateral disciplines for some modes of supply, particularly national treatment for FDI, would also be timely.

Another implication of Table 8.2 is that we can expect the goals of OECD countries to continue to focus on market opening – to deepen and broaden the limited commitments made in 1997, particularly for a wider range of choice of commercial presence in the suppliers of financial services (such as majority joint ventures, wholly owned subsidiaries and branches); to improve the scope of national treatment commitments; and in view of the explosion of Internet services since 1997, further commitments to the cross-border provision of financial services by electronic means.

While the protesters at the Seattle conference were not aiming at the FSA, their objections have significant implications for financial services. Objections to the negative list approach because it might 'put national health services on the table' and objections to the heavy weighting of the interests of developed countries and multinational firms are each relevant to future financial services negotiations. It is thus in the interests of the WTO to structure financial services discussions in the context put forward in this chapter: by asking how the FSA contributes to an emerging market economy's growth and development. Preparatory discussions in 1997 reflected this concern but sometimes lacked sensitivity to the importance of a country's sequencing of domestic reforms and market opening. However, the importance of sequencing is now firmly established as one of the central lessons for emerging market economies from the 1997–98 financial and economic crises.

Before concluding, it is also useful to stand back and look at the long-term strategic fundamentals of trade in services. The GATS framework suffers from architectural limitations that cast doubts on its ability to create a liberalisation-enhancing regime for trade in services, that is, one that exerts continuous pressure for opening. Market access in services is a basic issue in the management of globalisation that involves trade instruments and practices as well as policies directed at FDI and competition policy. The latter are crucial dimensions in a globalising economy with mobile factors of production. FDI remains the key to providing retail services, even though the information and communications technology revolution may facilitate cross-border trade. In addition, oligopolistic market structures and the potential for cross-border mergers increase the need for a multilateral approach to competition policy. This is another reason for extending the domain of multilateral negotiations to include liberalisation of direct investment regimes and better coordination of competition policy. Through the definition of broad principles in these areas that would apply to all goods and services, such an agenda would help to circumvent the limitations of the GATS and increase the liberalisation thrust of the multilateral trade regime.

Notes

1   This chapter draws on joint work with Pierre Jacquet in Dobson and Jacquet (1998).
2   Financial systems address the central problem of information asymmetry between the providers and users of funds. On the asset side, financial institutions take on risk in valuing projects and funding borrowers whose ability to repay is uncertain. On the liability side, creditors and depositors have imperfect information on the actual position of financial institutions yet must have confidence in those institutions. When these institutions are highly leveraged, lack liquidity or provide little information on their assets, they are vulnerable to losses in confidence, and depositors have an incentive to flee when confidence is eroded (Lindgren *et al.* 1996).
3   In the Asian crisis, short-term capital flows, particularly inter-bank loans, were a volatile form of capital.
4   All OECD countries have now eliminated capital controls. By the end of 1993, a quarter of developing country IMF members had removed restrictions on capital transactions, while seventy-six members maintained comprehensive controls on capital outflows and seventeen on inflows (IMF 1995).
5   New Zealand is one exception; its banks are 98 per cent foreign-owned. Argentina also has a high degree of foreign ownership of its banks.

References

Claessens, S. and Glaessner, T. (1998) 'Internationalization of financial services in East Asia', World Bank Working Paper No. 1911, available online at http.//www.world-bank.org/.

Dobson, W. and Jacquet, P. (1998) *Financial Services Liberalization in the WTO*, Washington: Institute for International Economics.

Hoekman, B. (1999) 'Services liberalisation and the Millennium Round', Washington: World Bank.

International Monetary Fund (1995) *Capital Account Convertibility*, Occasional Paper 131, Washington: IMF.

Kaminsky, G. and Reinhart, C. (1995) 'The twin crises: the causes of banking and balance of payments problems', Board of Governors of the Federal Reserve System and International Monetary Fund.

Key, S. (1997) *Financial Services in the Uruguay Round and the WTO*, Group of Thirty Occasional Paper No. 54, Washington: Group of Thirty.

Levine, R. (1996) 'Foreign banks, financial development and economic growth', in C. Barfield (ed.) *International Financial Markets*, Washington: American Enterprise Institute Press.

Lindgren, C.-J., Garcia, G. and Saal, M.I. (1996) *Bank Soundness and Macroeconomic Policy*, Washington: IMF.

Mattoo, A. (1999) 'Developing countries in the new round of GATS negotiations: from a defensive to a proactive role', Washington: World Bank.

9 International trade in telecommunications and transportation services

Christopher Findlay and Tony Warren

Introduction

Until the mid-1980s, services such as telecommunications and transport were seldom viewed through the prism of international trade. Governments developed domestic policy and regulations within the parameters of national monopolies. International concerns were confined to technical matters and were handled either through international organisations such as the International Telecommunications Union and the International Civil Aviation Organization or through bilateral agreements between national governments.

However, as telecommunications and transportation services have become increasingly contestable, a host of regulatory impediments to international trade and investment have come to light. Many of these barriers affecting telecommunications and aviation services are similar to those affecting other services in that laws and regulations impede the ability of producers and consumers to interact across borders through cross-border trade or foreign direct investment (Hill 1977; Sampson and Snape 1985). Other barriers of particular importance to transportation and telecommunications services involve the effective regulation of access to essential facilities (Warren *et al.* 1999).

The General Agreement on Trade in Services (GATS) has begun the process of applying international trade disciplines to the first set of impediments affecting telecommunications and is considering the application of these disciplines to aviation and maritime services. These are welcome developments for global economic welfare. However, unless the issue of access to essential facilities is also tackled the potential gains for consumers of telecommunications and transportation services will not be fully realised.

In telecommunications, current schedules do not reflect the actual policy environment. Negotiators have an opportunity to extend the scope of the agreement dramatically without engaging in significant domestic reform. Binding current policy is valuable. It insures against rollback. It also means that when conditions are again conducive to liberalisation negotiations on market access and national treatment can start at a far more advanced stage.

The shipping negotiations in the previous round failed to reach a conclusion and are scheduled to resume in 2000. This chapter reviews the implications of further reform and also notes some options for the process of negotiations in this sector. An important issue in maritime transport will be the treatment of multi-modal services.

With respect to air transport, the observation is made that the regulatory arrangements in that sector are now under pressure for reform. The so-called hard rights of air transport are currently excluded from the GATS. There is a possibility that a multilateral exchange of rights will be possible, at least in a series of regional exchanges.

It is argued in the final section that there may be still other competition policy issues in these sectors that demand attention. The paper concludes that the importance of access to essential facility legislation is yet to be fully addressed at the level of the multilateral trading system. The contribution of the telecommunications reference paper in this context is also discussed.

Commitments in basic telecommunications

Assessing GATS commitments

The core of the GATS is the specific commitments made by each member country. To a very large extent, the impact of the GATS for producers and consumers alike depends upon the commitments that have been made. Unfortunately, the GATS schedules remain largely opaque documents, with many countries failing to follow the drafting guidelines issued by the GATT Secretariat. However, there is a burgeoning literature that seeks to quantify the extent to which various economies have sought to bind themselves to GATS disciplines. Various weighting techniques have been adopted to bring some clarity to GATS schedules and allow for comparison across countries.

Quantification of the GATS schedules commenced with the pioneering work of Hoekman (1995), who developed a relatively simple three-category weighting method. All GATS schedules were examined, and for quantification purposes a number was allocated to each possible schedule entry (i.e. each possible market access or national treatment commitment in each mode in each industry sub-sector), specifically:

- Where a member has agreed to be bound without any caveats, a weighting of 1 is allocated. A weighting of 1 is also allocated in circumstances where a member declares that a particular mode of supply is 'unbound due to lack of technical feasibility' if other modes of supply are unrestricted. A common example of this situation is the cross-border supply of construction and related engineering services.
- Where a member has agreed to be bound but specific restrictions remain, a weighting of 0.5 is allocated. If a mode of supply is bound, but specific reference is made to the horizontal commitments, a weighting of 0.5 is also allocated. This is commonly the case for commitments on the movement of natural persons, where immigration constraints continue to apply.

- Where a member has explicitly exempted that particular entry from the operation of the GATS by recording an entry of 'unbound' or by simply failing to make any commitments at all, a weighting of 0 is allocated.

There are many limitations with this methodology, most of which are detailed by Hoekman and in the other studies such as that by PECC (1995) that have adopted this approach. Importantly, the Hoekman methodology does not distinguish between barriers in terms of their impact on the economy, with minor impediments receiving the same weighting as an almost complete refusal of access.[1] However, the method does provide a useful snapshot of cross-national differences in commitments made in industries such as basic telecommunications.

Commitments in basic telecommunications

Marko (1998) uses a variant of the Hoekman methodology to assess the commitments made as part of the Agreement on Basic Telecommunications in 1997, the last time that the telecommunications components of a significant number of member countries' schedules were altered. Marko examined the sixty-nine member countries that made commitments on basic telecommunications. She found significant variation in the extent of commitments across countries, with some making very extensive commitments (notably the European Union, New Zealand and Malaysia) and others few if any unequivocal commitments.

On average, less than 32 per cent of the total number of services in the sixty countries potentially covered by the agreement actually were subject to binding commitments to free market access and national treatment. The remainder were either not scheduled or were scheduled with limitations on the application of the multilateral disciplines.

This finding is concerning, but it is useful to compare this figure with the results of PECC (1996) and Hoekman (1995). Hoekman found that high-income countries scheduled only 25 per cent of services without listing any exceptions to national treatment or market-access obligations, while the figure for developing countries was 7 per cent. In the PECC report, 22.4 per cent of services markets in the APEC region were found to be open to trade. Consequently, it can be concluded that the basic telecommunications market fares reasonably well compared with the average for the services sector as a whole.

It is generally believed that high-income countries made more commitments than low-income countries; that the extent of GATS commitments varies by real income levels. This is reported by Hoekman (1994a) and PECC (1996), who show a generally high correlation with income per head. They conclude that richer economies tend to have more open service sectors. Marko (1998) found that this pattern does not hold for the Agreement on Basic Telecommunications. She found no evidence of a positive relationship between per capita GNP and frequency measures for the sixty-nine countries in relation to basic telecommunications services.

Interestingly, several countries have noted dates for future liberalisation in their schedules. This kind of grandfathering of existing prohibitions is a welcome development, as it helps to strengthen the commitment to future reform. However, until these reforms are undertaken, market-access and national treatment disciplines are not in force for the telecommunications sectors in many developing economies.

Remaining barriers to trade and investment

The mixed picture in terms of telecommunications liberalisation that emerges from the GATS schedules is reinforced when national telecommunications policies are examined directly. While some progress has been made towards the development of competitive telecommunications markets, in many countries large segments of the industry remain closed to competition, indicating that there is significant scope for improved commitments from the region in any future multilateral negotiations.

In 1998, the International Telecommunications Union undertook a detailed study of the regulatory environment affecting the telecommunications industry in most countries around the world. Table 9.1 details some of the key findings of this survey for selected East Asian economies, specifically:

- The percentage of the incumbent operator that is privately owned. Privatisation is important in a competitive market, where private ownership of the incumbent will result in some additional efficiency gains arising from capital market disciplines.[2]
- For six key market segments – local, long-distance, international, data, leased lines and cellular mobile services – information is provided on whether the market is characterised as a monopoly, partially competitive or a competitive market. Partial competition refers to situations where countries retain certain 'non-technical' restrictions, which can lead to limits on the number of operators or on geographical coverage. Competition refers to the introduction of legislation that allows for unrestricted entry. Unfortunately, the ITU has, in the case of mobile cellular services, listed all countries that allow more than one competitor as competitive on the grounds that bandwidth availability limits the number of licences that can be issued.
- Information is also provided in the table on whether or not callback services are allowed.

From the data in Table 9.1, the variety in regulatory regimes around the region is immediately apparent. Developed economies such as Australia, Japan and particularly New Zealand have very liberal policy environments in which all key segments of the telecommunications industry are exposed to competition.

Table 9.1 Telecommunications policy environment in selected economies, 1997

	Incumbent privatised (%)	Local[a]	Long-distance[a]	Int'l[a]	Data[a]	Leased lines[a]	Mobile[a]	Callback allowed
Australia	33.30	C	C	C	C	C	C	yes
Brunei	0.00	M	M	PC	M	M	PC	no
Cambodia	0.00	PC	M	M	PC	M	C	no
China	0.00	PC	PC	M	PC	PC	C	no
Hong Kong	100.00	PC	M	M	C	PC	C	yes
Indonesia	23.15	PC	M	PC	C	C	C	no
Japan	34.60	C	C	C	C	C	C	yes
Korea	28.00	PC	PC	PC	PC	PC	C	no
Malaysia	33.00	C	C	C	C	C	C	no
New Zealand	100.00	C	C	C	C	C	C	yes
PNG	0.00	M	M	M	C	C	M	no
Philippines	100.00	C	C	C	C	C	C	no
Singapore	17.00	M	M	M	PC	PC	C	yes
Thailand	0.00	M	M	M	PC	M	C	no
Vietnam	0.00	PC	PC	M	PC	M	C	no

Source: International Telecommunications Union (1999) *Telecommunication Reform, 1998* Volume IV, Geneva: ITU.

Note:
[a] Competition (C) equates to unrestricted access; partial competition (PC) refers to 'non-technical' restrictions that can lead to limits on the number of operators or on geographical coverage; and monopoly (M) refers to restricted market situations.

However, both Australia and Japan continue to resist the full privatisation of their incumbent operators (Telstra and NTT, respectively). Competition is being introduced in the newly industrialised economies of Hong Kong, Korea and Singapore, but many barriers remain. Indeed, some of the less industrialised economies such as Malaysia and the Philippines appear to have more liberal policy regimes than their more developed counterparts. Finally, there are a group of economies in the region where the core telecommunications industry remains isolated from competitive forces.

The extent to which the reforms engendered by the Asian financial crisis have changed this picture is impossible to assess from these 1998 data. However, what these data do indicate is that GATS commitments are yet to reflect the actual policy landscape accurately. The GATS framework does not pick up some restrictive policies that advanced countries have in place, while many developing economies are significantly more liberal than their GATS schedules indicate.

This observation offers a road map for the immediate future of multilateral negotiations on telecommunications. In the aftermath of Seattle, gradualism appears to be the preferred method for taking negotiations forward as indicated above.

Transportation services

Maritime services[3]

The General Agreement on Trade in Services is the most recent example of an instrument aimed at opening markets and creating a fair trading environment for all providers of maritime services. That is, the international service sector, including maritime transport services (MTS), is governed by the GATS under the WTO regime. The GATS has emerged as the most important institutional force pushing the international MTS sector towards freer trade. Although the Uruguay Round failed to reach an agreement on MTS, the round was fruitful since the application of the framework provisions of the GATS to MTS was agreed upon and the liberalisation of trading in MTS was promoted through bilateral negotiations (Choi *et al.* 1997). We review the outcome of the WTO negotiations later in this chapter. Before that, we provide an outline of recent empirical work on the significance of impediments to trade and investment in shipping services.

Impediments to trade and investment

McGuire *et al.* (2000) review the nature of restrictions on trade and investment in maritime transport and also provide an assessment of their impact. Common types of restriction are illustrated in Table 9.2. McGuire *et al.* then develop and apply a methodology to measure the significance of these types of measures. The data on policy came from a variety of sources, and separate indexes were developed to quantify restrictions on foreign suppliers of maritime services and those that apply to all suppliers.[4] The gap between the scores for these two types of entrant indicates the extent to which there is discrimination against foreign suppliers.

Results reported for thirty-five economies in the Asia-Pacific region, the United States and Europe show a large range in the degree of restrictiveness. The conclusions are based on information on restrictions from 1994 to the end of 1998. McGuire *et al.* (*ibid.*) report the following:

Table 9.2 Examples of restrictions on maritime services

Restriction	Description of restriction
Right to fly the national flag	Requires ships to be registered or licensed to provide maritime services on domestic and international routes. The conditions on registration may include having a commercial presence in the domestic economy, the ship being built and owned domestically, and meeting seaworthiness and safety requirements.
Cabotage	Restricts shipping services on domestic or coastal routes to licensed vessels that meet certain conditions. Shipping services between domestic ports may be required to be carried out by domestically owned, operated, built and crewed ships.
Cargo sharing	Stipulates the allocation of cargo on particular routes between parties to bilateral and multilateral agreements.
Bilateral agreements	Agreements between two economies that primarily restrict the supply of shipping services and the allocation of cargo. Some bilateral agreements also restrict the use of port facilities.
UN Convention on a Code of Conduct for Liner Conferences (UN Liner Code)	Stipulates that conference trade between two economies can allocate cargo according to the 40:40:20 principle: 40% of tonnage is reserved for the national flag lines of each economy, and the remaining 20% is to be allocated to liner ships from a third economy. The code also entitles any national flag shipping line to be a member of a conference and to fix freight rates.
Conferences	Restricts the free and open participation of maritime service suppliers. Conference members set freight rates and schedules. Conferences may be open or closed. Open conferences have unrestricted entry and exit, and freight rates are set on a route. Closed conferences set freight rates, allocate cargo and restrict membership. Governments usually permit the existence of conferences through exemptions from price setting and collusion provisions of domestic competition legislation.
Port services	Requires ships to use a designated supplier of port services. These services include pilotage, towing, tug assistance, navigation aids, berthing, waste disposal, anchorage and casting off.

Source: McGuire *et al.* (2000).

- Brazil, Chile, India, Indonesia, Korea, Malaysia, the Philippines, Thailand and the United States, among the sample of economies examined, have the most restricted markets against foreigners. Important restrictions in these cases include strict conditions on the right to fly the national flag; rules on the carriage of certain cargoes; permission to liner conferences to form and operate; and reservation of the right to impose discretionary retaliatory measures and restrictions on foreign equity participation in domestic maritime service suppliers to a minority.

- Chile, the Philippines, Thailand, Turkey and the United States are the most discriminatory in the sample in their application of policy. These economies treat foreign maritime service suppliers significantly less favourably than domestic suppliers.

Although empirical studies of price or quantity-impact measures for services are limited, Kang (2000) sought to develop a price-impact estimation model for international shipping services in manufacturing trade. The theory underlying the approach is that if the market is competitive and has no restrictions on trade in MTS then prices can be expected to approach a service supplier's long-term marginal costs, defined as the cost of keeping a particular service supplier operating in the long run. However, with restrictions or impediments, there will be a wedge between prices and marginal costs. Not only the margin over costs but also the costs themselves might be affected. Costs might be higher because low-cost suppliers are excluded from the market or because protected firms are not producing at the lowest possible cost. For all these reasons – the marginal effect, the cost-difference effect and the cost-reduction effect – prices observed in the presence of impediments may exceed those in their absence.

Kang's (2000) pilot model for price-impact analysis used the FOB/CIF[5] ratio in bilateral trade, which is defined as the shipping margin, as a benchmark to compare price differences in the presence of different levels of restriction on MTS in bilateral trade. The underlying presumption of this econometric model is that less restrictiveness in either exporting or importing countries will be associated with lower shipping margins. This model includes several explanatory variables, such as distance between trading partners and the scale of the bilateral trade, among which the components of the restrictive indexes developed by McGuire *et al.* (2000) are of major concern. Kang found evidence to support a negative relationship between the extent of restriction and the size of the shipping margin.

WTO negotiations

Choi *et al.* (1997) reviewed the negotiations on maritime transport services. Participants agreed to suspend negotiations on 28 June 1996 and to resume on the basis of existing or improved offers at the time of a further round of comprehensive negotiations, which has been scheduled to begin in the year 2000. They reviewed some of the stumbling blocks in the negotiations, including the implications of the application of m.f.n. risks in liberalisation perceived by developing economies, the treatment of restrictive measures applying to domestic shipping, the management of access to port facilities, and the terms of commercial establishment. Another issue was the recognition of multi-modal services as a fourth pillar of the negotiations, the others being international shipping, auxiliary services and port services.

Choi *et al.* also conclude that despite this outcome, the Uruguay Round negotiations achieved significant results. They led to substantial offers of liberalisation by a large number of economies. These deepened their understanding of the issues involved in liberalisation and also reinforced their commitment to resuming negotiations on this sector. They note that during the Uruguay Round negotiations on MTS, thirty-two countries submitted their final commitments to be included in the schedule of specific commitments as an integral part of the GATS. Members of the WTO should enter new rounds of negotiations by no later than 2000, and periodically thereafter, with a view to achieving a progressively higher level of liberalisation in MTS.[6]

If the negotiations in 2000 proceed successfully, a new paradigm for MTS could be created. Under this regime, summarised in Table 9.3, the principle of m.f.n. treatment will be more widely applied and the GATS schedule will be universally adopted in the settlement of trade frictions. Allowing time for negotiations to proceed and for an implementation period, one scenario is that international shipping could be completely liberalised by 2010. Before this time, domestic routes would also be targets for liberalisation.

Table 9.3 New shipping regime under GATS general principles

	GATS *general principles*	*Relevance to shipping regime*
m.f.n./non-discrimination	Unconditional application	Removal of cargo reservation and other discriminatory measures
Transparency	Prompt (at least by the time of enforcement) announcement of all relevant measures pertaining to or affecting the operation of the GATS	Transparency in government practices in cargo preference, private agreement/measures between operators, any measures for cargo reservation and subsidies, technical standards, and so on
Increasing participation of developing countries	Promotion of service industries in developing countries	Removal of cargo allocation in developed countries; promotion of technology transfer and application; support for staff training; investment in ships
General exceptions	When related to national security or culture	For example, transportation of military items

Source: Kang and Findlay (2000).

A further question about the WTO process is how the negotiations might proceed. Formula-type approaches to negotiations have been proposed (see, for example, Adlung 1999; Thompson 1999). Formulas could be used to produce common sets of undertakings. As Adlung explains, this would help to fill gaps and improve the quality of commitments. One of these formulas is a cluster approach where commitments are made for a set of related activities. Multi-modal transport, including maritime transport services, has been proposed as a cluster, and model schedules were prepared to cover this category during the maritime negotiations (Prieto and Burrows 1999).

Air transport[7]

The regulation of international trade in air transport services involves an elaborate structure of bilateral agreements (there are over 3,500 such agreements) that fix a set of rules:

- to identify the airlines of the contracting parties with the rights to fly on each route;
- to determine the capacity that can be provided by each of those designated airlines; and
- to limit the capacity that can be offered by airlines from third countries.

The system therefore imposes a set of country-specific quotas in each market, where markets are defined in terms of routes between pairs of countries and in terms of the two-way traffic flow. Competition on each route is limited to those suppliers designated by the relevant bilateral air services agreements. When privately owned, effective ownership and control of the designated carriers must rest in the countries negotiating the agreement.[8]

Features of this current system can be highlighted by considering the options for providing services, which are summarised in Table 9.4.

A typical bilateral agreement will:

1   place limits on access in option A1: the capacity available to carriers based in one of the end points of a route is often restricted;
2   place limits on access in option A2: only those carriers allocated rights under the bilateral agreement are allowed to pick up passengers on a route, and rights of access to third parties are usually tightly constrained;
3   ban options B and C (option C might be sought by a carrier based in a high-cost economy that seeks to maintain its competitiveness);
4   not permit foreign carriers access to domestic routes (not illustrated in the table as an option); and
5   note the possibility that a signatory will want to nominate more than one domestic operator for mode D.

Table 9.4 Options for the provision of air transport services

Status of firm	Operating from a foreign base	Operating from a local base adjacent to the consumer
Foreign ownership (i.e. ownership of a different nationality to that of the consumers)	A1. *Cross-border supply*: e.g. Singapore Airlines operating out of Singapore picks up Australians on Singapore–Australia routes. A2. *Consumption abroad*: e.g. Singapore Airlines carries Australians between two foreign points.	B. *Commercial presence*: e.g. Singapore Airlines establishes an Australian operation to serve routes to and from Australia.
Domestic ownership (i.e. the same nationality as the consumers)	C. *Commercial presence*: e.g. Qantas establishes a business in Singapore to serve routes to and from Australia.	D. *Home delivery*: e.g. Australian airline Qantas operates on routes to and from Australia.

In terms of WTO principles, m.f.n. is not satisfied, since there is discrimination between foreign suppliers. Nor is national treatment satisfied, since foreigners operate on different terms to domestic carriers, for example in terms of access to domestic markets. Clearly, market access is restricted.

Trade liberalisation refers only to options A1 and A2: this scope is appropriate for goods where it is generally assumed that there is free entry in the domestic market. In that case, the main issue is related to the terms of access of goods coming over the border from whatever source (including those produced by capacity owned offshore by local firms). Investment liberalisation covers options B and C. Neither trade nor investment liberalisation covers conditions of entry for domestic firms (D).

Of the modes of supply as they are described in the GATS, namely cross-border supply, consumption abroad, commercial presence and presence of natural persons, the first three are noted in the table. Mode 4 is also important, e.g. for the movement of airline staff and those who work for suppliers of complementary services, and of interest to countries at different stages of development.

Treatment of air transport in the GATS

The General Agreement on Trade in Services included an Annex on Air Transport, which stipulates:

1   This Annex applies to measures affecting trade in air transport services, whether scheduled or non-scheduled, and ancillary services. It is confirmed that any specific commitment or obligation assumed under this Agreement shall not reduce or affect a

member's obligations under bilateral or multilateral agreements that are in effect on the date of entry into force of the WTO Agreement.

2   The Agreement, including its dispute settlement procedures, shall not apply to measures affecting:

a   traffic rights, however granted;
b   or services directly related to the exercise of traffic rights, except as provided in paragraph 3 of this Annex.

3   The Agreement shall apply to measures affecting:

a   aircraft repair and maintenance services;
b   the selling and marketing of air transport services;
c   computer reservation system (CRS) services.

4   The dispute settlement procedures of the Agreement may be invoked only where obligations or specific commitments have been assumed by the concerned members and where dispute settlement procedures in bilateral and other multilateral agreements or arrangements have been exhausted.

5   The Council for Trade in Services shall review periodically, and at least every five years, developments in the air transport sector and the operation of this Annex with a view to considering the possible further application of the Agreement in this sector.

The annex spells out that the GATS shall not apply to traffic rights. Its coverage is therefore limited to the provision of complementary services. Following paragraph 5 of the annex, the WTO Council for Trade in Services recently agreed to schedule negotiations on air transport for October and December 2000.

Reform options

One extreme option for reform is to remove completely the Annex on Air Transport by its integration into the GATS.[9] The Australian Productivity Commission (1998) made the following points about the further use of the GATS process as a procedure for reform:

• If air services were to be covered by the general provisions of the GATS, then the bilateral agreements between WTO members could become redundant, although bilateral agreements might be maintained with economies that are not WTO members.
• If m.f.n. treatment were to be applied to air transport, economies could not discriminate between WTO members except as a result of commitments to a regional arrangement.
• M.f.n. treatment would not require open access to domestic routes, but an economy could not discriminate in the arrangement of the terms of that access between WTO members.

- Controllers of air space or managers of airports could not discriminate between foreign airlines on the basis of nationality.

If the annex were to be removed, then the provisions of the GATS relating to market access and national treatment would then also apply.

A number of other proposals have been made about routes to reform. One is to take a first step towards clarifying current coverage of the annex by considering a more detailed classification of the air transport sector, including related activities (IATA (1999) presents a more detailed discussion of the issues of definition in the current annex). There have also been proposals to gradually draw various parts of the annex into the GATS. The less controversial modes of delivery could be drawn into the GATS, while more difficult ones, such as supply across a national border, could remain exempted. Also, various types of services could be drawn into the GATS, starting with express delivery, charter and all-cargo services, for example.[10]

Bilateral 'open skies' agreements and regional arrangements

Another route to reform is from within the structure of bilateral agreements. An example of this approach is the large number of so-called 'open skies agreements' that the United States has negotiated worldwide. The open skies strategy grows out of the bilateral system and retains the key feature of that system, which is discrimination against third parties.

Countries that do not enter into such agreements with the United States risk a loss of traffic because of the diversion of travellers to routes that are more competitive, where frequencies are higher and service is better. The process of reforming international air transport by this bilateral route therefore creates some real advantages for those who move first or furthest in relation to neighbours, and in particular for US carriers. In this way, the development of open skies agreements is expected to put pressure on those who have not signed up.

The problem is that these 'hub-and-spokes' agreements do not necessarily achieve an adequate standard of openness. For example, open skies agreements do not cover domestic routes. Therefore, the US carriers have the advantage of being able to draw on their extensive domestic networks, to which Asian carriers do not have direct access. Moreover, the United States continues to insist that those on US government business use US airlines. Finally, these agreements do not cover rules on ownership and rights of establishment.

At the same time, a sequence of open skies agreements, by themselves, give US carriers much more liberal access to routes between economies that have signed open skies agreements. In fact, this access could be even more open than agreed between the signatories themselves.

A series of bilateral 'hub-and-spokes' open skies agreements with the United States (or any other hub) does not lead smoothly towards a progressively more open, competitive and non-discriminatory international system for trade in international air transport. The 'spokes' need to cooperate between themselves in similar terms as with the hub. In fact, many have already begun to do so.[11] These arrangements vary significantly in their scope and timetables.

Reform of the air transport system requires the removal of restrictions on capacity on sets of routes between economies. One option discussed by Elek *et al.* (1995) is to develop an open club. The rules of the club explain to whom this unrestricted access is available and to whom it is not available. Club members would exchange unrestricted market-access rights with each other. As a consequence, members and non-members will be treated differently: the rules of the club will divert activity away from, deny opportunities to and therefore discriminate against outsiders. The only way for outsiders to prevent this consequence is to join arrangements pioneered by others. A key feature of an open club regime is that its rules should also specify how new members can join. The rules for this process have to be transparent, and there should also be a regular review process. Further work is required on the links between these club rules and positions taken in the Annex on Air Transport in the GATS.

For reasons discussed above, these regulatory arrangements are now under pressure for reform. There is a possibility that a multilateral exchange of rights will be possible, at least in a series of regional exchanges. Even if that particular concern is resolved, other competition policy issues may still demand attention.

Essential facilities

In the longer term, the progress on market access and national treatment, while likely to be beneficial to consumers, is unlikely to lead to fully contestable markets for telecommunications or transport services in many countries. This is because most countries lack an effective essential facilities regime.

Essential facilities regulation refers to a set of legislative instruments that provide open access to an essential input into the production process that is owned and operated by another firm and that exhibits natural monopoly characteristics.[12] This form of regulation first arose with the common law doctrine of prime necessities, which is generally traced back to a mid-seventeenth-century decision of Lord Hale that established the principle in the case of monopoly wharves. He made the point that if people were constrained to use a particular private wharf because it was the only wharf at the port of the licensed wharf, then the wharf owner had an obligation not to set arbitrary and excessive or immoderate duties. That is, as an obligation under common law, monopolies providing essential commodities must charge reasonable and moderate prices. The 'essential facilities' doctrine has not yet been formally adopted by either the US Supreme Court or the European Court of Justice, but some lower courts in the United States and the European Commission have done so. Countries such as Australia have such a doctrine enshrined in legislation.

Access to essential facilities is of critical importance in relation to service industries. Most services that require access to a network, such as telecommunications, gas, electricity, water and transport, find that some part of that network exhibits natural monopoly characteristics (at least in the short to medium term). Issues also arise with respect to airport or port access in the transport sectors.

In countries where effective essential facilities legislation is not operating, potential entrants into these industries often claim that they cannot compete effectively with the incumbent operators that control the natural monopoly components of the network.[13] For these competitors, such failure to regulate can operate to prevent entry into a market in much the same way as constraints on entry captured by the national treatment and market-access provisions of the GATS.

If the GATS is to seek to build a credible and contestable global market for transport and telecommunications services, then it must seek to ensure that members provide appropriate regulation of access to essential facilities. This would represent a radical extension of the multilateral regime and is likely to run into extensive political and practical difficulties. Not least among these difficulties is the need for cross-national agreement on what a minimum acceptable regime would look like. The developments in US and European case law will be critical here.

Of more immediate importance for the purpose of this paper is the extent to which the GATS framework would be capable of encompassing such a complex set of issues. Fortunately, there is some precedent in the GATS itself for this type of agreement on basic regulatory principles. Of the sixty-nine governments that signed the Agreement on Basic Telecommunications in February 1997, fifty-seven incorporated a reference paper on regulatory principles developed by the GATS negotiators. The regulatory paper is an attempt by negotiators to bind members to a series of regulatory principles considered necessary for effective market access in an industry characterised by incumbents with significant market power. It outlines a set of six broad principles designed to ensure that service providers can compete on equal terms once they have been allowed to enter a particular market. These include:

- Competitive safeguards that prevent incumbent suppliers engaging in anti-competitive conduct towards entrants, such as anti-competitive cross-subsidisation, use of network information or failure to supply necessary technical or commercial information to be maintained.
- An interconnection regime to ensure that entrants can connect with the incumbent on non-discriminatory and cost-oriented rates[14] that are transparent and reasonable, have regard to economic feasibility and are sufficiently unbundled so that the supplier need not pay for network components or facilities that it does not require for the service to be provided.
- Universal service obligations that are administered in a transparent, non-discriminatory and competitively neutral manner.
- Licensing criteria that are transparent, with reasons for denial made known to the applicant.

- A regulator that is independent of any supplier of basic telecommunications.
- Procedures for the allocation of scare resources (e.g. bandwidth) that are objective, timely, transparent and non-discriminatory.

Those countries that have attached the reference paper to their schedule of specific commitments agreed to adhere to these regulatory principles. In principle, this should help ensure a neutral regulatory playing field for competitors entering a market dominated by a large incumbent carrier.[15] In practice, these principles do not ensure a neutral regulatory playing field and will require significant expansion before minimum essential facility regime requirements are guaranteed by multilateral agreement. Nevertheless, the reference paper represents a promising precedent for the type of issue that the international trade community must address if a fully contestable global market for services is to be achieved.

Notes

1   Recently, several studies have attempted to develop, at a sectoral and modal level, a more nuanced weighting system that seeks to quantify differences in the effect of different partial commitments. See, for example, the contributions to Findlay and Warren (2000).

2   In a market that retains monopoly characteristics, privatisation is generally equivalent to a transfer of monopoly rents from the public to the private sector and hence is unlikely to result in significant allocative or dynamic efficiency gains, although technical efficiency may improve.

3   This section is an updated and extended version of some material in Kang and Findlay (2000). A more detailed review of the outcome of the Uruguay Round on maritime services is provided by Choi et al. (1997). Details of the GATS commitments are also recorded in background papers by the WTO Secretariat (1998a, b).

4   Restrictions are grouped into two broad categories of those on commercial presence and 'other'. The former includes rules on forms of presence, investment in onshore service suppliers and permanent movement of people. The latter includes cabotage, port services, the UN Liner Code, treatment of conferences and temporary movement of people.

5   FOB: free on board; CIF: cost, insurance and freight.

6   However, no mention is made of a schedule for negotiations on maritime transport in the report of the WTO Council for Trade in Services held in April 2000 (see http://www.wto.org/wto/new/Services2.htm).

7   This section draws on material reported in Findlay and Nikomborirak (1999) and Findlay (1999). See also the background paper by the WTO Secretariat (1998a).

8   A recent description of the system is provided by Australia's Productivity Commission in its report on international air transport and by the UNCTAD Secretariat (1999).

9   Johnson et al. (2000) have estimated a model of this type for air transport services. They have included a series of markets over which airlines are likely to construct networks. They capture network choices explicitly and they incorporate forms of imperfect competition that make explicit mark-ups over costs. This model is used to simulate the effects of the entry of another carrier into routes to and from Australia. They estimated that prices would fall by between 2.4 and 7.7 per cent and that total net passenger movements would increase by nearly 4 per cent. Both Australian and foreign welfare improves in this simulation. Losses of airline profits are more than offset by gains in consumer surplus.

10 IATA (1999) asks the question of whether such services could be dealt with by a conditional m.f.n. agreement and refers to the WTO Agreement on Government Procurement as an example of how to proceed. However, further attention is required to the scope of an agreement of this type that was attached to the GATS and that was relevant to air transport. More likely to be observed are the regional routes to reform discussed in the next section.

11 The ICAO has identified fifty groupings of states that are, or could become, involved in the regulation of aviation. These include the Arab Civil Aviation Commission, the Latin American Civil Aviation Commission, the Common Market for Eastern and Southern Africa, the Economic and Monetary Community of Central Africa, the Andean Pact, the Caribbean Community, the Fortaleza Agreement, the Banjul Accord and an agreement between Cambodia, the Laos People's Democratic Republic, Myanmar and Vietnam. The APEC leaders have also committed themselves to a programme of work on air transport.

12 A natural monopoly occurs when one enterprise can supply a service or a bundle of services at a lower cost than two or more enterprises, generally as a consequence of economies of scale or scope (see Baumol *et al.* 1982). A monopoly may also occur as a result of significant barriers to entry (high start-up costs) and barriers to exit (high costs of converting sunk assets to alternative uses).

13 New Zealand, for example, which does not have an essential facilities regime, came under significant pressure during the WTO negotiations on basic telecommunications because US carriers argued that they could not get access to Telecom New Zealand's network on a timely and cost-effective basis. The validity of these claims is open to question, but the point remains that a failure to regulate can be seen as an important a barrier to entry as policies that explicitly restrict entry.

14 Importantly, the reference paper does not define cost.

15 Note that the objective is to ensure that regulations do not favour any industry participant. There should be no regulatory favouring of the incumbent nor any attempt to stimulate entry artificially through favourable regulation of potential entrants.

References

Adlung, R. (1999) 'Liberalizing trade in services: from Marrakech to Seattle', *Intereconomics*, September/October: 211–22.

Baumol, W., Panzar, J. and Willig, R. (1982) *Contestable Markets and the Theory of Industry Structure*, New York: Harcourt Brace Jovanovich.

Choi, D.-H., Kim, J. and Findlay, C. (1997) 'Transport service liberalization in APEC', *Asia-Pacific Economic Review* 3(2): 52–61.

Elek, A., Findlay, C., Hooper, P. and Warren, T. (1999) 'Open skies or open clubs? New issues for Asia Pacific economic cooperation', *Journal of Air Transport Management*, June.

Findlay, C. (1999) 'International air transport', paper presented to the expert meeting on air transport services, Commission on Trade in Goods, Services and Commodities, UNCTAD, 21–23 June.

Findlay, C. and Nikomborirak, D. (1999) 'Air transport', paper prepared for the East Asia Conference on Options for the WTO 2000 Negotiations, 19–20 July, Manila: PECC/TPF and World Bank.

Findlay, C. and Warren, T. (eds) (2000) *Impediments to Trade in Services: Measurement and Policy Implications*, London: Routledge.

Hill, T. (1977) 'On Goods and Services', *Review of Income and Wealth* 24(3): 315–38.

Hoekman, B. (1995) 'Tentative first steps: an assessment of the Uruguay Round agreement on services', paper presented for the World Bank Conference, The Uruguay Round and the Developing Economies, 26–27 January.

Hoekman, B., Low, P. and Mavroidis, P. (1996) 'Antitrust disciplines and market access negotiations: lessons from the telecommunications sector', paper presented at the Oslo Competition Conference, Oslo, 13–14 June.

International Air Transport Association (IATA) (1999) 'Liberalisation of air transport and the GATS', IATA discussion paper, October.

International Telecommunications Union (1998) *Telecommunications Reform*, Volume IV, Geneva: ITU.

Johnson, M., Gregan, T., Belin, P. and Gentle, G. (2000) 'Modelling the benefits of increasing competition in international air services', in C. Findlay and T. Warren (eds) *Impediments to Trade in Services: Measurement and Policy Implications*, London: Routledge.

Kang, J.-S. (2000) 'Price impact of restrictions on maritime services', in C. Findlay and T. Warren (eds) *Impediments to Trade in Services: Measurement and Policy Implications*, London: Routledge.

Kang, J.-S. and Findlay, C. (2000) 'Regulatory reform in the maritime industry', in C. Findlay and T. Warren (eds) *Impediments to Trade in Services: Measurement and Policy Implications*, London: Routledge.

Marko, M. (1998) 'An evaluation of the Basic Telecommunications Services Agreement', CIES Policy Discussion Paper 98/09, Centre for International Economic Studies, University of Adelaide.

McGuire, G., Schuele, M. and Smith, T. (2000) 'Restriction of trade in maritime services', in C. Findlay and T. Warren (eds) *Impediments to Trade in Services: Measurement and Policy Implications*, London: Routledge.

OECD (1997) *The Future of International Air Transport Policy: Responding to Global Change*, Paris: OECD.

Pacific Economic Cooperation Council (1995) *Survey of Impediments to Trade and Investment in the APEC Region*, Singapore: APEC Secretariat.

Prieto, F.J. and Burrows, A. (1999) 'Chile and Australia: GATS 2000 – towards effective liberalisation of trade in services: proposals for action', paper presented to the World Services Congress, Atlanta, November 1–3.

Productivity Commission (1998) *International Air Services*, Inquiry Report, 11 September, Melbourne.

Sampson, G. and Snape, R. (1985) 'Identifying issues in trade in services', *The World Economy* 8(2): 171–82.

Thompson, R. (1999) 'Formula approaches to improving GATS commitments', paper presented to the World Services Congress, Atlanta, November 1–3 (downloadable from www.worldservicescongress.com).

UNCTAD Secretariat (1999) 'Air transport services: the positive agenda for developing countries', Report TD/B/COM.1/EM.9/2, 15 April.

Warren, T., Tamms, V. and Findlay, C. (1999) 'Beyond the bilateral system: competition policy and trade in international aviation services', Paper presented at the American Economic Association annual meeting and meeting of the Transportation and Public Utilities Group, New York, 3 January.

WTO Secretariat (1998a) 'Air transport services', background note by the secretariat S/C/W/59, 5 November (downloadable from http://www.wto.org/services/services.htm).

—— (1998b) 'Maritime transport services', background note by the secretariat S/C/W/62, 16 November (downloadable from http://www.wto.org/services/services.htm)

10 Electronic commerce

A need for regulation?

Stefan Bach and Georg Erber

Introduction

The main function of the WTO is to ensure that international trade flows as smoothly, predictably and freely as possible. Its historical role was to lower trade barriers – reducing tariffs and dismantling non-tariff barriers to entry. E-commerce poses major new challenges because it transforms the entire international transaction system. The new economy emerging on electronic networks is currently highly unregulated and is developing very rapidly. However, efficient markets need an appropriate institutional and regulatory framework. This paper addresses the question of how the WTO Millennium Round negotiations might deal with these questions.

Products that are bought and paid for over the Internet but are delivered physically are subject to existing WTO rules on trade in goods and services. In contrast, products that are delivered digitally over the Internet – computer software and increasingly music, video and related kinds of new media – a variety of issues arise concerning the appropriate policy regime and regulation. Both the supply of Internet access services and many of the products delivered over the Internet fall within the ambit of the General Agreement on Trade in Services, but there is a need to clarify how far particular activities are covered by the members' market-access commitments.

In a recent working paper by WTO staff (Pérez-Esteve and Schuknecht 1999), it was estimated that the share of added value that lends itself to e-commerce is about 30 per cent of GDP. In 1996, the last year for which data are currently available, international exports in potentially digitisable media amounted to $44 billion and had risen at an average annual rate of about 8.5 per cent from 1990 to 1996. The share of digitisable media as a proportion of total imports worldwide was less than 1 per cent, and during the next couple of years, global e-trade will not transform international trade as much as public media coverage or the statements of politicians have sometimes suggested. However, e-commerce will become an important topic on the WTO agenda in the Millennium Round negotiations.

Two approaches to regulating global e-commerce

There are two general approaches to regulating issues such as global e-commerce, currently followed by two key international actors in the world economy.

The first approach, which is pursued mainly by European governments and the European Union, relies on government ex-ante regulation. This would require the establishment of an international regulatory framework in the form of bilateral or multilateral agreements. By applying a deductive set of fairly abstract principles following the tradition of the Roman law system, this approach attempts to solve legal conflicts by subsuming actual cases under this set of general legal principles. The success of such an approach depends mainly on the level of understanding of the regulatory conflicts that might occur in practice.

The other approach is more open to experiments with regulatory environments. It believes in self-regulating market organisations. This kind of liberal inductive method is preferred by countries following the Anglo-Saxon legal tradition[1] (US government 1999), where quarrels are to be resolved in a case-by-case manner. This tradition is suspicious of general principles, which do not deal adequately with the intricacies of a particular case. This more empirically oriented approach to regulation believes in the process of social learning first before more abstract rules emerge later on. Therefore, one should be cautious in establishing general principles, especially in an environment that was not well understood at the beginning of e-commerce.

Obviously, one side believes that e-commerce is like traditional commerce and is just a technical problem of implementing the existing legal rules and solving enforcement problems. The other side believes that e-commerce transforms traditional transactions. By simply attempting to apply the legal framework of traditional commerce to e-commerce, regulators tend to create regulatory inefficiencies. Since e-commerce changes more in the transaction process of an economy, it is assumed that the regulation of e-commerce needs a particular time span for social learning. Without a clear understanding, it would be preferable to adopt a 'wait-and-see' position in order to determine how global e-commerce develops and how actors in e-markets find ways of self-regulating their transactions.

The regulatory authority could be chosen according to the principle of subsidiarity and left to nation-states or by delegating the authority to an international institution. The WTO is one possible international organisation able to solve international disputes on e-commerce. Since the WTO covers the largest number of countries in the world, it would be best suited to guarantee the universality of a global regulation of e-commerce, in the same way that it is already doing in traditional trade disputes. This is why major players argue that e-commerce should be dealt with by the WTO.

The USA, as a front runner in global e-commerce, is eager to keep its momentum and avoid any regulation that might slow down the development of global e-commerce (see, e.g., White House 1997a, b). The USA follows the paradigm of a more inductive, self-regulatory and social learning regulatory approach. Conversely, the EU prefers regulation based on general principles.

The USA and the EU take into account the interests of two major constituencies that need protection from inappropriate regulation in e-commerce. The USA seems to be most worried about the fact that e-commerce in its infancy could be crippled by regulations that are too restrictive (*ibid.*). Excessive protection of civil privacy and consumers might put the burden on companies starting up in e-commerce and significantly reduce the advantage of e-commerce against traditional commerce. If the WTO negotiations were to settle on a regulatory model that would simply create a level playing field with the existing rules for traditional commerce, the USA would be worried that global e-commerce could not use its full potential.

In contrast, the EU seems to be concerned that the power of multinational players in e-commerce, in particular those of US origin, will tilt the balance to the disadvantage of weaker players such as consumers and small and medium-sized companies, which could lose out badly in a fairly unregulated global environment. The EU prefers to grant them more protection against the more powerful players in e-commerce early on, because they cannot cope with the more intense competition from abroad. Even the idea of a gradual social learning process in the area of global e-commerce does not seem to be very attractive to them, because this process will create situations that can hardly be reversed later. At the Seattle ministerial conference, potential losers voiced their concerns.

Two types of lobbying organisation are attempting to have some impact on the WTO negotiating process addressing global e-commerce. On the one hand, there is the Global Business Dialogue (GBD 1999) and the Alliance for Global Business (AGB 1999a–c), which represent a community of large multinational corporations. On the other hand, there are consumer and civil rights organisations such as EPIC (Electronic Privacy Information Center) and GILC (Global Internet Liberty Campaign) in a coalition with representatives of trade union organisations such as TUAC (Trade Union Advisory Commission) and organisations from SMEs, in particular sectors such as agriculture and textiles from the developed countries, or even big companies from developing countries, which feel better protected under current circumstances than under a more liberal, highly unregulated global regime of e-commerce (OECD 1999a). This coalition, which embraces a more defensive stand towards global e-commerce, illustrates the problem of reaching an agreement that takes care of the two main objectives: social justice and economic efficiency.

The costs and benefits of an early general global regulation of e-commerce following the European model of regulation according to general principles could be summarised by the following considerations:

- The costs involved are the potential loss in efficiency, because a regulatory competition as an exploratory search process to identify best practices cannot take place. This may increase the social costs of such a regulation.

- Conversely, a regulation would reduce transaction costs for most participants in the market, because regulatory regimes would become more homogeneous. Even if one group develops a more favourable way of self-regulating its e-commerce, market participants will always have to invest in search costs to find out which method is best for them. The more the regulatory environments differ, the more costly this search process will be for everybody. There are positive network externalities associated with a more general regulatory framework than with a more limited one.

To sum up, one might conclude that the negotiating process at the coming WTO Millennium Round will become a highly controversial topic concerning global e-commerce. Time will work for those countries and companies that are already leading. They create situations that are difficult to reverse afterwards. The key players are already sitting in the driver's seat. It would need major countervailing powers to rebalance such a process. What will be needed most is for the two different views on regulation to be blended into a more comprehensive approach, where the aim should be to integrate the comparative advantages of both lines of thinking. Based on historical experience, Kindleberger's law will apply; as he put it:

> I have developed Kindleberger's law of alternatives, based on historical example. Often after extended policy debate, the powers that be end up doing both.
>
> (Kindleberger 1999: 22)

That would also legitimise such an agreement in the eyes of the world community and could significantly reduce enforcement costs.[2]

Intellectual property rights

E-commerce implies big challenges for the enforcement of intellectual property rights at the national but even more so at the international level. Immaterial goods and services that are traded electronically often affect intellectual property rights. The current system of the Internet is not well suited to providing an effective framework for enforcing the protection of these rights. The basis for a multilateral framework was set in 1995 with the TRIPs (Trade-Related Intellectual Property Rights) Agreement, which was part of the Uruguay Round. The TRIPs Agreement established a minimum standard of protection for a broad range of intellectual property rights, including patents, copyright, trademarks and trade secrets. One important step forward in the TRIPs Agreement was that it established the m.f.n. principle for the area of intellectual property rights.

Even if all countries at the WTO were to come to an agreement according to the international agreements signed at the WIPO (World Intellectual Property Organization), it still would be very hard to enforce these rights. Obviously, it is technologically very easy to illegally copy and distribute media content such as films, music, software, books and databases on a multitude of channels (Callan 1998). The production costs of the first copy are extremely high, but the reproduction costs of additional copies are extremely low. As the initial production costs are high sunk costs to the producers and can only be recovered by selling large numbers of additional copies to a mass market afterwards to break even, this kind of media content has become a key target for people who want to make an easy profit from copying these items illegally.

The Internet enables these illegal copiers to distribute such forms of media content without having to face the necessity of building up their own distribution channels at local levels or in different countries. Therefore, it becomes much more difficult for the police, who should enforce the protection of intellectual property rights, to catch people on the supply side, which is often outside the country's legal borders.

Even attempts to block websites disseminating illegally copied electronic goods such as these would make it necessary to establish a permanent surveillance of information flows on the Internet and control websites to find out their locations.

Criminal organisations, which make their money by illegally distributing electronic media content, have a high incentive to overcome the barriers set up by law enforcement agencies. As they constantly find new ways to overcome these barriers, many observers of the scene believe that the fight to enforce legal protection will always end like the race between the hare and the tortoise. Whenever enforcement agencies believe that they have found a successful way to keep illegal distributors out, they soon learn that criminals have found a way to work around the barriers. In its current structure of openness, the Internet has the impact of raising the enforcement costs for the protection of intellectual property.

It will be a highly controversial issue in the Millennium Round as to who will have to carry these costs. Large numbers of developing countries are especially reluctant to enforce the protection of intellectual property rights of mainly foreign nationals or foreign organisations. They see the protection of intellectual property rights of mainly OECD countries as a threat to their economic development. Developing countries would transfer resources to the owners of those rights. Also, developing countries face restrictions on the diffusion of knowledge, and they fear being left behind in development. To reach an acceptance of the TRIPs Agreement by developing countries, the OECD countries have had to accept long transition periods. All developing countries have been granted a five-year transition period, and the least developed countries have been given ten years.

A further weakness of the current TRIPs Agreement is that it does not cover intellectual property rights on genetic technologies and Internet publications. If intellectual property rights on Internet content are to be respected, this problem will have to be resolved. A flood of activity is currently taking place in the USA to patent Internet technologies and Internet business models at the national level (*New York Times* 1999). The US government prefers to establish international intellectual property rights in these areas in the Millennium Round, something that will challenge all other countries, including EU countries, lagging behind in this development (WIPO 1999).

Further requirements for national and international legislation

Enlarged international business activities raise questions concerning the legal framework of national and international civil law. In a global environment, consumers and SMEs especially cannot cope with the multitude of different legal systems in all WTO member countries. This would make it necessary to establish a certain level of harmonisation in the legal systems so that uncertainties regarding the quality of legal contracts are reduced. Otherwise, the transaction costs of international e-commerce will be unfavourably high and hamper its development.

Claims and responsibilities must be clear and enforceable by law if e-commerce is to function without friction. Selling to or buying from abroad, by all kinds of firms and consumers that are not specialists in international trade, will raise questions: what are the relevant rules regarding contract law, general terms of business, business conventions, enforcement of claims, and guarantees, including liability for faults and jurisdiction?

In the case of transactions involving large payments, the risks concerning the creditworthiness of contractual partners become very important. This makes it necessary to create a more transparent world financial system. This includes a technically reliable system of e-money, including anonymous small payments. In particular, the creation of liquidity by private financial institutions or even large multinational companies through electronic payment systems will increasingly restrict the ability of central banks to control the money supply.

In many of these areas, there is still a considerable need for international coordination on minimum standards and for regulations to prevent abuse, as well as to ensure that the market is transparent with regard to the services agreed upon. This is also in the interests of those offering goods and services, as user confidence in these new forms of trading needs to be developed.

In the context of the WTO negotiations, other international agreements and treaties should be adapted to the new business environment of e-commerce. Adequate worldwide regulation of consumer protection and privacy issues will become key factors for successful global e-commerce. At the level of the OECD countries, a consensus has emerged recently by establishing guidelines for consumer protection and privacy in e-commerce (OECD 1999b). The EU is developing directives according to these principles (EU 1995; 1997; 2000). These principles and guidelines could easily be adopted at the WTO level.

Taxation issues of global e-commerce

The effects of e-commerce on public revenue, in particular on taxation, have been highlighted in recent years and are still being publicly debated. Existing taxation systems refer to a large extent to home markets of traditional commerce. Therefore, national legislation is still predominant, although complemented by regulations on double taxation and indirect taxation. With respect to taxation, the emerging new economy is characterised by two crucial issues:

- Suppliers are becoming less and less present at the point of sale.
- Added value is shifting in favour of immaterial goods and services.

As the ongoing debate about globalisation shows, it can be difficult to tax international mobile resources like capital and related services. E-commerce will lead to problems for the taxation of indirect consumption when consumers go shopping abroad over the Internet. This is particularly true if the whole distribution process goes online: in the long run, the Internet seems to integrate separate media such as computer software, music, video and television into a comprehensive digital multimedia channel, where distance plays a decreasing role.

This creates new demands on taxation with regard to the adaptation of tax regulations and enforcement. The question arises of whether existing national tax regulations can be adapted or whether a completely new harmonised global tax system should be established. To address the major topics:

- Business taxation is affected in so far as foreign suppliers refrain from being present in the country of destination. Governments deal with this problem by signing international tax treaties. It is being discussed whether a server or even a website can be considered a 'permanent establishment', thus making the supplier liable to domestic taxation. This shows that in practice it is not easy to apply existing principles and definitions. In addition, the scope and scale for creative accounting to avoid tax, although not limited to electronic commerce, can be expected to increase as it is used more intensively, e.g. between subsidiaries of multinationals by transfer pricing, shifting costs and financing. Accordingly, via the Internet private investors may easily transfer their assets to offshore locations to evade domestic taxation.
- Cross-border online sales imply big risks for the future of indirect consumption taxation according to the destination principle. Even if at present such transactions with private individuals make up only a small proportion of e-commerce, seen over the longer term, a considerable potential for evading VAT or sales taxes is clearly emerging. OECD and EU member states in particular agreed that in the case of cross-border e-commerce, consumer taxes should apply in the country where consumption takes place. However, the question arises of whether the taxman will still be able to enforce his tax claims in a new world economy.

Therefore, enforcement and compliance costs seem to be the crucial issues in taxing e-commerce. In the case of purely electronic transactions, the tax authorities are no longer able to seize the object of taxation. Taxpayers may also dematerialise. In technical terms, it is nearly impossible for tax officers to monitor communication via the Internet efficiently, even more so if encryption procedures are used. Website domain names and e-mail addresses sometimes give no hint to identify the location of their owners.[3]

Against this background, enforceable international taxation schemes have to take care of these problems. To minimise enforcement problems, suitable hardware and software solutions are needed, and, clearly, such solutions will have to be agreed upon and enforced at an international level. This should be done within the framework of the EU, the OECD and the WTO.

In Europe, it is undisputed that within the next few years a level playing field should be created for both traditional and e- commerce. The OECD ministerial conference in October 1998 came to an agreement that consumption tax regulations should be applied to cross-border e-commerce (OECD 1998) The EU supports this proposal (EU 1998), and the European Commission put forward a draft for a corresponding directive in summer 2000. Furthermore, there is a consensus that additional levies and duties on electronic commerce should be avoided (WTO 1998). The initiative of the US government to establish the Internet as a global free trade area is supported by the EU and the WTO.

In 1998, the US Congress adopted the Internet Freedom Act, which included a three-year ban on 'new Internet taxes'. A debate on a general sales taxation arrangement for traditional and e-commerce has just started. At present, US public opinion supports the idea of keeping e-commerce completely free of indirect taxation. The idea is on the one hand to foster growth of the new economy and on the other hand to place downward pressure on taxation in general in order to restrain governments' 'leviathan' appetite for raising money and spending it inefficiently (see, e.g., Becker 2000). Other US economists, such as Varian (1999) propose that all state and local sales taxes be discarded and replaced by direct state taxes, taking income or consumption expenditures as its tax base. The latter should be measured as annual income minus savings.

Yet these arguments are not convincing: the growth of e-commerce should be driven by its comparative advantage, not by subsidies. Moreover, historical experience as well as matters of tax practicability show that a well-suited mix of direct and indirect taxation is indispensable. Merely relying on one scheme seems to neglect the problem of tax avoidance. Besides this, direct taxation has come under pressure due to globalisation and tax competition, so there are sufficient incentives for politicians not to maintain inefficient tax systems. If both tax bases are eroding, this will diminish the capability to supply public goods and services as before.

To sum up, existing tax schemes should in principle be applied to e-commerce to guarantee a level playing field. E-commerce should be integrated into an economically sound and just taxation framework. Yet the specific environment of e-commerce has to be considered; in particular, compliance should be eased by adopting administrative procedures that taxpayers already use or develop to meet their markets. This could be accomplished efficiently by international standardisation of taxation procedures, in particular with regard to indirect taxation. One possibility is to reach a framework agreement and leave the actual design and certification of the required hardware and software components to the suppliers and users affected (Dittmar and Selling 1998). Furthermore, closer international cooperation between tax authorities is required. Only time will tell to what extent such improvements will enable authorities to prevent electronic 'smuggling' and 'virtual black markets'.

Development implications of electronic commerce: technology transfer and education

An important topic for the WTO will be the impact of e-commerce on trade and the economic perspectives of developing countries. Are there ways of enhancing their participation in e-commerce in order to integrate the developing countries better into the world economy and share the benefits?

Starting with a more general point of view, e-commerce seems to be useful to producers and consumers in developing countries. It helps them to overcome traditional barriers of access to foreign markets and enhances their capabilities to obtain information about market opportunities. Producers and traders no longer need to maintain physical establishments requiring large capital outlays. Increased advertising possibilities worldwide may help small and medium-sized businesses in developing countries, which may have found it difficult before to gain access to customers abroad. E-commerce may enable such firms to avoid middlemen and try to sell their products to the end customer.

E-commerce in particular makes it possible for consultant-type work such as software development and other business-related services to be carried out in developing countries as well, rather than in countries where these services are in demand. This should facilitate sales of services in which developing countries have at present a comparative advantage but which could not be fully utilised because of restrictions on the international mobility of labour.

This requires a well-functioning and modern telecommunications infrastructure, a satisfactory electricity supply, and access to hardware, software and servers. Access to telecommunications at low prices and the availability of telecommunications equipment are problems in many developing countries, where the infrastructure often remains at a low level and is monopolised by public or privately owned companies, which levy high charges on their services because efficient competition does not exist. Sometimes, high tariffs make IT products there even more expensive than in developed countries.

A global digital divide?

In the long run, the new economy paradigm implies an increasing share of knowledge production. The spread of information technology and e-commerce does not take place at equal speed across all nations and societies. Therefore, they are currently a facilitator for more inequality at a global scale (Van Alstyne and Brynjolfsson 1996), termed in the USA the 'digital divide' (US Department of Commerce 1995; 1999). The US government has already begun to develop policies to narrow this widening gap inside the USA (US Government Working Group on Electronic Commerce 1999). However, similar efforts to bridge the gap internationally between developed and developing countries is even more challenging (see World Bank 1999). This will make it necessary to increase the investment in the human capital of skills worldwide (*ibid.*).

Illiteracy and cultural differences are still high barriers to selling knowledge goods and doing commerce across national boundaries, especially in the developing countries. The less developed countries, as well as unskilled people worldwide, currently run the risk of becoming further marginalised in a world driven by global e-commerce. Therefore, technology transfer, education and vocational training will become even more important in both the developing and the developed world. It will become another important topic for development policy, and it will be necessary for international institutions such as the UN and the World Bank to cope with it early on. Support for an agreement from developing countries would become more enthusiastic if developed countries would offer their support to solve the problems set by the global digital divide internationally and inside developing countries.

The role of the secretariat

What kind of position could the WTO Secretariat have at the WTO negotiations? Obviously, its position should be closely coordinated with the main players, the USA, the EU, Japan and the developing countries. Moreover, it could try to act as a mediator between the two distinct positions taken by different countries.

With respect to TRIPs negotiations and efforts to extend intellectual property rights to new areas such as genetic technologies and Internet technologies, many European countries will have reservations about granting excessive property rights early on, as will many developing countries. As in the regulation debate over e-commerce, one should take time for a process of social learning to determine for how long and with what scope the protection of intellectual property in these areas should be granted at the WTO level in order to accomplish a high degree of global social welfare. Moreover, the WTO should encourage and monitor the discussion and negotiation process on creating an appropriate legal framework for e-commerce regarding civil law, financial services, consumer protection and privacy.

Taxation of global e-commerce should avoid high enforcement and compliance costs. The search for common standards has to take into account the current huge international differences in taxation. Setting up a global framework for e-commerce taxation could become a crucial leveller for greater harmonisation of worldwide taxation, at least concerning minimum standards. The WTO should try to develop efficient guidelines for this process.

Finally, accomplishing a successful accord at the WTO on global e-commerce would become easier if the developed countries were to combine this with commitments to help developing countries to overcome the global digital divide. Reasonable development policies by national and international development organisations targeting these problems could convince leaders of developing countries more easily that global e-commerce is for the mutual benefit for all people in the world.

If negotiations at the WTO level were to stall – because of reluctance, especially by developing countries – the OECD would become the major forum where international agreements could be worked out. This is possible because currently more than 90 per cent of e-commerce takes place inside the OECD area.

Notes

1   The five principles guiding US policy on e-commerce are part of the White House declaration (White House 1997b) and were signed by the British government soon afterwards:

> 1. The private sector should lead in the development of electronic commerce and in establishing business practices. 2. Governments should ensure that business enjoys a clear, consistent and predictable legal environment to enable it to do so, while avoiding unnecessary regulations or restrictions on electronic commerce. 3. Governments should encourage the private sector to meet public interest goals through codes of conduct, model contracts, guidelines, and enforcement mechanisms developed by the private sector. 4. Government actions, when needed, should be transparent, minimal, non-discriminatory, and predictable to the private sector. 5. Co-operation among all countries, from all regions of the world and all levels of development, will assist in the construction of a seamless environment for electronic commerce.
>
> (US government 1999)

2   Mr Schlögl, OECD deputy secretary-general, in summing up new trends identified as one of the four major new developments since the last meetings in Ottawa and Turku in the report of the last OECD Forum on Electronic Commerce (OECD 1999c), remarked:

> The issue of regulation and self-regulation. People no longer speak of a dichotomy – rather the challenge is to get the mix between these complementary approaches right. The mix has to be effective. 'Co-regulation' and an 'integrated approach' were discussed as means of achieving this. A basic legal framework upon which self-regulatory approaches can be built which give scope to innovation and competition. Responsibility stays with national governments, notably to protect vulnerable groups, but the regulatory environment should be a balance between self-regulation by industry and regulation by government

and international bodies developed co-operatively by government, business and the public voice.

(OECD 1999b: 13)

3   *The Economist* (2000: 4) recently pointed this out, quoting a magazine cartoon where two dogs are sitting in front of a computer screen. One tells the other: 'On the Internet, nobody knows that you're a dog'.

References

AGB (1999a) 'A discussion paper on trade-related aspects of electronic commerce in response to the WTO's e-commerce work programme', Alliance of Global Business, April.

—— (1999b) *A Global Action Plan for Electronic Commerce, Prepared by Business with Recommendation to Governments*, 2nd edn, Alliance of Global Business, October.

—— (1999c) papers of the conference at the OECD on Electronic Commerce: Maximizing the Opportunities, Paris, 11 October.

Becker, G.S. (2000) 'The hidden impact of not taxing e-commerce', *Business Week*, 28 February 2000, p.12.

Callan, B. (1998) 'Pirates on the high seas, the United States and global intellectual property rights', study group paper of the Council of Foreign Relations, New York.

Dittmar, F. and Selling, H.-J. (1998) *How to Control Internet Transactions? A Contribution from the Point of View of German Tax Inspectors*, Intertax.

Economist, The (2000) 'Survey "Globalisation and Tax"', by M. Bishop, 11 January.

EU (1995) Directive 95/46/EC of the European Parliament and of the Council of 24 October 1995 on the protection of individuals with regard to the processing of personal data and on the free movement of such data. Official Journal L 281 of 23/11/1995.

—— (1997) Directive 97/7/EC of the European Parliament and of the Council of 20 May 1997 on the protection of consumers in respect of distance contracts. Official Journal L 144 of 04/06/1997.

—— (1998) 'E-commerce and indirect taxation', communication by the Commission to the Council of Ministers, the European Parliament and to the Economic And Social Committee: COM(98)374final, 17/6/98.

—— (2000) Directive 1999/93/EC of the European Parliament and of the Council of 13 December 1999 on a Community framework for electronic signatures. Official Journal L 13/12 of 19/1/2000.

GBD (1999) 'Answering the challenges of the emerging online economy', 'Global business dialogue on electronic commerce', summary statements of working groups of the conference, Paris.

Kindleberger, C. (1999) 'The Manichaean Character of Economics', *Challenge* 42: 21–38.

New York Times (1999) 'Patents multiply and web sites find lawsuits are just a click away', 11 December: A1 and C14.

OECD (1998) *Electronic Commerce: Taxation Framework Conditions*, Paris: OECD.

—— (1999a) conference papers presented at the Third Public Voice Conference, 11 October, Paris: OECD.

—— (1999b) 'Recommendation of the OECD Council concerning guidelines for consumer protection in the context of electronic commerce', 9 December, Paris: OECD.

—— (1999c) OECD Forum on Electronic Commerce, Report SG/EC(99)12, 24 November, Paris: OECD.

Pérez-Esteve, R. and Schuknecht, L. (1999) *A Quantitative Assessment of Electronic Commerce*, Staff Working Paper ERAD-99–01, Geneva: World Trade Organization, Economic Research and Analysis Division.

US Department of Commerce (1995) *The Digital Divide, A Survey of the 'Have Nots' in Rural and Urban America*, Washington.

—— (1999) *Falling Through the Net: Defining the Digital Divide, report on the telecommunications and information technology gap in America*, Washington: National Telecommunication and Information Administration and US Department of Commerce.

US government (1999) US–UK joint statement on electronic commerce, 30 January, Washington.

US Government Working Group on Electronic Commerce (1999) *Toward Digital Equality*, second annual report, Washington.

Van Alstyne, M. and Brynjolfsson, E. (1996) *Communication Networks and the Rise of an Information Elite. Do Computers Help the Rich get Richer?* Cambridge, Mass: MIT Sloan School of Management, available online at http://www.mit.edu/marshall/www/home.html.

Varian, H.R. (1999) *A Proposal to Eliminate Sales and Use Taxes*, available online at http://www.sims.berkeley.edu/~hal/Papers/tax-proposal.txt.

White House (1997a) *Presidential Directive on Electronic Commerce*, memorandum for the heads of executive departments and agencies, Washington, 1 July.

—— (1997b) *A Framework for Global Electronic Commerce*, Washington, 1 July.

WIPO (1999) *WIPO Digital Agenda*, Geneva: World Intellectual Property Organization.

World Bank (1999) 'Knowledge for development, entering the 21st century', *World Development Report 1998/1999*, Washington.

WTO (1998) *Declaration on Global Electronic Commerce*, WT/MIN(98)/DEC/2, 20 May 1998, Geneva.

11 Competition policy and the WTO

Phedon Nicolaides

Introduction

Competition policy was on the agenda of the Seattle meeting of the World Trade Organization, and it met the same fate as most other issues under discussion. That is, there was neither tangible progress nor any agreement on future work. However, even if the meeting would otherwise have been declared a success, it is very doubtful whether any consensus would have been reached on competition policy. Not only were there the usual fault lines separating industrial and developing nations but, perhaps more significantly, there was hardly any common ground among the major trading nations and in particular between the United States and the European Union.

As the process of globalisation gathers pace and as international competition intensifies, slight differences in the terms of access to the various markets can have a substantial effect on the commercial success or failure of a firm. Market access can be decisively influenced by the presence or absence of competition rules and the rigour with which they are enforced. The WTO is seen as becoming anachronistic for not being able to address competition issues. Some have suggested that it is time the multilateral trade system acquired a global competition authority. Others, most notably the United States, are very much against anything that could encroach on their policy prerogatives.

The purpose of this paper is threefold. First, it reviews the positions of the two largest WTO members, the European Union and the United States, with respect to whether the WTO needs competition rules or not. Second, it examines the merits of the various proposals for the internationalisation of competition policy and their chances of success. Third, it considers what may happen if there is no agreement on multilateral disciplines on competition policy. The paper concludes that it is hard to see how market access could be achieved effectively through nationally based competition provisions and without any common rules and a WTO-based enforcement authority. However, the slim chance of agreement on this issue in the WTO does not mean that competition rules will continue to be enforced within national jurisdictions. On the contrary, this paper suggests that competition rules are likely to spread and will be shared between like-minded countries outside the framework of the WTO.

The dimensions of the debate[1]

The case against

The inclusion or not of competition provisions in the WTO has sparked a vigorous debate. Those against have basically advanced two broad arguments. The first argument claims that there is no need to internationalise competition law and that the cost of doing so will be high. The second emphasises the fundamental incompatibility between trade and competition policies.

The first argument has been strongly advocated by the United States. Although many markets and anti-competitive practices transcend national borders, the USA believes that US law and cooperation with its trading partners are almost always adequate to deal with those practices that may have a negative impact on its international transactions.

It is not difficult to understand why the USA has taken that position. US anti-trust law has a wide extraterritorial reach. Not only does the US extend it to foreign parties that harm US consumers but also US anti-trust law prohibits foreign agreements and acts on foreign soil that raise significant hurdles for US exporters trying to sell into foreign markets, if those acts restrict competition. In addition, the USA has the opportunity and power to conclude bilateral agreements with trading partners of its choice.

Jurisprudence and anti-trust thinking are also highly developed in the United States, which in the past has experimented with several directions of competition policy and has reached an orthodoxy that it does not wish to abandon in the name of an international agreement as to the meaning, aims and methods of competition policy. That orthodoxy is predicated on the pursuit of efficiency and promotion of consumer welfare.

The incorporation of binding competition rules in the WTO is seen from the American perspective as dangerous because it could come into conflict with the principles already enforced in the USA. The potential dilution of the purity and correctness of US anti-trust policy is perceived as imposing too high a cost on the USA, a cost that would also have to be added to the cost of the bureaucracy that is claimed would emerge as a result.

The second broad argument against the internationalisation of competition law is the claimed incompatibility between competition and trade law. While competition law in most jurisdictions protects consumers and the competition process (meaning that markets are kept open and users are not tied to any particular supplier or product), trade law, it is argued, protects competitors and markets. Again, it is feared that the protectionism that lurks beneath many trade instruments and in many of the institutions that enforce these instruments will corrupt and blur the focus of competition policy.

A related strand of that argument is that the WTO itself would not be able to handle the additional competence. Its institutional structure, which prevents it acting autonomously, its cumbersome decision-making procedures and its lack of in-house expertise raise serious question marks about how the WTO could deal with competition policy without extensive institutional reform.

Finally, it should be noted that many developing countries are against the inclusion of competition provisions within the WTO because they do not believe in the merits of competition as a process of development and because they fear that the internationalisation of competition policy would force them to open up their markets further and be exposed to greater 'exploitation' by multinational companies, most of which are American or European.

The case in favour

The European Union is the principal proponent of the incorporation of competition provisions in the WTO. The EU is aware that harmonisation of national competition laws is a long way off. However, it advocates a gradual convergence of national practices. It perceives market access or, rather, restricted market access to be the most pressing trade and competition problem. Market access is a problem not only because competition law is absent but also because competition law is not enforced.

Hence, the EU's proposals are more precisely a series of steps beginning with adoption and enforcement of national competition laws, then progressing to adoption of common competition principles and only in the distant future does it suggest the granting of any substantive investigative or enforcement powers to the WTO.

Indeed, the most controversial of all ideas that have been debated over the past few years concerns the creation of a global competition authority. Although there are many seasoned observers of the multilateral trade system who are convinced that the application of competition policy will be uneven unless the WTO is given real powers to investigate and enforce alleged anti-competitive practices, very few believe that there is any possibility that the WTO will acquire such powers in the near future.

In addition to the adoption and rigorous enforcement of national competition laws, the EU also proposes a series of other measures, the most significant of which are non-discriminatory application of national provisions, transparent and objective national administrative procedures, cross-border cooperation and exchange of information between competition authorities, and mechanisms for dispute resolution.

A preliminary assessment

Although the US view has its merits (e.g. concern about costs), it is motivated by the USA's unique position, which enables it to dictate its terms and policies to other, smaller countries. It cannot do the same with the EU, and it is for this reason that trade and other commercial disputes between the two often escalate to the brink of a full-scale 'trade war' (with unilateral sanctions taken against each other). It is also for this reason that the EU and the USA have signed an agreement of cooperation on competition issues.

To non-Americans, and especially to Europeans, it seems obvious that not all countries can rely on the extraterritorial application of its laws to remove any obstacles that its firms or products may encounter in trying to gain access to foreign markets. Moreover, even if each country could in theory enforce its own rules, one cannot necessarily conclude that it would be good for the world economy as a whole. Multinational companies and other traders would be subject to a multitude of rules with unpredictable results.

The problem with the EU view is not so much that its ultimate aim may be unreachable but that even though its progressive application theme sounds sensible, here too it presupposes the existence of a doubtful consensus. Enforcement of national competition laws will never be enough to eliminate problems of market access without some common understanding of the industries, sectors and practices that they cover and the standards of competitive behaviour that they should aim to uphold. The EU and the USA have signed their cooperation agreement because fundamentally they trust each other, even though the operational principles of their competition policies may differ. The experience of the EU itself in creating an internal common market testifies to the difficulty of bringing about that common understanding.

National competition laws are replete with exceptions and special cases. Competition policy within the EU has been a powerful instrument of integration because the European Commission has pursued a single-minded mission of eliminating all barriers to trade in whatever form they appear. In those industries where the authorities of member states have had involvement, integration has been delayed for years because the member states could not agree on a legitimate role for state intervention. In these cases, such as telecommunications and air transport, barriers have been removed only as a result of vigorous Commission action and use of the direct powers that are conferred to it by the EC Treaty, which forced member states grudgingly to make the necessary concessions.

So international cooperation in the field of competition policy can hardly succeed in an institutional and professional vacuum. Unless the enforcing authorities share the same views as to the usefulness of competition policy and unless they intend to enforce it vigorously, it is very doubtful whether agreement on any general principles would lead to tangible results. Indeed, it is revealing that international cooperation has been achieved only between like-minded countries (EU–USA; EU–EFTA; Australia–New Zealand) or between countries where one has been the driving force (the EU and associate members in Central and Eastern Europe).

However, it is also disingenuous to claim that the WTO cannot accommodate competition rules because somehow trade policy and competition policy are incompatible.[2] Although there are many differences between the two policies, and although some of their objectives are fundamentally at odds – e.g. trade policy may promote national champions, while competition policy attacks the creation of monopolies – it should be remembered that the primary objective of the WTO is to discipline national trade policies so as to facilitate international transactions. In this respect, competition rules can only strengthen existing WTO trade rules.

Elements of feasible future progress

Given the magnitude of the differences that separate the main industrial countries and the even more extreme differences that keep industrial and developing countries apart, it is probably unrealistic to expect any significant progress in the near future. To put it differently, progress will be achieved only at the expense of substance, because agreement will be feasible only after extensive dilution of the multilateral disciplines under discussion. However, the purpose of this paper is not only to speculate on the chances of an agreement being reached in the near future but also to explore the dimensions of a possible agreement and ask what might be the elements on which differences might be bridged. The rest of the paper reviews such elements in the various proposals that have been put forward and considers their merits.

The kind of agreement that appears to be feasible after the debacle of the Seattle ministerial conference is one that bypasses the objections raised by the major trading nations. This means that unless there is a sudden change in the US position, binding international competition provisions are unlikely to be agreed in the foreseeable future. This is even more likely with respect to a global competition authority.

It is not surprising, therefore, that most proposals on the internationalisation of competition policy have put forward 'softer' options, such as strengthening existing WTO rules, enhanced cooperation and institutionalised multilateral discussions on competition problems. These options are grouped in the following five categories.

Expansion of existing competition provisions

The WTO already incorporates a number of rules to discourage anti-competitive practices. The primary examples are the GATS provisions on monopoly and exclusive service providers (Article VIII) and on commercial practices (Article IX), as well as the provisions on competition safeguards in the reference paper concerning basic telecommunications. These rules are expressed at a high level of abstraction and generality. They need to be elaborated and made more specific and operational so that they can be useful in practice. Even then it is hard to see what tangible benefits might be delivered if any new rules were not binding on member countries. The crux of the problem is the rejection of adoption of new and binding rules.

Reduction of the anti-competitive effects of trade rules

Many tomes have been written over the past five years or so on the relationship between competition policy and trade policy. Most of these analyses conclude that the application of trade policy and especially contingent protection measures generate serious anti-competitive effects. Most of the problems are caused by anti-dumping measures, which pervert competition even though they are implemented in the name of fair competition. A restriction of the discretion of importing countries to apply anti-dumping measures, which are often based on dubious calculations and pseudo-scientific methods, would go a long way towards containing the anti-competitive effects of trade policy.

However, precisely because anti-dumping is such an emotive issue and holds an important position in the trade armoury of importing countries, there is likely to be little support, if not outright opposition, to any attempt to reform anti-dumping rules for the purpose of making them more compatible with competition policy.

Elaboration of general principles

Since most countries have some form of competition law on their statute books, the idea here is to get them to enforce their laws in the first place and to do so in a non-discriminatory manner. As the EU has argued, it is not even necessary at this stage to elaborate unique competition provisions within the WTO. It is sufficient to have non-discriminatory enforcement of national provisions.

The weakness of this idea, as explained in the previous section, is that it is very hard to prove non-enforcement or discriminatory treatment unless there is recourse to an independent authority or agency with powers to examine the facts of the case. Moreover, treatment that discriminates against foreigners is often mandated by law. It is unclear how any general WTO principles could apply to statutory restrictions of market access.

Fostering of a common understanding

Knowing that proposals for a global competition authority are a non-starter, many competition experts have suggested instead the establishment of various international competition forums to discuss competition problems. Such forums may take the form of plurilateral agreements attached to the WTO but without being binding on all WTO members.

Although the idea of multilateral discussion forums has been touted on many occasions, their precise nature is still sketchy. It seems naive to expect that discussion will somehow change the entrenched views of countries, which are steadfastly against what they perceive as further erosion of their economic sovereignty.

Sectoral market-access initiatives

None of the ideas outlined above can solve the problem of access to markets that are dominated by monopolies, which are often owned or sanctioned by the state. Here the problem is one of statutory discrimination, possibly justified on grounds of national security or broader public interest.

It would be exceedingly difficult to persuade developing countries to open markets that they see as vital to their national interests. Irrespective of whether they are justified or not in that belief, the only way forward is probably that of plurilateral agreements on a sectoral basis.

However, there is a danger that the pursuit of global integration through plurilateral agreements may harm the WTO itself. Many countries are not convinced of the case in favour of internationalisation of competition policy. They do not see benefits that can compensate for their loss of national policy autonomy. Their exclusion from any plurilateral agreements would cut them off further from the learning experience of analysing and appraising competition problems in a multilateral setting.

The fundamental dilemma for the WTO

Competition policy cannot function properly unless someone is responsible for its enforcement. The principles on which it is based are often too general to have any immediate applicability of their own. Therefore, any alleged infringement of competition law has to be examined individually and each case assessed on its own merits. It is very doubtful that any competition provisions that are inserted into the WTO would be of any value unless someone is responsible for their investigation and evaluation.

It may be argued that investigations will be done by the member countries themselves and that the evaluations could be carried out by WTO panels like those that are involved in the procedures for the resolution of disputes. However, this argument misses the fundamental point that the general competition principles have to be elaborated with more specific rules. This elaboration cannot be left to each country, because there will never be a homogeneous body of law applying to all member countries.

There is also the problem of how investigations are to be carried out. The investigations carried out by trade authorities in relation to anti-dumping cases are not examples to be followed. The latter are unfair to foreign producers and replete with arbitrary calculations. In the EU, there is currently a proposal for decentralisation of the enforcement of competition policy so that national authorities will assume some of the obligations and powers of the European Commission. This decentralisation is feasible in the EU because there is a large body of detailed case law to guide national authorities and because the Commission can always intervene if something goes wrong. Can this process be replicated by the WTO without having any mandate to act autonomously?

If the WTO were to be given autonomous powers it would eventually develop more detailed implementation rules and guidelines and would be able to intervene in cases of lax enforcement by the national authorities of member countries. The problem is that no one considers that a serious option, at least for the time being.

Indeed, there is no easy option, because at the heart of the issue there is an unresolved dilemma. On the one hand, competition principles need to be continuously interpreted and elaborated and the merits of each case individually assessed. On the other hand, no one wants to discuss the establishment of yet another institution or international bureaucracy. If the process of interpretation and elaboration is to be done through bilateral channels and informal cooperation between like-minded countries, then there will be no truly global rules. It may even alienate further the countries that are at present distrustful of any suggestion to expand the WTO's mandate.

What is likely to happen?

Previous sections have explained that there are no easy or obvious options. As long as the USA and developing countries maintain their positions, no substantive competition rules will be adopted by the WTO. This means that any progress will be achieved either in the form of a plurilateral agreement with restricted membership or in the form of much softer cooperation and consultation provisions.

For the reasons that were also explained above, neither of the two options is likely to prove satisfactory. Unless cooperation is based on common or shared ideals, it would only lead to interminable debate with no tangible results. It should be noted that behind the EU proposals of softer options there is the assumption that cooperation will eventually lead to the adoption of more explicit competition rules and that multilateral discussion will foster the development of common views and perceptions of the usefulness of competition policy. However, there is no guarantee or reason why that process will follow such a progressive path.

The fact that the WTO is unlikely to adopt competition provisions in the near future does not necessarily mean that competition policy will be a predominantly national issue. Because a global economy requires global rules and because cross-border transactions create problems that require cross-border solutions, countries will explore other means of addressing cross-border competition problems. Since tackling anti-competitive behaviour on a systematic basis needs a set of rules that are enforceable in the partner countries, it appears that two such sets of rules will inevitably spread outside the WTO framework: one on a more cooperative basis, the other in a more *ad hoc* manner.

The first is the competition policy of the European Union. All recent association agreements and trade agreements of the EU with third countries contain provisions on competition. The association agreements with the countries of Central and Eastern Europe explicitly require that those countries adopt EU rules and practices on competition policy. And as thirteen countries are now formally recognised as candidates for membership of the EU, the whole framework and procedures of the EU will soon spread to virtually all of the continent of Europe.

The second is US anti-trust policy. The USA appears determined to pursue an active extraterritorial application of its policy. It is also keen to assist other countries to adopt anti-trust laws similar to its own. However, even if other countries do not prove eager to enforce competition law, the extraterritorial reach of US anti-trust law will most probably ensure that in the end foreign firms will be subject to some competition discipline.

Conclusion

None of the proposals reviewed in this paper is perfect. Indeed, there is little chance of their adoption in the near future by WTO members after the disheartening outcome of Seattle.

All of the proposals try to bypass the objections of the USA and developing nations by putting forward softer options that centre on enhanced cooperation, the gradual strengthening of existing rules and the conclusion of agreements with like-minded nations. Although there is merit in these proposals, it is difficult to see how they can generate tangible results if they are not binding. Despite their good intentions, there is also a danger that they may contribute to undermining the WTO by deepening the divisions between its members.

One thing is clear, however. Competition policy will be internationalised in a *de facto* manner. The USA appears to be determined to apply its own anti-trust law extraterritorially. At the same time, the competition rules of the EU are spreading gradually but systematically to those countries that have either applied for membership of the Union or who have entered into a trade agreement with it (the trade agreements of the EU with third countries contain provisions on anti-trust and state aid). So two models of competition policy are becoming predominant.

Perhaps for most of the industrialised world (with the notable exceptions of Japan, Australia and New Zealand), in the end, competition problems will be addressed through an upgraded version of the current cooperation agreement on competition issues between the EU and the USA.

Unfortunately, that would leave out in the cold the rest of the world. But as long as other countries do not see any benefits from enhanced competition policy, the role of the WTO will be minimal in this respect. Those countries ignore at their peril that one of the main reasons for the existence of the WTO is not only to propagate rules that benefit the immediate interests of its members but also, to a greater extent, to protect them from the arbitrary actions of the bigger and more powerful trading countries.

Notes

The views expressed in this article are strictly personal and should not be attributed to any institution with which the author is affiliated.

1   The following provide extensive reviews of the arguments and positions of the main players in the WTO: Nicolaides (1996); Graham and Richardson (1997); Janow (1998); Fox (1998); Bilal and Olarreaga (1998); Shelton (1999). See also the WTO website (http://www.wto.org) for the various official documents. Note that given the general level of presentation adopted in this paper no references to specific position papers will be made.

2   For a full analysis of the similarities and differences between trade and competition policies, see Nicolaides (1994).

References

Bilal, S. and Olarreaga, M. (1998) *Competition Policy and the WTO*, Maastricht: European Institute of Public Administration.

Fox, E. (1998) 'International antitrust', *The Antitrust Bulletin*, Spring: 5–13.

Graham, E. and Richardson, D. (1997) *Global Competition Policy*, Washington: Institute for International Economics.

Janow, M. (1998) 'Unilateral and bilateral approaches to competition policy', *Brookings Trade Forum*, Washington.

Nicolaides, P. (1994) *An Analysis of the Objectives and Methods of Trade and Competition Policies*, Paris: OECD.

—— (1996) 'For a world competition authority', *Journal of World Trade* 30: 131–45.

Shelton, J. (1999) 'Competition policy: what chance for international Rules?', *OECD Journal of Competition Law and Policy* 1: 57–72.

12 Anti-dumping and trade remedies

A necessary reform

Patrick A. Messerlin

Introduction

Almost everybody agrees nowadays that the use of anti-dumping measures has increased and spread among WTO members to such an extent that it represents a systemic threat to the WTO system. The average number of countries routinely initiating anti-dumping cases has more than quadrupled, from five in the late 1980s to more than twenty today (Miranda *et al.* 1998). The average annual number of cases has almost doubled between the late 1980s and late 1990s. Since 1993, seven new users (Argentina, Brazil, India, Korea, Mexico, South Africa and Turkey) have initiated as many cases as the five 'old' users (Australia, Canada, the European Community, New Zealand and the United States). Although quite dramatic, these figures still underestimate the true extent of the problem. They ignore the fact that the average number of tariff lines covered by anti-dumping cases has increased during the 1990s. They ignore the many 'reviews' of previous or existing cases, which extend initial measures almost systematically and indefinitely (the 'sunset' clause being quite ineffective).

The protectionist drift of anti-dumping may be dramatic, but it should not hide a similar evolution among some of the many trade remedies allowed by the international trading regime. Some remedies have a broad intent and scope: general exceptions (GATT XX and GATS XIV), provisions dealing with changes in commitments (GATT XXVII and GATS XXI), and balance-of-payments provisions (GATT XII and XVIII, and GATS XII). Others have a strong sectoral focus: Article V of the Uruguay Round Agreement on Agriculture or Article VI of the Agreement on Textiles and Clothing. Lastly, regional agreements provide their batch of similar instruments, with often weaker disciplines (e.g. the safeguard provisions included in the agreements between the EU and Central European countries).

As a result, reforming all the trade remedies existing in the WTO regime (not only anti-dumping) is an urgent need amplified by the following considerations. The coming round will have to deal with industries skilful and powerful enough to have escaped the progressive trade liberalisation brought by the last eight rounds (textiles and clothing, steel, farm and food products). Developing countries will increasingly be under the same pressure to renege on their commitments as industrial countries, since the next round is likely to see a narrowing of the gap between their applied and bound tariffs. In the absence of robust negotiating techniques, liberalisation of services will require the 'safety net' of an 'emergency safeguard' clause. As a result, there is a need for both the establishment of principles guiding a bold strategy for reform and for a progressive implementation of these principles.

A strategy for reform

There is an implicit – unrealistic and counterproductive – assumption in the current WTO regime: once liberalised, industries should remain open for ever. Interestingly, each WTO member does not follow this assumption in its own domestic affairs: it recognises the need for 'recontracting' the commitments that are the basis of the free trade regime between its various regions, and it uses a range of different instruments in this respect – flexible local regulations (federal regime), public investment, subsidies of all kinds, etc.

Such a realistic approach should be extended to the GATT–WTO regime, which is now robust enough to adopt it. In the international trade system, there is one key instrument available for recontracting: renegotiating existing commitments under GATT Article XXVIII (for goods) and GATS Article XXI (for services). Currently, trade remedies are implicitly used as unilateral recontracting of the commitments of the countries implementing them – making them an implicit substitute for GATT–GATS renegotiation provisions. In fact, the use of the GATT renegotiation procedure declined in the early 1980s, precisely at the time when anti-dumping procedures were increasingly being used (Finger 1998).

Renegotiating commitments should therefore be recognised as the ultimate trade remedy. However, making renegotiation the strategic pillar for addressing the problem of trade remedies raises three practical problems. If trade remedies are necessary only for a limited period, renegotiation looks a 'disproportionate' instrument. Trade remedies should be available rapidly, whereas renegotiations require time. Too many and frequent renegotiations might blur the long-term movement towards liberalisation to a dangerous extent.

There is therefore a need to limit the frequency of renegotiations, hence the following proposal: trade remedies would continue to exist (subject to improvements, see sections below), but all would be 'locked' by the renegotiation process so that they could be used for only a limited period. In other words, a WTO member would not be allowed to escape for 'too long' its commitments through trade remedies: after a predetermined period, it would be forced either to eliminate its 'transitory' reprotection or to renegotiate its existing commitments.

Such an approach has several decisive advantages in the long run. First, by putting renegotiations as the direct source of disciplines on WTO trade remedies, it relies on the most powerful discipline possible in the WTO forum:

reciprocity. Second, it does not require an (impossible) rewriting of the existing GATT–GATS texts: rather, it makes full use of them by combining them in the most logical way (instead of leaving them side by side). Third, this approach can easily be applied to services, where trade remedies are likely to play an even more important role for several reasons: existing instruments of protection can rarely be fine-tuned (unlike tariffs); their values as concessions are almost impossible to compute; and their expected impact is very hard to assess. All these features will make the liberalisation process less incremental to implement and more difficult to control in services than in goods. By the same token, they make the combination of transitory trade remedies (GATS X) and renegotiation (GATS XXI) an argument even more compelling in services than in goods.

This approach has also advantages in the short to medium term. It would be a strong force in favour of a progressive shift towards *one* trade remedy: safeguards. Being substitutable, the many trade remedies currently available compete between themselves to provide relief (*de jure*) and permanent protection (*de facto*). The success of anti-dumping comes from the fact that it guarantees the best deal (the highest level of protection) for complainants and hence the greatest damage to existing WTO commitments. Almost all empirical economic studies, including those from agencies involved in anti-dumping procedures (US ITC 1995; CBO 1998) show that the vast majority of anti-dumping cases are driven by the will to provide protection to industries claiming to be in trouble: less than 10 per cent of EU and US anti-dumping cases would have a chance to succeed without arguments associated with protection, as shown by Morkre and Kelly (1994), Finger (1995), Greenaway *et al.* (1995), Shin (1998), Bourgeois and Messerlin (1998) and Winters *et al.* (1998) (quoting only a few studies covering a large number of cases).

To sum up, the world trade regime of the early 2000s is robust enough to recognise the need for recontracting in some circumstances. All the trade remedies should be subjected to the same discipline: being transitory and, at the end of the transition period, being locked by the choice between elimination or renegotiation of the corresponding commitments. Moreover, there should be a progressive shift from the existing trade remedies to an unified safeguard procedure – and a shift from trade remedy to competition law for the tiny portion of cases raising competition issues (less than 10 per cent in the case of anti-dumping).

Progressive implementation: a minimal programme

The most difficult task will be to implement the above principles progressively. This section aims at sketching a minimal programme of reforms. In this respect, the opposition (from the US government) to official negotiations on such issues for the coming round is not such a severe obstacle because a lot of the work could be initiated in the *ad hoc* WTO committees, so that once enough material has been accumulated, it could be shifted to a full negotiating working group.[1] However, these *ad hoc* committees should meet in joint sessions in order to ensure that potential reforms in one trade remedy are not ruined by the absence of reforms in other trade remedies (since all are substitutable). A minimal programme should include three sources of improvement.

Anchoring safeguards to renegotiation

GATT XIX on safeguards has been largely unused precisely because it was not a back door to protection as 'efficient' as GATT-illegal VERs (during the 1970s) or as anti-dumping procedures (since the 1980s). The reasons for its relative 'inefficiency' are well known: strictly non-discriminatory and transitory measures; a high risk of retaliation by trading partners; and the fundamental recognition that the protection to be granted flows from the failure of the domestic industry. All these features are in sharp contrast to anti-dumping measures, which allow almost unlimited discrimination for unlimited periods, which run almost no risk of retaliation, which are based on the assertion that the protection to be granted is caused by 'unfair' foreign behaviour, and which ignore the need for 'adjustment'.

The Uruguay Round Safeguard Agreement has been a notable effort to 'revitalise' the safeguard instrument while trying to maintain intact its key positive features. On balance, it has brought net benefits, and it constitutes a valuable basis on which to build additional progress (it is consistent with the strategic choices described above). It has introduced two essential improvements: a clarification of the notion of transitory measures (for a period of four years, renewable once), and the elimination of all VERs and other 'grey' measures (although effective elimination may have been notably related to substituted anti-dumping measures). The silence of the Safeguard Agreement on the 'ongoing liberalisation' and 'unforeseen development' conditions included in GATT XIX are rather positive: it has made safeguard a possible competitor to anti-dumping, not only for the limited period of ongoing liberalisation but also in much wider circumstances. This is a reasonable move if one accepts the notion that recontracting is a 'natural' phenomenon, and a necessary move if one wants a progressive elimination of anti-dumping.[2] The only real cost of the Uruguay Round Safeguard Agreement has been to allow a more discriminatory use of quotas.

An improved Safeguard Agreement should make more robust the concept of transitory protection. It should specify that, at the end of the second period of enforcing safeguard measures, the country will have the choice between only two alternatives: to renegotiate the tariffs on the goods subject to safeguard measures, or to eliminate these measures. In the latter case, shifting to other trade remedies should be prohibited – a first recognition of the fact that all trade remedies should converge to a single type. Lastly, the two transition periods of safeguards should be reduced from four to three years in order to fit explicitly with the renegotiation procedure under GATT XXVIII.

Disciplining anti-dumping reviews

Anti-dumping reviews represent the strongest systemic threat to the WTO regime because they perpetuate what was meant to be transitory protection. Reviews leading to renewed anti-dumping measures would make sense in only two situations: import-competing firms aim at perpetuating reprotection; and alleged dumpers and import-competing firms aim at implementing long-term VER-type deals under anti-dumping regulations. Both situations have little to do with alleged anti-dumping logic but a lot to do with protection.

As a result, introducing more disciplines in anti-dumping reviews should be a priority. There is a wide spectrum of possible reforms. The minimum effort would consist of closing all existing procedural loopholes, such as the obligation (weaker for reviews than for initial cases) to compare domestic and foreign prices on an average-to-average or transaction-to-transaction basis. A bolder approach would consist of introducing all the improvements of substance that are suggested below in the reviews – making disciplines in reviews a test for disciplines to be introduced later in initial anti-dumping cases. The boldest reform would be to eliminate anti-dumping reviews completely and replace them with safeguards (in turn, this would require limiting the time frame of the initial anti-dumping cases to three years): this shift is the logical consequence of the absence of an anti-dumping rationale in the case of reviews (as mentioned above), and it corresponds to another step towards a single trade remedy.

Reducing the current biases in favour of dumping determination

Finding dumping is the key step in anti-dumping cases: it comes first in the investigation procedure (hence it heavily determines the next stages), and it is potentially the most 'objective' to the extent that, compared with subsequent stages (injury determination and causal relationship), it relies more on facts. Focusing on dumping determination is also justified, because dumping margins have shown a tendency to increase (CBO 1998; Bourgeois and Messerlin 1998), which underlines the urgent need for improved disciplines.

A minimal programme could include several 'minimal' reforms. First, the exceptions to the requirement that price comparison should be average-to-average or transaction-to-transaction (an almost certain recipe for finding dumping) should be eliminated. Second, existing biases in the definition of foreign normal value should be reduced. For instance, when there are no (or negligible) domestic sales but when there are export sales, export prices should be considered the mandatory source of information. The exclusion of an exporter's home-market sales at a loss from 'actual data' (through the notion of 'ordinary' course of trade, which is a systematic way of inflating constructed values) should be eliminated. Third, the period to be taken into account by the investigation should be extended, a reform essential in anti-dumping cases dealing with cyclical activity (an important source of anti-dumping activity in developing countries).[3] It is possible to have a sense of the potential impact of certain reforms. For instance, out of the 208 EU and US anti-dumping cases initiated between 1995 and 1998 (with the necessary information), only thirteen (6 per cent) have been based exclusively on a direct price comparison, and there is a (monotonously) increasing average margin of dumping when one departs from price comparison – from 3 to 95 per cent in the USA and from 22 to 74 per cent in the EU (Lindsey 1999; Messerlin 2000).

Two additional reforms not directly related to dumping determination could be envisaged. First, it would be important to reduce (preferably eliminate) the possibility of accumulating allegedly 'dumped' imports over countries. Prusa (1998) has provided evidence that mandatory (since 1984) accumulation in the US regulations has caused an extra 100 cases to be filed between 1984 and 1994, but it has also changed the ITC's determination in about sixty cases (all other things being constant). Similar results have been found for the EU (Tharakan *et al.* 1998). A weaker variant would be to ban accumulation of imports from countries representing less than a given percentage of total imports. For instance, WTO members could agree to start from a low threshold and increase it during the enforcement period of the coming round, or they could agree to increase it in the negotiations of future rounds (a first example of a 'threshold-based' approach, see below). The other additional reform would consist of prohibiting the initiation of anti-dumping cases if the allegedly dumped imports are already subject to quantitative restrictions, price surveillance or any other severe constraints on trade (such as public procurement representing a substantial portion of the market), which could be put on a list to be agreed on by WTO members. In other words, accumulating trade remedies is not acceptable – a prohibition consistent with the long-term strategic choice of a unique trade remedy.

This minimal programme deserves a final remark. Because anti-dumping and safeguards are substitutable and competing, reforming safeguards and anti-dumping has to be conducted in parallel. All the above reforms for anti-dumping should therefore be introduced in safeguards (and *vice versa*). They could be introduced in similar terms when the two procedures are very similar (such as the definitions of the like-product or of the domestic industry). Or they could be introduced under a stronger form if required by the specifics of safeguards. For instance, the 'unforeseen development' condition could suggest that the *de minimis* share condition allowing small imports to be put out of anti-dumping reach could be higher in the case of safeguards (hence mirroring the fact that the development has to be unforeseen).

Progressive implementation: a more ambitious programme

Even if fully successful, the above minimal programme has no chance in the long term of curbing the number of anti-dumping cases and the derived protectionist drift. Sooner or later, all reforms of the anti-dumping component will be eroded or circumvented by complainants using the opportunity of new cases.

More ambitious reforms require the support of economic analysis. Economic issues associated with anti-dumping enforcement are related to price discrimination, cyclical dumping, and predatory and strategic pricing (Willig 1998). Substantive reforms in anti-dumping should therefore reflect the economic analysis of these four issues. In a nutshell, this means that the new anti-dumping agreement should contain provisions making it difficult or impossible to open anti-dumping cases related to price discrimination and cyclical dumping, whereas it should prepare for the handling (probably in the distant future) of the very few predatory and strategic dumping cases by competition authorities under national competition laws. Ultimately, substantive reforms in anti-dumping should lead to the elimination of anti-dumping regulations and a progressive reallocation of existing anti-dumping cases into a red box (no economic or political justification), an orange box (no economic justification, but political constraints requiring the use of safeguards), and a green box (economic justification requiring the use of competition law).

This process could be eased substantially by using an approach based on negotiated quantitative 'thresholds'. A threshold-based approach has three key advantages: it is easily negotiable (negotiators can talk in terms of figures or percentages); it gives a sense of the magnitude of the concessions granted by both sides; and it can be tightened (through more binding thresholds) in future rounds – hence it can deliver the progressive liberalisation that WTO members are looking for. Moreover, it can be used in trade-offs, including issues other than anti-dumping or trade remedies: for instance, heavy users of anti-dumping measures could trade stricter reforms in anti-dumping in exchange for better access to foreign markets in goods or services.

Limiting the number of anti-dumping complaints

Anti-dumping complaints depend upon three key definitions: a major proportion of the industry, *de minimis* conditions, and like-product.

Complaining firms should constitute the major proportion of the domestic industry. 'Domestic' firms and the 'major proportion' have no unequivocal definitions. For instance, requiring that complaining firms represent a large (25 to 50 per cent) aggregate market share may minimise the number of potential complainants, but it implies that potential oligopolies or monopolies can complain more easily than the many firms in a competitive environment. And it does not exclude a small firm if the definition of the product is narrow enough. Rather, what counts is the aggregate market share of the complainants and defendants (and its breakdown by firm), because this information will reveal the risks of making the investigated market less competitive by imposing anti-dumping measures (as a reminder, complainants and defendants having a combined market share larger than 95 per cent represent almost a third of the total number of EU and US cases (Messerlin 1996)). Asking for public information on the market shares of all major firms involved in the anti-dumping proceedings looks to be a minimal requirement. A stronger variant would be to prohibit the initiation of anti-dumping cases with an aggregate (complainants and defendants) market share above a given threshold. This threshold could be tightened up progressively – an illustration of the 'threshold-based' approach suggested above.

Anti-dumping cases with 'negligible imports' (3 per cent of total imports on an allegedly dumping country basis, with a collective cap of 7 per cent for all the countries involved) are not permitted under current anti-dumping regulations. However, this *de minimis* provision makes little sense (particularly, in terms of predatory and strategic pricing), because it refers to import shares: market shares should be defined in terms of *domestic consumption* in the importing country. Agreeing on a *de minimis* threshold of 5 per cent of domestic consumption would be a relatively conservative decision – and WTO members could agree to increase this threshold during the implementation phase of the round (or to negotiate further increases during subsequent rounds).

Anti-dumping investigations start by defining whether domestic and foreign products are *like-products*. In economic terms, like-products are defined in terms of substitution (the magnitude of their price cross-elasticities determines the 'relevant' market). This market-based definition has already surfaced in a few dispute settlement cases, when the like-product definition has been linked to 'competition in the marketplace' (*Japanese Liquor Taxes II, Korean Liquor Taxes*) (Bronckers and McNelis 1999: 75). However, it would be difficult to extend this link to anti-dumping in general because of the absence of robust legal ground – and because the benefits of such an extension on the number and outcome of anti-dumping cases are far from clear.

Rather, an acceptable reform could consist of simply imposing transparency in these matters: a list of the like-products tabled by the complainants/defendants but excluded by the investigating authorities, and a detailed description of the markets and of the firms operating in them (firms' market shares, and connections between firms, if any). Such transparency would almost provide the information necessary for a preliminary assessment of the relevant market in a typical competition case, but without requiring the complex and sophisticated procedures of competition cases.

Injury determination

Existing anti-dumping regulations have no clear methodology when estimating injury: what counts today is less a matter of economic assessment than of political opportunity and clout. The existing criteria for injury determination are potentially redundant (relative price changes can explain market share changes, and *vice versa*), and they can reflect quite healthy evolutions (a declining market share of a domestic monopoly or dominant firm is the healthy outcome of competition).[4]

Ideally, reforms should aim at making a distinction between competitive trade shocks (healthy because they provide benefit to domestic users, even if they require adjustment from inefficient domestic producers) and competition 'distorted' by the strategic behaviour of foreign firms (based on predation or on the existence of a protected 'sanctuary' market in the exporting country). The best compromise between the existing legal framework and minimal economic analysis is the use of partial equilibrium models, allowing the estimation of firms' revenue losses related to dumping (and the benefits for users), all other things being constant. The simple criterion of revenue losses could be privileged. The use of such models could be made mandatory, or it could merely be seen as a systematic source of information. In both cases, the model used and the estimates obtained by the model should be published in the official anti-dumping proceedings of each case in order to fulfil the transparency objective (and to give ammunition to the supporters of the national interest clause, see below).

If WTO members are sufficiently reform-minded, they could introduce thresholds in the use of partial equilibrium models. For instance, no measure should be imposed in cases where the level of injury losses is less than an agreed threshold (x per cent) of the revenues of the initial year – a threshold that could be increased later by new negotiations (as a reminder, complainants with losses larger than 5 per cent of their 'pre-dumping' revenues represent only one-third of the total number of EU and US anti-dumping cases, including those dealing with non-competitive market structures (Messerlin 1996).

As already noted, it is essential to make parallel reforms in anti-dumping and safeguard. As is well known, GATT XIX refers to serious injury (as opposed to material injury in anti-dumping). The specific definition of serious injury could be reflected by a slightly different threshold for revenue losses than for material injury: for instance, material injury would occur when the losses of domestic firms were larger than 10 per cent of their revenues, whereas serious injury could be said to occur when their losses were larger than 15 or 20 per cent (possibly to be strengthened in future negotiations).

Anti-dumping and safeguard measures

A substantial proportion of anti-dumping *measures* do not consist of duties but of price or quantity undertakings (underlining the safeguard nature of anti-dumping). Re-establishing the pre-eminence of tariffs, which do not generate those private rents capable of fuelling long-term protection (in particular, when shared between foreign and domestic firms) seems essential.

Banning anti-dumping measures other than duties could be envisaged. However, it may run the risk of triggering private rent-sharing agreements before the official termination of the case (Prusa 1992; Panagariya and Gupta 1998). Such a risk could be managed to a certain extent by requiring a stricter and more complete notification procedure of the anti-dumping cases not terminated by anti-dumping duties, and by imposing a cross-examination of these cases by the WTO Safeguard Committee after three years in order to check for the absence of any 'grey' measure. But there is a better alternative to such a ban: that anti-dumping investigations not terminated by tariffs should not be subject to anti-dumping reviews, or that they could be prolonged only under the same conditions as those imposed on safeguards during their second period of enforcement (again implying that they could last only three years).[5]

Measures are where anti-dumping and safeguards differ the most: anti-dumping allows for endlessly discriminatory measures, whereas sticking to GATT XIX would impose non-discriminatory measures – a sure recipe for maintaining the current primacy of anti-dumping for ever. Among the many possible reforms, the most logical would be to limit the non-discriminatory requirement on safeguards to initial negotiators or principal countries. It maintains the non-discrimination discipline for the major existing competitors (it opens the door to discrimination only in favour of emerging competitors. It substantially reduces the gap between anti-dumping and safeguards, because anti-dumping tends *de facto* to target all the major competing countries (the gap remains unaltered to the extent that anti-dumping can impose different measures on different firms from every trading partner). Lastly, it has a legal logic: renegotiation (one of the two possible ultimate results of a safeguard action) is subject to a provision of the same nature (the right to compensation under GATT XXVIII is essentially reserved for countries with the status of initial negotiators or principal suppliers).

The 'national interest' clause allows a WTO member that has demonstrated the existence of dumping and injury not to take protectionist measures on the grounds that such measures would harm other parts of the domestic economy. In other words, this clause opens the door to the introduction of domestic consumers' interests, which so far have been excluded from the anti-dumping procedure. As mentioned above, this clause has not worked well (Moore 1999): it comes too late in the procedure, at a time when it is very hard for the authorities to say 'no' to the complaining firms requesting protection.

Many reforms proposed above (in particular, those about more information and transparency) will *de facto* reinforce the national interest clause. One could add a last reform with a systemic dimension: each WTO member that has enforced more than a given number of anti-dumping actions during a defined period would be required to provide an economic report on all the cases investigated for the WTO Council. Ideally, these reports (due, say, every three years) should include an assessment of the estimated costs of the anti-dumping measures adopted during the period and an analysis of the impact of the measures on the domestic market structure. These reports would constitute the economic basis for a pluri-annual review of anti-dumping practices to be done within the WTO – and, hopefully, the basis for future reforms.

Concluding remarks

This brief presentation deserves two final remarks. First, re-examining trade remedies in goods has an inescapable echo in services. There is no anti-dumping provision in the GATS and – following the disastrous experience of anti-dumping in goods – one can only hope that there never will be.[6] But there is an embryonic safeguard clause: GATS Article X on 'emergency safeguard measures' merely states that 'there shall be multilateral negotiations on the question of emergency safeguard measures', and that future GATS X shall be 'based on the principle of non-discrimination'.

As a result, WTO members should not miss the unique opportunity to create a safeguard regime for services parallel to what should ideally exist in goods: locking the use of GATS X with GATS XXI (renegotiations), making transitory safeguard measures under GATS X (with only one renewal) possible. Most of the detailed provisions (like-services, a major proportion of the industry, etc.) do not raise specific issues for services, at least conceptually (enforcement may be more difficult).

However, safeguards in services raise two specific problems. The first is the 'cross-modality' of GATS X: should emergency safeguard measures be defined by mode of delivery, or not? The economically sound answer is that GATS X should be 'cross-modal', that is, enforced across all modes. Like the need to define *de minimis* shares in terms of domestic consumption, any 'surge' in service imports should be judged on the basis of the domestic consumption of the service in question (independently of the mode of delivery): what counts is the domestic situation, not the fact that 'disturbances' have been created by imports, the movements of consumers or producers, or commercial presence.

The second problem is as follows: could safeguard measures take all the possible forms (including quantitative restrictions), or should they be limited to certain forms (*ad valorem* tariffs). Some caution seems necessary here. In particular, quantitative restrictions may deserve a fresh look in the case of services: although they are likely to have the same downsides in services as in goods (opaqueness, rents creating permanent vested interests, a capacity to isolate the domestic market from world markets, etc.), they may have 'good' sides (relative to other instruments) because they may be easier to enforce in a non-discriminatory way and to monitor in a transparent manner.

The last comment is that this paper has adopted a very pragmatic tone. It should be made clear that, from the economist's perspective, the best proposals are the most radical – or alternatively that any departure from the maximum programme will have a price to pay in domestic and world inefficiencies and/or conflicts. The economist's stance flows from the fact that, although it is always possible to find cases where, at least in theory, anti-dumping might not be welfare-deteriorating (see Messerlin and Tharakan 1999 for a review of the literature), a careful study of existing cases suggests a quite different story.

Notes

1 The fact that anti-dumping has not been put clearly on the Punta del Este programme has not been an obstacle to intensive discussions on this issue during the following seven years (Horlick and Shea 1995).

2 Two recent rulings of the WTO Appellate Body have clearly stated that the 'unforeseen development' condition remains, without offering any insight into its precise definition.

3 The thrust of the reform would be to base the investigation on the whole price cycle, not on the usual one-year (or less) basis (a provision that allows dumping to be

found with almost certainty since it is just a matter of lodging the complaint at the right time to get the desired protection). The anti-dumping regulations of some countries (e.g. Chile) have indirectly introduced this provision by considering a 'price tunnel' based on the last three or four years.

4   The 1992 panel report *Salmon from Norway* has added to ambiguity by suggesting that there was no need to identify other factors and assess the specific impact of dumping on injury (Palmeter 1996: 53).

5   The increasingly frequent proposal of systematically imposing price undertakings to allegedly dumped developing countries' exports (under the fallacious argument of 'educating' exporters in developing countries in terms of pricing) should be rejected: it is a machine to generate VERs.

6   However, many domestic regulations (including competition laws) could be used as anti-dumping instruments in services. For instance, competition regulations on 'abnormally low' prices in retail distribution are frequent among WTO members.

References

Bourgeois, J.H.J. and Messerlin, P.A. (1998) 'The European Community experience', *Brookings Trade Forum*, Washington: Brookings Institution.

Bronckers, M. and McNelis, N. (1999) 'Rethinking the "like-product" definition in the WTO anti-dumping law', *Journal of World Trade* 33(3): 73–92.

Congressional Budget Office (1998) *Anti-dumping action in the US and around the world: an analysis of international data*, Washington: Congressional Budget Office.

Finger, J.M. (1995) 'Legalized backsliding: safeguard provisions in the GATT', in W. Martin and L.A. Winters (eds) *The Uruguay Round and the Developing Countries*, Washington: World Bank.

—— (1998) 'GATT experience with safeguards: making economic and political sense of the possibilities that the GATT allows to restrict imports', World Bank, Development Research Group, Policy Research Working Paper No. 2000.

Greenaway, D., Lloyd, T.A., Milner, C.R., Morrissey, W.O., Reed, G.V. and Hutton, G. (1995) *The European Union's Anti-dumping Policy and Non-Tariff Barriers to Trade*, CREDIT, University of Nottingham, mimeo.

Horlick, G.N. and Shea, E. C. (1995) 'The World Trade Organization Antidumping Agreement', *Journal of World Trade* 29(1): 5–31.

Lindsey, B. (1999) 'The US anti-dumping law rhetoric versus reality', Cato Institute, Center for Trade Policy Studies No. 7.

Messerlin, P.A. (1996) 'Competition policy and anti-dumping reform', in J.J. Schott (ed.) *The World Trading System: Challenges Ahead*, Washington: Institute for International Economics.

—— (2000) 'Anti-dumping and safeguard', in J.J. Schott (ed.) *The WTO after Seattle*, Washington: Institute for International Economics.

Messerlin P.A. and Tharakan, M. (1999) 'The question of contingent protection', *The World Economy* 22(9): 1251–70.

Miranda, J., Torres, R.A. and Ruiz, M. (1998) 'The international use of anti-dumping: 1987–1997', *Journal of World Trade* 32(5): 5–71.

Moore, M. (1999) 'Anti-dumping reform in the United States – a faded sunset', *Journal of World Trade* 33(4): 1–19.

Morkre, M. and Kelly, K.H. (1994) *Effects of Unfair Imports on Domestic Industries: US Anti-dumping and Countervailing Duty Cases, 1980–1988*, Washington: Federal Trade Commission, Bureau of Economics.

Palmeter, D. (1996) 'A commentary on the WTO anti-dumping code', *Journal of World Trade* 30(4): 43–69.

Panagariya, A. and Gupta, P. (1998) 'Anti-dumping duty versus price negotiations', *The World Economy* 21(8): 1003–19.

Prusa, T.J. (1992) 'Why are so many anti-dumping petitions withdrawn?', *Journal of International Economics* 33: 1–20.

—— (1998) 'Cumulation and anti-dumping: a challenge to competition', *The World Economy* 21(8): 1021–33.

Shin, H.J. (1998) 'Possible instances of predatory pricing in recent US anti-dumping cases', *Brookings Trade Forum*, Washington: Brookings Institution.

Tharakan, P.K.M., Greenaway, D. and Tharakan, J. (1998) 'Cumulation and injury determination of the European Community in anti-dumping cases', *Weltwirtschaftliches Archiv* 134(2): 320–39.

US International Trade Commission (1995) *The Economic Effects of Anti-dumping and Countervailing Duty Orders and Suspension Agreements*, Publication 2900, Washington: US International Trade Commission.

Willig, R.D. (1998) 'Economic effects of anti-dumping policy', *Brookings Trade Forum*, Washington: Brookings Institution.

Winters, L.A., Rubin, M. and Bond, A.R. (1998) 'Anti-dumping action on American imports from Russia', *Post-Soviet Geography and Economics* 39(4): 183–224.

13 Investment in the WTO

Stephen Woolcock

Introduction

This chapter considers the case for including investment in the agenda of a future Millennium Round of WTO negotiations. At the time of writing, shortly after the failure to reach agreement on the launch of a new round of WTO negotiations at the ministerial conference in Seattle in December 1999, it is not clear when or whether a new comprehensive round of WTO negotiations will begin. The inclusion of investment in WTO negotiations will in part depend on there being a comprehensive agenda. If WTO member countries opt for a more modest round of negotiations based on those policy issues on which consensus already broadly exists, then the prospects for any of the 'new commercial' agenda items, including investment, will not be good. Inclusion of new issues is more likely in a multilateral round that provides for trade-offs over coverage.

It is not really accurate to describe investment as a 'new' issue, since it has been on the GATT and WTO agenda for some time. The Havana Charter of the International Trade Organization (ITO) included provisions on investment. Even the General Agreement on Tariffs and Trade of 1948 covered some aspects of investment policy, but these were not applied until the United States brought a case against the Canadian Foreign Investment Review Agency (FIRA) in 1983. Before the 1980s, all GATT contracting parties maintained controls on capital flows and foreign direct investment, so there was no interest in seeking to apply the GATT rules. From the late 1970s onwards, however, there has been a progressive shift towards more liberal investment policies, starting with the United States and Britain in the late 1970s, followed by Japan and the rest of the European Union member states in the mid-1980s, then Scandinavia and a number of leading newly industrialising countries (NICs) in Latin America.

Flows of foreign direct investment increased significantly in line with this liberalisation (Julius 1994).[1] During the 1980s, US efforts to include investment in the coverage of the Uruguay Round had only limited success, due to the opposition of some leading developing countries and less than wholehearted support from EU Member States. As a result, the Uruguay Round covered only trade-related investment measures (TRIMs).

Independently of the GATT talks, all OECD countries and a large number of NICs had made the shift to liberal investment policies by the end of the Uruguay Round in 1993. This liberalisation involved removing controls or screening of incoming FDI in manufacturing, more liberal regulation of services, such as financial services and telecommunications, and privatisation of 'sensitive' or 'strategic' sectors, such as transport and energy, which had been excluded from investment liberalisation even under the OECD codes.

The modest results of the Uruguay Round on TRIMs were therefore seen by those in governments and the private sector, which constituted the rather narrow policy-making community in international investment regimes, as being at odds with the liberal paradigm that prevailed at the time. There was little interest, let alone opposition, from the non-governmental organisations that were to figure in the failure of negotiations on a multilateral agreement on investment (MAI) in the OECD in 1998. The prevailing and apparently uncontested view in 1994 and 1995 was therefore that there was an opportunity to agree on a strong set of rules for investment that would ensure the rules kept pace with market and policy developments and rationalise the patchwork of bilateral, plurilateral, regional and multilateral rules that had been put in place in the absence of a comprehensive multilateral regime.

This broad consensus among OECD countries concealed differences, particularly between the USA and the EU, over what the regime should cover and in which forum it should be negotiated. The United States pressed for negotiations in the OECD, with the aim of extending the model of the North American Free Trade Agreement (NAFTA) rules on investment to the multilateral level. The NAFTA model offered progressive liberalisation, high standards of investment protection and dispute settlement that included provision for investor–state action. The European Union favoured multilateral negotiations within the WTO on the grounds that the main barriers to investment were in developing countries and that these needed to be involved in negotiations from the start rather than being asked to sign up to a *fait accompli* negotiated by OECD countries.

The outcome of these differences was a two-track approach, with negotiations beginning in the OECD on an MAI in May 1995 and the establishment of a working group on trade and investment in the WTO at the Singapore ministerial conference in December 1996. The MAI negotiations stalled in 1997 and finally failed in 1998. The EU's hopes of including investment in the WTO agenda were lost, along with the new round, in the debacle of the Seattle ministerial conference in December 1999.

What is the next step? Should investment be included in a new round of the WTO, if and when it is launched? Is there likely to be enough support for an ambitious agreement on investment? If not, what elements of the menu of topics included in regional, plurilateral and bilateral investment agreements should be included in modest negotiations? I will argue that there is a need for a multilateral framework for investment within the WTO, because the existing patchwork of investment rules cannot, in the long run, provide the predictability and confidence that is needed for FDI flows to continue, which is in the interests of both investors and host countries.

The multi-layer patchwork of investment rules

The current debate is not whether there should be international rules on investment or not, but whether there can and should be a consolidated framework of principles accommodating the existing patchwork of rules at plurilateral, regional, bilateral and multilateral levels. This patchwork of rules already constrains national investment policy options and grants rights to – and imposes far fewer obligations on – international investors.

Before looking at this patchwork of rules, it is helpful to summarise the provisions of existing investment agreements and what has been proposed for future agreements at whatever level. The following box summarises some of the key substantive provisions.

A menu of provisions in investment agreements

Definition of investment: can be broad asset-based definitions, including intangible assets such as intellectual property; or narrow definitions limited to FDI and excluding portfolio investment.

Transparency: information on host country rules and regulations affecting investment and/or requirements to list exceptions to provisions of agreements; is thought to assist liberalisation by obliging governments to defend restrictions on investment.

National treatment and m.f.n. status: core elements of all agreements that require non-discriminatory treatment of FDI, if national treatment is provided for investors (i.e. new incoming FDI) this is equivalent to right of establishment.

Bans on performance requirements: partial or total bans on conditions attached to investment, such as local content, export or trade balancing requirements.

Control of investment incentives: provisions banning or controlling subsidies and tax incentives.

Movement of key personnel: right of entry into a host country for the managerial and technical staff needed to support an investment project.

Monopolies and competition/anti-trust policy: provisions aimed at ensuring that national monopolies do not deny access for FDI or at ensuring that national competition law and practice ensure contestable markets.

Coverage/sector exceptions: coverage defined by top-down or negative lists, which list all sectors or horizontal measures (such as FDI screening) excluded; or bottom-up or positive lists, which list everything covered.

Negative listing is generally considered to be more liberal.

Exceptions for regional integration agreements: provisions for preferential or regional agreements, such as the EU or NAFTA.

National security exemptions: exemptions for control of investments or acquisitions contrary to security/foreign policy interests.

Investment protection: provisions against uncompensated expropriation or controls on payments or other capital transfers. Can include *de facto* expropriation and measures having the equivalent effect to expropriation, i.e. denying the investor the benefits of his/her investment.

Corporate governance: provisions that seek to ensure that market practice, such as cross-shareholdings, does not effectively block FDI.

Dispute settlement: provisions to enforce agreements, which may be state–state (only governments can initiate actions) or the more intrusive investor–state (private companies can challenge governments).

Social and environmental policy: provisions aimed at preventing regulatory arbitrage as investors choose locations with low standards of employment or environmental protection, such as policy harmonisation or approximation. These may involve obligations on investors rather than obligations on states.

The OECD instruments

The most extensive multilateral rules on investment can be found in the OECD codes and instruments. Work on investment issues in the OECD dates from the establishment of the organisation in 1961 but more specifically from 1964, when the codes on liberalisation of capital movements and current invisible operations were adopted (OECD 1987). These codes are binding on OECD members and require the progressive liberalisation of controls on capital movements. The basic approach of the codes has been to improve transparency by requiring member countries to notify any 'reservations' or exceptions from free movement of capital. Until the late 1980s, these reservations were quite extensive and covered sensitive sectors such as energy and telecommunications as well as horizontal controls or screening of inward and outward investment. Once barriers to investment were identified, peer pressure, in the shape of reviews of exceptions in OECD committees, then served as the 'enforcement mechanism'. In practice, this meant that the pace of liberalisation was really determined by each national government. However, the codes had a 'ratchet effect' in that they precluded any reintroduction of an investment control or liberalising measure.

The codes have developed and been strengthened to cover more issues:

- In 1984, the codes were strengthened to effectively require OECD countries to offer the right of establishment to signatories of the codes, subject to the remaining reservations, although investors still have to comply with host country regulations. At the same time, there was a debate about whether national monopolies, such as in telecommunications services, were compatible with liberal investment policies, but the right to allow such monopolies was retained.

- In 1986, changes were made requiring notification of 'reciprocity' provisions in national regulations (the conditioning of access for FDI upon equivalent access to the home country). Existing reciprocity rules were 'grandfathered'.

- In 1990, there was a review of the national treatment instrument (NTI) by the OECD. The NTI originates from the so-called Declaration and Decisions on International Investment and Multinational Enterprises of 1976, and together with the MFN provisions in the codes provides for non-discrimination between OECD countries. The NTI employs the same approach as the codes in that it ensures transparency through notifications of exceptions to national treatment. Progressive liberalisation is then encouraged through peer pressure (OECD 1993). However, unlike the codes, the NTI is not binding, so new laws can be introduced that discriminate against inward investors. The 1990 review led to efforts to strengthen the NTI by making it binding and extending its scope. The negotiations failed because of US–EU differences over the inclusion of sub-federal level government (sought by the EU) and provisions on regional preferences. The NTI review only succeeded in strengthening procedural rules that made notification of exemptions to national treatment binding.

The OECD approach is therefore based on transparency, requiring notification of reservations or exceptions to m.f.n., non-discrimination and national treatment requirements. Transparency facilitates peer review of exemptions from national treatment and m.f.n. (primarily in the Committee on International Investment and Multinational Enterprises). Together with the 'ratchet mechanism', which precludes the reintroduction of an exception to the right of establishment once it has been removed, this has contributed to a progressive liberalisation. But the pace of liberalisation has been determined predominantly by OECD governments acting unilaterally. Failure in the 1990/91 negotiations on a binding NTI did not mean the end of debate in the OECD. Work continued on the feasibility of what was at the time called a 'wider investment instrument' that would consolidate and strengthen the codes and NTI and address unresolved issues. The negotiations on an MAI in 1995 can therefore be seen as a continuation of existing OECD work.

Regional agreements

The treaties establishing the European Community offered *de jure* national treatment and the right of establishment anywhere within the Community

(Article 58, EEC), with a very limited number of exceptions, such as national security and broadcasting. Notwithstanding these rules, there was no *de facto* right of establishment due to national regulation of services, investment screening and controls in manufacturing and an absence of contestable markets. During the 1980s, liberalisation by member states, competition in markets and the liberalisation of capital controls through an EU directive in 1988 brought about more or less complete liberalisation of investment within the EU.[2] With the exception of France and Greece, this liberalisation was extended *erga omnis*, at least to other OECD countries. This left monopolies or oligopolistic market structures in such sectors as telecommunications, gas distribution, power genera‑ tion and distribution, postal services and rail and air transportation, which have been addressed through specific-sector directives and European competition policy. European competition policy has also been deployed to control the use of investment subsidies or incentives to attract FDI. Within the EU, there has been a harmonisation of environmental and to a lesser degree social and tax policies, which has reduced, but by no means removed, regulatory competition between investment locations in the EU (Thomsen and Woolcock 1993). This approach to investment has been adopted by countries neighbouring the EU, especially those that have negotiated or are seeking accession and that are therefore obliged to adopt the European *acquis*.

Much of the impetus behind negotiations on rules for investment has come from North America, and from the USA in particular. As early as 1970, ideas had been emanating from the United States for a 'GATT for investment'. The United States pushed the idea of GATT coverage of investment in the Consultative Group of 18 in 1981, and at the (failed) 1982 GATT ministerial conference the USA pushed for a code on investment in the GATT covering, among other things, 'performance requirements' (Graham 1990). The USA was motivated by a desire to remove controls such as those operated by the Canadian FIRA. In 1982, the USA brought a case against Canada before the GATT claiming that the FIRA infringed, among others, GATT Article III.4 (national treatment). The GATT panel on the case ruled in favour of the USA but limited the effective coverage of GATT by also arguing that developing countries could use GATT Article XVIII.c (government assistance to promote economic development) to justify the imposition of performance requirements. Such limitations motivated US interests to press for stronger GATT rules on investment, pressure that ultimately led to the inclusion of TRIMs in the Uruguay Round negotiations.

Not surprisingly, in the light of the FIRA case, the 1988 Canada–USA Free Trade Agreement (CUSFTA) provided for national treatment of investment and the phasing out of export and production-based performance requirements. It also eliminated Canadian screening of all but large investments. For its part, the USA had no general controls on investment other than those for reasons of 'national security', which were indeed revised in the 1988 Omnibus Trade Act. Given the USA's role in global security, it has retained considerable discre‑ tionary power to block inward FDI on grounds of national security. Concern about the potential for abuse of such provisions as a means of blocking foreign takeovers in 'sensitive' sectors for commercial reasons has resulted in a desire to tighten rules, in the MAI negotiations, for example. This is especially true when, as in the case of the United States, there is no independent review of decisions taken by the Committee for Foreign Investment in the United States (CIFIUS), the inter-agency US committee that makes judgements on such questions. In line with the approach taken by OECD countries, the CUSFTA excluded certain sensitive sectors, such as energy, mining, air transport and fishing, from the national treatment obligation. The automobile sector was also excluded from the obligation to remove performance requirements because of the desire to retain local content rules.

The NAFTA extended the approach used by the CUSFTA to include Mexico and provides for national treatment at a federal and state/province level and m.f.n. status. Performance requirements are prohibited, and the agreement explicitly cites export performance requirements, domestic content, local preferences, trade balancing requirements (with regard to both exports and foreign exchange), domestic sales requirements, the obligation to transfer technology, and exclusive sales requirements. The granting of incentives depending on location of investment is possible, but these cannot be conditional upon performance requirements, such as using a certain percentage of local products. There are also provisions on investment protection, including expropriation and transfer of funds. One whole section of the NAFTA is concerned with dispute settlement, which provides for investor-to-state actions. The dispute settlement procedures are detailed and include use of the arbitration procedures under the ICSID (the World Bank-based International Centre for Settlement of Investment Disputes)[3] and UNCITRAL.[4]

The NAFTA uses the top-down, negative list approach to coverage, with Mexico understandably having the longer list of exceptions. Both Canada and Mexico have exceptions for cultural industries. As in the case of the EU – and as discussed below, the GATT – the NAFTA has specific provisions for financial services and telecommunications. In broad terms, the NAFTA provisions offer a considerable degree of liberalisation over time. They require governments to ensure that public monopolies comply with the NAFTA and that market strength through regulated monopolies is not used to distort competition in other sectors. But there is no NAFTA level competition policy that can work to ensure that private restraints on access do not replace public regulatory restrictions. The first draft of the NAFTA negotiated by the parties in 1992 included only passing reference to labour and environmental issues. But the negotiation of NAFTA provoked considerable controversy among labour and environmental organisations in the United States. These saw NAFTA as a threat to the high standards of labour and environmental protection that they had worked years to establish. Lobbying from these NGOs (non-governmental organisations) influenced opinion in Congress, particularly among Democrats, who look to such groups for votes and funding during elections. Congress then blocked ratification of NAFTA until 'side agreements' on labour and environmental protection had been negotiated by the incoming Clinton administration. The NAFTA undoubtedly provided a model for the USA in future investment negotiations because it embodied US business interests in high standards for liberalisation, investor protection and investor–state dispute settlement. It has perhaps been overlooked that the NAFTA also possibly provided a model for NGOs seeking to ensure that labour rights and environmental standards are not undermined by investment agreements.

The GATT and investment

The General Agreement on Tariffs and Trade was designed for trade in goods. Investment provisions in Articles 11 and 12 of the Havana Charter were lost with the International Trade Organization (ITO). Even when the ITO was being negotiated, there was a reluctance to extend the scope of trade agreements to include foreign companies for fear that this would undermine sovereignty. The GATT's narrow coverage of goods and like-products traded meant greater simplicity in the application of national treatment and m.f.n. Reviews of the GATT's coverage of investment in the 1950s, 1960s and even 1970s did little to change this view.

Trade-related investment measures in the Uruguay Round

The idea of including investment in the GATT re-emerged during the 1980s. The progress made in the OECD led some countries to favour extending this to the GATT. But ideas to include investment in the Uruguay Round negotiations were opposed by some leading developing countries, which feared that GATT rules would limit their ability to use investment policy as an instrument of development. At the launch of the Uruguay Round in Punta del Este in September 1986, a compromise was reached with the effect that only those investment measures that had an effect on trade, or trade-related investment measures (TRIMs), would be the subject of negotiations. It was further agreed that the negotiations would first examine how the existing GATT operated with regard to TRIMs and only then elaborate, as appropriate, further provisions that may be necessary to avoid such adverse effects.[5]

US negotiators, backed by leading US multinational corporations in sectors such as information technology and in the service sector in general, were the ones making the demands in TRIMs – they sought the prohibition of fourteen TRIMs. At the other end of the spectrum, India and Brazil argued that developing countries should continue to have the right to use performance requirements as legitimate instruments of development policy, and that the GATT already covered key TRIMs. The EU assumed an intermediate position, favouring the prohibition of a shortlist of five TRIMs, some of which, such as local content requirements, were arguably already covered by the GATT, with a longer list being 'actionable' (i.e. subject to complaint) under the GATT. This position was also adopted by Japan and some of the NICs. Japan was mainly concerned about local content requirements in the USA and EU. Confirmation that the GATT already covered certain TRIMs was not sufficient to satisfy the Americans, but developing countries opposed any extension of GATT rules. As a result, there was no agreement on investment for four years during the Uruguay Round (Croome 1995). Even in the run-up to what should have been the concluding ministerial conference in Brussels in December 1990, there was still no text on investment/TRIMs. Following Brussels, views converged towards a compromise position, which enabled a draft TRIMs Agreement to be included in the so-called Dunkel text of December 1991, the draft final agreement of the round as a whole.

The Dunkel text and final agreement required all TRIMs contrary to the GATT to be notified to the GATT. An annex to the agreement provides a non-exclusive list of TRIMs that fall foul of the existing GATT. This includes local content and trade balancing requirements (contrary to Article III:1); trade balancing requirements (contrary to Article XI:4); and foreign exchange restrictions and export requirements (contrary to Article XI).

Developed countries had to eliminate such measures by 1997, developing countries by January 2000, and the least developed countries by 2002 (Article V). Finally, the agreement establishes a committee on TRIMs to review progress towards the objectives of the agreement. Any dispute is subject to the general dispute settlement provisions of the WTO, which means state–state only. There was also provision for a review of the agreement after five years. This, along with the question of whether some developing WTO members should be given longer to implement it (as well as other Uruguay Round agreements), now forms part of the WTO's ongoing work post-Seattle.

From the point of view of those who demanded a comprehensive agreement on investment, the TRIMs Agreement was well short of the target and did little more than agree to prohibit measures that had been contrary to the GATT for fifty years. This lack of satisfaction in progress in the GATT/WTO had an important bearing on the post-Uruguay Round debate, in which the USA opted for a plurilateral OECD forum for the next push to establish comprehensive international rules for investment. However, before looking at the post-Uruguay Round debate, we must first complete the patchwork of agreements by looking at the General Agreement on Trade in Services (GATS) and bilateral investment treaties.

Other WTO rules governing investment

In addition to the TRIMs Agreement, other WTO agreements have a bearing on investment. The most important of these is the GATS, which is concerned with opening markets in services, but because a presence or establishment in a market is important for access to many service sectors, effective access can only be assured through direct investment. In fact, the GATS envisages four modes of supply for services, one of which (mode 3) is through the establishment of a branch or subsidiary. The GATS also includes obligations on host country regulators to treat foreign-owned companies in the same way as nationally owned companies (national treatment) after establishment.

In contrast to the OECD codes and regional agreements such as NAFTA, the coverage of GATS is determined by a combination of the positive (or bottom-up) listing of sectors covered by the general agreement and of the negative listing of exceptions within each of the sectors covered. This makes for a complex set of schedules determining coverage, but on balance coverage is less comprehensive, which is what developing countries wanted. As in regional agreements, certain key service sectors, such as financial services and telecommunications, are covered by sector-specific agreements, which go further than national treatment and require a degree of policy harmonisation. In other words, in these key service sectors the GATS represents a considerable degree of multilateral rule making.[6]

Comparing the GATS agreement with the menu of provisions of investment agreements, we find that although national treatment, m.f.n. and transparency are all present, as indeed are exceptions for regional agreements (Article V, GATS). There are no provisions on investment protection, and dispute settlement is state–state rather than investor–state. Even if the coverage of GATS were to be extended, those interested in these aspects of investment agreements would find the GATS a weak agreement. As the GATS has been signed by all WTO members, it is unlikely that there will be revisions that include such investment protection measures.

The WTO agreement on trade-related intellectual property rights (TRIPs), on the other hand, does provide some elements of investor protection, at least with regard to intellectual property. As one of the major motivations for FDI is to exploit the intellectual property of the investing multinational company, protection against the 'expropriation' of intellectual property rights is of considerable importance in some sectors. However, in line with other WTO agreements, there is no investor–state dispute settlement provision in the GATS, so those investors seeking such means of ensuring their intellectual property is not 'expropriated' may still prefer bilateral investment treaties that include such provisions over TRIPs.

Bilateral investment treaties

In the absence of comprehensive and effective multilateral investment agreements, bilateral investment treaties or BITs have grown to fill the vacuum. This has occurred mainly during the 1990s, when two-thirds of the total of 1,513 BITs agreed up to 1997 were concluded (WTO 1996). BITs were initially used by a number of OECD countries to ensure more predictable climates for investment in developing economies. From the host country perspective, BITs helped to promote the confidence of investors and thus growth in inward FDI. More recently, the developing and transition economies have begun to negotiate BITs among themselves. Indeed, of the 153 BITs concluded during 1997, most were between developing countries or developing and transition economies (UNCTAD 1999).

The substantive elements of BITs vary from treaty to treaty, but generally speaking they tend to use a broader definition of investment than that used in multilateral investment agreements. Investment is often equated with property, so both moveable and immovable property are covered, as are ownership rights, claims on money and intellectual property rights. Most BITs include provision for m.f.n. and a majority national treatment, but the formulation of these rights varies from BIT to BIT. Almost all BITs include investment protection provisions covering expropriation, transfer of funds and in many cases general provisions that protect investment from any impairment of the use or disposal of assets. These provisions mean that host state regulations that reduce the value or ease of access to assets could be covered by BITs. However, only a minority of BITs, mainly those concluded by the United States, cover performance requirements and provisions ensuring the temporary right of entry of key personnel. Finally, almost all BITs include dispute settlement provisions, usually providing for arbitration, and they provide reference to ICSID and/or UNCITRAL and ICC (International Chamber of Commerce) procedures.

Summing up, judging by the growth in investment agreements at various levels over the past twenty years, it would seem that there is a demand for international rules governing investment. In the absence of a comprehensive international or multilateral agreement, there has been a growth of bilateral and regional agreements, which tend to be of a 'higher standard', offering greater protection for investors. This has resulted in the basic elements of the OECD rules being extended to developing and transition countries via bilateral agreements, or implemented through more binding regional agreements. Rule making has taken place at all levels: bilateral, regional, plurilateral (OECD) and multilateral. In each case, the rules have used different combinations of the menu of provisions in investment agreements offered above, so that although the agreements have common elements, there is a considerable degree of inconsistency across agreements. This inconsistency creates uncertainty for investors and may have a dampening effect on investment. Rules developed on one level have also tended to provide models for other levels. For example, there appears to be some evidence that the approach developed in the USA for bilateral agreements helped to shape the CUSFTA and NAFTA. The NAFTA, in turn, was seen as a model for the 'multilateral' OECD negotiations on an MAI (see below).

The post-Uruguay Round debate

In the period following the conclusion of the Uruguay Round in 1993/94 there was a consensus in the international investment policy community (largely consisting of government officials and private sector experts) on the desirability of new negotiations on a comprehensive multilateral agreement on investment. It was felt that this offered a window of opportunity for a regime change (Julius

1994). The expectation was that the negotiations on investment would not be controversial (Henderson 1999). However, as noted above, the Uruguay Round negotiations were a disappointment for those pressing for effective, multilateral rules of a high standard. There was also support among the policy makers for the liberal view that 'investment [could] provide the next great boost to the world economy following the powerful impulse given by the removal of trade barriers during the Uruguay Round' (Brittan 1995). But before this could happen, there was a need to establish a more predictable environment for FDI through the replacement of the patchwork of partly contradictory agreements that had grown up with a multilateral agreement.

Although there was a consensus on the desirability of further negotiations, differences of view remained over the right forum (WTO or OECD) for negotiations, and sharp differences continued over some of the issues that contributed to the collapse of the 1991 OECD negotiations. As will be shown below, the cohesive nature of the international investment policy community was irreversibly changed from 1997 onwards when labour, environment, development and other NGOs chose to enter the debate. The choice of forum pitted the United States against the European Union. The USA pressed for negotiations in the OECD on the grounds that the kind of high-standard multilateral agreement that it wished to negotiate could not be negotiated anywhere else. The NAFTA model that the USA was basing its negotiating position on called for investor protection extending to *de facto* expropriation provisions, investor–state-based dispute settlement and a top-down (negative list) approach to coverage. The USA also wanted to have another attempt at prohibiting European discrimination against US film and audio-visual products and services, which escaped GATS disciplines thanks to the EU sticking to its GATS Article II exemption for this sector. Developing country members of the WTO were not ready to negotiate on these issues and were probably not even ready to consider the extension of the list of performance requirements sought by the USA. By building on past OECD work, most recently the feasibility work on a 'wider investment instrument' undertaken in the OECD from 1991, the USA believed that a high-standard agreement could be concluded, which would then be open for non-OECD countries to sign.

The European Union preferred negotiations in the WTO on the grounds that most barriers to EU investors were in developing countries and not in the OECD. As set out in a European Commission discussion paper (EU 1994), the balance of opinion in the EU favoured the WTO because it was more inclusive and because it was unrealistic to expect developing countries to sign up to a *fait accompli* negotiated in the OECD. Negotiating in the WTO inevitably meant a more modest agenda, which would in any case make it easier for the EU to maintain a consensus among its member states. The EU agenda therefore included transparency, national treatment and m.f.n., as well as effective dispute settlement. Issues such as a ban on further performance requirements and expropriation provisions were seen as secondary. The EU sought continued exclusion of 'cultural industries' and exceptions for regional preferential agreements while pressing for the inclusion of 'sub-federal' government. The states and provinces of the USA, Canada and Australia are not generally covered by OECD or WTO rules, and the EU wanted to ensure that they would be covered by any investment agreement. Finally, the EU wanted to deal with the issues of the extraterritorial reach of national laws governing investment. The longstanding European opposition to the extraterritorial reach of US law had been further strengthened by US efforts to deny European investors in the United States rights that they could expect under OECD and WTO agreements, because they failed to comply with US sanctions against Cuba (The Helms–Burton Act) and Iran and Libya (ISLA).

The MAI negotiations

Despite its preference for the WTO as a forum, the EU agreed to begin negotiations in the OECD. The OECD ministerial conference in May 1995 launched the MAI negotiations and set 1997 as the target completion date. From this it was clear that any OECD text would be concluded before WTO negotiations could realistically be started, since the next WTO ministerial conference (at which a working group on trade and investment was established) would not be held until December 1996. The view in the OECD at the time was that there had to be an ambitious agenda to make the MAI exercise worthwhile (Henderson 1999). Presumably, this meant that the effort and risks involved in a new negotiation would have to be justified in terms of results that improved on the existing OECD instruments and WTO agreements.

The mandate for the MAI was to negotiate a comprehensive and fully binding agreement at the highest standard in every respect. This meant that the negotiations had to succeed where the earlier OECD negotiations in 1991 had failed in agreeing on a binding coverage of national treatment. In order to achieve this, the negotiations had to deal with the unresolved issues, including, for example, coverage of sub-federal government, which the US administration could not deliver in the face of Congressional opposition but which the EU sought. An ambitious agenda also meant resolving the issues of carve-outs for cultural industries and regional preferential agreements, on which the EU was not ready to move, and finding compromise wording for security exemptions from the agreement. On top of resolving these old issues, the negotiations had to agree on a range of new issues. In practice, the MAI negotiations had to find a consensus on all the issues listed on our menu of potential provisions for investment agreements.

Progress was made with this ambitious agenda until 1997, when a draft negotiating text was produced. This showed progress on many fronts:

- the definition of investment was to be a broad asset-based one including FDI and portfolio investment;
- there was to be national treatment and m.f.n. for investors and rules for transparency;

- coverage was to include all sectors and all levels of government, but subject to 'a balance of commitments' (in other words key issues of coverage such as the cultural exclusion and sub-federal government would depend on the final package);
- there were to be additional disciplines for performance requirements, privatisation, monopolies and key personnel;
- investment protection was to include provisions on expropriation and measures having an equivalent effect to expropriation; and
- dispute settlement was to be based on state–state and investor–state actions.

However, a number of key issues, such as 'cultural exclusions' and definitions of the security exemptions, continued to cause difficulties. It has also been suggested that governments began to get cold feet about conceding so much control over investment policy in a multilateral agreement.

During 1997, opposition from NGOs began to grow, and the posting of the draft negotiating text on the Internet provided a rallying point for organised labour and environmental groups with concerns about the agreement. These NGOs feared that the agreement would undermine national standards of environmental protection and labour conditions. There was also opposition from development NGOs, which feared that developing countries would have little choice but to sign the agreement, and in doing so they would significantly limit the scope for development policies. The negotiations and the OECD were damaged by claims that the MAI negotiations, which would have far-reaching effects on a range of interests, had been conducted in secrecy. This is inaccurate, since the negotiations had been launched with public statements by the OECD ministers. But as noted above, the policy community that was engaged in the negotiations was a fairly select group. In defence of those responsible for negotiating the MAI, few people outside business and even few people in business had paid much attention to previous OECD negotiations. The negotiators probably continued to assume that there would be little public interest.

With hindsight, it is perhaps surprising that the NGO response was not anticipated. The NAFTA negotiations had generated considerable opposition from labour and environmental groups, and if the NAFTA could be seen as a model for investment negotiations in the MAI, why could the negotiation of the side agreements not be seen as a model by labour and environmental groups? The opposition from development NGOs was anticipated in the sense that it was known that LDCs would resent being excluded from negotiations and then presented with an agreement to sign. Perhaps the fact that the NAFTA and the results of the Uruguay Round had been ratified in the US Congress and other parliaments led negotiators to believe that there would be little opposition. Perhaps negotiators were too busy listening to private sector interests, which favoured proceeding with the negotiations. But the political masters of those negotiating the MAI were certainly surprised by popular opposition to the MAI, which had been coordinated by NGOs at an international level via the Internet. Such opposition meant that the negotiations could turn out to be a vote loser, with the result that governments had to act.

In an attempt to defuse the opposition, concessions were made to environmental and labour interests, in particular, with general wording inserted into the draft agreement covering these issues. But these amendments did little to placate NGO opposition, which saw the MAI as promoting globalisation in the interests of multinational companies. However, the inclusion of social and environmental provisions was not welcomed by multinational companies, which opposed binding obligations on themselves. Furthermore, difficulties in finding consensus on some of the substance of the agreement meant that the agreement would have to be watered down (from the high standards sought by business) if it was to find a consensus among governments. Together, these developments reduced the value of the MAI for international business, so support among the agreement's main supporters ebbed away. Growing doubts on the part of the governments negotiating the text, opposition from NGOs and a weakening in support from business combined to bring negotiations to a halt in the spring of 1998. A six-month pause was agreed, during which opposition only grew. In the end, the French government, under strong pressure from public protest, formally withdrew from the negotiations just before they were due to resume in October 1998, which had the effect of killing the MAI. The report produced by a French parliamentarian on the MAI provides an indication of the kind of watering down that was being called for in the public debate. The Lalumière Report argued that France should withdraw unless a number of conditions were met. These included a more limited definition of investment (excluding portfolio investment and asset-based definitions), removal of provisions on investor–state dispute settlement, more limited provisions on expropriation (which would effectively preclude the inclusion of the provisions on *de facto* expropriation), an abandonment of the 'ratchet', and limits on the coverage of TRIMs (so that the MAI would only extend the prohibition of TRIMs agreed in the Uruguay Round to services). The recommendations of the report were that the negotiations be started anew and that developing countries be included. In effect, this meant that the WTO would be the forum and that the scope of the agreement would have to be much more modest.

Investment in the WTO

Thanks in large part to the EU, a WTO working group on the relationship between trade and investment was established at the Singapore ministerial conference in December 1996. Given the continued opposition from many developing countries to anything that might be seen as the first step towards comprehensive negotiations on investment in the WTO, and the prevailing US view that a WTO agreement on investment would be too weak to be of any value, the remit of the working group was constrained to studies. The mandate given to the group was that it should consider (1) the implications of the relationship between trade and investment for developing countries and economic growth; (2) the economic relationship between trade and investment; (3) the existing instruments and activities regarding trade and investment; and (4) identification of common features, differences, advantages and disadvantages of entering into bilateral, regional and multilateral rules on investment. The work of the group between 1996 and 1999 provided little by way of convergence of views.

In the preparatory work in Geneva on the agenda for the Seattle ministerial conference and the draft communiqué to launch the WTO Millennium Round, it was the EU that remained the main party demanding the inclusion of investment in an ambitious round. In the Council of Europe conclusions of October 1999, the Council called for negotiations to begin in the WTO on investment. While the conclusions do not indicate a great deal of detail concerning the Council's mandate to the Commission on this issue, they do appear to limit investment to FDI (excluding negotiations on portfolio investment) while calling for negotiations to address access to investment opportunities, non-discrimination and protection of investments. The United States was opposed to including investment and was seeking a more modest agenda that reflected its own interests. Given the legacy of the MAI, the US administration wanted to avoid provoking US labour, environmental and anti-globalisation NGOs in agreeing to negotiate an agreement that US business was convinced would not be worth the paper it was written on (Barshevsky 1999). Leading developing countries such as India also continued to actively oppose including investment in the WTO agenda, while most LDCs simply had more pressing objectives, such as improving access to developed country markets. The Geneva process failed to make any real progress on the investment issue, as was the case with other sectors, although the draft communiqué, which was all in square brackets (meaning that it had not been agreed), appears to reflect the general EU line as reflected in statements by the Commission.

In Seattle, the EU, jointly with Hungary, Japan, Korea and Switzerland, tabled a common paper. This also reflected the EU's objectives and its assessment of what sort of investment coverage would be acceptable to the LDCs. The paper called for a multilateral framework for investment in the WTO that would be based on non-discrimination, ensure transparency, address the relationship between WTO rules and those of the OECD and regional and bilateral agreements, seek progressive liberalisation using a positive list approach, address policies and practices not covered by the existing WTO, and exclude investor–state dispute settlement and take into account developing country needs. This text was presented to the negotiating group on 'new issues', but the group made little progress on this or other issues in Seattle as most negotiating effort went into addressing agriculture. It should be stressed that the WTO framework, proposed by the EU and supported in the end by about fourteen WTO members, was very different from the agreement proposed in the MAI. But there can be little doubt that the fact and the manner in which the MAI failed contributed to the absence of support for the inclusion of a framework for investment on the WTO agenda.

Future prospects

Is an agreement in the WTO needed? There is certainly a rational case to be made for rules on investment to keep pace with developments in global markets in order to provide a stable and predictable environment for investment. If this case holds for goods and services, it should hold for investment, which is a major element in the internationalisation of markets. There is also a growing risk of conflict between bilateral, regional, plurilateral and multilateral rules governing investment. On the other hand, FDI is increasing anyway, despite the patchwork of rules that exists today (WTO 1996).

At present, there is no consensus in favour of a WTO framework for investment. In the absence of such a consensus, the alternative approach of using existing WTO agreements, particularly the GATS, is likely to be followed in the short to medium term. As noted above, the GATS covers much the same issues for services as a WTO agreement on investment would. As much of the growth in FDI is in services, an extension of the GATS to include more sectors and perhaps some more horizontal rules provides an alternative route to coverage of investment through probably stronger rules than would have been possible in a new overarching framework agreement for investment. As the controversy over investment has not (yet) affected services, this option is likely to be attractive to some negotiators. In the field of goods, the parallel option of extending the coverage of the TRIMs Agreement seems somewhat less likely, given the limited agreement achieved only recently in the Uruguay Round. Finally, in theory, the TRIPs Agreement could also be used to provide further protection for intangible assets of investment. But this option will be limited by opposition from development NGOs and LDCs and the disinclination of multinational companies to reopen the intellectual property rights debate at the present time. Making use of existing WTO agreements would not deliver the investor–state dispute settlement that is sought by the USA, but this is probably too intrusive into national sovereignty anyway. The risk with such an approach is that if these alternative WTO agreements are to be used to at least partially fulfil the aims of an investment agreement, why should there be less opposition in these negotiations than to a negotiation on investment? If the opposition stems from concern about WTO rules intruding into national regulatory competence, why should it be easier in GATS than an investment negotiations? Is this really in line with the spirit of transparency? Is it feasible for investment to be included on the WTO agenda? The legacy of the MAI makes the likelihood of being able to negotiate anything approaching an ambitious agreement highly unlikely.

Governments, in particular the US government, have become wary of the issue and are not generally willing to risk political capital to negotiate an agreement that would be short of what is desired by the private sector. If investment is to get on to the WTO agenda, it will have to be in the shape of a modest package along the lines of the paper tabled by the EU and other states in Seattle. This would have to focus on transparency, the core principle of non-discrimination. Coverage would have to be limited to FDI and not include, for example, portfolio investment or broad asset-based definitions of investment as used in the MAI or NAFTA. Dispute settlement would have to be limited to state–state actions, because it is not on the cards that a consensus of WTO members would agree to the precedent of private rights of action under the WTO. Such an agreement would do little more than provide a multilateral framework for what will probably continue to be unilateral decisions to liberalise. But then this has been the practice in investment since the 1960s.

If the agenda for investment in the next round has to be of such a modest nature, it may be better to continue work on investment in the working group on the relationship between trade and investment with a view to preparing the ground and public opinion for inclusion in the round after next. This would be especially appropriate if the next round takes the form of a more modest mini-round than the one envisaged or proposed by the European Union in Seattle. In such a modest round, it is unlikely that new issues, on which there is no broad consensus on the need for stronger WTO rules, will get on to the agenda. In any case, a consensus first needs to be achieved on the scope of a WTO framework for investment. This may be as easily achieved in the working group as in formal negotiations.

The difficulty with this pragmatic approach is that in the absence of any consolidated multilateral framework, the patchwork of investment measures will continue to expand. This could at some point in the not too distant future begin to create real tensions between the different regimes. Therefore, there remains a need to develop a clear multilateral framework, although for such a framework to have any effect, it must discipline or at least provide firm guidelines for bilateral, regional and plurilateral agreements. While the pace of liberalisation will be decided by WTO members unilaterally, any WTO agreement would also have to be binding in the sense of preventing the reintroduction of discriminatory policies that had been liberalised. If national policies can switch between liberalisation and control, there would be no predictable climate for investment and arguably a greater risk of governments using deregulation to attract investment. In short, the model for a WTO framework agreement is perhaps not the NAFTA, with its high standards, and certainly not the MAI, but the approach of the earlier OECD codes.

Notes

1   DeAnne Julius identifies five historical phases in the evolution of what she calls international direct investment (IDI): (1) the heyday of the nineteenth century, 1870 to 1914, when there was an essentially liberal regime; (2) the collapse of IDI and trade during and between the two world wars, 1914 to 1945; (3) trade growth with investment controls, 1945 to 1973, but some recovery of IDI, especially US investment in Europe; (4) the years of recession induced by soaring oil prices during the period 1973–1983; and (5) the current phase of explosive growth in IDI post-1983.

2   The OECD (1993) describes three waves of liberalisation in Europe. The first national and unilateral from 1979; the second from the mid-1980s as a result of the

European Single Market; and the third from the late 1980s, in which Scandinavia and other applicant countries followed the trend.

3 The convention establishing the ICSTD has 126 signatories. It is referred to as a possible means of resolving disputes in no less than 350 regional and bilateral agreements as well as NAFTA, but it had dealt with only thirty-five cases in the thirty years of its history up to 1996.

4 The United Nations Centre on Investment and Trade Law.

5 The wording of the relevant Punta Del Este declaration of September 1986 was:

> Following an examination of the operation of the GATT article related to the trade restrictive, distortive effects of investment measures, negotiations should elaborate as appropriate, further provisions that may be needed to avoid adverse effects on trade.

6 It is worth noting in passing that neither the GATS nor the sectoral agreement on financial services prevents a government introducing capital controls, maintaining essential prudential regulation or managing exchange rates. This is worth mentioning because opponents of multilateral investment agreements have argued that these would make it harder for governments to deal with financial crises.

References

Barshevsky, C. (1999) 'Toward Seattle: the next round and America's stake in the trading system', speech to the Council of Foreign Relations, New York, 19 October.

Brittan, L. (1995) 'Smoothing the path for investment worldwide', speech in Washington, January.

Croome, J. (1995) *Reshaping the World Trading System: A History of the Uruguay Round*, Geneva: WTO.

Graham, E. (1990) 'Trade related investment measures in the Uruguay Round of multilateral trade negotiations', paper prepared for Foro Internacional: Mexico y sus perspectiveas de negociacion exterior, Institute for International Economics, May.

Henderson, D. (1999) *The MAI Affair: A Story and Its Lessons*, London: The Royal Institute of International Affairs.

Julius, D. (1994) 'International direct investment: strengthening the policy regime', paper for the Conference on Managing the World Economy of the Future: Lessons of the First 50 Years of Bretton Woods, Washington: Institute for International Economics, May 19–21.

OECD (1987) *Introduction to the OECD Codes of Liberalisation*, Paris: OECD.

—— (1993) *Foreign Direct Investment: Policies and Trends in the OECD Area during the 1980s*, Paris: OECD.

Thomsen, S. and Woolcock, S. (1993) *Direct Investment and European Integration: Competition Among Firms and Governments*, London: Royal Institute of International Affairs.

United Nations Conference on Trade and Development (1999) *Preparing for future multilateral trade negotiations: issues and research needs from a development perspective*, Geneva, 18 May.

World Trade Organization (1996) *Trade and Foreign Direct Investment*, Geneva, October.

14 Trade-related intellectual property rights

From Marrakech to Seattle

Carlos A. Primo Braga and Carsten Fink

Introduction

One of the most significant developments of the Uruguay Round (1986–94) was the inclusion of trade-related intellectual property rights (TRIPS) issues on the agenda of the multilateral trading system. To many outsiders, it may have been surprising that something as 'esoteric' as intellectual property would find its way on to the agenda of an institution that has traditionally been mainly concerned with the reduction of trade barriers. Yet, due to the growth of trade in knowledge- and information-intensive goods, the economic implications of imitation, copying and counterfeiting had in many industries become at least as relevant for international commerce as conventional border restrictions to trade.

Intellectual property is a generic term for a set of legal instruments that delineate the exclusive rights granted to creators of, broadly defined, new knowledge and information. These instruments seek to address certain failures of private markets to provide for an efficient allocation of resources. It is useful to distinguish between two categories of intellectual property rights (IPRs) in this respect. First, patents, industrial designs, copyright, plant breeders' rights and layout designs for integrated circuits grant exclusive rights to new innovations and original works of authorship for a limited period. They thus provide an incentive for innovative businesses, authors and artists to commit resources to the creation of new consumer products, technologies, software packages, books, musical recordings, and so on – without the fear of intellectual theft once the results of these innovative and creative activities have been disclosed to the public. Second, trademarks and geographical indications protect the use of words, signs and symbols associated with a particular product or company. They thus facilitate market transactions by assuring consumers that they are purchasing what they intended to purchase.[1]

Intellectual property rights are always granted on a territorial basis. That is, each nation protects IPRs only in so far as these rights are exercised in the domestic economy. However, new ideas, copies of books, musical recordings and software code easily cross national boundaries. Hence, conflicts arise if domestic IPR regulations discriminate against foreign nationals or if standards of protection are weaker abroad than they are at home. To address these conflicts, governments have, for a long time, negotiated international treaties on IPRs, such as the Paris Convention for the Protection of Industrial Property (1883) and the Berne Convention for the Protection of Literary and Artistic Works (1886). Most of these treaties are administered by a specialised agency of the United Nations, the World Intellectual Property Organization (WIPO). At best, these WIPO conventions have achieved some degree of non-discrimination with regard to the application of IPR regulations, but they have failed to establish minimum international standards of protection. With the growing economic significance of IPR-sensitive goods in international commerce, the largest producers of intellectual property have become increasingly dissatisfied with the WIPO's ineffectiveness. This is why TRIPS issues were included on the agenda of the GATT – a more powerful institution that offered the possibility of cross-sectoral trade-offs and an effective enforcement mechanism in case a country did not live up to its committed obligations.

The resulting TRIPS Agreement was signed at the ministerial conference in Marrakech in April 1994 as part of the final act of the Uruguay Round. TRIPS is one of the three multilateral agreements that form the tripod serving as the basis for the WTO and hence is binding on all WTO members (135 countries up to February 2000) and all future entrants to the WTO.[2] As with previous WIPO conventions, it requires non-discrimination with regard to the application of IPRs,[3] but TRIPS also defines minimum standards of protection and sets out basic procedures that deal with the enforcement of rights. Moreover, the Agreement makes disputes between member governments with regard to their TRIPS obligations subject to the WTO's integrated dispute settlement system, with the possibility of cross-sectoral retaliation (i.e. trade sanctions) in the case of non-compliance.

What came out of the Uruguay Round?[4]

The TRIPS negotiations were characterised by significant North–South disagreement. Developing countries, which are mostly consumers of intellectual property, originally resisted the inclusion of TRIPS issues on the negotiating agenda, arguing that it went beyond the mandate of the GATT and that WIPO represented the appropriate discussion forum for IPRs. However, developed countries, led by the United States, made the inclusion of intellectual property one of their top priorities and insisted on an agreement that would not only combat trade in counterfeit goods but also establish minimum standards of protection and detail mechanisms for the enforcement of IPRs.

Why in the end were developing countries willing to put their signatures to the TRIPS Agreement? Two considerations were paramount. First, the acceptance of TRIPS has to be understood in the context of the overall package of agreements that came out of the Uruguay Round. Specifically, TRIPS has been characterised as a 'price' that developing countries had to pay in return for concessions on market access in the areas of agriculture and textiles trade.[5]

Second, some developing countries preferred multilateral disciplines on IPRs to being nakedly exposed to unilateral pressure from economically powerful industrial countries. Especially in the late 1980s and early 1990s, the United States, through Section 301 of its Omnibus Trade and Competitiveness Act of 1988, had raised the issue of weak foreign protection for US intellectual property to a priority status for negotiations concerning trade preferences and as a basis for potential trade retaliation.

For each type of IPR, the TRIPS Agreement defines the main elements of protection, namely the subject matter to be protected, the rights to be conferred and permissible exceptions to those rights. The minimum standards in the TRIPS Agreement are, in most cases, stronger than the standards that prevailed in nearly all developing countries during the Uruguay Round. For developed countries, the picture is more heterogeneous. For some industrial countries, the TRIPS standards more or less reflected the existing state of IPR norms, with some adjustments required in some areas. For others, these standards were significantly below the kind of protection that domestic laws conferred on IPR holders (e.g. US patent protection for biotechnology inventions).

It is important to point out that not all aspects of the TRIPS Agreement were marked by North–South divisions. The biggest controversy between developing and developed countries existed in the area of patents, where developed countries insisted that TRIPS should extend patent protection to pharmaceutical and chemical products. Other areas were characterised by North–North disagreement, such as the protection of geographical indications, where the EU argued in favour of strict rules to protect European producers of wine, spirits and foodstuffs. Again, other areas were largely uncontroversial, such as the protection of trademarks and industrial designs.

A rigorous overall assessment of the TRIPS standards of intellectual property protection is difficult. Economic guidance on the optimal scope of patent or copyright protection, for example, is scarce. In technologically advanced countries, which have the longest experience with intellectual property policies, the current standards of protection are largely a historical outcome, determined by educated 'rules of thumb', the influence of vested interests and the evolution of technology. Given this uncertainty, negotiators had to make pragmatic choices.

It is also important to point out that it is difficult to speak of 'TRIPS standards' of protection. In various areas, countries have some leeway in adjusting their IPR systems to country-specific needs while meeting their international obligations. For example, the criteria used to determine the novelty, non-obviousness and usefulness of patentable inventions can to some extent be defined differently across nations – as can the reasons for the use of compulsory licences (official permissions to use protected intellectual property without authorisation of the title holder). Another example would be that there are no specific obligations regarding the exhaustion of intellectual property (aside from non-discrimination), thus leaving the choice open of whether or not to restrict parallel imports of IPR-protected goods.[6]

For the first time in an international agreement, TRIPS incorporates obligations pertaining to the enforcement of rights. This is motivated by the fact that the ownership of an intellectual property title can indeed be meaningless unless IPR holders have the possibility of defending their exclusive rights in a court. The approach taken by the Agreement is to set general standards on, among other things, enforcement procedures, the treatment of evidence, injunctive relief, damages, and provisional and border measures. However, it does not require countries to put in place a specialised judicial authority for IPRs. Besides enforcement, TRIPS also contains an article on the acquisition and maintenance of intellectual property, which demands that IPRs are administered so as to avoid unwarranted delays in the granting or registration of an IPR.

As already mentioned, the Agreement makes disputes over TRIPS matters subject to the WTO dispute settlement body (DSB), with the possibility of cross-sectoral retaliation if members are found to be in violation of their obligations. However, a moratorium on the use of so-called non-violation disputes had been set, but this expired at the end of 1999. Such disputes concern measures that may nullify or impair the benefits of the TRIPS Agreement without being a direct violation of its specific provisions.

The provisions of the TRIPS Agreement became applicable to all signatories at the beginning of 1996. However, developing countries and economies in transition were entitled to a four-year transition period. Developing countries are also entitled to an additional five-year transitional period for product patents in fields of technology that were not protected at the date of application of the Agreement. However, for pharmaceuticals and agricultural chemicals, developing countries have to accept applications for product patents immediately and to grant exclusive marketing rights for five years or until the patent is granted or rejected, whichever is shorter. This so-called 'mailbox' provision of the TRIPS Agreement effectively denied developing countries a transition period for the most sensitive issue negotiated during the Uruguay Round. The least developed countries are entitled to a ten-year transitional period to comply with the Agreement. Moreover, the Agreement allows for the possibility of extending this period upon 'duly motivated' request by an LDC member.

TRIPS in the WTO: the experience 1996–99

The pursuit of minimum standards in TRIPS requires that governments take positive action on IPRs. In this respect, the Agreement differs from the more discipline-based approach for trade in goods (GATT 1994) or trade in services (GATS), which do not require governments to pursue specific policies. Moreover, the implementation of TRIPS obligations requires changes in domestic laws, which typically entail legislative proceedings and the approval of a parliamentary majority. Improvements in enforcement mechanisms can necessitate reforms of the judicial system, and enhancements in administrative procedures may require significant organisational restructuring. In comparison, simple tariff reductions can often be achieved with the 'stroke of a pen' from the government's executive branch.

For many developing countries that did not have TRIPS-consistent IPR systems at the end of the Uruguay Round, implementation of the Agreement therefore poses significant institutional and financial challenges. This point is made strongly in a recent study by Finger and Schuler (1999), who point to the significant costs of TRIPS implementation in developing countries. However, it should be noted that this study does not take into account that an upgrade of the IPR system also generates income for a government – principally from the enhanced revenues of patent offices due to more applications and administrative improvements. We would argue that the bigger challenge for developing countries is how to design IPR systems that are conducive to the needs of domestic producers and consumers, rather than simply to focus on pure TRIPS compliance, which may benefit only the dominant players.[7] Good advice on how to do this is scarce.

How has implementation progressed since the Agreement came into force in 1996? Undoubtedly, the conclusion of the TRIPS Agreement has motivated many changes in IPR systems around the world in the second half of the 1990s. However, it is difficult to assess how many countries can be considered TRIPS-compliant and how many still fall short of the Agreement's standards, as to some degree this requires interpretations of laws and regulations that may or may not be sustained by potential dispute settlement proceedings. With these difficulties in mind, we present some crude indicators of compliance in Table 14.1. The first four columns indicate whether a WTO member is party – as of January 2000 – to the WIPO conventions referred to in the TRIPS Agreement.[8] Note that this is inevitably a very limited measure of compliance, as TRIPS goes far beyond the obligations of these treaties. The fifth column shows the WTO member countries that were on the 'priority watch list' and 'watch list' of the 1998 Special 301 Report compiled by the US Trade Representative (USTR). The sixth column presents an assessment of compliance by the Transatlantic Business Dialogue (TABD), a coalition of European and North American companies. Both of these indicators are necessarily subjective and do not tell anything about the severity or extent of the alleged violations. Moreover, countries that are not 'negatively marked' in these two columns cannot necessarily be considered as compliant. They may simply not represent a commercial priority for the USTR or the TABD – which, however, is in itself insightful.

With regard to the WIPO conventions, only one developed country (Portugal) is not signatory to an agreement referred to in TRIPS.[9] The vast majority of developing countries and least developed countries are members of the Paris and Berne Conventions, whereas membership in the Rome and Geneva Conventions is confined to a minority of these countries. A significant number of developing countries have joined these conventions since 1995 – just under twenty in the case of both the Paris and Berne Conventions. With respect to the USTR and TABD indicators, several developed countries are perceived to be not compliant with TRIPS. Among developing countries, both indicators are biased towards larger or economically more advanced countries. Similarly, the fact that no least developed country is mentioned by the USTR

Table 14.1 Some indicators of TRIPS compliance

WTO member	Paris	Berne	Rome	Geneva	USTR	TABD
Developed countries						
Australia	yes	yes	yes	yes	WL	NC
Austria	yes	yes	yes	yes		
Belgium	yes	yes	yes*	no		
Canada	yes	yes	yes*	no	WL	NC
Denmark	yes	yes	yes	yes		
European Communities	n/a	n/a	n/a	n/a	PWL	n/a
Finland	yes	yes	yes	yes		
France	yes	yes	yes	yes		
Germany	yes	yes	yes	yes		
Greece	yes	yes	yes	yes	PWL	
Iceland	yes	yes	yes	no		NC
Ireland	yes	yes	yes	no		
Italy	yes	yes	yes	yes	WL	
Japan	yes	yes	yes	yes	PWL	NC
Luxembourg	yes	yes	yes	yes		
Netherlands	yes	yes	yes	yes		
New Zealand	yes	yes	no	yes		NC
Norway	yes	yes	yes	yes		NC
Portugal	yes	yes	no	no		
Spain	yes	yes	yes	yes		
Sweden	yes	yes	yes	yes		
Switzerland	yes	yes	yes	yes		NC
United Kingdom	yes	yes	yes	yes		
United States	yes	yes	no	yes		
Developing countries and economies in transition						
Antigua and Barbuda	yes*	yes*	no	no		
Argentina	yes	yes	yes	yes	PWL	NC
Bahrain	yes*	yes*	no	no	WL	NC
Barbados	yes	yes	yes	no		
Belize	no	no	no	no		
Bolivia	yes	yes	yes	no		NC
Botswana	yes*	yes*	no	no		
Brazil	yes	yes	yes	yes	WL	NC
Brunei Darussalam	no	no	no	no		
Bulgaria	yes	yes	yes*	yes*		NC
Cameroon	yes	yes	no	no		

Table 14.1 Continued

WTO member	Paris	Berne	Rome	Geneva	USTR	TABD
Developing countries and economies in transition						
Chile	yes	yes	yes	yes	WL	NC
Colombia	yes*	yes	yes	yes	WL	NC
Congo	yes	yes	yes	no		
Costa Rica	yes*	yes	yes	yes	WL	NC
Côte d'Ivoire	yes	yes	no	no		
Cuba	yes	yes*	no	no		
Cyprus	yes	yes	no	yes		NC
Czech Republic	yes	yes	yes	yes		NC
Dominica	yes*	yes*	yes*	no		
Dominican Republic	yes	yes*	yes	no		NC
Ecuador	yes*	yes	yes	yes	WL	NC
Egypt	yes	yes	no	yes	WL	NC
El Salvador	yes	yes	yes	yes	WL	NC
Estonia	yes	yes	no	no		NC
Fiji	no	yes	yes	yes		
Gabon	yes	yes	no	no		
Ghana	yes	yes	no	no		
Grenada	yes*	yes*	no	no		
Guatemala	yes*	yes*	yes	yes	WL	NC
Guyana	yes	yes	no	no		
Honduras	yes	yes	yes	yes		NC
Hong Kong, China	yes	yes	no	yes		NC
Hungary	yes	yes	yes*	yes		NC
India	yes*	yes	no	yes	PWL	NC
Indonesia	yes	yes*	no	no	PWL	NC
Israel	yes	yes	no	yes		NC
Jamaica	yes*	yes	yes	yes		
Kenya	yes	yes	no	yes		
Korea	yes	yes*	no	yes	PWL	NC
Kuwait	no	no	no	no	WL	NC
Kyrgyz Republic	yes	yes*	no	no		
Latvia	yes	yes*	yes*	yes*		
Liechtenstein	yes	yes	yes*	yes*		
Macau	yes	yes	no	yes		
Malaysia	yes	yes	no	no		NC
Malta	yes	yes	no	no		
Mauritius	yes	yes	no	no		

Table 14.1 Continued

WTO member	Paris	Berne	Rome	Geneva	USTR	TABD
Developing countries and economies in transition						
Mexico	yes	yes	yes	yes		NC
Mongolia	yes	yes*	no	no		
Morocco	yes	yes	no	no		NC
Namibia	no	yes	no	no		
Nicaragua	yes*	no	yes	no		NC
Nigeria	yes	yes	yes	no		NC
Pakistan	no	yes	no	no	WL	NC
Panama	yes*	yes*	yes	yes		NC
Papua New Guinea	yes*	no	no	no		
Paraguay	yes	yes	yes	yes	WL	NC
Peru	yes*	yes	yes	yes	WL	NC
Philippines	yes	yes	yes	no	WL	NC
Poland	yes	yes	yes*	no	WL	NC
Qatar	no	no	no	no		
Romania	yes	yes	yes*	yes*		NC
Saint Kitts and Nevis	yes*	yes*	no	no		
Saint Lucia	yes*	yes	yes*	no		
Saint Vincent and the Grenadines	yes*	yes*	no	no		
Senegal	yes	yes	no	no		
Singapore	yes*	yes*	no	no	WL	NC
Slovak Republic	yes	yes	yes	yes		NC
Slovenia	yes	yes	yes*	yes*		NC
South Africa	yes	yes	no	no		NC
Sri Lanka	yes	yes	no	no		
Suriname	yes	yes	no	no		
Swaziland	yes	yes*	no	no		
Thailand	no	yes	no	no	WL	NC
Trinidad and Tobago	yes	yes	no	yes		
Tunisia	yes	yes	no	no		NC
Turkey	yes	yes	no	no	PWL	NC
United Arab Emirates	yes*	no	no	no	WL	NC
Uruguay	yes	yes	yes	yes		NC
Venezuela	yes*	yes	yes*	yes	WL	NC
Zimbabwe	yes	yes	no	no		

Table 14.1 Continued

WTO member	Paris	Berne	Rome	Geneva	USTR	TABD
Least developed countries						
Angola	no	no	no	no		
Bangladesh	yes	yes*	no	no		
Benin	yes	yes	no	no		
Burkina Faso	yes	yes	yes	yes		
Burundi	yes	no	no	no		
Central African Republic	yes	yes	no	no		
Chad	yes	yes	no	no		
Dem. Rep. of Congo	yes	yes	no	yes		
Djibouti	no	no	no	no		
Gambia	yes	yes	no	no		
Guinea	yes	yes	no	no		
Guinea Bissau	yes	yes	no	no		
Haiti	yes	yes*	no	no		
Lesotho	yes	yes	yes	no		
Madagascar	yes	yes	no	no		
Malawi	yes	yes	no	no		
Maldives	no	no	no	no		
Mali	yes	yes	no	no		
Mauritania	yes	yes	no	no		
Mozambique	yes*	no	no	no		
Myanmar	no	no	no	no		
Niger	yes	yes	yes	no		
Rwanda	yes	yes	no	no		
Sierra Leone	yes*	no	no	no		
Solomon Islands	no	no	no	no		
Tanzania	no	no	no	no		
Togo	yes	yes	no	no		
Uganda	yes	no	no	no		
Zambia	yes	yes	no	no		

Sources: World Intellectual Property Organization (www.wipo.int); United States Trade Representative (www.ustr.gov); and Transatlantic Business Dialogue (www.tabd.com).

Notes: Paris, Berne, Rome, and Geneva refer to membership of the respective WIPO conventions as of January 2000. An asterisk indicates that the country joined a convention after 1 January 1995. Developed countries are defined as high-income OECD countries according to the World Bank; the classification of least developed countries is from the World Trade Organization. All remaining countries were classified as developing countries. 'PWL' and 'WL' indicate that a country was on the priority watch list or watch list, respectively, of the 1998 Special 301 Report compiled by the United States Trade Representative. Finally, 'NC' indicates that a country was found to be non-compliant with TRIPS obligations for at least one type of intellectual property by the Transatlantic Business Dialogue, a coalition of companies from Europe and North America.

or TABD reflects the relative economic insignificance of IPR violations in these countries, together with the longer TRIPS transition periods foreseen for least developed countries.

Table 14.2 provides an overview of TRIPS-related disputes that, up to February 2000, have been brought to the WTO DSB. The first observation from this table is that only four of the nineteen disputes involved a defendant from a developing country, and two of these four related to the same subject matter – the so-called Indian 'mailbox' disputes. This compares with forty-seven out of 189 disputes with a developing country defendant for all WTO disputes and reflects the transition period for developing countries referred to above. The Indian 'mailbox' disputes stand out in that they were the only TRIPS-related disputes that, so far, have led to the adoption of panel reports. With regard to the US complaint, India decided to appeal against some legal interpretations of the panel report, but the appellate body largely upheld the findings of the original panel. India subsequently complied with the recommendations of the DSB and brought its patent regime into compliance with its TRIPS obligations.

All TRIPS-related disputes so far have been raised by developed countries (in fact, by only three WTO members), compared with around 75 per cent for all WTO disputes (Hoekman and Kostecki 2000). This reflects the 'comparative advantage' of developed countries in commercialising intellectual property in foreign countries. What seems particularly striking about the disputes between developed countries is the extent of reciprocal disputes on closely related matters between the United States and Canada on the one hand, and the EU on the other. These transatlantic rows are a sign of the resolution of mainly the United States and Europe in enforcing the provisions of the TRIPS Agreement but are probably also intended to deter the initiation of future disputes by establishing the threat of credible counter-disputes.

As pointed out by Hoekman and Kostecki (*ibid.*), developing countries are generally disadvantaged in the dispute settlement process because they can commit fewer resources to defending their interests at the WTO, and their enforcement power is significantly weakened by their smaller economic size. In the context of TRIPS-related disputes, this dilemma is probably of less relevance with regard to the initiation of disputes, as hardly any developing economy counts as an important 'exporter' of intellectual property. Nonetheless, there is a potential danger that the few legal resources available to developing countries will be drawn into the defence of their IPR systems, such that little room exists for defending their own export interests.[10]

Has TRIPS and multilateral dispute settlement eliminated or at least reduced unilateral trade measures targeted at alleged IPR violators? As we recall, this expectation represented an incentive for developing countries to sign up to the Agreement. There is undoubtedly an improvement in transparency and objectivity, as disputes on issues covered by TRIPS must go through the WTO dispute settlement mechanism, and trade preferences committed under any WTO agreement can only be removed as determined by the DSB. In this context, the bilateral consultations built into the dispute settlement process

Table 14.2 TRIPS-related disputes at the WTO (as of February 2000)

Month of initial request	Complainant	Respondent	Name of dispute	Status
February 1996	United States	Japan	Measures concerning sound recordings	Mutually agreed settlement
April 1996	United States	Portugal	Patent protection under the Industrial Property Act	Mutually agreed settlement
April 1996	United States	Pakistan	Patent protection for Pharmaceutical and Agricultural Chemical Products	Mutually agreed settlement
May 1996	European Communities	Japan	Measures concerning sound recordings	Mutually agreed settlement
July 1996	United States	India	Patent protection for pharmaceutical and agricultural chemical products ('mailbox')	Panel report found India in violation of its TRIPS obligations. India decided to appeal. Appellate body report largely upheld findings of the panel report. Both reports were adopted in January 1998.
April 1996	European Communities	India	Patent protection for pharmaceutical and agricultural chemical products ('mailbox')	Panel report found India in violation of its TRIPS obligations. Report was adopted in September 1998.
May 1997	United States	Sweden	Measures affecting the enforcement of IPRs	Mutually agreed settlement
May 1997	United States	Ireland	Measures affecting the grant of copyright and neighbouring rights	Pending consultations
May 1997	United States	Denmark	Measures affecting the enforcement of IPRs	Pending consultations

Table 14.2 Continued

Month of initial request	Complainant	Respondent	Name of dispute	Status
December 1997	European Communities	Canada	Patent protection of pharmaceutical products	Active panel
January 1998	United States	European Communities	Measures affecting the grant of copyright and neighbouring rights	Pending consultations
April 1998	United States	Greece	Enforcement of IPRs for motion pictures and television programmes	Pending consultations
April 1998	United States	European Communities	Enforcement of IPRs for motion pictures and television programmes	Pending consultations
December 1998	Canada	European Communities	Patent protection for pharmaceutical and agricultural products	Pending consultations
January 1999	European Communities	United States	Section 110(5) of the US Copyright Act	Active panel
May 1999	United States	Canada	Patent protection term	Active panel
May 1999	United States	Argentina	Patent protection for pharmaceuticals and test data protection for agricultural chemicals	Pending consultations
June 1999	United States	European Communities	Protection of trademarks and geographical indications for agricultural products and foodstuffs	Pending consultations
July 1999	European Communities	United States	Section 211 Omnibus Appropriations Act (related to trademarks)	Pending consultations

Source: World Trade Organization (www.wto.org).

Note: Only those disputes that are centrally related to the TRIPS Agreement are listed. Thus, the dispute on the Indonesian automobile industry, for example, where an alleged violation of the TRIPS Agreement was part of a broader set of measures contested by the complaining members, is not listed here.

have proved to be an effective force of mediation and consultation, defusing differences between members at a technical rather than a political level. However, nothing prevents countries applying unilateral pressure by threatening the removal of trade preferences that go beyond WTO commitments or by other political means, such as threatening cuts in development aid or simple moral persuasion.

Indeed, the United States has continued to put unilateral pressure on countries where it felt that weak IPR systems disadvantaged US companies. The two most prominent cases in this context were the dispute with Argentina on pharmaceutical patents, which in 1997 led to the removal of 50 per cent of Argentina's benefits under the generalised system of preferences (GSP); and the dispute with South Africa, also on pharmaceutical patents, where the USA reached a 'joint understanding' with South Africa in late 1999. The US government did not initiate dispute settlement proceedings under the WTO in these cases, partly because both countries were still under transition with regard to their TRIPS obligations and partly because some aspects of these disputes related to matters where the TRIPS Agreement has no specific obligation (e.g. parallel imports) or where the outcome of WTO arbitration would be highly uncertain (e.g. compulsory licences).[11] Interestingly, the settlement with South Africa was mainly prompted by domestic pressures in the United States, criticising the government's use of trade policy with regard to sensitive health policy issues in developing countries.

Future unilateral actions on TRIPS will to some degree depend on the effectiveness of enforcing compliance with the Agreement through the WTO route. As with other WTO disputes, there is a potential danger that TRIPS violators will employ delaying tactics in implementing the recommendations of the DSB, such as in the widely publicised EU 'bananas' dispute. Moreover, various IPR issues that are economically important (e.g. exhaustion) are not covered by TRIPS, and developed countries may resort to unilateral measures in defending the interests of their IPR producers. Nonetheless, we would argue that the short experience since 1996 points to a positive role of the TRIPS Agreement in terms of enhancing transparency and objectivity with regard to international IPR disputes.[12]

The way to Seattle

In reviewing the 'new' intellectual property agenda that emerged in the context of the ministerial conference in Seattle in December 1999 and that, presumably, would form the basis of a future round of negotiations on IPRs, it is useful to distinguish between two kinds of matter. First, there are issues that are raised by the so-called built-in agenda of the Agreement and by the expiry of various deadlines embedded in the TRIPS Agreement. Second, there are issues where members may seek revisions to the text of the Agreement, either because they are dissatisfied with existing provisions or because they would like to include new articles on matters that are not covered by the existing Agreement.

As for the first set of issues, the expiry of the transition period for developing countries at the beginning of 2000 appears to be the most pressing. Although we recognise the many limitations of the indicators shown in Table 14.1, it seems clear that many developing countries have not yet upgraded their IPR systems to the TRIPS level, raising the possibility of new disputes at the WTO. While no specific proposal was submitted to the Seattle conference, many developing countries have demanded that they be given more time to implement the provisions of the Agreement. This demand has also been reinforced by the dissatisfaction of developing countries with the implementation of the Agreement on Textiles and Clothing by developed countries – the tacitly understood *quid pro quo* for adopting stronger IPRs. Although developed countries are technically compliant with their obligations under the textiles agreement, the extent of actual liberalisation has so far been minimal.[13]

Any extension of deadlines, even on a case-by-case basis, would require changes to the TRIPS Agreement and thus could only be reached by consensus. If developed countries give in to prolongation demands, they are likely to use this concession as a bargaining chip in other areas. This could include the general consent of developing countries on launching a new trade round or relate to specific market-access concessions. Developed countries could be receptive to such a bargain, as they may not be willing to commit the necessary resources to bring a sizeable number of TRIPS disputes to the WTO. An important consideration in this regard is the kind and extent of violations of the TRIPS Agreement. For example, the 'mailbox' provision has already led many developing countries to adopt stronger patent protection for pharmaceutical and chemical products, making prolongation concessions on other less sensitive areas of the Agreement less 'painful'.

As mentioned in the previous section, a second deadline that expired at the end of 1999 was the moratorium on non-violation disputes. In preparation for the Seattle ministerial conference, several developing countries and Canada submitted proposals for an extension of the moratorium, arguing that more time was needed to determine the nature of such disputes in the context of TRIPS. Many countries fear that non-violation disputes may be used to fill certain 'loopholes' in the Agreement or to address IPR-related matters that are not covered by TRIPS. Although the United States signalled that it would veto any extensions of the moratorium, the draft ministerial declaration at Seattle (which was never adopted) contained a recommendation to extend the moratorium until the end of 2002. Judging from the overall experience with non-violation disputes at the WTO, one can also argue that heavy use of such disputes in the TRIPS context appears unlikely in the near future. There seem to be a sufficiently large number of cases of direct violation of the Agreement to be pursued first before launching complicated non-violation proceedings, where the outcome would be highly uncertain and a defeat quite costly.

The third issue of the built-in agenda concerns the patentability of biotechnology inventions. Article 27.3(b) of the TRIPS Agreement foresees patent protection for micro-organisms and non-biological and microbiological processes but allows for the exclusion of patent coverage for plants and animals as well as essentially biological processes for the production of plants and animals. This article also contains a clause that calls for a review of these provisions in 1999. This compromise solution was mainly due to the legal uncertainty in the EU, which at the time of the TRIPS negotiations had not yet passed its biotechnology directive. Although this directive was passed in 1998, and some of the legal uncertainty has been removed, no international consensus has emerged on how to define patentability in this area – in part due to the various controversies over genetically modified food in Europe and elsewhere. As of early 2000, deliberations in the TRIPS Council on Article 27.3(b) had not led to any significant progress towards concluding the review. Given the limited experience with IPRs in this new field of technology, it may be that members decide simply to maintain the *status quo*.

Fourth, the TRIPS Agreement calls for the establishment of a multilateral system of notification and registration of geographical indications for wines and spirits. Moreover, countries agreed to continue negotiations aimed at extending the kind of protection granted to wines and spirits under the TRIPS Agreement to other product areas. However, little progress has been made on both these issues, which reflects to a large degree divisions between the EC, the trading block that hosts the largest number of geographical indications, and the United States, which, in many product areas, is mostly a 'consumer' of such indications and prefers relatively weak levels of protection. During the TRIPS negotiations, which focused mostly on wines and spirits, most developing countries showed little interest in establishing strong provisions on geographical indications. In preparation for the Seattle ministerial conference, several developing countries expressed their support for moving forward with the built-in agenda, mainly with a view to extending strong protection to their own export products (e.g. Darjeeling tea). The draft ministerial declaration recommended that further work be undertaken with regard to geographical indications, in line with the built-in agenda. The EU has also indicated that further negotiations on geographical indications represented one of its priorities. Yet, since there is no consensus on how to proceed between the major trading blocks, it seems likely that strengthening current TRIPS obligations would require trade-offs in other areas that may be negotiated. In addition, it needs to be pointed out that many disputes on geographical indications are on specific names (e.g. with regard to their generic or semi-generic use), which can be resolved effectively only on a bilateral basis, not by a multilateral agreement.

Turning to possible amendments to the TRIPS Agreement, it is first interesting to note that developed countries did not submit any proposal to the Seattle ministerial conference that would strengthen existing provisions or bring new IPR issues under the TRIPS umbrella. This pledge for the *status quo* is certainly not due to complete satisfaction with the reach of the existing agreement. IPR producer lobbies in developed countries have pointed to various areas where they would like to see revisions to the TRIPS Agreement. The most important ones include an obligation for national exhaustion, that is the prevention of parallel imports; more restrictive criteria on the use of compulsory licences; a strengthening of the provision on test data exclusivity; an obligation for patent term restoration, when product marketing is delayed because of government approval procedures; and the incorporation into the TRIPS Agreement of the recent WIPO conventions addressing copyright questions related to electronic commerce.

There are two main reasons why the governments of developed countries have not so far advanced these issues at the WTO. First, before further strengthening the TRIPS Agreement, they would like to see the existing agreement implemented by all WTO members. Arguably, some of the most sensitive issues are already covered by the existing provisions, and enforcing compliance with these provisions is likely to yield the greatest and most immediate benefits to intellectual property producers in industrial countries. The second reason has to do with changes in the political environment and the campaigns of non-governmental organisations (NGOs) with regard to WTO matters. While IPRs were one of the top priorities before and during the Uruguay Round, new governments in the United States and Europe shifted their focus to labour standards, environmental concerns and other topics. NGO criticism targeted the TRIPS Agreement regarding its potential impact on access to medicines in developing countries and its role with regard to genetically modified food.

The only proposals for amendments to the Agreement have actually come from developing countries. The most far-reaching of these concerns the establishment of a multilateral framework within the TRIPS Agreement with regard to the use of genetic resources and traditional knowledge. The motivation behind this initiative stems from concern that the contribution of indigenous resources and knowledge in developing countries to potentially patentable inventions may not be adequately acknowledged and that the owners may not receive appropriate compensation if such inventions lead to commercially successful products. Indeed, so-called 'bio-prospecting' has become a way for some large agricultural and pharmaceutical companies to target new research activities. The Convention on Biological Diversity (CBD) – one of the outcomes of the 1992 Rio Earth Summit – established some guidelines on the use of genetic resources and traditional knowledge, but the specific obligations resulting from this convention remain vague at best.[14]

The various proposals for amending the TRIPS Agreement in this context range from harmonising the text of the Agreement with the provisions of the CBD to, more ambitiously, requiring that patents disclose the origin of genetic resources and establishing a system within the TRIPS Agreement for the protection of the traditional knowledge of local and indigenous communities. However, there is little consensus on how to design such a system, because important questions such as how benefits would be shared within a community have not been addressed in sufficient detail. Only a few countries have considered establishing a legal framework for traditional knowledge at the national level. Moreover, there is great uncertainty with regard to the potential value of indigenous resources and traditional knowledge, raising the risk that developing countries would pay a high negotiating price at the WTO for relatively little economic benefit.

Conclusion

The conclusion of the TRIPS Agreement at the end of the Uruguay Round represented a milestone in two distinct ways. For the multilateral trading system, it was one of the most significant of the so-called 'new issues' that marked the departure from narrow negotiations on border measures towards the establishment of multilateral rules for trade-affecting measures beyond borders. For intellectual property policy making, it represented an international agreement that, for the first time, established minimum standards of protection for all forms of intellectual property and detailed obligations regarding the enforcement of IPRs. Given the diverging interests of countries with regard to IPRs and the uncertainty on the optimality of many IPR standards, this can be considered as no minor achievement. As IPR policies are heavily debated in all jurisdictions around the world and the evolution of technology poses new questions and challenges for existing IPR systems, there is no doubt that the TRIPS Agreement will continue to be a point of contention.

Nonetheless, the Agreement represents an important component of the multilateral trading system, providing fundamental ground rules for international commerce in knowledge- and information-intensive goods. It strikes a pragmatic balance between the enforcement of exclusive rights of IPR holders in WTO member countries on the one hand and the necessary flexibility for countries to design national IPR systems according to their economic needs. The large number of cases on TRIPS matters brought to the WTO's dispute settlement body indicates the willingness of developed countries to use the agreement to advance the commercial cause of their intellectual property producers in foreign countries. In this respect, the TRIPS Agreement has enhanced transparency and objectivity with regard to international IPR disputes and has reduced – but not eliminated – the use of unilateral measures by countries producing intellectual property.

For many developing countries, implementation of the Agreement poses significant institutional and financial challenges. However, we would argue that these challenges relate to achieving pure TRIPS compliance to only a certain extent, being mostly about taking ownership of IPR reforms and establishing a system that serves the needs of local businesses. For example, the WIPO provides technical assistance to developing countries in drafting industrial property laws consistent with the TRIPS Agreement. But how does one address the broader task of creating awareness and designing incentives for using IPRs to stimulate innovation and technology transfer in a developing country context? Only a few developing countries, such as South Korea, have made advances in this regard. For the least developed countries, the TRIPS Agreement is unlikely to become a contentious issue for the foreseeable future. Their transition period expires only in 2005 and may be extended on a case-by-case basis. In addition, the importance of IPR-sensitive goods in their international trade is relatively small, and they do not represent a commercial priority for countries producing intellectual property to pursue.

The prospects for future negotiations on TRIPS in a 'post-Seattle' world are highly uncertain. Among other things, they depend on political developments and future changes in governments; the willingness of WTO members to engage in a broad round of negotiations, thus raising the scope for cross-sectoral trade-offs; the implementation of the Agreement on Textiles and Clothing by developed countries; and the outcomes of current and future WTO disputes related to TRIPS. For the immediate future, it seems likely that developed countries will devote most of their resources to securing implementation of the existing agreement. Developing countries may push for an extension of the implementation deadline, but are unlikely to pay a high 'price' for prolongation if it would only relate to some minor provisions of the Agreement.

For the longer-term future, developed countries may seek to fill some of the 'loopholes' of TRIPS or create obligations on matters that are not covered by the Agreement. Progress on establishing a framework with regard to the use of genetic resources and traditional knowledge will to a large extent depend on the ability of developing countries to define and form a consensus on what should be protected and who owns indigenous resources and knowledge.

Notes

This paper has benefited from interactions with Owen Lippert and comments from Jayashree Watal. The views, interpretations and conclusions expressed here are the authors' own and should not be attributed to the World Bank, its Executive Board of Directors, its management or any of its member countries.

1   Trade secrets also belong to the family of IPRs. They differ from the other types of intellectual property in that no exclusive right is granted to the holder of the trade secret. They only protect the secret holder from acquisition by others using dishonest means, for example through industrial espionage.
2   The other two multilateral agreements are the Multilateral Trade Agreement (MTA) on trade in goods – encompassing the GATT 1994 – and the General Agreement on Trade in Services (GATS). All other WTO Agreements are plurilateral agreements, that is they are only binding to the respective signatory countries.
3   Note, however, while previous the WIPO convention only required national treatment (equal treatment of nationals and non-nationals), TRIPS added the principle of m.f.n. treatment (equal treatment of foreign right holders regardless of their national origin).
4   For a more comprehensive review of the TRIPS Agreement, see Primo Braga (1996). See Primo Braga *et al.* (2000) for a survey of some of these newer economic studies.
5   This view is contested by a recent study analysing market-access commitments made during the Uruguay Round, however. Finger and Schuknecht (1999) found that developing countries scheduled tariff bindings comparable in scope to industrial countries and that tariff reductions were actually deeper than those of developed nations. See also Chapter 5 in this book, by Finger and Schuler.
6   The exhaustion doctrine defines the territorial rights of intellectual property owners after the first sale of their protected products. For a detailed discussion, see Fink (2000).
7   This argument is further elaborated in Primo Braga and Fink (1998).
8   Technically, the TRIPS Agreement does not require ratification of these conventions but only calls for adherence to the principles of these conventions.

9 The Geneva Convention for the Protection of Producers of Phonograms (1971) is not mentioned in TRIPS, but it can be seen as an alternative to the Rome Convention for the Protection of Performers, Producers of Phonograms and Broadcasting Organizations (1961) (which *is* mentioned in TRIPS), as it implies even stronger protection.

10 An additional, potentially significant role of intellectual property with regard to dispute settlement pertains to the removal of TRIPS benefits as a retaliatory device by developing countries to enforce obligations of developed countries under other WTO Agreements. In a ground-breaking ruling related to the EU 'bananas' dispute, the arbitrators in March 2000 granted Ecuador the right to impose $201.6 million worth of trade sanctions against intellectual property rights protecting EU products. At this stage, however, it is still too early to predict the implications of this ruling.

11 Note, however, that in May 1999, the United States initiated a dispute against Argentina at the WTO (see Table 14.2).

12 Even in the US disputes with Argentina and South Africa, the TRIPS Agreement was used – by both sides – as an international benchmark of intellectual property standards.

13 See the discussion by Finger and Schuler in Chapter 5 of this book.

14 See Primo Braga *et al.* (2000) for more information.

References

Fink, C. (2000) 'Entering the jungle of intellectual property rights exhaustion and parallel imports', in O. Lippert (ed.) *Competitive Strategies for Intellectual Property Protection*, Vancouver: Fraser Institute.

Finger, M.J. and Schuknecht, L. (1999) *Market Access Advances and Retreats: The Uruguay Round and Beyond*, Policy Research Working Paper No. 2232, Washington: World Bank.

Finger, M.J. and Schuler, P. (1999) *Implementation of Uruguay Round Commitments: The Development Challenge*, Policy Research Working Paper No. 2215, Washington: World Bank.

Hoekmann, B. and Kostecki, M. (2000) *The Political Economy of the World Trading System*, Oxford: Oxford University Press.

Primo Braga, C.A. (1996) 'Trade-related intellectual property issues: the Uruguay Round agreement and its economic implications', in W. Martin and L.A. Winters (eds) *The Uruguay Round and the Developing Economies*, World Bank Discussion Paper No. 307, Washington: World Bank, 381–411.

Primo Braga, C.A. and Fink, C. (1998) 'Reforming intellectual property rights regimes: challenges for developing countries', *Journal of International Economic Law* 4: 537–54.

Primo Braga, C.A., Fink, C. and Sepulveda, C.P. (2000) *Intellectual Property Rights and Economic Development*, World Bank Discussion Paper No. 412, Washington: World Bank.

15 Agriculture

New wine in new bottles?

Stefan Tangermann

The background

Agriculture was a problem sector in the GATT for a long time. It was often said to have remained largely outside the disciplines governing international trade. Although this view was not quite correct in a legal sense, as the GATT has always applied in full to agriculture as well, it was true that in practice the agricultural policies of many countries had found ways to escape the disciplines that the GATT was meant to establish. Until the early 1990s, most tariffs on agricultural products remained unbound in the GATT; in many cases, agricultural imports were constrained by grey area measures such as variable levies and minimum import prices; some countries maintained quantitative restrictions, whether legal under the special agricultural exception of GATT Article XI:2(c) or not; export subsidies played an important role in agriculture, covered by the agricultural exception of GATT Article XVI:3, and the discipline of the 'equitable share of world export trade' that agricultural export subsidies were supposed to honour proved futile in a number of GATT disputes; domestic subsidies, not disciplined very effectively in the GATT, abounded in agriculture (Josling *et al.* 1996: 111–32).

This situation was changed fundamentally in the Uruguay Round. The Agreement on Agriculture, and the country schedules that went with it, required all members of the newly created WTO to convert all non-tariff measures in agriculture into bound tariffs, to be reduced by agreed rates over an implementation period. To guard against prohibitively high tariffs, minimum access conditions were also agreed. Export subsidies, although not yet prohibited in agriculture, now have to remain within well-defined quantitative limits, also to be gradually reduced over time. Domestic support to farmers, to the extent that it has a noticeable effect on trade, is now constrained by upper bounds and is also declining during the implementation period (*ibid.*: 175–216). The Uruguay Round Agreement on Agriculture did not come easily. Indeed, throughout the negotiations agriculture was one of the most difficult sectors, and when the first attempt was made at concluding the Uruguay Round, in December 1990, the inability to find agreement on agriculture caused a deadlock and required three more years of negotiating effort to bring the overall round to an end.

However, the Uruguay Round Agreement on Agriculture also contained the seeds for another round of negotiations. Some countries (mainly the United States and members of the Cairns Group) would have wanted to go much further in agriculture than proved possible in the Uruguay Round. They managed to convince their more conservative negotiating partners that a clause should be entered into the agreement that required a continuation of the agricultural reform process, in the form of a new round of negotiations to be initiated in 1999. Along with an equivalent provision in the new WTO agreement on services, this requirement to conduct further negotiations in agriculture was one of the reasons why an attempt was made in Seattle, in December 1999, to agree on a new round of WTO negotiations, dubbed the Millennium Round by the European Union, which is interested in using this opportunity to enter into a comprehensive set of negotiations going far beyond the 'built-in' agenda for agriculture and services.

To the surprise of many, the difficulties faced at the Seattle ministerial conference of the WTO had little to do with agriculture. To be sure, agriculture was certainly not an easy sector in the run-up to Seattle and during the conference. However, based on the extensive pre-negotiations that had taken place informally since mid-1997, in the process of 'analysis and information exchange' pursued in parallel with the meetings of the WTO Committee on Agriculture, and taking into account the country positions on agriculture that had already been submitted to the WTO General Council in the course of 1999, negotiators in Seattle came fairly close to agreement on a text that could have formed the starting point for the agricultural element of the Millennium Round. However, the failure of the Seattle ministerial conference to find overall agreement on a new round of comprehensive negotiations eventually took the pressure off the agricultural negotiators, and the draft agenda for the forthcoming agricultural negotiations, which had already been nearly agreed, was dumped. Though some media reports saw a relation between the overall breakdown at Seattle and difficulties in agriculture, this was not really the case. Yes, some agricultural negotiators were happy to construct a link between their interest in the concept of 'multifunctionality' in agriculture and the environmental concerns expressed on the streets of Seattle (although what happened on the streets of Seattle had little to do with the breakdown of the conference). Yes, some developing countries made the point that the repeated dominance of the quarrels between the USA and the EU in the agricultural negotiations was a typical example of how the participation of smaller countries in WTO proceedings is deficient (although it is exactly in agriculture where, through their membership in the Cairns Group, some developing countries have exerted and continue to exert a particularly strong influence on what happens). However, it was pretty clear that – unlike the Brussels ministerial conference in December 1990 – the Seattle ministerial conference did not break up over agriculture.

In fact, it may now turn out that the agricultural negotiations revive the overall talks on a Millennium Round. In spite of the Seattle disaster, WTO agricultural negotiators got together in Geneva on 23–24 March 2000 to begin the process of negotiations mandated in the Uruguay Round Agreement on Agriculture. Though falling somewhat behind the schedule for the agricultural negotiations that had already been drafted in Seattle, they still agreed constructively on at least the programme for a first phase until March 2001, with a minimum of four more negotiating meetings before then (back to back with the regular meetings of the WTO Committee on Agriculture), a call on all countries to submit detailed negotiating proposals by December 2000, and a request to the WTO secretariat to table a number of background papers on various issues. WTO Director-General Michael Moore's comment on the outcome of this agricultural meeting was 'this is the WTO working at its best ... the goodwill shown at this meeting is a good omen for the future' (WTO 2000). If everything goes well, constructive negotiations on agriculture (and services) might now spark progress towards a comprehensive new Millennium Round.

Does this mean that agriculture has moved from its retarding role on the back benches of the GATT to the function of an accelerator at centre stage of the WTO, that agriculture is already in the mainstream of the international trading order, and that all outstanding issues in agriculture will be easily solved in the coming round of negotiations? Unfortunately, this is not really the case. In spite of all the good new rules for agriculture that were agreed in the Uruguay Round, agriculture is still one of the few remaining sectors where market access is restricted by extremely high rates of protection; new forms of import barriers have been created as a by-product of tariffication in the Uruguay Round; export subsidies still play an important role in some countries' agricultural policies and are an exclusively agricultural anomaly of the international trading regime; trade-distorting domestic subsidies to farmers can still be granted at high levels in some countries; the Uruguay Round Agreement on Sanitary and Phytosanitary Measures has not done away with disruptive technical standards in agricultural trade, and new issues such as biotechnology create significant problems; 'non-trade concerns' in agriculture threaten to become a stumbling block in future trade talks; and what is most important, the views of countries on what should happen in the next round of agricultural negotiations still differ widely.[1] The following sections of this chapter will briefly discuss these issues and the resulting agenda for, and options in, the coming round of agricultural negotiations.

Market access

As far as tariff bindings are concerned, agriculture is now ahead of most other sectors because tariffication as agreed in the Uruguay Round has meant that in agriculture almost no cases are left where tariffs are not bound or where quantitative restrictions are still used. Even the most prominent exception from the 'tariffs only' rule in agriculture, i.e. rice in Japan, disappeared in April 1999 when Japan converted its import quota on rice into a (rather high) tariff. However, conversion of the former non-tariff barriers into bound tariffs has, despite an average reduction of 36 per cent (for developed countries) agreed in the Uruguay Round, resulted in many extremely high and often prohibitive tariffs in agriculture, where tariffs in the order of several hundred per cent still exist in many cases. Moreover, tariff rates differ significantly between individual agricultural products in many countries, with the resulting large distortions of allocation in production and consumption. Nearly all countries agree that significant tariff cuts will have to be agreed in the next round. Some countries have also proposed that something needs to be done about tariff peaks. As a minimum, the Uruguay Round approach should not be repeated, because it allowed countries quite some latitude as to how they wanted to allocate average tariff reductions to individual products (with the resulting tendency to cut high tariffs least for the most 'sensitive' products). A much better approach would be to apply a tariff-cutting formula, such as the 'Swiss formula' used for industrial tariffs in the Tokyo Round, that would reduce high tariffs by more than low ones and thereby result in more even tariff profiles.

An issue often discussed in this context is the prevalence in agriculture of applied tariffs significantly below bound rates, as is often found particularly in developing countries. Reducing bound tariffs by agreed rates in such cases would do little to improve actual market access. However, it could be counter-productive in the longer run to adopt this approach, as it might act as a disincentive to implement tariffs below the bound rates in the future. It may be best to agree that future reduction rates have to be applied to the base tariffs from which reductions also started in the implementation period following the Uruguay Round. This would have the additional obvious (and hence political) advantage that reduction rates do not need to be very high in order to achieve significant cuts (as they are applied to a higher base). Another round of 36 per cent reductions on average would then bring agricultural tariffs down to no more than 28 per cent of their Uruguay Round base level, and a third round of reductions by that percentage could then finally eliminate all tariffs in agriculture.

A new phenomenon, brought about as a by-product of tariffication in the Uruguay Round, is the large number of tariff rate quotas now existing in agricultural trade. To guard against prohibitive tariffs resulting from the tariffication of the many rather restrictive non-tariff barriers that existed prior to the Uruguay Round, and in order to counteract 'dirty tariffication' by using 'comfortable' statistical data in the calculation of the new tariff equivalents, minimum access commitments were agreed in the Uruguay Round in the form of tariff rate quotas with lower within-quota tariffs for agreed shares of domestic consumption. While succeeding in opening up new trade opportunities that would not have arisen under the new high tariff bindings, the many tariff rate quotas that now govern agricultural trade have also created new problems. In particular, administration of the licences under these quotas can cause significant discrimination between sources of supply and trading companies, and the implicit distribution of quota rents to licence holders causes headaches (IATRC, forthcoming). The disputes that have arisen over the EU's banana-trading regime (which has not strictly resulted from tariffication in the Uruguay Round – it also involves a large set of other issues) are an illustrative case in point. Agreement on transparent rules for the administration of tariff rate quotas has already been identified by some countries as an item on the agenda for the next round of agricultural negotiations. From the point of view of economics, auctioning of licences would appear to be a particularly attractive approach. However, it would have to be clarified whether (or agreed that) auctioning of licences is legal under the GATT. At the same time, decisions need to be taken in the next round of negotiations on what should happen to within-quota tariff levels and quota volumes. The relationship between within-quota and above-quota tariffs, which was not explicitly regulated in the Uruguay Round and hence differs from country to country and product to product, could now be agreed, for example such that within-quota tariffs must not be above x per cent (say, 10 per cent) of the base tariffs set in the Uruguay Round. On quota volumes, a decision to expand them (by, say, 50 per cent) would mean that, in particular if repeated in a further round of negotiations, the lower within-quota tariffs would gradually take over from the high above-quota tariffs, thus increasingly opening up market access.

Another by-product of tariffication in the Uruguay Round was the introduction of a special safeguard provision in agriculture that allows the newly bound tariffs to be augmented by additional duties if either world market prices decline strongly or the quantities imported rise beyond a certain threshold. Some countries have argued that this provision should be eliminated in the next round, while others are absolutely determined to maintain it. This agricultural anomaly will certainly have to go in the longer run, but for the immediate future a compromise might be to change the parameters in the special safeguard provision in such a way that the additional duties can be charged less frequently, and only at lower rates.

Finally, state trading entities are still used in many countries' agricultural market policies, and even though their import activities should also be disciplined through the market-access commitments that were adopted in the Uruguay Round, it is not quite clear whether that is the case in practice. More stringent rules for importing state trading entities will therefore be on the agenda for the next round of agricultural negotiations.

Export assistance

A big step forward was made in the Uruguay Round when the old GATT provision that essentially gave *carte blanche* for countries to subsidise their agricultural exports was replaced by strict and declining limits on both quantities of subsidised exports and outlays on export subsidies. This new rule in agricultural trade has by and large been honoured to date during the Uruguay Round implementation period (with the exception of Hungary, which sought and obtained a waiver for a few years). In fact, of all the agricultural innovations agreed in the Uruguay Round, the new provisions on export subsidies were expected and turned out to be the ones that were most effective in terms of imposing tangible constraints on the agricultural policies of a number of countries. In the EU, for example, the need to agree to some limits on export subsidies triggered the so-called 'MacSharry reform' of the Common Agricultural Policy in 1992 during the Uruguay Round after the traumatic breakdown of the negotiations in December 1990 had driven the message home to the EU that it had to give something sensible in agriculture before the round could be concluded. Moreover, the further reforms to the EU's agricultural policies agreed as part of the Agenda 2000 package were also largely motivated by the need to bring policies into line with the increasingly tight constraints on export subsidies.

The United States and the Cairns Group would ideally like to see export subsidies in agriculture banned altogether in the next round of agricultural negotiations. Indeed, at some point this agricultural anomaly in the WTO will have to go. However, the EU is not ready for this step in the coming WTO round. To a large extent, export subsidies in agriculture are the EU's problem. For many agricultural products, the EU holds more than 50 per cent of all worldwide 'rights' to export subsidies in the WTO (see Figure 15.1).

However, not all countries make full use of their 'rights' to agricultural export subsidies. For example, the USA has so far made far less than full use of its commitments in this area. The EU, on the other hand, has tended to use its export subsidy commitments fully for many product groups in agriculture. As a

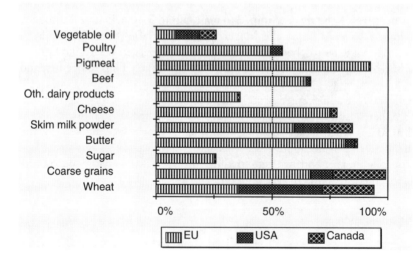

Source: GATT Secretariat (1994), GATT (1994), European Communities (1995).

Figure 15.1 Shares of the EU, the USA and Canada in total worldwide export subsidy commitments (by quantity) on selected agricultural products for 2000

result, the EU's share in worldwide export subsidies actually granted is even higher than its share in commitments. In 1996 (the most recent year for which comprehensive data are available), it stood at 83.5 per cent (see Figure 15.2).

Hence the EU will be the primary target for further negotiations on export subsidies in agriculture. At the same time, the EU's agricultural policies are not yet in a state where the EU could easily agree to very large cuts in this area. For cereals, cereal-based livestock products (such as pork and poultry products) and beef, the reform decisions taken under Agenda 2000 may make it possible for the EU to live without export subsidies, at least in years with favourable world market conditions. For other product groups, such as dairy products, however, the Common Agricultural Policy has not yet been reformed enough to allow the EU to live without export subsidies (Tangermann 1999b). On the other hand, it is clear to EU negotiators that further significant cuts in export subsidies will have to be agreed in the next round, and the EU has already indicated a willingness to negotiate constructively in this area.

As a *quid pro quo*, the EU will want to use the next round to impose discipline on other forms of export assistance that went unconstrained in the Uruguay Round. In particular, some countries, most notably the USA, provide subsidised guaranteed credit for their agricultural exports. The Uruguay Round

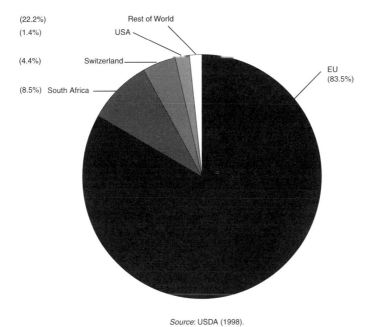

Source: USDA (1998).

Figure 15.2 Countries' shares of total worldwide export subsidies (by value) actually granted in 1996

Agreement on Agriculture contains a clause in which WTO members undertook to work towards the development of internationally agreed disciplines on measures such as export credits. However, nothing was achieved in this area, and hence the next round will have to deal with this unfinished business.

Equally, after the Uruguay Round some countries have changed their policies such that formerly overt export subsidies were granted in less direct forms, mainly financed through price pooling between high-priced domestic sales and lower-priced exports. Canada's dairy regime was found, in a WTO dispute, to have violated the rules on circumvention of export subsidy commitments under the Uruguay Round Agreement on Agriculture. However, negotiators may not want to leave such cases to be dealt with in disputes but may prefer to review the WTO provisions on agricultural export subsidies so that such practices are clearly ruled out.

In the area of agricultural export competition, some countries are also concerned about the activities of state trading entities, typically acting in the form of single-desk sellers (such as the Canadian Wheat Board). The aim in the next round of negotiations is to impose discipline on these agencies. However, it is not exactly clear why such disciplines, rather than being specifically addressed to exporting state trading entities, should not come in the form of more general rules outlawing their criticised practices, such as stringent provisions on export subsidies (preventing price pooling, for example, by exporting state traders, or more effective international rules on competition (guarding against price discrimination and other forms of restrictive business practice).

Domestic support

On domestic subsidies, the Uruguay Round Agreement on Agriculture created a situation in which agricultural policies are in some regards more, in others less, constrained than policies in other sectors. On the one hand, there are now definite quantitative and declining constraints on the extent to which governments can grant certain forms of domestic support to their farmers – a situation that does not exist in other sectors. On the other hand, some agreed types of agricultural subsidy are explicitly exempted from that discipline and are in addition protected under a 'peace clause' until 2003. Moreover, in most countries the quantitative limits on accountable forms of domestic support (i.e. support falling in the so-called 'amber box') have so far proved to be so generous that they have not effectively constrained the policies currently pursued.

The latter factor may gradually change with the further reductions to 'amber box' support that are likely to be agreed in the next round of negotiations. Most countries agree that such reductions should be made, although their rate will not be negotiated easily. Potentially more contentious is the future of the rules for those forms of agricultural subsidy that are exempt from commitments to reduce. They come in two categories. First, there is the 'green box', embracing subsidies that are notionally not, or only minimally, distorting production and trade. Such subsidies, 'decoupled' from production and input use (in the sense of being made not in relation to the volume of production or input use) are generally considered a modern form of agricultural policy far less undesirable than old-fashioned price support. There are good reasons for maintaining the incentive, in the form of exemption from reduction commitments, for governments to change their agricultural policies in the direction of decoupled support. Hence the 'green box' will certainly survive the next round of negotiations.

However, some countries want to define the 'green box' criteria more narrowly, so that support falling in this category is truly not distorting production and trade. Other countries, by contrast, aim at a more generous framework that would allow them to bring some of their preferred policies into that safe haven. It is not at all clear what will come out of this part of the agricultural negotiations.

Second, there is the 'blue box' of domestic support measures also exempt from reduction commitments, although not necessarily production- or trade-neutral. This provision in the Agreement on Agriculture is clearly an anomaly, not least because essentially it was targeted at the policies of only two specific WTO members, the USA and the EU (although a few other countries then also made use of this provision). It was negotiated in the Uruguay Round in order to make it possible for the EU to maintain its compensation payments to farmers, introduced under the MacSharry reform in exchange for the price cuts implemented, and for the USA to cover its deficiency payments to grain producers.

The USA has since, under its agricultural policy reform of 1996 (the 'FAIR Act'), arguably decoupled its payments completely from production and thereby put it in the WTO 'green box'. For a while, therefore, the USA argued strongly against survival of the 'blue box' beyond the next round of negotiations. However, since mid-1999 the USA has been conspicuously silent about the 'blue box', possibly because it is not quite sure whether the large extra 'disaster' payments it made to its farmers in 1998 and 1999 (and may make again in election year 2000) are really 'green' (Tangermann 1999a). This has left the Cairns Group, for the time being, as the only strong opponent of the 'blue box'. It will be interesting to see whether this provides the EU with a better opportunity to defend the further existence of this provision – a matter of significant importance for the EU as its 'amber box' is not nearly large enough to cover all the payments it is making to its farmers (Tangermann 1999b).

Another extremely important matter for the EU is an extension of the 'peace clause' beyond its current expiry date in 2003. The protection from WTO proceedings against domestic subsidies that the 'peace clause' now provides is far from complete but also far better than nothing. The EU is therefore strongly interested in an extension of the 'peace clause'. In a way this is understandable, because the meaning of the provisions on domestic support contained in the Agreement on Agriculture, and of the quantitative country commitments going along with them, is not really clear if domestic support that is in line with these provisions can still be attacked under other provisions of the GATT and the WTO. In any case, the expiry of the 'peace clause' in 2003 provides a healthy stimulus, for the EU and other countries interested in that provision, to conduct constructive negotiations in the next few years, because there will be little if any chance to extend the validity of the 'peace clause' after 2003 if the rest of agriculture has not yet been successfully negotiated.

'Non-trade concerns' and other new issues

In the preparations for the next round of agricultural negotiations, a new term has been injected into the international debate about agricultural policies – 'multifunctionality' of agriculture. This new catchphrase refers to the notion that farmers not only produce agricultural products for the market but also provide other services to society, such as maintenance of the countryside, economic stability for rural regions, and provision of food security. Countries that strongly advocate this concept in international debate, such as the EU, Japan, Norway and Korea, refer to those clauses in the Uruguay Round Agreement on Agriculture that mention 'non-trade concerns' in the context of current and future reforms of agricultural policies and argue that these concerns will have to play a crucial role in the next round of negotiations.

It is reasonably clear why the advocates of 'multifunctionality' stress this concept so much – at the international level they want to guard against much stronger constraints on their agricultural policies in the next round of WTO negotiations, and at home they try to signal to their farmers that their interests will be taken care of in international negotiations. However, it is far less clear whether and how this concept could possibly be integrated into the WTO rules for agriculture in any meaningful way that does not yet exist. Economics speaks clearly against allowing a country higher tariffs or larger export subsidies because its agriculture plays a (larger than international average?) 'multi-functional' role. The proponents of agricultural trade liberalisation, such as the USA and the Cairns Group, know this and will strongly resist such attempts. It is at best in areas of domestic support where policies targeted at 'multifunction-ality' could possibly be justified, but in this regard the 'green box' already provides sufficient shelter for policies that respond to these 'non-trade' concerns. It is also notable that none of the devoted friends of 'multifunction-ality' has so far come up with a concrete proposal for how this concept should be integrated into the next round of negotiations. If all goes well, therefore, at the end of the next round 'multifunctionality' will be seen to have been nothing more than a red herring.

Much more real, however, and at the same time more difficult to deal with, are other issues that have recently plagued international trade in agricultural and food products, completely unrelated to traditionally contentious factors such as tariffs and subsidies. For example, in some parts of the world consumers are increasingly concerned about modern food production technologies.

As such, this would not necessarily become a trade problem if all countries were in the same situation in this regard. Markets would then universally respond to these concerns by supplying those products that consumers want to eat, or governments would step in and set corresponding standards. However, different countries feel differently about these issues and hence adopt different standards and production technologies. As a result, some countries do not want to open up their markets to products that are considered completely innocent in other parts of the world. The dispute over beef hormones between the USA and the EU is one such case, and much larger volumes of trade are potentially affected by different views on the desirability of food produced using genetic technology.

It was hoped that the Agreement on Sanitary and Phytosanitary Measures negotiated in the Uruguay Round would overcome differences in the regulatory standards of different countries in agricultural and food products trade. However, one central concept in this agreement, i.e. scientific evidence as a basis for acceptable standards, does not cover consumer concerns of this kind, because they do not necessarily rely on scientific evidence.

The standard response of economists and others to this problem is that labelling can do the trick where consumer concerns are not supported by any scientific evidence that would call for, or at least justify, government-regulated standards. However, there are a number of cases where labelling is neither an effective or desirable response (Tangermann 1999a). In such cases, international agreement on standards that go beyond scientific evidence may be appropriate. It will be interesting to see whether the next round of negotiations can come up with new solutions to these types of problem.

Somewhat similar are issues that arise where concerns for environmental goods or animal welfare differ between countries. As long as it relates to environmental goods of a local nature, economics does not speak for international trade measures to support national environmental policies, although producers 'suffering' from demanding domestic standards, and politicians sympathising with them, tend to argue for compensation for what they see as competitive disadvantages in comparison with producers in countries with less stringent legislation. However, where global environmental commons and animal welfare (arguably a global common) are concerned, the situation is different. Countries enacting national standards that protect such global commons make life more difficult for domestic producers, and may then find that their objectives are not reached because production moves to other countries where the same global commons are not protected.

A case in point is the new rules on minimum space per laying hen in batteries recently decided in the EU. This regulation will mean that production costs for eggs in the EU are considerably above those in the USA and other countries where hens can be held in much smaller space. Under certain conditions, this could mean that the EU market is swamped by imports from countries with less demanding standards. If this were to happen, the intended benefit of the EU regulation for animal welfare would not materialise, because production of eggs for the EU market would move to countries where hens are not held in accordance with the conditions the EU considers appropriate. Could the EU then use economic measures that would ensure that egg production in the EU could continue, so that the intended benefit for animal welfare materialises? Under current WTO rules this would not be possible. Discussions on issues like these may also (have to) play a role in the next round.

Conclusions

In some regards, the coming agricultural negotiations in the WTO may appear like old wine in new bottles. The framework for these negotiations, i.e. the Uruguay Round Agreement on Agriculture, is new, but with the large slack existing in most quantitative commitments agreed for the current implementation period, it has not yet imposed very demanding constraints on agricultural policies. Moreover, country positions still appear to resemble the traditional attitudes, with the EU, Japan, Norway, Korea and other countries defending their protectionist agricultural policies, while agricultural free traders like the USA and the Cairns Group push for rapid liberalisation. The result of the negotiations could then be minor amendments to existing rules and minimal further reductions of protection and support for agriculture. There is certainly some likelihood in this perspective, and in the end it may turn out that this is exactly what the Millennium Round negotiations on agriculture were about.

However, if everything goes well, agriculture in the Millennium Round can also become new wine in new bottles. After the Uruguay Round had yielded the Agreement on Agriculture, multilateral agricultural negotiations will never again be like they were. There is no longer any need to consider what should be done about traditional agricultural import protection in the form of variable levies and quantitative restrictions: they have all given way to bound tariffs. Debates about the appropriate nature of disciplines on agricultural export subsidies are a matter of the past: the well-defined quantitative commitments agreed in the Uruguay Round will not be done away with. Whether there should be quantitative constraints on trade-distorting domestic support in agriculture need not be discussed: they do exist. And it is very reassuring in this regard to note that in the preparations for the next round of agricultural negotiations no single country, and not even one with the most protectionist agricultural policy makers, has indicated the slightest inclination to fall back fundamentally behind the new rules and commitments for agricultural policies that were agreed in the Uruguay Round (Tangermann 1999a).

Without doubt, the next round of negotiations on agriculture starts from the *status quo post* the Uruguay Round, not where the deficient GATT rules for agriculture stood in the mid-1980s. It is a completely different matter to negotiate refinements to the new rules and further reduction rates for bound tariffs, constrained export subsidies and limited domestic support than to start from scratch in a negotiating environment in which none of these fixed points exists. This different starting position alone will make the agricultural negotiations of the Millennium Round very different from those of the Uruguay Round.

Meanwhile, the state of affairs in international agricultural policy making has moved on. Agricultural policies are being reformed worldwide (Josling 1998a). The reforms to the EU's Common Agricultural Policy decided in 1992 and 1999, the FAIR Act adopted in the USA in 1996, and the many policy reforms implemented in Latin America since the 1980s are cases in point. This is not to say that agricultural protectionism has already disappeared altogether. Protection is still far too high in many countries' agriculture, and the direct government payments that have replaced some part of the old-fashioned price support and export subsidies in a number of countries are still both too high and not sufficiently decoupled from production in many cases.

However, it appears that the trend has been reversed in agricultural policies on a global level, and there is now a much better understanding of the need to get away from heavy-handed government interference in agricultural markets. With some cautious optimism, it is conceivable that on this basis it will be possible in the next round of agricultural negotiations to agree on significant further reductions of protection and support.

This does not necessarily mean that the negotiations on agriculture will be easy. The refinements of the Uruguay Round rules on agriculture that are on the agenda for the next round of trade talks will require negotiators to look into technically complicated matters. Countries still like to ride their hobby horses in agriculture, and the new emphasis that some governments place on 'non-trade concerns', alias the 'multifunctionality' of agriculture, will cause headaches for the negotiations. Moreover, new issues such as differences between countries in the areas of consumer concerns about modern food production technologies, environmental policies in agriculture and standards for animal welfare are complex and difficult to deal with.

However, it appears that most countries are seriously committed to negotiating these matters in a constructive way. If that continues to be the case when negotiations enter their decisive phase in late 2002 or early 2003, then it may turn out that agriculture is no longer a stumbling block in multilateral trade negotiations but can make a productive contribution to overall progress in the Millennium Round.

Notes

1   On implementation of the Uruguay Round Agreement on Agriculture in major countries and the current state of play in agricultural trade policies, see IATRC (1994; 1997), Tangermann (1996), Josling and Tangermann (1999) and Sumner and Tangermann (forthcoming). Issues and options for the next round of agricultural negotiations are also discussed in Tangermann (1997) and Josling (1998a). Positions of major developed countries on the next round of agricultural negotiations are reviewed in Tangermann (1999a).

References

European Communities (1995) *Schedule CXL, Part IV – Agricultural Products: Commitments Limiting Subsidization* [provisional Schedule revised after EU enlargement]. Brussels: European Commission.
GATT (1994) *Schedules of Market Accession Concessions*, electronic version.

GATT Secretariat (1994) *The Results of the Uruguay Round of Multilateral Trade Negotiations. Market Access for Goods and Services: Overview of the Results*, November.

International Agricultural Trade Research Consortium (IATRC) (1994) *The Uruguay Round Agreement on Agriculture: An Evaluation*, IATRC Commissioned Paper No. 9, St Paul, Minn.: IATRC.

—— (1997) *Implementation of the Uruguay Round Agreement on Agriculture and Issues for the Next Round of Agricultural Negotiations*, IATRC Commissioned Paper No. 12, St Paul, Minn.: IATRC.

—— (forthcoming) *Issues in the Administration of Tariff-Rate Import Quotas in the Agreement on Agriculture in the WTO*, IATRC Commissioned Paper No. 13, St Paul, Minn.: IATRC.

Josling, T. (1998a) 'The Uruguay Round Agreement on Agriculture: a forward looking assessment', paper presented at the OECD workshop on emerging trade issues in agriculture, Paris, 26–27 October 1998, Paris: OECD (Document COM/AGR-/CA/TD/TC/WS(98)100).

—— (1998b) *Agricultural Trade Policy: Completing the Reform*, Washington: Institute for International Economics.

Josling, T. and Tangermann, S. (1999) 'Implementation of the WTO Agreement on Agriculture and developments for the next round of negotiations', *European Review of Agricultural Economics* 26(3): 371–88.

Josling, T., Tangermann, S. and Warley, T.K. (1996) *Agriculture in the GATT*, Houndmills and New York.: Macmillan and St Martin's Press.

Sumner, D. and S. Tangermann (forthcoming) 'International trade policy and negotiations', in B. Gardner and G. Rausser (eds) *Handbook of Agricultural Economics*, Amsterdam: Elsevier Science.

Tangermann, S. (1996) 'Implementation of the Uruguay Round Agreement on Agriculture: issues and prospects', *Journal of Agricultural Economics* 47(3): 315–37.

—— (1997) *A Developed Country Perspective of the Agenda for the Next WTO Round of Agricultural Negotiations*, SFIO Occasional Paper, WTO Series No. 5. Geneva: Institute of Graduate Studies.

—— (1999a) 'Interests and options in the WTO 2000 negotiations on agriculture: developed countries', paper prepared for the conference on 'Agriculture and the New Trade Agenda from a Development Perspective: Interests and Options in the Next WTO Negotiations', organised by the World Bank, Geneva, 1–2 October 1999.

—— (1999b) 'Europe's agricultural policies and the Millennium Round', *World Economy* 22(9): 1155–78.

US Department of Agriculture (USDA) (1998) *Agriculture in the WTO*, Economic Research Service, International Agriculture and Trade Reports, Situation and Outlook Series, WRS-98-4, December, Washington: USDA.

WTO (2000) *What's New*, press release 172. [http://www.wto.org/ wto/new/ Press172.htm. Geneva, 27 March 2000.]

16 Regionalism and multilateralism – side by side

Gerhard Fisch

Introduction

Multilateralism is dead. We are at the beginning of a new wave of regionalism. Is this the conclusion that can be drawn from the failed negotiations in Seattle? Presumably not, but the negotiations dramatically revealed the major shortcomings of the WTO as a multilateral forum for advancing trade liberalisation. And Seattle showed something else: trade negotiations are becoming increasingly complex. International trade impinges on all areas of national policy making. The debate about environmental and social standards in Seattle is just one example of this. This phenomenon can also be observed in the day-to-day work of the WTO in Geneva. National patent rights, competition policy, health standards and their potentially negative effects on trade show the growing interaction between trade policy and other policies.

This raises the question of whether a multilateral institution can achieve such an ambitious task, which requires a huge amount of policy coordination. The internal decision-making process, in particular the principle of 'one country, one vote' and the increasing heterogeneity of member countries, makes it virtually impossible to reach an agreement. In addition, major players like the USA, which previously had actively supported further trade negotiations, were very reluctant to take the lead in Seattle. The outcome of Seattle was disappointing. But will this be the end of multilateral trade negotiations? Do we stand at the beginning of a new wave of regional trade agreements (RTAs)? There is no clear answer, but presumably RTAs will become more appealing following Seattle, and the phenomenon of RTAs is likely to be discussed in greater depth in the future. The traditional discussion has to be broadened. We have to recognise the positive impact that RTAs have on international integration. We have to ask how this positive role in international trade can be enhanced. And we have to consider the role of the WTO in a world in which regionalism and multilateralism coexist.

New developments in regionalism

Since the early 1990s, the number of RTAs has increased rapidly in scope and coverage. The number of RTAs notified to the GATT/WTO has exceeded the total number of WTO members and reached 198 in 1999. Almost all WTO members are party to one or more RTAs. During the 1990s, regional and multilateral trade liberalisation have progressed side by side, with regional integration increasingly driving the growth in international trade and liberalisation efforts.

What's new in the process of regionalism?

1.   Almost all RTAs show an inherent dynamic towards greater liberalisation and open markets. The modern motivation for forming RTAs is to open up markets and promote competition; this contrasts sharply with the inward-looking, import-substituting regionalism of the 1950s and 1960s. In fact, RTAs have brought about liberalisation in areas such as services and investment on a scale unlikely to be seen at the multilateral level for some years to come. Increasing competition is seen as a source of economic growth that will ultimately benefit the non-members of RTAs as well. The best example of this free market orientation is the EU, where a single market and a common currency were introduced to strengthen internal competition and external competitiveness, among other reasons. The best-known exception is the EU's Common Agricultural Policy.

In the Americas, trade has increased significantly between the USA, Mexico and Canada as a result of NAFTA. Recently, regionalism has received a major boost from the plans to create the Free Trade for the Americas (FTAA). The negotiations, aimed at progressively eliminating barriers to the trade in goods, services and investment, are to be concluded no later than 2005. The four members of MERCOSUR have decided to introduce a common external tariff by 2006.

In Asia, the geese are flying again. Members of the Association of South-East Asian Nations (ASEAN) are accelerating trade liberalisation within the ASEAN Free Trade Area (AFTA). In the common effective preferential tariff of AFTA, each of the six founding members agreed to achieve a minimum of 85 per cent of the tariff lines of its inclusion list in the 0–5 per cent range by 2000, covering 90 per cent of intra-ASEAN trade. The targets of APEC to open their markets in trade and investment are very ambitious.

Regional integration has also gained importance in Africa. The initiatives of the Southern African Customs Unions (SACU), the Common Market for Eastern and Southern Africa (COMESA) and the progress towards regional integration in the West African Economic Monetary Union (WAEMU) show the growing significance of regional cooperation in a continent where trade flows have traditionally been oriented towards the former colonial powers in Europe.

These global trends show that regionalism is very much on the march worldwide. The liberalisation process is advancing far more quickly at the regional level than at the multilateral level. However, it must be recognised that the political will to achieve greater liberalisation varies across regions. Each RTA has its own history, its own motivation and its own dynamic. Differences in the level of development, culture and the degree of regional division of labour play an important role in determining the specific speed of integration, as do the level and dynamic of internal heterogeneity.

2. The new regionalism is bringing with it an increase in the size of regional groupings, and there are a variety of reasons for this. The political objective of stabilising reform processes in neighbouring countries is one of the central arguments for enlargement. Others are the desire to wield greater negotiating power, the self-perpetuating momentum of institution building and economic motives, such as opening up new markets in neighbouring countries. As RTAs discriminate against outsiders, non-members may respond to this situation by trying to join the club, which gives rise to a domino theory of regionalism (Winters 1998). Whatever the specific reason, more and more countries are ultimately participating in regional trade liberalisation and benefiting from it. This tendency contradicts the thesis of regionalism as a stumbling block.

The best example of the inherent enlargement dynamic can be seen in the EU. The accession negotiations with Cyprus, the Czech Republic, Estonia, Hungary, Poland and Slovenia are well underway. In December 1999, the EU opened the door to future membership to another group of countries, including Turkey. The success of the EU's enlargement process depends to a large extent on the success of the necessary institutional reforms. This touches on the very sensitive topic of national sovereignty.

3. There is the emergence of overlapping regionalism or, in the words of Bhagwati, the spaghetti bowl of regional integration. The best-known example of this is APEC, but it can also be observed in Europe as well as in Africa (WAEMU and ECOWAS), where countries belong to more than one RTA. This can be interpreted as another step towards open regionalism. Taking a more critical view, however, overlapping regionalism can be said not to promote transparency in international trade at all. Rules of origin, in particular, are a source of concern, as they impose additional requirements and costs on firms with international operations.

4. Modern regional integration is about more than just building a free trade area or a customs union. Regionalism covers many issues beyond the removal of barriers to trade in goods and services, such as social policy, environmental policy and competition policy. The issues on the Seattle agenda, namely the differences in environmental and social standards and their impact on international trade, are also on the agenda of RTAs. Higher levels of regional integration automatically raise the question of system competition or harmonisation of national standards. From this standpoint, virtually all policy areas and practices are affected by RTAs. The internal dynamic of each RTA is therefore becoming increasingly difficult to predict. There is no guarantee that the process of regional trade liberalisation is automatic and irreversible.

In this context and as a consequence of the growth in number and scope of RTAs, the heterogeneity of the regional grouping takes on greater significance. Heterogeneity of development levels, together with the desire for policy coordination, impinge on the internal decision-making process. Free internal trade with different levels of environmental and social protection rules might cause conflicts between member states. The general issue of the division of labour between countries at different stages of development is connected to this.

5. RTAs exist in all regions of the world. They are no longer the privilege of industrialised countries. Developing countries are becoming active players in the game of regionalism. Increasing trade between developing countries might be one result.

6. RTAs follow a strategy that combines internal liberalisation with external liberalisation agreements. This is not only the case in the EU, where the large number of external agreements is a very dynamic element of integration. Under the Euro-Mediterranean free trade area initiative, bilateral free trade agreements with a number of countries have either been concluded or are about to be concluded. In order to foster cross-regional integration, there are ongoing negotiations with the USA, Mexico, MERCOSUR, APEC and ASEM. This underlines the thesis that modern regionalism is not oriented towards bloc building or protectionism but at creating open markets.

7. Regionalism in its present form can be described as a process driven by many motivations. Reasons for the rapid expansion of RTAs include frustration with the slow pace of multilateral negotiations, a desire to benefit from stronger competition and economies of scale, a response to the formation of RTAs in other regions, the prospect of increasing one's negotiating power within the international community and the prospects of enhanced growth as the larger markets attract both domestic and foreign investment.

8. Regionalism is undoubtedly on the rise. The depth and breadth of regional integration has far exceeded the expectations originally entertained when Article XXIV of the GATT was formulated. What was thought to be an exception to the rule of multilateralism and non-discrimination became the rule. However, modern regionalism is generally of a benign character that is compatible with the overall aims of the multilateral trade order.

Experience with existing WTO rules

The GATT has always allowed some exceptions to the guiding principle of non-discrimination (m.f.n. status). The relevant rules concerning RTAs are (1) Paragraphs 4 to 10 of Article XXIV of GATT, which refer to the formation and operation of customs unions and free trade areas, (2) the so-called enabling clause, which governs preferential trade arrangements between developing country members; and (3) Article V of the GATS, which covers the formation of RTAs covering trade in services.

WTO members are required to give notification of the RTAs in which they participate. In the period 1948–94, GATT members gave notification of 118 RTAs, and since the creation of the WTO in 1995, eighty additional RTAs have been notified. Of the 198 RTAs notified to the GATT/WTO, 119 are currently in force (WTO 1999).

All RTAs notified are examined by the Committee on Regional Trade

Agreements (CRTA), founded in 1996. In these reviews, the other WTO member states seek to obtain information on the legal and procedural aspects of the implementation of these agreements and on their economic dimension. The RTA under review must be shown to conform with the relevant WTO rules. In addition, the CRTA is responsible for examining the systemic implications of RTAs for multilateral trade and making appropriate recommendations to the General Council.

The work of the CRTA has not been a resounding success. Ongoing CRTA examinations have been delayed, and not a single report has been adopted since the establishment of the WTO. The CRTA admitted in its report to the General Council in 1998 that the delay in examination was 'slowed, *inter alia*, by a lack of consensus on the interpretation of certain elements of those rules relating to regional trade agreements' (*ibid.*).

The CRTA has also failed to make progress in addressing systemic issues. One example that illustrates the difficulties encountered is the discussion within the working group about the interpretation of the terms 'substantially all the trade' and 'substantial sectoral coverage'. A similar level of controversy surrounds the interpretation of the requirement that the level of trade barriers be 'not on the whole higher or more restrictive'.

There are a number of reasons for this lack of progress. First, existing WTO rules are open to a variety of interpretations and lack the precision necessary to form the basis for any credible examination process. In its report on regionalisation, the WTO states: 'The Uruguay Round made only limited progress in removing the ambiguities plaguing the interpretation of Article XXIV, while adding similarly worded provisions for services' (WTO 1995). Moreover, the WTO principle of consensus makes the search for operational solutions difficult. Second, most countries are members of at least one RTA. Their interest in binding WTO rules is very limited. So it was not surprising that only a few countries actively attempted to bring RTAs on to the agenda of a comprehensive new round of trade negotiations after Seattle. Only Hong Kong, China, Hungary, Turkey, Japan, Korea and Australia had formulated proposals to improve the existing rules.

Why regions matter

The academic interest in RTAs is dominated by the question of whether regionalism is a building block or a stumbling block for multilateralism. A conclusive answer to this question has not yet been found – and the chances of this happening are slim. In assessing a world of 'second best', Lawrence's (1996) verdict is positive, while Bhagwati and Panagariya (1996) are less confident about the benefits of RTAs in general. Numerous empirical studies on this issue have also produced a variety of outcomes. One cannot but support Anne Krueger when she says that 'it is to be hoped that empirical examination and analysis of outcomes will greatly expand in the next few years' (1999).

What is common to most of the studies about RTAs is the negative comments they draw from trade economists. Primarily, this is because most economists regard total liberalisation at the multilateral level as the right point of reference for assessing regional integration. Another common feature of these studies is their focus on rather narrowly defined and specific aspects, while other aspects receive little attention. Much has been said about the relationship between regionalism and multilateralism, but there is a big black box concerning a positive theory of regionalism (Speyer 1997). The further development of theory relating to regionalism seems to be of no interest to researchers.

This will probably change following the failure of negotiations in Seattle and the growing awareness of the inherent structural deficits in the WTO. A renewed academic interest in RTAs is therefore more than welcome. Theoretical and empirical studies about RTAs must be broader and less dogmatic. RTAs have always been part of economic reality and will continue to be so. They are part of a very dynamic process of trade liberalisation, so greater emphasis needs to be placed on research into RTAs *per se*, not only on their interplay with multilateral trade negotiations.

Regional integration is about much more than trade creation and trade diversion. Although traditional integration theory has been extended with dynamic elements of the so-called new trade theory, and although new elements like economies of scale and intra-industry trade have enriched the discussion about regional integration, there is still some scope for further analysis. In the following, I shall contribute to this discussion and attempt to show why RTAs *per se* are not a bad thing.

One reason for the bad press that regionalism receives is the reference point of global liberalisation. From the neo-classical point of view, there is no reason to question the validity of this reference point. RTAs are a second-best solution. But maybe it is better to have a second-best solution than a third-best solution gained from striving for the best solution. Many RTAs have been created because of the disappointing results of multilateralism. They are created and enlarged because the member countries aim to improve the competitiveness of their economies in an open market. The open-minded character of modern regionalism is demonstrated by the numerous preferential arrangements with outsiders. Meanwhile, the web of trade agreements between different regional groupings is growing rapidly, so it has to be said that as long as no further progress is made towards multilateral liberalisation, RTAs represent one means of pursuing a strategy of open markets and free trade.

A second issue that has been discussed is deeper integration. Lawrence (1996) was one of the first to focus on this. Regional integration is often much more than simple trade liberalisation. Rather, RTAs are one possible answer to the challenges of deeper integration issues. From a trade policy point of view, the idea is that international trade includes more issues than just trade barriers such as tariffs and non-tariff measures. It encompasses all the political actions of individual countries and raises the question of how to deal with cultural and geographical differences.

Underlying this perspective is the notion that comparative advantages are not the result of hidden hands. They are man-made. We do not live in a world of neo-classical economics, in which societies are considered as black boxes connected by exchange rates. What goes on inside the box is quite important (Lorenz 1998). National tax systems, the social order, domestic institutions and the system of state intervention all combine to produce comparative advantage. International trade policy cannot be separated from the general policy mix of a country. Therefore, it is not surprising that international trade negotiations at the WTO are now concerned with many issues, such as health standards, national patent law and national competition rules, that go far beyond the removal of traditional trade barriers. And there is often a conflict between trade objectives and other political objectives, which can lead to the imposition of non-tariff trade barriers. A closer alignment of national policies is necessary to help to reduce tensions arising from differences in national policies and their impact on trade.

Ultimately, this leads to the fundamental question of whether a particular national policy measure is motivated by trade considerations. Do national environmental standards reflect a special desire of the population for a safe environment and sustainable growth? Are they an attempt to keep out products from other countries with lower environmental standards for environmental reasons or are they merely protectionist measures? The conflict of policy targets is obvious. The quest for national autonomy conflicts with WTO obligations as well.

The concept of deeper integration focuses on the question of the balance between trade liberalisation and policy coordination. It also points to additional criteria for RTAs. Efficiency and optimal factor allocation are the only criteria for assessing integration and should remain so. What we need is a balance between free trade and national preferences for independent policy making, in other words a balance between the welfare-enhancing power of competition and the desire of societies to devise an adequate policy mix, including environmental and social standards as well as distribution and adjustment policy (Rodrik 1997).

Why then is regionalism a better way of solving this inherent conflict? To the neo-classical economist, the optimum economic space is the world. Global liberalisation leads to optimum factor allocation, the most efficient use of resources and, consequently, to optimum global welfare. An alignment of economic and other policies is not on the agenda at all. This seems insufficient. In the following, I will discuss some factors supporting the idea that the optimal economic space is somewhere between the world and the nation-state: the region. I will focus on three aspects: internal decision-making structures, economic geography and the advantages of North–South integration in a regional context.

Internal decision-making structures need to be addressed in connection with the issue of deeper integration. Deeper integration can best be realised in regions of like-minded countries with overlapping preferences. It is unreasonable to imagine that a global institution like the WTO, with 136 member states at very different stages of economic development and with widely differing economic, political and cultural traditions, can effect the necessary policy coordination. The heterogeneity of WTO members, which will probably increase further with the accession of China and other countries in transition, not only prevents efficient further liberalisation of trade but more significantly also prevents policy coordination. The analysis of the political economy of integration supports this argument (Guerrieri and Padoan 1989). The classical prisoner's dilemma problems are less relevant at a regional level.

Countries are generally unwilling to give up major aspects of their political sovereignty, but they may be less resistant at the regional level. Regionalism is one way of encouraging greater convergence of policies and standards.

The second reason for focusing more heavily on the regions as the relevant economic space has emerged with the renewed academic discussion about economic geography and the issue of natural integration areas. Geographical and cultural proximity have a positive impact on trade, and this argument still has its validity in the modern world of information and communications technology. The economic space replaces the nation-state when regional integration policy reduces restrictions based on national borders. Agglomeration effects and regional spillover will become more important in determining location. National trade policy will have less impact on the direction of trade flows (Krugman 1993; Lorenz 1992).

The concept of economic proximity is based on the relevance of transaction costs. In recent years, the ideas of economic geography have gained relevance in the discussion about trade and growth theory. The empirical phenomena of clusters and centres of gravity are not congruent with political borders.

This brings us to the third factor, the integration of the less developed countries. The concept of economic proximity is based on economies of scale and spatially limited spillover effects. In such an imperfect world, there is no guarantee of economic convergence or, therefore, overall development. Trade liberalisation between countries with different levels of development does not automatically lead to a rapid catch-up by the less developed countries.

Multilateral liberalisation, even with some privileges for developing countries, has not led to a universal convergence of income levels. Since the degree and speed of global North–South integration leave something to be desired, it might be helpful to ask whether and under which conditions RTAs can play a less universal but more successful role in the integration of developing countries into the international division of labour.

Geographically and spatially limited North–South integration relates to the issue of the optimum size of a region. One decisive factor is the heterogeneity of the group, or, in terms of economic geography, the relative size of the centre and the periphery (Schott and Hufbauer 1999).

The process of catching up by less developed countries depends to a large extent on their ability to compete in the global market. The increased relevance of capital-intensive production, economies of scale and technological infrastructure as determinants of comparative advantage lead to different views on the division of labour between countries at different stages of development. Cheap labour – the traditional comparative advantage of developing countries –

plays a central role, together with the ability of these countries to imitate and adapt the technologies from industrialised countries.

In connection with the imitation and adaptation of new technologies, the process of development depends on the cycle of innovation and imitation. Time is the decisive factor. The earlier imitation sets in, the greater the competitive pressure in the innovating countries. A natural reaction to such pressure to adjust is the call for protectionism: either countries and firms try to hinder the diffusion of innovation in order to safeguard their innovation rents, or national governments support the development of new technologies in a neo-mercantilist manner with all kinds of state aid. Thus, neo-protectionism reflects exactly the balance of innovation and imitation.

Competitive pressure also grows with an increasing number of imitating countries. Conversely, this means that with less adjustment pressure the desire for protectionism decreases. This raises the questions of the optimum size of an RTA and the optimum combination of centre and periphery.

At a regional level, this problem can be ameliorated by the redistribution of resources to poorer areas, e.g. by the financing of infrastructure projects. The success of north–south integration in the EU is a good example of how this can work. The positive effects of the NAFTA on Mexico also show that geographically limited North–South integration can work effectively.

Coexistence of regionalism and multilateralism

We have to accept that we live in a world of RTAs. If multilateral negotiations are unsuccessful and the multilateral level proves an inadequate forum, regionalism might be one way to promote and secure trade liberalisation. Regionalism has its own justification as a strong element in a liberal world economy (Speyer 1997).

In particular, the regional level can be the appropriate arena for deeper integration. It is a viable base for the geographically limited but potentially more successful integration of developing countries. Regionalism might be an appropriate base for further trade liberalisation and more dynamic competition, where the side effects of adjustment and the willingness to adjust can be dealt with effectively. It is one potential means of safeguarding the increased prosperity generated by trade liberalisation, as long as the WTO is unable to find solutions to the conflict resulting from the connection between trade policy and national policy mix and as long as there is no real progress in further multilateral negotiations. Regionalism and multilateralism can coexist, and in fact both can play constructive roles in creating a framework for further increases in prosperity.

Acknowledging the existence and the positive function of RTAs, the question is: what role should the WTO play? In a world of RTAs, the role of the WTO and other multilateral organisations consists of devising regulations that specify how much RTAs can deviate from multilateral rules of non-discrimination. Krueger (1999) has pointed out that there is little reason to advocate that the WTO should seek to outlaw RTAs, because RTAs are here to stay. Rather, research should focus on finding ways of avoiding regional bloc building. What does this mean in practical terms?

First, clear and transparent rules must be established for RTAs. The starting point should be the amendment of Article XXIV of the GATT in order to reduce the broad scope for its interpretation. In particular, the meaning of the term 'substantially all the trade' needs to be clarified in both quantitative and qualitative terms. The term 'on the whole not higher or more restrictive' should also be defined more clearly.

Second, the WTO must carry out its monitoring and surveillance role more effectively. RTAs must be made to comply with WTO rules. Stricter and more binding rules for notification and reports to the CRTA could help.

Third, the WTO has to develop methods for assisting the coordination of different RTAs. The WTO should be a forum for international negotiations in order to maximise the benefits of the system of coexistence of regionalism and multilateralism.

Finally, and on a more positive note, the WTO should monitor where and how RTAs manage to achieve a greater degree of liberalisation than has been possible at the multilateral level. The experience gained from RTAs could then serve as a useful example for multilateral trade agreements, as has already been the case.

References

Bhagwati, J. and Panagariya, A. (1996) *The Economics of Preferential Trade Agreements*, Washington: American Enterprise Institute.

Fisch, G. (1994) *Integration und Kohäsion heterogener Staaten in der EU*, Wiesbaden: Gabler.

Guerrieri, P. and Padoan, P.C. (1989) *The Political Economy of European Integration*, London: Harvester Wheatsheaf.

Krueger, A.O. (1999) 'Are preferential trading arrangements trade liberalising or protectionist?', *Journal of Economic Perspectives* 13(4): 105–25.

Krugman, P.R. (1993) 'On the relationship between trade theory and location theory', *Review of International Economics* 1: 110–22.

Lawrence, R.Z. (1996) *Regionalism, Multilateralism and Deeper Integration*, Washington: Brookings Institution.

Lorenz, D. (1992) 'Economic geography and the political economy of regionalisation. The example of Western Europe', *The American Economic Review* 82(2): 84–7.

—— (1998) 'The impact of regional integration on the international division of labour', in J. Scherpenberg and E. Thiel (eds) *Towards Rival Regionalism? US and EU Regional Regulatory Regime Building*, Baden-Baden: Nomos, 40–59.

Rodrik, D. (1997) *Has Globalisation Gone Too Far?* Washington: Institute for International Economics.

Schott, J.J. and Hufbauer, G.C. (1999) 'Whither the free trade area of the Americas', *Journal of International Economics*, 765–82.

Speyer, B. (1997) *Regionale Integration*, Wiesbaden: DUV.

Trebilcock, M.J. and Howse, R. (1998) *The Regulation of International Trade*, London: Routledge.

Winters, A. (1998) 'Regionalism and the Next Round', in J.J. Schott (ed.) *Launching New Global Trade Talks. An Action Agenda*, Washington: Institute for International Economics, 47–59.

WTO (1995) *Regionalism and the World Trading System*, Geneva.

—— (1999) *Regional Integration and the Multilateral Trading System*, Geneva.

17 Trade and labour standards

Harnessing globalisation?

Philip von Schöppenthau

Introduction – labour standards in a globalised world

The heated debate at the WTO Conference in December 1999 about linking trade and labour standards and President Clinton's call for trade sanctions against countries that violate labour standards demonstrated:

- that calls for labour standards in international trade agreements are not a fashion that will simply fade away;
- that politicians, business and the public will have to reassess their approach to this controversial issue and to engage in a dialogue rather than confrontation; and
- that a new facet of globalisation has gained the potential to impact upon trade policy initiatives such as a new round of WTO trade negotiations.

A few years ago, globalisation was still perceived as merely an economic phenomenon binding national economies into a global net of interdependence. Today, however, globalisation has spread to the societies of these economies. Using the Internet as a means of global communication, human rights activists, trade unions and other 'civil society' groups exchange information and coordinate their activities across national frontiers, mustering ever-wider support and sympathy for their cause. Both government and business have difficulties keeping pace with this development.

This new facet of globalisation is undoubtedly changing the traditional 'triangle' of politicians, officials and business as the main shapers of international trade policy. Today, civil society groups are trying hard to 'square' this triangle wherever possible, and Seattle is the latest trophy that they claim as their own. Although the failure to launch a new WTO round was not due to civil society protesters in the streets, Seattle showed that the debate about trade and labour standards will increasingly be shaped by civil society groups. Both politicians and business will have to be prepared.

The Seattle ministerial conference

The road to Seattle

Calls for a GATT social clause to allow trade sanctions were first voiced in the late 1970s, but it was not until the early 1990s that trade unions and some sectors of industry were able to push through a social side accord to the agreement setting up the North American Free Trade Agreement (NAFTA). US trade unions also prompted President Clinton to call for a social clause to become part of the final agreement of the GATT Uruguay Round in 1993. Strongly resisted by developing countries, the USA failed to get its way, but the issue of trade and labour nevertheless found its way into the work programme of the newly created WTO.

It therefore came as no surprise when the issue became one of the most controversial topics at the first WTO conference, in Singapore in December 1996. Whereas the USA and the EU pushed for a working group on trade and labour standards in the WTO, developing nations resisted fiercely. They feared that such a working group could eventually open the door for trade sanctions. After long negotiations, both sides finally agreed that developing countries should not be deprived of their comparative advantages based on abundant cheap labour and that social protectionism must be avoided. They also agreed that the International Labour Organization (ILO) is the competent forum for dealing with labour issues but asked the secretariats of both the ILO and the WTO to start a dialogue. While everybody could live with this compromise, it clearly failed to narrow the differences between North and South.

Towards consensus in Seattle?

When in December 1999 ministers convened in Seattle to launch a new WTO round of trade negotiations, their fundamental positions had not changed. However, some new developments had taken place in the meantime that eventually allowed for some elements of consensus to emerge in Seattle before the ministerial conference broke down.

The most significant developments had occurred in the European Union. The advent of socialist governments in many European countries during the second half of the 1990s had created a political climate in favour of demands for labour standards. However, EU member states were divided on how to position this demand in the WTO. Whereas some member states supported a more 'fundamentalist' approach, others insisted that the developing countries' fear of protectionism must be addressed. This constellation finally enabled the European Commission to propose and obtain a balanced negotiating mandate for the Seattle meeting. Its key objective was the 'creation of a Joint ILO–WTO Standing Forum on trade, globalisation and labour issues to promote a better understanding of the issues involved through a substantive dialogue between all interested parties' (Council of Ministers 1999).

This forum would be serviced jointly by the Secretariats of the ILO and WTO to carry out analyses of the relationship between trade policy, development and core labour standards, while ruling out any kind of trade sanctions. It would not aim at rule making within the WTO but at clarifying the issues at stake through an ongoing dialogue involving governments, trade unions and employers' representatives, calling upon the expertise of academics and other international organisations, such as UNCTAD (Lamy 1999).

In addition to this mandate, Trade Commissioner Pascal Lamy mapped out the EU's longer-term vision. He suggested that the 'social incentive clause' of the EU's Generalised System of Preferences (GSP) could become the model for a multilateral system of additional trade preferences for those developing countries that comply with core labour standards (*ibid.*). These core standards would include the right of trade unions to organise and bargain collectively (ILO Conventions Nos 87 and 98), and the bans on child labour (No. 138), on forced and prison labour (Nos 29 and 105) and on discrimination in the workplace (No. 111). With this approach, the EU hoped to be able to bridge the gap between those developing nations that object to a link between trade and labour issues and its civil society groups insisting precisely on such a link to be established in the WTO.

In Seattle, the EU actively pursued its aim of building consensus around its proposal. Not surprisingly, the developing countries rejected the proposal. Most outspoken were India and Hong Kong, which accused the EU of opening the door to social protectionism. Supported by many other developing countries, such as Egypt, Pakistan and Indonesia, they insisted that labour issues have to be dealt with by the ILO, which has the necessary competence in this area, whereas the WTO should keep out of labour issues. They saw the EU attempt to establish a standing joint ILO–WTO forum as a poorly disguised attempt to get labour standards into the WTO by the back door, leading eventually to the possibility of trade sanctions.

Such a reaction was to be expected. What was unexpected was that the objections of developing countries were by no means unanimous. Largely overshadowed by the noisy opposition from India, Hong Kong and others, some countries indicated that they would be open to considering the EU proposal in a constructive manner. While still opposed to linking trade and labour in the WTO, they were prepared to discuss the merits and drawbacks of an ILO–WTO forum. The EU therefore received small openings from Chile, Brazil, South Africa and Singapore, although the permanent character of such a forum worried some of them. Other countries, such as South Korea, believed that a decision about a joint forum should be made by the ILO, whereas Hungary and Switzerland openly supported the EU proposal.

However, Seattle failed to bring these divergent positions to the light, largely because of a lack of structured debate. In fact, some countries tried to set up an informal working group on 'trade, globalisation and labour' to discuss whether the Seattle conference declaration should call for some kind of permanent body to be established to study the issue of trade and labour. Tentatively set up under the chairmanship of Costa Rica, this group was quickly denounced by India and others and was finally broken up. Hence, no structured debate could take place, and no formal text was agreed.

However, Seattle demonstrated that a small split is emerging in the ranks of developing countries, with some starting to see a link between trade and labour as a potential opportunity for better access to the markets of industrialised countries. Developing countries where labour standards are relatively high – e.g. in Latin America and some of the more advanced Asian countries – can therefore be expected to be more open to the idea of studying the relationship between trade liberalisation, labour standards and social development.

However, the openness of developing countries will largely depend on which stance the United States will adopt in future. In the run-up to Seattle, the USA was under strong pressure from trade unions, the textile industry and protectionist members of Congress to adopt a tough stance on a new WTO round as well as on China's WTO accession. In Seattle, Clinton's call for trade sanctions against countries that do not respect labour standards was the result of this pressure, which became most apparent in the large street protests staged by the American trade union AFL-CIO during the conference. Clinton's remarks were disastrous. They not only suffocated the good will that some developing countries had shown in Seattle but also poured water on the mills of those who suspected that industrialised countries are protectionist wolves in social clothing.

On the other hand, Clinton and his administration were keen to downplay his remarks on trade sanctions. In fact, much of his rhetoric was a result of the presidential elections, where the Democrats depended on trade union support. Although trade unions, protectionist industrial sectors and congressmen can be expected to continue their fight for trade sanctions, a new administration will be freed from its electoral strings. This should enable the new administration to take a less hawkish stance on trade and labour issues and play a more constructive role on the international stage.

The post-Seattle situation can therefore be summarised as follows:

- The US government will remain constrained by domestic protectionist interests but can be expected to adopt a more constructive approach in the future;
- Taking advantage of the US paralysis and pushed by civil society groups, the EU has taken the lead on the trade and labour front and will continue to do so; and
- A number of developing countries are becoming less hostile to discussing trade and labour issues. This could encourage other developing countries to join in, provided that they feel they can get something in return, and trade sanctions are not up for discussion.

The way forward: carrot or stick?

Sanctions versus incentives

Calls for trade sanctions against countries that do not respect basic labour standards are counter-productive for a number of reasons:

- They discourage developing countries from engaging in a constructive dialogue on trade and labour. However, without their cooperation, little progress can be expected either in the WTO or the ILO.
- The possibility of imposing trade sanctions tempts powerful producer lobbies and trade unions to urge politicians to use them to protect jobs at home. Trade history has shown that once there is an instrument allowing trade restrictions, those who can benefit from it make sure it is used.
- Trade sanctions do not improve social conditions in the targeted country. Instead, they often have severe adverse social consequences for those who lose their export-related jobs. Trade sanctions block social progress instead of promoting it.

A more constructive approach consists of offering incentives in the form of additional market access for countries that are committed to improving labour standards. First, better market access allows producers in developing countries to export more and to earn additional hard currency, which can contribute to improving working conditions. Second, linking additional market access to improvements in domestic labour legislation and its implementation in the workplace encourages governments to make progress in this respect. Finally, 'social preferences' for one country worsen the relative competitive position of other countries, encouraging the latter to make efforts to become eligible for preferences as well. However, the extent to which social preferences have these effects very much depends on the exact format of the incentive scheme.

Social clauses – a mixed success

The only major importer in the industrialised world to offer social preferences is the European Union (European Communities 1998; 1999; von Schöppenthau 1998). Since June 1998, the EU has used a so-called 'social incentive clause', which is part of its GSP. Offering tariff preferences on top of those already granted under the GSP, this incentive clause is intended to encourage developing countries to abide by internationally accepted labour standards. On average, the clause offers a doubling of the normal GSP tariff reductions for manufactured goods and a number of agricultural products. The social preferences are granted to a country as a whole, although in some cases they can be given to selected production sectors only.

The precondition for granting these additional preferences is that an interested country formally requests them, providing proof that it effectively applies legislation incorporating certain labour standards set by the ILO (ban on child labour, trade union rights). Moreover, the beneficiary country's government must have taken measures to enable it to implement and monitor the application of the legislation and to properly certify its exports as socially 'clean'. Once these conditions have been met, the products of the country concerned will receive the social preferences. In addition, the EU's GSP provides for trade sanctions to be applied to countries that show a systematic use of forced or prison labour with Myanmar being the only country to have lost its GSP preferences so far.

The EU's incentive clause does not, however, seem to be a success. During the first years of its existence, not a single developing country applied for the preferences. Only Moldova and Russia did so. After more than a year of examination, in the summer of 2000, Moldova eventually became the first and only country to have been granted additional market access under the clause.

To some extent, the lack of interest from developing countries does not surprise given their widespread opposition to any kind of link between trade and labour. Applying for the social preferences would be inconsistent with this stance and require breaking ranks with other developing countries. Such a step can therefore only be expected if the economic benefits of the social clause are large enough.

However, they are not. A doubling of the existing GSP margins sounds impressive, at least on paper. In practice, however, this translates into only very limited additional social preferences for so-called 'sensitive' and 'highly sensitive' products, such as textiles, due to the already very small GSP margins for such products. As it is precisely the more sensitive products where developing countries have a comparative advantage and an interest in exporting under more favourable conditions, the incentive offered by the social clause is simply not attractive enough to make them apply. As long as the social preferences do not at least partly outweigh the economic costs of adapting an economy to the required ILO standards, few countries can be expected to apply (von Schöppenthau 1998).

Another conceptual weakness of the EU's social clause is that it does not reward social progress. Instead, it offers preferences to those 'happy few' who already have adequate legislation and the necessary enforcement mechanisms in place. All other countries that make slow but steady progress, such as ratifying the relevant ILO conventions or introducing domestic labour legislation, but cannot show full compliance, are left out.

This insistence on full compliance disregards the fact that the improvement of social standards is a complex, long-term process embedded in the general economic development of a country. The strict conditions attached to the granting of social preferences are therefore in contrast to the aim of the clause itself, i.e. to set a process of social progress in motion and to offer an incentive to continue (*ibid.*).

How does the US approach compare with that of the EU? The main difference between the two is that the US system does not offer incentives but allows for the withdrawal of tariff preferences should labour standards be violated (USTR 2000; Elliott 1998; Noland 1999). Based on so-called 'country practice petitions' filed by interested parties who believe that labour standards are not respected in a GSP beneficiary country, the USTR can propose to withdraw the GSP partly or entirely, subject to approval by the US president. Only if the country concerned has taken steps to guarantee that labour rights are effectively respected can it be readmitted. The wish to regain the GSP is therefore the main motive to improve labour standards.

In practice, this approach has a number of drawbacks. First, it often takes these countries many years to comply with the conditions to get back into the GSP. Second, during these years, the withdrawal of preferences harms the workers that depend on exports to the USA, and the negative social consequences can easily outweigh the intended positive ones. Third, the system of country practice petitions offers organised interests an opportunity to obtain protection against imports from developing countries through the withdrawal of GSP. Fourth, the American GSP does not apply to 'sensitive' sectors, such as textiles, and the social clause therefore does not reach sectors where standards are often particularly low. This reduces its effectiveness as a tool for improving labour standards. Finally, the American GSP is an unpredictable instrument. In recent years, it had lapsed several times without being renewed in time, and once renewed it only applies for one or two years. Without continuity, however, the social clause can be neither an effective nor a credible instrument to raise labour standards in developing countries. The US approach therefore does not seem to offer a viable alternative to the EU's incentive clause.

How to overcome the opposition of developing countries

Today, both the EU and the US approaches have been rejected by developing countries. They consider them as attempts to link trade and labour standards, and it is safe to assume that the sanctions-based US approach will continue to face stiff opposition. Trade incentives stand a better chance of receiving sympathetic consideration, provided that developing countries see considerable benefit for themselves.

To make developing countries understand that they can actually benefit from a link between trade and labour, the two major trading powers will have to offer a down payment:

1   The US government has to state publicly that trade sanctions are not the most effective means of improving labour conditions internationally and that alternative approaches need to be explored. This would help to reassure developing countries about US motives and therefore pave the way for an international dialogue on incentive schemes. At the same time, it would leave the USA the option of continuing its sanctions-based GSP scheme until international consensus has been found.

2   The EU has to make its social clause more acceptable and attractive to developing countries, providing better 'social' market access than is the case today. This will help developing countries to see trade and labour in a different light, making it easier to engage them in a constructive dialogue.

Being the one that has an incentive scheme already in place, the EU will have to take the lead when it comes to a concrete down payment. And there is a unique window of opportunity for doing so: the coincidence of the expected start of a new round of WTO negotiations and the renewal of the EU's GSP. The current GSP scheme ends in December 2001, and internal EU talks about a new scheme (2001–04) will gain momentum in 2001. This is also the time when substantive negotiations on the agenda for a new WTO round are expected to start and when calls for placing trade and labour high on this agenda will be made again.

Linking these two sets of negotiations in an intelligent way by using the EU's down payment as a bargaining chip would help to get developing countries closer to the EU position. At the same time, the EU could demonstrate to its civil society that it is serious about promoting labour standards. To be able to link the two, the EU would have to address the main shortcomings of its social clause:

- Social preference margins should be increased to a level where they provide a real incentive to engage in the costly exercise of raising labour standards. Duty-free access to the EU for all goods would be the most effective incentive, but a political non-starter due to the protectionist tendencies of various EU governments. The EU should therefore reserve zero duties for those products that are not sensitive or highly sensitive, while offering a 50 per cent reduction of the common customs tariff on the latter.
- The clause's strict entry conditions, which require the effective implementation of ILO standards, should be replaced by 'convergence criteria' that reward progress towards implementation instead of reserving preferences for those who have already done their job. This 'progress-oriented' approach would have to include the possibility of taking sanctions, such as withdrawal of the entire GSP, to prevent countries dragging their feet once they obtained the preferences.

Making these changes *now* is a matter of urgency. First, the window of opportunity created by the parallelism of GSP renewal and WTO agenda setting will not be open for long. Second, the GSP is rapidly losing its effectiveness as an instrument for encouraging improvements in labour conditions. Already today, the value of its preferences has decreased as a result of continuous tariff reductions agreed under the GATT/WTO. As this trend is to continue, the room for offering additional social preferences is becoming smaller by the year. Should the EU fail to reform its social clause today, its only instrument for promoting social concerns in international trade will be lost. Convincing developing countries that they can gain from linking trade and labour will be even more difficult in the absence of such an instrument.

The role of the private sector

Codes of conduct – a fashionable trend?

The confrontation between politicians from North and South about whether trade and labour issues should be linked misses the fact that in the day-to-day business relations between their countries trade and labour have often already become closely linked.

In fact, many companies in developing countries are required by importers in the North to observe certain labour standards in the production of the goods they sell them. Whereas five years ago such requirements were still rare exceptions, a rapidly increasing number of companies in industrialised countries are adopting policies of "corporate social responsibility". In many cases, this involves the establishment of social codes of conduct for their business partners, be they from developing or other countries. The potential impact that their code of conduct can have on labour conditions in the companies concerned is very high. Policy makers in the North and South will therefore have to address this trend, which offers opportunities but also risks for all involved.

A social code of conduct normally defines a set of labour standards that the company pledges to respect in relation to its own employees as well as to employees in companies that they do business with. As the standards are widely respected in most industrialised nations, their practical relevance relates to developing countries, where standards are lower. Business partners in these countries therefore have to make an effort to comply with the code of conduct's labour requirements. If they do not, they risk losing their client.

Private sector initiatives like this therefore seem to many to be a welcome 'fast track' to raising labour standards in developing countries while governments continue their war of words in international forums. Moreover, as they are a direct result of the 'civil society' facet of globalisation, such private sector initiatives are more than a passing fashion.

In fact, most companies adopted policies of corporate social responsibility due to high-publicity campaigns by civil society groups, such as human rights activists, trade unions, and development and consumer groups, blaming the companies for turning a blind eye to the exploitative labour practices of their third world business partners. These civil society groups have discovered that large multinationals have a key weakness and a key strength to be exploited. First, multinationals have considerable buying power and business interests in many developing countries, which can be instrumental in promoting social change in these countries. Second, large, well-known corporations do not wish their brand name to be associated with child or prison labour in far-away factories, given the harm to reputation and future business. By exploiting this 'weakness' through 'name-and-shame' campaigns as well as dialogue, civil society groups have developed the power to convince companies to adopt codes of conduct. Once in place, the code serves as a vehicle to project the company's 'strength' towards generating social change with their business partners in developing countries. While blaming economic globalisation for all kinds of evils, civil society groups very intelligently use the leverage that multinationals – the incarnation of globalisation – can offer.

Another reason why the trend towards policies of corporate social responsibility is more than a fashion is that companies are starting to understand that such policies can have considerable commercial benefits. They realise that their business will be increasingly affected by changes in societal values. As their customers are citizens who act according to values and societal changes, future business opportunities will depend on the 'citizen-customer' being satisfied not only with the product itself but also with the company's societal behaviour. Recent changes in values towards greater concern for the environment, the quality of life and human and labour rights mean that sustainable competitive advantage can be secured only by addressing these changes through a 'citizen orientation' of their business strategies (Hamilton 1999). Policies of social responsibility are therefore slowly but increasingly understood as an investment in the company's competitive positioning for tomorrow.

Codes of conduct – a panacea?

Codes of conduct are by no means a magic formula for raising labour standards throughout the world. Despite the positive contribution that they can make, they also have drawbacks and leave many problems unresolved. For example:

- Codes of conduct reach only those workers in developing countries who are employed in export-oriented industries. However, export-oriented industries account for less than 5 per cent of the world's estimated 250 million working children, so 95 per cent of child labour remains outside the code's reach.
- Most codes of conduct apply only to the final product purchased in a developing country, because checking the 'social cleanliness' of input materials is practically almost impossible. Even making sure that the final product has been manufactured in compliance with set labour standards is very difficult. To expect 100 per cent compliance is therefore unrealistic, even if sophisticated monitoring and verification systems are in place.
- Codes of conduct are easier to implement by large companies, which have the necessary resources, than by smaller ones. As the latter account for a considerable share of world trade, this share remains largely outside the codes' reach.
- Codes of conduct are often introduced without proper warning and preparation of the business partners in developing countries. As raising labour standards is a costly and time-consuming process, the sudden introduction

of a code of conduct can cause considerable harm to the companies and workers concerned.

- There is a lack of standardisation, as each company draws up its own code of conduct. Whereas flexibility is needed to allow for sector specifics to be reflected in a code of conduct, many firms in developing countries have to produce one and the same product according to several different sets of standards, depending on the client and their code of conduct. More harmonisation is therefore needed.
- Codes of conduct do not tackle the roots of the problem: poverty and decades of government policy failures. This can only be done through adequate development policies and better government policy. Codes of conduct can play only a secondary role.

Despite these drawbacks and problems, civil society groups will continue to press companies to adopt and implement codes of conduct, and more and more companies will understand that corporate social responsibility can increase shareholder value. The challenge is therefore how to make codes of conduct more effective and more beneficial to developing countries while avoiding placing companies into a straitjacket of exaggerated expectations or government legislation.

First attempts to meet this challenge are underway. Since the late 1990s, the European Commission and US Department of Labour have been organising regular transatlantic conferences to address the practical problems associated with codes of conduct and to exchange experiences between companies, civil society groups and policy makers. Similar dialogues are encouraged at national level in the EU, the USA and other countries.

Given the potential benefits as well as the risks associated with codes of conduct, governments in both the North and the South will have to pay more attention to private sector initiatives. While governments can encourage the spread of codes of conduct and help to improve their effectiveness, they should tread carefully when considering legal steps. Attempts to create stringent enforcement mechanisms for companies that fail to live up to their codes of conduct would be counter-productive as they deter companies from setting up codes of conduct in the first place. Instead, dialogue and exchanges of experience between stakeholders from both the North and the South should be further encouraged.

Conclusion

As demonstrated by events in Seattle, the trade and labour issue can easily degenerate into outright confrontation, putting at risk the launch of a new trade round. Both industrialised and developing countries would lose out.

Both sides are therefore well advised to engage in dialogue to create confidence to identify both risks and opportunities associated with linking trade and labour standards, and to find solutions that address opportunities and risks alike.

For such a dialogue to take place, the EU and the USA as the main 'demandeurs' for the trade and labour issue to be addressed will have to make the first steps to build confidence.

A key for success is that the USA follow the EU in publicly stating that trade sanctions are not the way forward. This would not only address the concerns of developing countries about 'social protectionism' but would also keep those pressure groups at bay that are mainly interested in protecting their markets against cheap imports from developing countries.

In addition, the EU and the USA will have to back down from their demand that the WTO is given a prominent role. The WTO should be left out altogether to address the fears of developing countries that the WTO could be asked to legitimise trade sanctions.

On their part, developing countries will have to accept that dialogue on trade and labour is not a one-off exercise but an ongoing process based on a clearly defined set of objectives and a set timetable. The timetable should be the same as for the new WTO round. The dialogue would thence take place separately from the WTO negotiations but would allow for positive cross-fertilisation between the two sets of talks. If properly managed, this could bring advantages for both industrialised and developing countries.

Also, developing countries need to understand that linking trade and labour can bring substantial economic and social benefits. For this, the EU will have to make its GSP social clause more attractive to developing countries, increasing the social preference margins and introducing 'convergence criteria' that reward social progress in developing countries, rather than full compliance.

Finally, governments in both the North and the South should encourage voluntary private sector initiatives such as codes of conduct, help to improve their effectiveness and integrate them into their overall strategies for improving labour standards.

Note

This article expresses the author's personal view and does not engage EPPA in any way.

References

Anderson, K. (1998): 'Environmental and labour standards: what role for the WTO?', in A.O. Krueger (ed.) *The WTO as an International Organization*, Chicago: University of Chicago Press, 231–55.

Council of Ministers (1999) *Preparation for the Third WTO Ministerial Conference – Council Conclusions*, Brussels, 25 October.

Elliott, K.A. (1998) 'International labour standards and trade: what should be done?', in J.J. Schott (ed.) *Launching New Global Trade Talks. An Action Agenda*, Washington: Institute for International Economics, 165–77.

European Communities (1998) Council Regulation No. 1154/98 of 25 May 1998, *Official Journal* C 160/1, 4.6.

—— (1999) *Official Journal* C 176/13, 22.6.

Hamilton, S. (1999) speech at seminar of the Global Public Affairs Institute (GPAI), London, 7 October.

Lamy, P. (1999) 'The EU's approach to trade and core labour standards in the new WTO round', speech given at ICFTU conference in Seattle, 29 November.

Noland, M. (1999) 'Learning to love the WTO', *Foreign Affairs* 5: 78–92.

USTR (2000) *Trade Policy and 1999 Annual Report of the President of the United States on the Trade Agreements Program*, Washington.

Vellano, M. (1999) 'Full employment and fair labour standards in the framework of the WTO', in P. Mengozzi (ed.) *International Trade Law on the 50th Anniversary of the Multilateral Trade System*, Milan: Guiffre, 379–419.

von Schöppenthau, P. (1994) 'Sozialklauseln: die falsche Waffe', *Internationale Politik und Gesellschaft* 3: 240–56.

—— (1998) 'Social clause: effective tool or social fig leaf?', *The European Retail Digest* 20: 44–5.

18 Delineating trade and environmental rules

Towards a new consensus

Cord Jakobeit

Although the WTO rules do not include an express reference to environmental protection, there is some consensus that this is implied in paragraphs (b) and (g) of the GATT general exception in Article XX. However, the potential clash between the ideals of free trade and environmental protection has lain largely dormant for decades.

Environmental regulators are mainly concerned with internalisation of the costs of pollution and environmental degradation. They want to tackle the environmental impact of a product's production process, use and disposal at both the domestic and the international level. By contrast, the GATT/WTO regime is based on the notions that exceptions to the rule of equal treatment of imported and domestic goods and to the extension of trade advantages to all contracting parties of the global trade regime are allowed only on the basis of a product's own characteristics, not the processes of its production.

The issue came up in the early 1990s, triggered mainly by the 1991 dispute settlement over the so-called tuna–dolphin case in the GATT. This settlement outlawed the US import ban on Mexican tuna caught in fishing nets that also happened to kill dolphins. In line with earlier decisions, the settlement only reconfirmed the reluctance of the GATT to allow protective measures directed against processes rather than products. Already at the time, and as a possible way out of this conflict, the GATT suggested that the US aim of protecting dolphins would be served better by labelling dolphin-safe tuna as such. But because of its powerful and media-relevant resonance with a broader public already alarmed by a number of other environmental issues in the preparations for the 1992 United Nations Conference on Environment and Development (UNCED), the tuna–dolphin case also brought the trade and environmental debate to the top of many agendas (Esty 1994).

The GATT was no exception to this rule, arguing for the easy way out to claim that economic growth based on the enlargement of the free trade regime would be the best way of generating the necessary funds to clean up the environment (GATT 1992). With a reaction similar to the *World Development Report*, released by the World Bank in the same year (World Bank 1992), even moderate environmentalists were upset that key international economic organisations such as the WTO and the World Bank more or less refused to recognise their concerns. Environmental aspects, or so they argued, should not be relegated to a distant future but rather should be incorporated in all economic and trade-related aspects from the outset. Rather than mitigating environmental damage, both efficiency and precautionary considerations would favour prevention in the first place.

However, as with social and labour considerations, and given the intensive efforts of internationally operating non-governmental organisations (NGOs) lobbying hard with OECD governments and increasingly with the WTO itself, the trade and environment issue is going to stay with the WTO for years to come. Since this debate mainly pitches developed against developing countries, this paper argues that a new consensus and better relationship should not be sought primarily within the WTO. A more appropriate vehicle for this seems to be the content of existing and future multilateral environmental agreements, whose (re)design will have to become more sophisticated to accommodate the conflicting views, rather than trying to agree sweeping and all-encompassing modifications of WTO rules, This would allow all sides involved to save face. The case-by-case approach inherent in multilateral environmental agreements might gradually pave the way for a new consensus. However, once such a consensus has been arrived at, the WTO should get involved again to grant it global reach. This pragmatism seems to be already behind the cautious approach favoured by the WTO so far. An international organisation operating on the basis of consensual decision making might be able to influence and guide a debate, but it is ill-placed to go against the expressed view of the majority of its members permanently.

The irresistible rise of the issue

The issue of trade and environment was not on the agenda of the Uruguay Round. Nevertheless, several environmental concerns were addressed in the results of the negotiations, such as the reference to sustainable development in the preamble of the WTO Agreement, the permission to exempt direct payments under environmental programmes from commitments to reduce domestic support for agricultural production, and the explicit taking into account of measures to protect human, animal and plant life and health and the environment in the new Agreement on Technical Barriers to Trade and Agreement on Sanitary and Phytosanitary Measures. As was the case with any other international organisation operating in the 1990s, the WTO was no longer able to treat the issue with benign neglect.

The most noteworthy institutional response consisted of the creation of a WTO Committee on Trade and Environment (CTE), which was given a broadly based mandate in Marrakech in 1994 to examine all aspects of the issue and to make recommendations on whether any modifications of the trade rules were required. However, the report produced by the CTE for the first WTO ministerial conference in Singapore in December 1996 largely failed to meet the high expectations of WTO critics and environmental NGOs alike. Both felt left out of the process and strongly criticised the secretive nature of the discussions in the CTE (Chaytor and Cameron 1999). The report merely summarised the different views of CTE members and contained no recommendations on modifications of WTO rules (CTE 1996). Subsequently, the CTE mandate and terms of reference were simply extended into the future.

Given the fundamentally opposed views of developing and developed countries, it should not come as a surprise that the CTE largely ducked many controversial issues. Notwithstanding the persistent differences between the EU and the USA over eco-labelling and the elimination of environmentally damaging subsidies, the avoidance of strong language by the CTE mainly reflected the substantial resistance of developing countries to any environmentally inspired modification of the global trade rules. Delegates to the WTO from developing countries see the issue as yet another protective barrier and an infringement of their sovereignty, whereas many environmentalists in the developed countries would like to piggy-back on the WTO and apply trade measures to enforce international environmental obligations from multilateral environmental agreements and establish or raise domestic environmental standards where they are not yet in place or are low. But since developing countries make up more than 70 per cent of WTO membership, it is difficult to imagine that the organisation can come up with a ruling that would go so openly against the majority. In addition, the pending accession of the People's Republic of China to the WTO is likely to strengthen the resistance from developing countries. China has acted as a central spokesperson and advocate for all developing countries, strongly rejecting most environmental positions pursued by the developed countries in all multilateral negotiations in the past.

However, it would also be misleading to portray the entire developed world as a homogeneous group or bloc willing to use the WTO to advance the environmental agenda. Nor are all developing countries equally adamant in their resistance to consideration of the issue in the WTO. On balance, however, poorer countries do set up more of a uniform front against any additional excuse to adopt protectionist policies. On the side of the richer countries, environmental experts, some industries (e.g. reinsurance and 'green' industries such as production of energy from renewable sources) and environmental lobby groups tend to make their increasing weight felt more with the USA than with the EU. At the same time, one should not underestimate the influence of interest groups in the developed world eager to defend the *status quo*, whereby the environment (or labour) should not interfere with the primary agenda of the WTO, i.e. the promotion of free trade.

In the preparations for the ministerial conference in Seattle, internationally operating NGOs, such as the World Wide Fund for Nature and Greenpeace, the most vocal of all the WTO's critics, once again accelerated their environmental lobbying with national trade representatives and the public in both the USA and Europe (Greenpeace 1999). Not least due to this pressure, which was increasingly felt within the WTO itself, the WTO Secretariat published a new report on the relationship between trade and the environment just weeks before the meeting in Seattle (WTO 1999). This report took up many of the suggestions that had emerged in the intensive academic debate over the last few years (Anderson and Blackhurst 1992; Cameron *et al.* 1994; OECD 1996).

This time around, the WTO openly conceded that trade can harm the environment. But the WTO also maintained that environmental issues should be tackled primarily at the domestic level, where they arise, rather than by blocking freer trade. The new report is most noteworthy for the attempts made to outline possible areas of agreement between the noisy environmentalists, the stern free traders and the fearful and *status quo*-oriented developing countries. While these lines of compromise were seemingly lost in the 'battle in Seattle', they will undoubtedly help to guide future decisions to accommodate the conflicting views. The significant reduction or elimination of subsidies to polluting activities (energy, agriculture, fishing), the scrapping of barriers to trade in environmental services, and a more open approach by the WTO to the labelling of eco-friendly products all seem to offer opportunities for compromise.

But even if these suggestions were to be put into practice, well knowing the significant domestic resistance that they would inevitably run into almost everywhere, environmentalists will still be tempted to use the uniquely binding dispute settlement mechanism of the WTO to pursue their own agenda. At the same time, developing countries will be immediately up in arms if they sense that yet another protectionist loophole is in the making.

Striking a new balance

For a new consensus between richer and poorer countries to emerge, the more flexible and pragmatic approach would be to leave the ground-breaking tasks to different forums, such as issue-specific agreements. While environmentalists toy with the idea of creating a global environmental organisation to offset the significant reach and power of the WTO and other existing international organisations, such a new organisation is unlikely to emerge soon. Developed countries are outspokenly against the creation of any new international bureaucracies. Existing organisations such as the United Nations Environmental Program (UNEP) and the UN Commission on Sustainable Development (CSD) will have a hard time expanding their limited mandate. The history of international cooperation on environmental issues seems to underline the merits of the issue-specific approach. And the effort, time and energy spent negotiating the mandate and aim of a new global environmental organisation would be better invested in trying to tackle existing environmental problems through existing multilateral environmental agreements.

The WTO has already signalled its sympathy with such a view in its 1998 appeal court ruling on the US import ban to protect sea turtles. Rather than by imposing unilateral import bans, the US right was recognised so long as it did this by negotiating turtle protection agreements. Such bilateral or preferably multilateral environmental agreements will be more acceptable to developing countries the more they include financial or technological transfers, thereby demonstrating the shared commitment of the developed world. Once the lessons learned from such agreements have triggered global environmental learning and increased global environmental concern, it should be up to the WTO to extend global reach to such a new-found consensus.

References

Anderson, K. and Blackhurst, R. (eds) (1992) *The Greening of World Trade Issues*, New York: Harvester Wheatsheaf.

Cameron, J., Demaret, P. and Geradin, D. (eds) (1994) *Trade and Environment: The Search for Balance*, London: Cameron May.

Chaytor, B. and Cameron, J. (1999) 'The treatment of environmental considerations in the World Trade Organization', in *Yearbook of International Co-operation on Environment and Development 1999/2000*, London: Earthscan, 55–64.

Committee on Trade and Environment (1996) *Report to the Ministerial Conference* (WT/CTE/1, 12 November), Geneva: WTO.

Esty, D.C. (1994) *Greening the GATT: Trade, Environment, and the Future*, Washington: Institute for International Economics.

GATT Secretariat (1992) *Trade and the Environment*, Geneva: GATT.

Greenpeace International and the Center for International Environmental Law (CIEL) (1999) *Safe Trade in the 21st Century*, Amsterdam: Greenpeace International. [http://www.greenpeace.org/politics/wto/]

OECD (1996) *Reconciling Trade, Environment and Development Policies. The Role of Development Co-operation*, Paris: OECD.

World Bank (1992) *World Development Report 1992: Development and the Environment*, Washington: World Bank.

WTO (1999) *Trade and Environment Report*, Geneva: WTO. [http://www.wto.org/wto/environ/environment.pdf]

Part III

Systemic and institutional issues

19 Clinton's legacy

US trade leadership languishes

Henry R. Nau

American leadership in trade policy is comatose. Although not solely at fault, the United States bears the major responsibility for the failure of the ministerial conference of the World Trade Organization (WTO) in Seattle in December 1999. The meeting broke up in chaos, not only figuratively but also literally. Protest groups rioted in the streets, disrupting the meetings. Participating nations went home, accusing one another of poor planning and a failure of leadership.

This appalling spectacle occurred despite the best domestic and international conditions America has ever known. The United States is experiencing the longest and most powerful economic boom in its history. The world at large is mostly at peace. No significant great power rivalries fragment world markets, as the Cold War did for four decades after World War II. North–South rivalries have faded. Emerging nations (or what we once called developing nations and which now also include the former communist nations) no longer resist free trade or call for an alternative new international economic order. Instead, they rush to join the existing global economic order and implement painful market reforms to gain access to global prosperity. Despite these unprecedented conditions, the world trading system is at a standstill and may have already shifted into reverse.

No country is more responsible for this state of affairs than the United States. The leader of the free world, which now includes practically the entire world, is no longer leading. In a world with only one leader, such failure is disastrous. What is more, it comes on the watch of a US administration that made international economic leadership its number one foreign policy priority. President Clinton came into office trumpeting a new economics-centred (or geo-economic) foreign policy. He raised trade and economic policy to the highest levels of national security policy and called upon the country to compete, not retreat. Today, the US economy is competing, but US leaders are retreating. Unlike Vice President Al Gore, who defended the earlier North American Free Trade Agreement (NAFTA) and Uruguay Round treaty against protectionist opponents, such as Ross Perot, President Clinton actually helped to scuttle the Seattle meeting. He not only legitimised the claims of domestic rioters that the trading system was inhuman (calling for 'globalisation with a human face', much as communist leaders once called for 'socialism with a human face'), Clinton directly undercut the negotiations in Seattle by supporting trade sanctions to enforce labour rights. In the process, he alienated almost the entire developing world.

Ultimately, Clinton sacrificed trade leadership for domestic political reasons. Approaching a decisive election year in which he would like to unseat the Republican Congress that impeached him, Clinton yielded to the protectionist and environmentalist interests of the left wing of the Democratic Party. As Henry Kissinger summed it up: 'Instead of assuming the mantle of President's Truman's leadership role in inspiring the structure of the post-World War II world, Clinton decided to play to the gallery' (Kissinger 1999; see also Bhagwati 1999).

Geo-economics self-destructs

Clinton's policy in Seattle was no accident. It was 'baked in the cake' of his foreign policy strategy from the beginning of his administration. Clinton's vision of an economics-centred foreign policy exaggerated the threat of global economic competition to American workers and provoked a backlash of special interests against new free trade initiatives throughout the Clinton years, despite unprecedented US economic prosperity (Nau 1995; Zoellick 1999).

Clinton articulated his geo-economic foreign policy to replace the containment policy of the Cold War era. The end of the Cold War, he argued, marked the passing of traditional geo-political military competition between states. The traditional great powers no longer competed over territory and military balances. They fought instead for trade and export market shares. The trading state replaced the territorial state, and the Cold War became the 'Cold Peace'. Whereas the Cold War united America and its allies, the Cold Peace divided them. A furious economic competition erupted between the United States and its former European and Asian allies to decide their geo-political status in the twenty-first century. The key to this competition was government-promoted competitiveness and export policies, creating jobs and grabbing world market shares from trading partners. The adversaries were not political rivals, such as China and Russia, but fellow democracies such as Japan, Germany and the European Union (EU).[1]

In its early years, the Clinton administration waged geo-economic 'warfare' against Japan and Europe. It negotiated numerous bilateral agreements to balance trade more equitably with Tokyo and used the Asia-Pacific Economic Co-operation (APEC) forum to head off the feared spread of the Japanese model of export-led growth to Southeast Asian countries.[2] The Clinton team also sharpened bilateral trade disputes with Europe. The president put NATO expansion and aid to Russia ahead of cooperation with the EU to expand global markets with Russia and other emerging nations. Trade disputes with Europe became so severe that European defence and trade ministers took the initiative in 1994–95 to call for a new transatlantic free trade initiative (Nau 1995).

Although they passed the multilateral trade agreements left over by the Bush administration (the NAFTA and the Uruguay Round), Clinton officials were sceptical about further steps to liberalisation through multilateral institutions (Tyson 1992). They did not consider these institutions to be effective dealing with complex new trade issues such as information services, investment and domestic regulatory policies.

Clinton was not wrong to promote a more assertive US trade policy. The end of the Cold War did increase the stakes in the world economy. And the United States was right to defend its trade interests against a querulous EU and mercantilist Japan. But tough policies have to lead the country somewhere. When Ronald Reagan adopted tough military policies towards the then Soviet Union, he eventually cashed in those policies to conclude historic arms control agreements with Moscow and end the Cold War. Clinton's tough trade policies yielded no comparable long-term benefits for US economic interests. He did not seem to have any objectives in mind beyond the specific agreement he was negotiating at the time (Zoellick 1995). As a result, he ended his presidency with no significant trade accomplishments, such as the NAFTA and Uruguay Round initiatives, which he inherited from the Reagan–Bush administrations. In short, he leaves without a trade legacy, even though he made trade the number one priority of his entire foreign policy.

The net result of Clinton's geo-economic foreign policy vision was to drain US trade policy of any larger geo-political rationale and increasingly to subject US trade policy to the narrow special interests of domestic protectionist and environmentalist forces (for a full critique along these lines, see Nau 1995). During the Cold War, free trade policies were always closely linked to America's containment of the Soviet Union and the need to strengthen the economic power and political integration of the Western allies. Once the Cold War had ended, Clinton's geo-economic approach offered no substitute rationale to justify free trade. While rhetorically supporting the enlargement of democracy and free market reforms, Clinton's geo-economic logic actually divided the democratic allies and missed the opportunity to align them with emerging nations to create new markets and enlarge the democratic peace. Some of Clinton's own officials recognised this failure. Ellen Frost, who served in the US Trade Representative's Office from 1993 to 1995, argued that Clinton missed 'the opportunity to inject shared foreign policy leadership and forward momentum into the post-Cold War global political-economic order'. 'For now', she concluded in 1997, 'the transatlantic partners are stuck in the trenches, fighting it out over relatively unimportant issues while a world of opportunities passes them by' (Frost 1997: 3, 5).

Clinton's geo-economic strategy caused him to lose the authority to negotiate free trade agreements. Three times, in 1995, 1997 and 1999, he failed to secure fast-track authority from Congress. Fast-track legislation allows US negotiators to conclude trade agreements that Congress cannot amend after the fact. Without such authority, Clinton has no credibility to make commitments in international negotiations. As a result, he botched one opportunity after another to move free trade negotiations forward: to expand NAFTA; to conclude an international investment treaty; to move APEC beyond mere rhetoric and whatever the least enthusiastic members might accept; to liberalise trade with African and Caribbean countries (which finally happened in the waning months of Clinton's term); and to energise the credibility and leadership of the new WTO.

Thus, Clinton's trade policies, the leading edge of his entire foreign policy strategy, languished and became increasingly captured by domestic labour and environmental interests. Many of these interests do not favour free trade at all.[3] But Clinton needs these groups for other purposes. They hold the key to his personal legacy. If the Democrats capture the House of Representatives in the 2000 elections, Clinton can argue that the American people repudiated the Republican Congress that impeached him. At Seattle, he was unwilling to jeopardise this chance for personal vindication. He staked his trade legacy almost entirely on an agreement with China. Signed just before the Seattle meeting, to admit China into the WTO and give it normal trade status. Labour and other Seattle protest groups, most within Clinton's own Democratic Party, strongly opposed the agreement. With strong business and Republican support, the bill passed. Republican support belied Clinton charges of an isolationist, do-nothing Congress, raised when Congress failed to ratify the Comprehensive Test Ban Treaty in the fall of 1999.

Clinton's geo-economic strategy is responsible for his tactics in Seattle.[4] If he was once sincere in his appeal to American business and labour to compete not retreat, he is now the victim of the political cynicism that he cultivated by bashing former Cold War allies and undercutting free trade-oriented emerging nations. He cannot blame this strategy on the need to defend American jobs. The argument propounded by labour and other protesters in Seattle that globalisation threatens American jobs is ludicrous (so ludicrous that media efforts to justify these concerns only damage their credibility further with an already distrustful American public).[5] Joblessness has never been lower in America, and real wages are growing. Workers are moving into more highly skilled occupations, exactly what one would hope for in an advancing, more equitable society. True, the less skilled workers have to be retrained. But acquiring better skills is in their interest. Globalisation actually creates pressure to improve labour conditions; it does not prompt a rush to the bottom or lowest common denominator of labour and environmental standards. Studies show that foreign investment goes to emerging nations that are raising, not lowering, labour standards (Rodrik 1997; Lawrence *et al.* 1998). The case against free trade is not credible, especially in the current economic climate. But facts and logic are no longer what matters; the issues are now politics and tactics. American leadership creates a sad spectacle. How did it come to this?

Globalisation mania

Part of the problem lies in the exaggeration of the process of globalisation and the assumption that this process is relentless and uncontrollable. A *Business*

Week article in 1999 repeats this often-expressed but ill-founded view of globalisation. Noting that a new architecture is emerging in Europe, the article concludes that 'the result is a much more vibrant and pluralistic continent, one in which the state is no longer the final arbiter of society'. 'The driving forces', the article stipulates, 'are technology and business, rather than ideology and geopolitics' (*Business Week* 1999). This perspective is patently overdrawn and probably false. If it were true that globalisation trumps national sovereignty, we would have never experienced the great wars of the twentieth century, both the hot and cold ones. For technology and business were in the driver's seat at the beginning of the twentieth century. Trade accounted for a larger share of world GNP just before World War I than it did in the mid-1970s. Only in recent years is today's global economy more tightly integrated than the world economy of a hundred years ago. Yet globalisation did not end ideology and geo-politics then, and globalisation is not outside the control of government and social forces today.

In fact, the opposite view is closer to the truth. Global ideological and geopolitical forces are driving technology and business. Globalisation mirrors the unprecedented triumph of industrial democracy and the spreading ethos of market competition and political openness. This unprecedented triumph mirrors, in turn, the dominant power and influence of the United States and other Western democracies. The geo-politics of a democratic security community, in which for the first time in history the great industrial powers (Russia and China are not yet great industrial powers) share a common political ideology, creates an environment in which business and technological innovation flourish, not the other way around. Business operates worldwide, and the Internet is poised to 'wire' the world not because technology is inevitable but because country after country is adopting market reforms, privatising state enterprises and slowly, in some cases (such as Russia) reluctantly, encouraging more open individual competition in both politics and economics. Were this not so, the technology of the Internet might be deployed for different reasons, to wage information wars, not wire the world for e-commerce. This is what happened to nuclear technology during the Cold War. That technology too had the promise to spark global integration through peaceful nuclear energy research and commerce. But sharp geo-political differences between the United States and the Soviet Union turned nuclear technology into a deadly weapon of mutual assured destruction. Something similar could still happen with information technology. If, for example, the ideology of democracy and individualism does not spread in China (or Iran), the technology of the Internet will not serve the purpose of opening up China (or Iran). The expectation that the Internet equals freedom of information assumes that individuals value information, but if there is no ideology or politics of individualism (or no opportunity for such politics), institutions, especially the state, control that information. The technology of the Internet may spread, just as the technology of nuclear power spread, but it will not spread with the consequence of emancipating individuals and widening free markets. It will spread to serve the interests of the state and authoritarian oligarchs.

Geo-politics has not been replaced by geo-economics. The latter which is itself a product of geo-politics. If the United States and other democratic countries falter, globalisation falters. Globalisation thrives where political communities exist. In the present world, globalisation reflects the convergence of all the major industrial powers in the world today around the common ideology of liberal politics and free market economics. This democratic convergence, in which mature democracies do not fight against one another, is the real revolutionary development of the modern world, not globalisation (Russett 1993; Ray 1996; Gowa 1999).[6] Free trade, individual entrepreneurship, freedom of information and the judicial settlement of disputes exist where liberal democratic societies prevail. Through these mechanisms, liberal societies manage peaceful political and economic competition within their own borders. Is it that surprising that they practise the same rules in their relations with each other, expanding international commerce and the role of international organisations in settlement of trade disputes (NAFTA, WTO, etc.)? To be sure, not all members of international trade organisations are democratic, and there are legitimate issues about how to operate institutions democratically that include non-democratic nations. But the core members of global institutions are liberal democracies, and these members exert the biggest influence on the process of globalisation. Thus, while globalisation may appear to arise outside the control of governments, it does so only because it reflects the prevailing influence of liberal democratic political cultures in which the role of government is sharply circumscribed and that of an independent civil society is given wide latitude to operate.

The real shortcoming of US leadership lies in failing to develop this alternative view of globalisation as an outgrowth of liberal democratic values and institutions. Clinton missed the opportunity to tell the American people that this world of democracy and free markets is exactly what they have fought to achieve over the past two hundred years. And they have achieved it only because they befriended and worked closely with other democracies, establishing and supporting integrated markets and international institutions such as NATO, the Group of Seven (G-7) and the EU. America should have every reason to feel more at home, not more threatened, in this globalising world of democratic peace (Nau, forthcoming). Yet instead of embracing this world, Clinton's geo-economics-based leadership has created a great fear among Americans that globalisation threatens US sovereignty and jobs. It was a serious miscalculation on the part of US leadership. Clinton, who godfathered the harsher Darwinian notion of globalisation as a struggle for geo-economic supremacy, is directly responsible.

Hence, the problem with US trade policy is not technical or political; it is conceptual and intellectual. That is a surprising conclusion to reach when one considers that Clinton may be the smartest of all American presidents. Still, he completely overlooked an alternative way to think about globalisation and

American foreign policy in the post-Cold War era. The reason for this conceptual failure may have been political: Clinton had a vested interest in distinguishing his policies from his Cold War Republican predecessors Reagan and Bush. He bought into the argument that these predecessors had pressed Cold War security policies at the expense of US economic interests, allowing America's democratic allies to gain an unfair economic advantage. He became convinced that US trade policy had to become more self-interested, mercantilist (job-oriented) and nationalistic if it was going to compete against the interventionist policies of Asian and German capitalism. But he is now paying the price for this Faustian bargain with nationalist and protectionist interests. Clinton has demonstrated once again that being smart is neither necessary nor decisive for effective leadership. 'Looking back over our history', James Chace concludes, 'it is evident that leadership, character and good judgement, not intellectual acumen, are the hallmarks of an effective presidency' (1999).

Clinton's focus on economic competition, rather than the democratic peace community, created an obsession with trade and global competitiveness. This obsession contributed to the heightened fear that international bureaucrats and organisations are deciding issues central to the sovereignty and well-being of the United States, but nothing could be further from the truth, especially in the trade policy area. The WTO is the weakest of the international economic institutions. It operates on the basis of consensus or unanimity. By contrast, international financial institutions such as the World Bank and the International Monetary Fund (IMF) have weighted voting (the US share is about 18 per cent), and the United Nations depends on the Security Council, in which the United States and the four other great powers exercise a veto. In practice, the United States exerts disproportionate influence in all of these institutions, including the WTO. And none of these institutions can change US law. If the WTO rules against the United States on a trade policy case, it cannot force the United States to change its offending legislation.[7] It simply requires the United States to compensate the offended country or authorises the offended country to impose trade sanctions on the United States. If the United States feels strongly about its national laws, it absorbs the sanctions or compensates the offended country in some other way. No national sovereignty is violated. In fact, the mobs in Seattle protesting against the infringement of US sovereignty by the WTO were advocating exactly the same powers for the WTO in labour and environmental areas that they were criticising in trade areas. If another country's laws did not meet WTO labour and environmental standards, the protesters wanted the United States to be authorised to impose sanctions against that country.

Neither global free trade nor international organisations pose the slightest threat to US sovereignty. The fiction that globalisation is out of control is a product of the flawed foreign policy vision of the Clinton administration. This vision not only sabotaged Clinton's own trade policy agenda, resulting in the fiasco in Seattle; it also caused the Clinton administration to miss an opportunity to portray globalisation in an entirely different light.

A caucus of democratic nations in global institutions

This alternative vision begins by recognising that mature democracies in Europe and Japan, which make up three-quarters of the world economy and dominate international economic institutions, share the same fundamental political and economic goals as the United States. They defend individual rights and free markets at home and share the same general foreign policy interests abroad: to safeguard the security and prosperity of Europe and Asia; to promote wider international peace and stability; and to consolidate and develop democracy and the rule of law (Gompert and Larabee 1997). Because they have similar domestic political and economic systems, they do not threaten one another militarily. Their sovereignty is not at stake. None of the major, mature (that is, reflecting the internal characteristics necessary for the democratic peace; see note 6) industrial democracies, which include the United States, Canada, Great Britain, Germany, France, Italy and Japan, use, threaten to use or plan to use military force against each other.

However, democracies have different interests on specific issues: they compete against one another economically and culturally; and they sometimes even talk in terms of balancing power against one another.[8] But they do not raise their disagreements to the level of military threat. True, they often differ in their assessment of relations with non-democratic countries. The United States and France, for example, differed recently over UN action towards Iraq. During the Cold War, the allies repeatedly disagreed over how to deal with the then Soviet Union. Today, they differ on how to deal with Russia and China, the two major democratising or non-democratic states that could pose a military threat to the democracies. Overall, however, the democracies coordinate their interests among themselves and towards non-democratic nations. That is the function of the major international institutions binding the democracies together – NATO, the G-7 and the EU. In these institutions, The United States and other liberal democracies already share considerable sovereignty (Risse-Kappan 1995).

A true strategic, as opposed to geo-economic, view of America's foreign policy interests would anchor American policies in these institutions and work though a caucus of democratic nations to influence wider UN institutions such as the WTO, the World Bank and the IMF, in which non-democracies also participate. NATO has expanded to include several new democracies in Central and Eastern Europe. The EU is planning to do the same, as soon as the new democracies meet the more stringent conditions of mature political and competitive economic systems. The G-7 brings Japan into the community of democratic nations and provides a vital bridge between US security commitments in Asia and its commitments in Europe. The G-7 also links US security and economic commitments in Europe. Because there is no Atlantic organisation in economic areas similar to NATO in military areas, the G-7 integrates Western economic and security interests. The United States often complains that it has no seat at the table of European economic decision making, while it has serious security commitments in Europe through NATO. But the G-7 closes this gap between NATO and the EU. Despite this critical role, the G-7 is the most poorly understood and under-used institution among the mature democracies.

The United States (and other G-7 countries) sees the G-7 as either a *symbolic* or a *substantive* institution. In fact, it is neither. It is best used as a *strategic* caucus to coordinate the policies of the major democratic nations towards one another and the wider family of UN institutions.

The *symbolic* view depicts the G-7 as a circle of great powers, but this leads to the premature inclusion of immature or not-yet-democratic countries in the G-7. This occurred when Russia was admitted to the political talks of the G-7, forming the so-called P-8. And it may be repeated if China is admitted to the P-8, as German and Japanese leaders have advocated (Tett *et al.* 2000). This dilution of the democratic character of the G-7 has been a mistake. This is the one institution in which the major democratic nations meet alone. Given their common systems and responsibilities, such an institution is warranted. It need not diminish the importance of other actors or institutions. For example, both Russia and China have great power status in the UN Security Council. The G-7 countries can deal with them in this forum and its regional affiliates, such as the Organisation for Security and Co-operation in Europe (OSCE). On the other hand, if the Security Council cannot act, given the wide differences that often exist between democratic and non-democratic states, the G-7 and its parallel institutions such as NATO remain available for action by like-minded democratic countries. These institutions proved to be indispensable in both the Balkans (Bosnia and Kosovo) and Middle East (Gulf War) when the UN was not able to act decisively.

The *substantive* view of the G-7 highlights its role in direct negotiations of international economic policies among the mature democracies. At annual summit meetings, G-7 heads of state and governments negotiate to harmonise or adjust their domestic economic policies to steer the world economy (coordinate interest and exchange rates, or expand and contract fiscal policies) (Bergsten and Henning 1996; Putnam and Bayne 1987). This view, popularised by the Bonn Summit in 1978 when the industrial democracies traded off policies to stimulate the world economy against measures to curb energy consumption, risks transferring responsibilities for key domestic economic policy decisions to international diplomats and bureaucrats who plan summit meetings. It feeds into fears that globalisation is taking place outside the control of democratic processes, particularly the close oversight by national parliaments. Since such international meetings and institutions are not yet subject to international parliaments, *substantive* summitry dilutes democratic accountability and encourages the view that globalisation weakens national sovereignty. The EU experienced a backlash against European integration when the Maastricht Treaty went too far towards usurping national responsibilities without strengthening international parliamentary accountability. And the public backlash against the WTO in Seattle was prompted in part by the perception that international bureaucrats and multinational corporations were escaping the scrutiny and control of national democratic parliaments.

The industrial democracies would be better off using the G-7 as a *strategic* caucus among democracies. G-7 summits would set broad guidelines and goals for economic and security policies (not negotiate detailed policy packages) and invite national parliaments to review these initiatives. European Parliament leaders suggested at the Seattle WTO meeting that the heads of national parliaments of G-7 countries meet together, similar to the annual summit meetings between G-7 heads of state and governments. While this idea needs to be developed (the heads of parliaments in parliamentary and presidential democracies carry different weight), it has merit. The democracies have to develop international institutions (executive and legislative) that mirror the contested and accountable institutions they use at home. Otherwise, international meetings usurp the responsibilities of elected representatives and contribute to the fear that globalisation threatens national sovereignty.

In the meantime, the G-7 should coordinate policies by a looser process of inward-first policy coordination (Nau 1984–85; 1985; 1990; forthcoming; Paarlberg 1995). This process emphasises taking responsible national (inward) actions first to implement security goals or economic initiatives. These actions then interact in the global marketplace, while the G-7 leaders (both heads of state and representatives of parliament) debate and monitor these actions at annual summit meetings. The parallel but interactive process of national decision making and international monitoring creates a more open and indirect style of policy coordination. National parliaments remain responsible for national action, but this action has to run the gauntlet of competitive market pressures and intense intergovernmental debate between both the executive and legislative officials of each country. This inward-first approach avoids the alienation of democratic control caused by outward-first approaches. The latter, represented by the Bonn Summit in 1978, emphasise reaching international agreements (outward) first, then using these agreements as a way of pressuring national parliaments to accept the results and change national legislation. National parliaments understandably feel alienated from this decision-making process.

The Williamsburg Summit of 1983 offers a good example of the inward-first style of foreign economic policy leadership. The United States and France adopted national policies in 1981 to correct their economic troubles, which ran in exactly opposite directions. The USA chose to rescue its economy through tax cuts, deregulation and tight monetary policy, driving up interest rates and the dollar; France chose to stimulate its economy through increased taxes, spending and regulation, weakening its currency. At summit meetings in 1981 and 1982, the G-7 countries hotly debated these alternatives. Eventually, market forces and international discussions convinced France to reconsider its policies. (The United States also retreated marginally from some of its policies, raising taxes modestly in 1983 and 1984.) In March 1983, France reversed course and adopted more market-oriented policies. At the Williamsburg

Summit in May 1983, the United States, France and other G-7 countries agreed on a programme of multilateral surveillance to move their economic policies towards converging goals of low inflation, reduced budget deficits and structural reforms. The programme was only imperfectly implemented. The United States consistently failed to meet reduced budget targets, but the overall result of this approach was a dramatic resurgence of Western economies, contributing to the economic outpacing of the Soviet Union and the eventual end of the Cold War.

Beyond Seattle

How could the United States and other G-7 countries utilise this alternative view of globalisation as an expression of the democratic peace to salvage international trade and economic diplomacy after the debacle in Seattle? The first step by a new US president must be to reconnect trade policy with strategic concerns. A free trade system remains imperative, not to strengthen Western countries in a Cold War but to express an integral part of what free democratic societies are all about and to extend the possibilities of greater economic and political freedom to other countries. From this perspective, trade is not the linchpin of economic prosperity, as geo-economic perspectives claim. National economic policies are far more important for national growth and competitiveness (Krugman 1996). Instead, trade and peaceful settlement of international disputes through litigation and compromise are the calling cards of free societies. These processes regulate competitive battles internationally and preserve the democratic peace. If the free trade system goes into reverse, or national governments consistently refuse to implement legal judgements by the WTO, it will reflect a rise of nationalism and an erosion of democracy in the G-7 countries, not the protection of their sovereignty against globalisation. The best measure we have of democracy is the ability of citizens to exercise their political and economic rights and to expect those rights to be adjudicated on in an open, legal process under the rule of law. Among the G-7 countries, therefore, which share the rule of law, there should be no complaints about accepting WTO legal rulings as long as those rulings are reached in a fair and open process (which is not yet the case in the WTO – see further discussion below).

However, the G-7 countries do not live in the world alone. They have to relate to non-democratic countries. It is legitimate to ask whether the United States should accept legal decisions by a WTO in which China, an authoritarian, non-democratic state that suppresses citizens' and workers' rights, exercises as much legal right as the United States. The choice to engage in free trade with non-democratic states is made on different grounds. The United States accepts WTO decisions not because it shares with China a respect for the rule of law but because the WTO may be an effective way of establishing and extending the rule of law in non-democratic societies. However, that will happen only if the WTO operates democratically. Thus, a first assignment of the G-7 in repairing the damage in Seattle is to reach and implement agreements that permit private groups to observe and submit opinions in WTO proceedings. These agreements should also be vetted by national parliaments to ensure that citizens who will be expected to abide by WTO decisions feel that their representatives have had an opportunity to scrutinise such agreements.

The next step is to get a new global trade round going. A successful strategy must be carried out on several fronts. First, a new US president must seek fast-track authority from Congress. This effort must have top priority and be based on strategic arguments. Free trade is still the best national security instrument that America and other democracies have to preserve the democratic peace (and avoid internecine military competition between democracies) and gradually extend this peace to non-democratic societies. Second, the traditional quadrilateral or 'quad' trade talks between the four major democratic powers (the United States, Canada, Japan and the European Union) must be reinvigorated. These talks degenerated before Seattle primarily because neither the US president nor any other head of state exercised any high-level leadership to make difficult compromises. Third, the G-7 countries need a high-level negotiating forum to discuss trade issues with emerging nations. Emerging nations are now the focus of US national security policy. They, especially Russia and China, are the principal potential external threats to the democratic peace. The next round should have the principal strategic purpose of integrating these countries slowly but steadily into the democratic peace community.

The G-20 is a new grouping that includes emerging nations. It was established in the wake of the Seattle debacle and could become a new high-level forum for intensive trade talks. At the moment, it deals largely with financial issues and is run by the US Treasury Secretary. The next president must find a way to link and integrate the cabinet-level responsibilities of trade (the Office of the US Trade Representative) and finance (US Department of Treasury), giving trade and finance the high-level personal and political attention that only the president can provide.

Negotiations at all of these levels need to be pressed vigorously and simultaneously. The WTO itself will be the beneficiary of such multi-tiered diplomacy. As a large (134 members) consensus organisation, it should not be expected to be the principal negotiating arena. It is the receptacle, not the originator, of trade negotiations. Future WTO ministerial conferences should be held, other than routine meetings, only if all of the other negotiating groups have done their jobs beforehand.

A fourth step to reverse the disastrous course of US trade policy in recent years is to maintain the sound direction of financial and structural reforms in the world economy that support free trade. Trade does not exist in a vacuum. Irresponsible domestic fiscal and monetary policies, excessive state intervention in pricing and production decisions, captive and non-competitive banking systems, undeveloped equity and bond markets – all contribute to exchange rate volatility, capital flight, financial corruption, low returns on capital and, ultimately, stagnating labour markets and wages. Since the early 1980s (spurred by the Williamsburg Summit), the world economy has been moving incrementally towards more efficient standards, converging around fiscal and monetary policy discipline, privatisation, competitive banking, equity and bond markets, deregulation, trade and capital market liberalisation, and labour training and mobility. The results of this restructuring are clearly evident in the United States and Europe. And despite growing pains, they are beginning to emerge in Asia as well. The lesson of the recent Asian crisis is not that international financial market liberalisation proceeded too rapidly. It is that domestic banking and equity market reforms in Asian countries proceeded too slowly.

A fifth and final step to rechart American trade policy is to initiate a single market exercise between the EU, the United States and Japan. Such an exercise would complement a new trade round, just as the EC's Single European Market in the late 1980s accompanied and complemented the Uruguay Round. An Atlantic single market would build on the European initiative in 1995 to create a transatlantic marketplace. The latter initiative started both government and business dialogues to identify behind-the-border barriers to trade, such as regulations and domestic business practices. But this approach lacked high-level leadership and excluded parliaments. Behind-the-border barriers are more difficult to reduce than traditional trade barriers at the border, such as tariffs and quotas. Behind-the-border barriers often reflect deep-seated domestic habits and private cultural practices. They grow out of national legislation, and attempts to modify them ignite strong domestic opposition and claims of threats to national sovereignty.

Hence, to reduce them, national parliaments need to be involved. Parliamentary involvement is an advantage of a single market exercise over traditional trade rounds, and why a single market exercise must accompany the next trade round. Unlike traditional trade negotiations, which take place on a fast-track basis (no official parliamentary approval until after the package has been negotiated), a single market exercise requires more regular parliamentary oversight and review of liberalisation measures. Not only local representatives but also domestic interest groups maintain closer and more regular contact with the negotiations. Their involvement may complicate and possibly slow down negotiations, but this need not be the case if governments exercise the necessary leadership. What is more, the closer contact develops civil society relations between parliamentary democracies and underpins intergovernmental institutions, such as the WTO, with inter-societal and transnational relationships that reflect citizens' involvement and choice. Rather than being left out on the streets to riot, domestic interest groups are absorbed into the process and led to understand that globalisation is a peaceful, competitive product of democracy, not a threat that justifies protectionism, nationalism and a return to traditional balance-of-power military rivalries.

Conclusion

At this most propitious moment of global economic prosperity and world peace, America's trade policy leadership languishes. This situation is not primarily a consequence of new and difficult technical issues involved in the agricultural, services and investment sectors. Nor is it a consequence of strong public opposition to free trade. A recent *Wall Street Journal*/NBC News poll showed that almost three-fifths of the American people (59 per cent) thought that trade was either good for the United States or did no harm (35 and 24 per cent, respectively). Only one-third thought that it was harmful (*Wall Street Journal* 1999). America's trade leadership languishes because it is based on a flawed foreign policy vision that misunderstands the true nature of globalisation. This vision stresses a zero-sum competition for export markets, which encourages citizens to fear loss of jobs and national sovereignty at the hands of the uncontrolled forces of globalisation in international markets and institutions. This fear has slowly eroded the Clinton administration's own trade policy agenda and left the president crippled by the extremist forces in his own party and other nationalists in Congress. As a result, President Clinton has been unable to move forward with trading partners in the WTO, NAFTA, APEC or G-7. His legacy, at least in terms of his trade policy based on geo-economics, is a shambles, and the next president faces a formidable task to re-energise American trade and foreign policy leadership.

This task, however, is doable. The next president has to offer a different vision. Globalisation is not the novel feature of world politics at the beginning of the twenty-first century. The democratic peace is. The most powerful countries in the world live in total peace with one another. They neither threaten to use nor use military force in their international relations with one another. They employ similar political and economic systems that spin off vigorous trade and non-governmental groups. These groups compete economically and culturally but solve their differences peacefully through international market and legal institutions without the slightest hint of military threat. They spawn the vast network of contacts we call globalisation. This network envelops other, non-democratic societies and develops tensions between low- and high-wage countries and societies that live by the rule of law and others that do not. But these tensions are not a threat to democratic sovereignty or national jobs. How can they be, when democratic nations are more powerful and have more jobs than they have ever had. The tensions are merely the promise that the democratic peace may be extended to include emerging nations that no longer resist free trade and former communist countries that seek to overcome the paralysing legacy of state oppression and interventionism. The democratic nations at the core of globalisation are certainly strong enough to relate to emerging nations without fear of losing their vitality and standard of living. On the strength of this vision of globalisation, the next US president can lead again in trade and foreign policy.

Notes

1   In developing this view, Clinton drew on a body of literature spawned in the late 1980s and early 1990s that saw America declining *vis-à-vis* its Cold War allies. This decline, it was argued, was due largely to free trade policies. While the United States provided security for its allies, Japan and Europe concentrated on economic competi-

tion and proceeded to eat America's economic lunch. Germany and Japan, in particular, pursued a model of government intervention that promoted domestic technology, restricted imports and subsidised exports. The United States, meanwhile, relied too heavily on free markets and fell behind in the new geo-economic warfare. Many of the proponents of this argument took high positions in the early Clinton administration. See, among others, Laura D'Andrea Tyson (1992), who was head of Clinton's Council of Economic Advisers and then his National Economic Council; Jeffrey Garten (1992), who was undersecretary of commerce for international trade; and Lawrence H. Summers (1989/1990), who was assistant, deputy and then secretary of the Treasury. For other classic statements of the geo-economic argument, see Eckes (1992) and Borrus *et al.* (1992). For an early critique of these geo-economic views in the Clinton administration, see Lavin (1993).

2   From 1993–95, the Clinton administration negotiated twenty-one bilateral agreements with Japan. While US exports to Japan in these sectors grew, global exports to Japan grew even faster, suggesting that general market conditions, not bilateral agreements, were more important for competitiveness. See Lavin (1996a); reply to Lavin by Kantor (then US trade representative) (1996); and reply to Kantor by Lavin (1996b).

3   Republicans as well as Democrats oppose free trade. But the president, not Congress, has the responsibility for leading on trade policy. Clinton's failure to do so is evident in his declining ability to persuade his own party members to follow him on trade. In late 1993, when the House passed the NAFTA legislation, 102 Democrats voted for the measure. In 1997, when Clinton sought fast-track authority for the second time, only forty-two Democrats indicated that they would support him. Meanwhile, the labour unions penalised Democratic defectors, withdrawing support for them in elections in 1996 and 1998. The threat to do this again in the 2000 elections doomed fast-track legislation for the third time in 1999 (see Broder 1999; Berlau 1999). For a view from the labour perspective, see Mazur 2000.

4   The media, which are endlessly impressed by Clinton's intellectual and political skills, tend to dismiss Clinton's failures as a consequence of tactical errors or technical complexities in the negotiations. The *Washington Post*, for example, editorialised in 1999 that at Seattle Clinton was right in principle but wrong on tactics. In fact, as this essay argues, he was wrong in principle, that is, his flawed geo-economic foreign policy strategy, while his tactics of siding with protesters and against emerging nations were perfectly consistent with that strategy.

5   The media seldom report on trade issues. Rather, they report on trade victims. The endless stories of individual workers losing their jobs are never offset by the 40 million or more workers who have gained new jobs over the past two decades. The steady drum beat over the loss of jobs systematically undercuts public support for free trade as well as broader globalisation.

6   The democratic peace is now a well-documented, if still unexplained, phenomenon. The statistical evidence that mature democracies do not fight one another is substantial, but the explanations are contested. Some analysts attribute it to the recent alliance of these countries against the former Soviet Union and expect these countries to resume military competition and balancing as soon as enough time has passed to adjust to the demise of the Soviet threat (Mearsheimer 1990; Waltz 1993). Others attribute the peace to economic and technological developments, which integrate these countries (Friedman 1999). These analysts see globalisation as an autonomous force acting outside the control of democracies. Still others see the peace as a consequence of the domestic norms and institutions in democracies that restrain power and place a premium on settling issues by the rule of law (Russett 1993; Owen 1994). Whatever the reason, the fact of the democratic peace is not disputed. Think of what the world would be like if the United States had to worry

about defending its territorial sovereignty against military threats from Great Britain, Germany, France or Japan.

7   In the two celebrated cases of shrimp and gasoline imports, the WTO did not rule that US laws protecting turtles caught in shrimp nets and setting high fuel standards for gasoline had to be changed. It ruled that the United States was applying these laws discriminatorily: giving some countries only four months, others three years, to adopt turtle protector devices; and imposing higher fuel standards on foreign than on domestic refiners (Irwin 1999).

8   French leaders are traditionally the most inclined to resort to balance-of-power language in describing relations between democracies, particularly with the United States. Recently, Foreign Minister Hubert Vedrine has talked about America's 'hyper-power', and President Jacques Chirac advocates a 'multipolar' world. But this language is largely rhetorical and is intended to wage a cultural, not a military, competition with the United States (see Whitney 1999).

References

Bergsten, C.F. and Henning, C.R. (1996) *Global Economic Leadership and the Group of Seven*, Washington: Institute for International Economics.

Berlau, J. (1999) 'How the trade battle was lost: interest groups sabotaged Seattle talks – from within', *Investor's Business Daily*, 14 December, p. 1.

Bhagwati, J. (1999) 'Did Clinton take a dive in Seattle?', *Washington Post*, 7 December, p. A31.

Borrus, M., Weber, S. and Zysman, J. with J. Willihnganz (1992) 'Mercantilism and global security', *The National Interest* 29 (Fall): 21–30.

Broder, D. (1999) 'The inescapable issue', *Washington Post*, 19 December, p. B7.

Business Week (1999) 'Europe: ten years later …,' 8 November.

Chace, J. (1999) 'Bush isn't an egghead – so what?', *Wall Street Journal*, 23 December, p. A18.

Eckes, A.E. (1992) 'Trading American interests', *Foreign Affairs* 71(4): 135–55.

Friedman, T.L. (1999) *The Lexus and the Olive Tree*, New York: Farrar, Straus & Giroux.

Frost, E. (1997) *Transatlantic Trade: A Strategic Agenda*, Washington: Institute for International Economics, May.

Garten, J. (1992) *The Cold Peace: America, Japan, Germany and the Struggle for Supremacy*, New York: Times Books (a Twentieth Century Fund book).

Gompert, D.C. and Larabee, F.S. (eds) (1997) *America and Europe: A Partnership for a New Era*, Cambridge: Cambridge University Press.

Gowa, J.S. (1999) *Ballots and Bullets: The Elusive Democratic Peace*, Princeton, NJ: Princeton University Press.

Irwin, D.A. (1999) 'How Clinton botched the Seattle summit', *Wall Street Journal*, 6 December, p. A34.

Kantor, M. (1996) letter to the editor, *Wall Street Journal*, 20 June, p. A11.

Kissinger, H. (1999) 'Making a go of globalization', *Washington Post*, 20 December, p. A33.

Krugman, P. (1996) *Pop internationalism*, Cambridge, Mass.: MIT Press.

Lawrence, R.Z., Litan, R.E. and Shapiro, R.J. (1998) *Globaphobia: Confronting Fears about Open Trade*, Washington: Brookings Institution.

Lavin, F.L. 1993) 'Clinton and trade', *The National Interest* 32 (Summer): 29–40.

—— (1996a) 'Boosting export figures, not exports', *Wall Street Journal*, 6 June, p. A12.

—— (1996b) letter to the editor, *Wall Street Journal*, 3 July, p. A11.

Mazur, J. (2000) 'Labor's new internationalism', *Foreign Affairs* 79(1): 79–94.

Mearsheimer, J. (1990) 'Back to the future: instability in Europe after the Cold War', *International Security* 15(1): 5–56.

Nau, H.R. (1984–85) 'Where Reaganomics works', *Foreign Policy* 85 (Summer): 144–53.

—— (1985) 'The state of the debate – Reaganomics the solution?', *Foreign Policy* 85 (Summer): 144–53.

—— (1990) *The Myth of America's Decline: Leading the World Economy in the 1990s*, New York: Oxford University Press.

—— (1995) *Trade and Security: US Policies at Cross-Purposes*, Washington: American Enterprise Institute Press.

—— (forthcoming) *At Home Abroad: Identity and Power in American Foreign Policy*, Ithaca: Cornell University Press, a Century Foundation book.

Owen, J.M. (1994) 'How liberalism produces democratic peace', *International Security* 19(2): 87–126.

Paarlberg, R. (1995) *Leadership Abroad Begins at Home: US Foreign Economic Policy After the Cold War*, Washington: Brookings Institution.

Putnam, R. and Bayne, N. (1987) *Hanging Together: Cooperation and Conflict in the Seven-Power Summits*, Cambridge, Mass.: Harvard University Press.

Ray, J.L. (1996) *Democracy and International Conflicts: An Evaluation of the Democratic Peace Process*, Columbia: University of South Carolina Press.

Risse-Kappen, T. (1995) *Cooperation Among Democracies: The European Influence on US Foreign Policy* Princeton, NJ: Princeton University Press.

Rodrik, D. (1997) *Has Globalisation Gone Too Far?* Washington: Institute for International Economics.

Russett, B. (1993) *Grasping the Democratic Peace: Principles for a Post-Cold War World*, Princeton, NJ: Princeton University Press.

Summers, L.H. (1989/1990) 'The Ishihara–Morita Brouhaha', *The International Economy* 3(6): 49–55.

Tett, G., Kynge, J. and Fidler, S. (2000) 'Beijing may have seat at July summit', *Financial Times*, 14 February, p. 4.

Tyson, L. (1992) *Who's Bashing Whom? Trade Conflict in High Technology Industry*, Washington: Institute for International Economics.

Wall Street Journal (1999) 'Most Americans don't distrust free trade', 2 December, p. A8.

Waltz, K.N. (1993) 'The emerging structure of international politics', *International Security* 18(2): 44–80.

Whitney, C.R. (1999) 'With a "don't be vexed" air, Chirac assesses US', *New York Times*, 17 December, p. A3.

Zoellick, R. (1995) 'Who Won the Trade War?', *The National Interest* 41 (Fall): 78–82.

—— (1999) 'Clinton's Seattle straddle', *Washington Post*, 14 December, p. A39.

20 Broadening WTO membership

Key accession issues

Rolf J. Langhammer and Matthias Lücke

WTO membership is still less than universal. Although most developed and many developing countries are WTO members, fully one-third of the world's population, accounting for about 10 per cent of world trade and 5 per cent of world GDP, lived in countries outside the WTO system at the end of 1999 (Langhammer and Lücke 1999: table 1).

The good news is that most of these countries (most prominently, China) have applied to join the WTO. However, while current WTO members have welcomed this move in principle, that welcome has not translated into swift and successful accession negotiations. From 1995 to 1999, only seven countries that were not previously contracting parties to GATT 1947 were admitted to the WTO (in chronological order: Ecuador, Bulgaria, Mongolia, Panama, Kyrgyzstan, Latvia and Estonia). Another thirty-three countries were at various stages of negotiating their terms of accession with current members; some, like Algeria and China, first applied to become a contracting party to GATT 1947 more than ten years ago. The thirty-three applicants are a fairly diverse group and include most CIS countries (prominently, Russia, Ukraine and Belarus), other transition economies in Asia and Europe (in addition to China, Vietnam, Laos, Cambodia and Albania), and an assortment of others, such as Chinese Taipei (Taiwan), the Gulf states, and African and Pacific island economies.

Unless accession negotiations are accelerated, many of the benefits of WTO membership will be denied to applicant countries for a prolonged period. This would be unfortunate because, particularly for the many transition economies among applicants, accession to the WTO becomes one important focus of efforts to implement market-oriented reforms in a wide range of trade-related policies. Furthermore, even if there is no full-blown Millennium Round of trade negotiations, forthcoming negotiations between current WTO members will inevitably tie up political attention and administrative capacity that would be required to complete accession negotiations with the new-comers.

Potential stumbling blocks in accession negotiations

Overview

Accession negotiations deal with two broad types of issue. First, the WTO Agreement and its annexes contain mandatory rules on the conduct of a wide range of national trade-related policies, e.g. the extension of m.f.n. treatment to WTO members, national treatment of imported goods with respect to indirect taxes, the general prohibition on quantitative import restrictions, and the protection of trade-related intellectual property rights. Accession negotiations therefore involve a detailed review of the relevant legislation and practice of applicant countries. Current members typically take the view that these must be substantially in line with WTO rules by the time an applicant joins the WTO. In recent accessions, the implementation of particular legislation was deferred until after accession in only a very few cases, with the exact timing specified in the acceding country's protocol of accession.

Accession negotiations have been protracted because, compared with GATT 1947, WTO rules are far more detailed and cover a wider range of topics, such as international trade in services (GATS) and trade-related intellectual property rights (TRIPs). Besides, many countries acceding to GATT 1947 in recent decades were developing countries that enjoyed considerable discretion in the conduct of their trade policies under Article XVIII of GATT 1947 and the amendments of 1965 (Part IV: Articles XXXVI–XXXVIII). Now, many candidates for accession to the WTO are transition economies that will be subject to the full set of (extended) disciplines of the WTO Agreement.

Second, accession negotiations deal with market access for imported goods and services in applicant countries. Among GATT 1947 and WTO members, the protection offered to domestic firms has been progressively reduced as a result of successive rounds of trade negotiations; nevertheless, the level of protection still differs widely across WTO members. Relevant policy instruments include the level and dispersion of import tariffs for goods and market-access commitments in services. Accession negotiations have become protracted, *inter alia* because some current WTO members are using their leverage in negotiations to extract concessions from acceding countries that go much further than the commitments made by current WTO members at a similar level of economic development.

Trade in industrial goods

Acceding countries are required to bind their import tariffs, i.e. to commit themselves to not setting tariffs above specified levels. Typically, they also commit themselves to reducing bound tariff levels over an implementation period, usually of seven years from their accession to the WTO. Negotiations between applicants and incumbent members focus on the import-weighted average tariff level, the dispersion of tariff rates across products, the number of zero-rated products and the number of tariff lines for which rates are not to be bound (normally very few).

The key demand by current WTO members has been that the major acceding economies (including China and Russia) bind their tariffs for industrial goods at roughly double the average rate for OECD countries (*cf.* Langhammer and Lücke 1999: 847). This would imply an import-weighted average of bound rates of no more than 10 per cent. Among countries that recently joined the WTO, the simple average of individual tariff bindings was between 7 and 13 per cent for Estonia, Kyrgyzstan, Latvia, Panama and Bulgaria, and approximately 20 per cent for Ecuador and Mongolia (WTO 1999: table 3).

By contrast, developing country WTO members still impose higher tariffs, even after implementing the Uruguay Round liberalisation. Finger *et al.* (1996) estimate the post-Uruguay Round trade-weighted applied average tariff on industrial goods for twenty-six developing countries at 13 per cent; the corresponding average bound rate is 20 per cent. Furthermore, in many of these countries, tariff bindings for industrial products are not nearly comprehensive, whereas recently acceded countries as well as applicants are strongly expected to bind all tariffs.

While it can be argued that current members are applying double standards in making far-reaching demands on applicants, a more benign view would focus on the implications of their position for the evolution of the world trading system. In the Uruguay Round and successive negotiations, tariffs on industrial goods have been cut and even eliminated for some groups of products (e.g. information technology). Tariff bindings were made far more comprehensive even by developing countries, which in the past had frequently either not bound tariffs at all or had bound them at far higher levels than were actually applied. Thus, in this benign view, current WTO members are requiring applicants to be at the forefront of global tariff liberalisation rather than possibly entering the WTO with a protectionist agenda that would create obstacles in the way of further liberalisation.

Agriculture

The WTO Agreement on Agriculture has brought that sector back into the discipline of the multilateral trading system. Essentially, members' commitments under the agreement are in three broad areas. First, quantitative import restrictions are to be replaced by tariffs that are bound and subsequently reduced. Second, domestic production subsidies that strongly impact upon trade ('yellow' subsidies) are to be bound and reduced over time. Certain other production subsidies that are regarded as not affecting trade ('green' subsidies) are not restricted, while yet another category ('blue subsidies') consists of measures that have been exempted only temporarily from reduction requirements. Third, export subsidies, while not outlawed as for industrial goods (Agreement on Subsidies and Countervailing Measures), are also to be bound and reduced.

Here, the Cairns Group of countries (mainly exporters of temperate-zone agricultural products, prominently including Australia) have gone further in committing themselves to the abolition of agricultural export subsidies.

With respect to the tariffication of quantitative restrictions, applicant countries are in practice free to abolish these and propose 'target bindings' for their tariffs on agricultural imports that need not be based on an exact calculation of the tariff equivalent of the quantitative restrictions. This procedure avoids the difficulties that most applicant countries would face in quantifying the effects of policy instruments based on weak data in the context of a rapidly evolving systemic transformation (for the bindings of recently acceded countries, see WTO 1999: table 3).

On domestic support, the binding of production subsidies entails the calculation of the aggregate measurement of support for each basic agricultural commodity in accordance with Annex 3 of the WTO Agreement on Agriculture. This raises a number of technical difficulties, which are easily appreciated by inspecting the format to be followed (downloadable WTO document WT/ACC/4; see WTO 1999: 17–18). Alternatively, acceding countries may make a *de minimis* commitment in accordance with Article 6.4 of the Agreement on Agriculture, i.e. restrict 'yellow' domestic subsidies for a basic agricultural commodity to 5 per cent of its value of production (10 per cent in the case of developing country members). Both routes have been followed by recently acceded countries.

Accession negotiations with respect to agriculture have become protracted mainly because some applicants were not willing to commit themselves to cutting domestic support much more quickly (e.g. by making *de minimis* commitments) than current WTO members have done in the Uruguay Round negotiations. Similar problems arise with respect to agricultural export subsidies, where the Cairns Group of agricultural exporters has pushed for an early elimination. While the Cairns Group of countries have done so themselves (they tend to be highly competitive producers of temperate-zone agricultural products), once again this demand goes further than most OECD countries (and the EU in particular) have been willing to go in restricting their own export subsidies.

Services

The General Agreement on Trade in Services (GATS) represents a first step towards liberalising international trade in services. The agreement defines four potential modes of international service supply (cross-border supply, consumption abroad, commercial presence and the presence of natural persons); lists the general obligations of members (such as m.f.n. treatment, transparency, due process in domestic regulation and conditions for economic integration agreements); describes in detail the measures that are subject to members' market-access commitments (such as limitations on the number of service suppliers or on the types of legal entity that may provide a service); and lists various exceptions to GATS obligations (such as m.f.n. exceptions, subsidies, public procurement, balance-of-payments restrictions and national security).

Accordingly, WTO members' schedules of specific commitments on services consist of three parts: first, horizontal commitments that affect all sectors, for example with respect to the movement of natural persons or payments abroad; second, sector-specific commitments, which may be differentiated by the four modes of supply; and third, exemptions from m.f.n. treatment. While the GATS represents the general framework for liberalisation in services, negotiations since the Uruguay Round on financial services and particularly on telecommunications have led to substantial further liberalisation in these sectors.

Incumbent WTO members expect applicant countries, as a precondition for WTO membership, to offer economically meaningful commitments for at least a limited number of important service sectors. Across service sectors, access to financial services and telecommunications are of particular interest, not least because WTO members have themselves negotiated further liberalisation in these fields since the conclusion of the Uruguay Round. Because of the wide variety of sectors and the different modes of supply under GATS, it is difficult to provide a summary measure of the quality of the commitments agreed in recent accessions; a survey is contained in WTO 1999 (Annex 2.3).

Reluctance to liberalise market access in services has been shown particularly by the transition economies among the applicants, where the service sector suffers from a double handicap. First, the central planning system has left many countries overindustrialised but with underdeveloped service sectors. This was true especially for financial and business services, which are now crucial for the functioning of a market economy. With free entry, local service firms would often be overwhelmed by international competition. Second, the services that were provided in the past were usually produced under state monopolies. Hence, the opening of service sectors to international competition, particularly through direct investment by foreign suppliers (commercial presence), has met powerful political resistance.

At the same time, the international competitiveness of manufacturing industries depends increasingly on the firms enjoying access to high-quality services. Hence it is in the national interest of applicant countries (whatever resistance may be articulated by sectoral lobbies) to make economically significant commitments on service liberalisation. Where regional governments and non-governmental sectoral associations can control market access, it is also in the applicant country's interest to ensure that these entities do not undermine the free supply of services across regions in each country.

TRIPs

The TRIPs Agreement mainly obliges WTO members to implement certain specified procedures for the effective enforcement of a wide range of intellectual property rights: copyright and related rights, trademarks, geographical indications, industrial designs; patents, and the layout designs of integrated circuits.

The agreement builds upon and extends the provisions of the relevant international conventions (Bern, Rome and Paris; and the Treaty on Intellectual Property in Respect of Integrated Circuits).

The effective implementation of the TRIPs Agreement encounters problems in both former socialist and developing countries, because both (albeit for different reasons) traditionally tended to view intellectual property as a public, or partly public, rather than a private good. This is in contrast to the position of industrialised countries, which is closely reflected in the TRIPs Agreement, that intellectual property is a private good to be protected through appropriate legislation.

In transition economies, most legislation on intellectual property rights is of very recent vintage. Extensive advice received from the World Intellectual Property Organization (WIPO) has normally ensured that the new legal texts correspond to the provisions of the relevant international conventions as well as the TRIPs Agreement. However, effective enforcement, which is central to the TRIPs Agreement, depends on effective institution building in the legal system as a whole, which in turn is part and parcel of the difficult process of systemic transformation.

Many developing countries have traditionally been reluctant to extend full protection to intellectual property created mainly by firms in high-income countries, particularly if this would have enabled those firms to extract monopoly rents on the use of technologies deemed crucial for development (such as pharmaceuticals to combat diseases). Problems in accession negotiations have arisen both from the reluctance of some applicants to account fully for the private good character of intellectual property rights in their legislation and from difficulties with enforcement.

While the appropriateness of including intellectual property rights in the WTO framework has been questioned, TRIPs is now, for better or worse, part of the multilateral trading system. Applicant countries have no choice but to bring their legislation and law enforcement into line with the provisions of the TRIPs Agreement. This may be helped by the fact that the legitimate interests of developing countries are reflected in several relevant provisions. For example, national legislation may permit the use of intellectual property by third parties without the owner's consent for public non-commercial purposes such as disease control (Articles 30 and 31 of the TRIPs Agreement).

State trading and economic transition

The WTO agreements assume implicitly that WTO members are market economies where economic agents are free to act according to commercial considerations. This is clear from Article XVII of GATT 1994, which stipulates that state enterprises, as well as enterprises with exclusive or special privileges, should be notified to the WTO and, furthermore, should be run solely in accordance with commercial considerations. The logic behind this provision is that enterprises directed by the state, or endowed with exclusive or privileged trading rights, can undermine a member's market-access commitments if they act on any other than a strictly commercial basis. Furthermore, the centrally planned economies that were members of GATT 1947 (Poland, Czechoslovakia and Romania) had special membership protocols that stipulated, *inter alia*, mandatory rates of import growth from GATT 1947 contracting parties; tariff bindings or similar commitments would have been meaningless in centrally planned economies.

State trading companies and exclusive trading rights are widespread in many applicant countries. Some transition economies among the applicants have made only limited progress in privatisation, so a large share of GDP is still produced by state-owned enterprises. In many countries, access to natural resources and the distribution of strategic commodities such as mineral ores or fuel are traditionally a domain of the state. In the case of Saudi Arabia, state trading companies are also instrumental in enforcing government controls on domestic sales of food and fuel products and setting domestic prices below international prices (WTO online document WT/ACC/SAU/6: 28–33).

For accession negotiations, the crucial criterion for the compatibility of a given enterprise structure with WTO rules is not ownership but the actual behaviour of enterprises. If state ownership is still widespread, applicants need to demonstrate that enterprises effect their purchases and sales solely on commercial grounds. In spite of some evidence of restrictive practices, international trade has been one area of systemic reform in nearly all transition economies where progress has been relatively rapidly sustained. As a result, goods markets in transition economies have become more contestable, and the behaviour of existing enterprises is based increasingly on commercial grounds.

One indication of continuing progress in this direction is an active programme of enterprise privatisation. Typically, therefore, applicants have provided detailed information on their privatisation programmes during accession negotiations. Besides notifying state trading enterprises and those with exclusive rights or privileges, transition economies acceding to the WTO have committed themselves to reporting regularly on progress in privatisation (for example, annually in the case of Kyrgyzstan). While there are no well-defined criteria that a privatisation programme needs to meet in order to be considered as conforming with WTO rules, a regular reporting requirement improves the transparency of the incentive systems under which enterprises operate.

Developing country status

The WTO agreements acknowledge that developing countries may find it particularly difficult to fully meet WTO obligations with respect to trade liberalisation. Developing countries are therefore allowed greater freedom to restrict trade in exceptional situations, to withdraw from existing commitments such as tariff bindings in order to protect infant industries, or to provide domestic subsidies to agriculture. Other special provisions for developing countries relate to extended implementation periods for various obligations and to particularly poor, 'least developed' countries. With respect to market access for their exports, developing countries benefit from the 'enabling clause', which permits WTO members to grant imports from developing countries 'special and differ-ential' treatment under the Generalised System of Preferences (GSP). Regional preferential trading arrangements between developing countries are permitted even when they do not meet the requirements of Article XXIV of GATT 1994.

All these provisions raise the obvious question of which countries are to be considered 'developing' and may thus benefit from more favourable treatment. Remarkably, criteria for developing country status have never been established either by the contracting parties to GATT 1947 or by WTO members. Whether a country is considered 'developing' depends on a unilateral decision of the trading partner (the US procedure for the GSP), or on membership in the Group of 77 (the EU procedure for the GSP), or on self-selection for other WTO purposes. Only the term 'least developed country' is clearly defined in the WTO context in accordance with the list drawn up by the UN.

In accession negotiations, developing country privileges such as under Articles XII and XVIII of GATT 1994 have been claimed by China in partic-ular. This Chinese position was strongly resisted by current WTO members, not least because of China's relatively large share in world trade; resort to devel-oping country privileges could have rendered Chinese market-opening commitments meaningless. In addition, the empirical evidence accumulated over the last several decades suggests that trade restrictions to promote infant industries or to protect the balance of payments provide no significant benefits to developing countries. Hence, applicants have nothing to lose from not using such measures.

The issue of extended implementation periods for developing countries is, in principle, more complicated. Developing countries (however defined) tend to possess limited administrative capacity, so extended implementation periods appear justified. However, in a formal sense, this issue will gradually die away because all implementation periods for new WTO members, as for current members, are calculated from the coming into force of the WTO Agreement (not from the date of accession to the WTO). This is now established practice and will most probably also apply to future accessions. In practice, therefore, all extensions to implementation periods for acceding countries are now subject to negotiation.

Key country perspectives

China and Chinese Taipei (Taiwan)

More than a decade has passed since the accession working party for China was established in 1987 under GATT 1947. Negotiations have dragged on tediously for a combination of reasons: China is a major exporter of traditional manufac-tures (especially textiles and clothing; see Langhammer and Lücke 1999: table 2), and these 'sensitive' exports are likely to grow further once restrictions stemming from the Multi-Fibre Agreement are removed (Uruguay Round Agreement on Textiles and Clothing). The consequent prospects for political trouble at home has hardened the determination of some current WTO member governments to push China, as a condition of WTO accession, towards a rather far-reaching liberalisation of market access for imported goods and services. With the large and growing size of the Chinese market, the liberalisation of market access is of far greater economic value to current WTO members than in the case of any other candidate country. However, pressure for rapid liberalisation was long resisted by the Chinese government, which pointed to the ongoing systemic transformation of the country with all its attending problems, in addition to China's low *per capita* income, which would traditionally have been accepted, in a GATT/WTO context, as justification for infant industry protection.

Up to the end of January 2000, China had concluded bilateral negotiations on its terms of accession with Japan, Canada and the USA, but the agreement with the USA is probably the most far-reaching (White House Office of Public Liaison 1999). Import tariffs are projected to fall from an overall average of 24.6 per cent in 1997 to 9.4 per cent by 2005, with an average of 7.1 per cent for some US priority products. Market access will also be enhanced in a wide array of service industries, including telecommunications, banking (with special provisions for auto finance), distribution and motion pictures. At the same time, the USA will be allowed to treat China as a non-market economy for another fifteen years in anti-dumping and countervailing duty examinations, and the USA may also apply a special safeguard mechanism (beyond that available under WTO rules) against imports from China for twelve years.

It remains to be seen whether these terms, which were described as particularly advantageous to US firms by the US negotiators involved, will be acceptable to China's other major trading partners, especially the European Union. While all commitments and concessions by China would automatically apply to all WTO members under the m.f.n. principle, other trading partners might emphasise market access in other products of particular interest to them and seek concessions similar in value to those obtained by the USA. Nevertheless, the bilateral USA–China agreement makes the successful conclusion of accession negotiations in the foreseeable future more likely.

Failure to conclude accession negotiations with China represents a critical, politically motivated accession barrier for Taiwan (officially called the 'Separate Customs Territory of Taiwan, Penghu, Kinmen and Matsu' – 'Chinese Taipei'). Most current WTO members recognise the People's Republic as the only legitimate government of China and therefore accept the Chinese government's position that Taiwan should only accede to the WTO after China. This position cannot be justified from WTO rules, which only require members to be in full control of all trade-related policies, which is the case for Taiwan (as it is for Hong Kong, which continues to be a WTO member). Substantially, negotiations in the accession working party for Taiwan, which started in 1992, have been concluded without any major issues remaining unresolved.

It is at present unclear what political leverage China will gain on the Taiwanese accession to the WTO if it formally joins the WTO before Taiwan is given the chance to do so. In spite of growing trade and capital flows, political relations between the two governments remain difficult. However, a further politicisation of Taiwanese WTO membership would be detrimental to the cause of freer trade in a rules-bound world trading system. Together, China and Taiwan account for approximately half of the international trade of current WTO non-members and for an even larger share of their combined population and GDP (Langhammer and Lücke 1999: table 1). Thus, their accession would bring the WTO a significant step closer to being a truly global institution.

Russia and other CIS countries

Accession negotiations with the larger CIS countries, especially Russia and Ukraine, have not progressed far and, significantly, little new ground has been covered during the last two years. This is in marked contrast to several smaller former Soviet republics (Kyrgyzstan, Estonia and Latvia) and Mongolia, which have managed to accede to the WTO since 1995.

In several ways, the slow pace of accession negotiations reflects the lack of progress made by most CIS countries in their transformation from centrally planned to market-based economic systems. First, accession to the WTO means that a very wide range of trade-related policies need to be formulated consistently. This has been particularly difficult to achieve for many newly independent states, whose administrative capacity is not well developed. Even if appropriate legislation is written (in which foreign advisors may play a helpful role) and passed, the subsequent implementation of WTO-consistent policies is still less than automatic. For example, Kyrgyzstan is still officially a member of a customs union with Russia, Kazakhstan and Belarus, although it has bound its tariffs on goods at very low levels that the other three countries say they find unacceptable.

Second, apart from unclear or conflicting legislation, even the implementation of existing, well-defined legal texts can be undermined by remnants of the old system such as pervasive and non-transparent state interference in the economy. For example, various types of barrier to internal trade have been documented in the case of Russia (Berkowitz and DeJong 1998). In Belarus, direct administrative intervention in the management of enterprises is widespread, and the resulting lack of transparency could easily undermine any commitments on market access that Belarus might undertake. The fact that published legal texts may not represent the full range of measures that affect international trade inevitably complicates accession negotiations.

Finally, the larger CIS countries have been reluctant to commit themselves to significantly liberalising access to their markets. For example, the initial import tariff offer by Russia would do little more than let bound rates decline to the current applied level during a seven–ten-year implementation period. Such insistence on protection for domestic firms, which extends to many service industries, contrasts sharply with the demands for market-access liberalisation by current WTO members as well as the examples of countries that recently acceded to the WTO.

Least developed countries

Up to November 1999, six out of a total of thirty-four applicants for WTO membership were defined by the WTO as least developed (Bhutan, Cambodia, Cap Verde, Lao PDR, Nepal and Vanuatu), with another two regarded as least developed by UNCTAD (Sudan and Western Samoa). In addition, twenty-eight least developed countries (UNCTAD definition) are already WTO members (Langhammer and Lücke 2000: table 1). Apart from a low *per capita* income, common characteristics include geographical remoteness (i.e. large economic distance from major markets: island and landlocked states), reliance on a small number of export goods, mostly raw materials, weak administrative capacity, economic and ecological vulnerability, lack of market-oriented institutional infrastructure, and often political instability compounded by civil disorder.

For such countries, the gains from WTO membership in terms of enhanced access to exports markets for traditional products are probably small. Raw materials already enjoy low or zero import tariffs in OECD countries; domestic supply bottlenecks (including inadequate transport facilities) probably hamper export expansion more than policy-induced barriers on the demand side. Furthermore, although some raw materials have been subject to anti-dumping procedures by industrial countries, the least developed countries are typically not leading suppliers of specific raw materials and are therefore not much affected by anti-dumping measures.

Nevertheless, there are several good reasons for least developed countries to join the WTO and for current WTO members to support this process. First, WTO membership requires transparency and consistency in a wide range of trade-related policies. At the same time, WTO membership constitutes an external commitment to enforce these rules, which may create additional momentum in favour of necessary economic reforms. For example, in many of the least developed countries, vested interests collect monopoly rents from their control of strategic sectors such as minerals, fuels, and maritime and tourist resources. Such practices conflict with WTO rules on state trading, and the implementation of these rules would lead to enhanced transparency and an opening of markets. Furthermore, greater transparency would also encourage incoming foreign direct investment.

Second, WTO membership may induce the least developed countries to liberalise market access for imports, even if they are not necessarily required to do so as they benefit from 'special and differential treatment'. Not only will reducing the implicit tax on exports increase allocative efficiency and stimulate export diversification but market opening will also reduce the power of privileged traders, who have frequently been found to drive up import prices in the presence of high import tariffs (Yeats 1990).

Third, the WTO offers some protection against unilateral pressure from powerful importers as conflicts can be made transparent by invoking the dispute settlement mechanism. This is of particular relevance for the smaller least developed countries that depend on transit routes through the territory of a large neighbour with whom they also conduct a major share of their international trade (such as Bhutan and Nepal with India, or Cambodia and Laos with Thailand).

Policy recommendations

Our discussion suggests that accession negotiations can be streamlined and accelerated if several rules of thumb, whose political and economic logic requires little justification, are obeyed. First, current members should not require applicants to liberalise market access substantially more than current members at a similar level of economic development have done. The essence of WTO rules is to ensure the transparency of national regulations and to provide for a progressive, negotiated reduction in the level of protection. There is no basis in WTO rules for requiring applicants to adopt an untypically low level of protection at the time of joining the WTO.

This rule of thumb could be questioned on the grounds that the outcome of USA–China bilateral negotiations vindicates those who call for a tough stance by current WTO members: the far-reaching liberalisation of market access agreed by China will be of long-term benefit to both China itself and its trading partners. However, this view would be short-sighted: First, accession negotiations with China could probably have been concluded long ago, with all the attendant benefits, had the US position been less out of touch with the trade regimes practised by other low-income countries.

Second, the bilateral USA–China agreement should not become a model for others, because it is heavily lopsided: despite the far-reaching Chinese commitment to trade liberalisation, the agreement allows the USA to continue to treat China as a non-market economy in anti-dumping proceedings and to subject imports from China to special safeguards. To treat China as a non-market economy is logically inconsistent because, as a WTO member, China will be subject to the restrictions on state trading contained in Article XVII of GATT 1994. Country-specific safeguards are fundamentally in contradiction with the m.f.n. principle, which requires safeguards to be applied without discrimination as to country of origin. The damage done to the WTO system by thus bending its rules cannot be justified by the short-term gains that US firms will derive from higher protection against Chinese competition.

As a second rule of thumb, applicant countries should fully accept the need for transparency in their trade-related policies and for the full implementation of relevant WTO rules. For many applicants, improvements in the transparency, coherence and consistent implementation of trade-related policies will represent the most important benefit of WTO membership. By contrast, market access for exports will only improve marginally, because most applicants already enjoy m.f.n. status with their trading partners and often benefit from preferential market access under the GSP.

As a third rule of thumb, in negotiating their commitments on market access for imported goods and services, applicants should consider benefits and costs to their economies as a whole rather than narrow sectoral interests. More often than not, more liberal market access will be beneficial overall, even if it hurts particular sectors. This applies especially to liberalisation of trade in services. Underdeveloped business services industries represent an important obstacle to growth in manufactured exports, because access to high-quality services is a key requirement for successfully entering international markets for differentiated goods.

A fourth rule of thumb is that negotiations can be accelerated if clearer priorities are set for necessary changes in national legislation and practice. While important adjustments might well need to be made early on, extended implementation periods for non-essential items could be tolerated given the complexity of WTO rules and limited administrative capacity of applicants. At the same time, the setting of priorities would focus the accession negotiations more clearly and thus ensure that applicants are not required to 'shoot at moving targets' as new demands are brought up time and again by current WTO members.

Note

Some parts of this paper have been updated from an earlier and much longer article by the same authors (Langhammer and Lücke 1999). Interested readers are invited to consult this longer article for a more detailed discussion of many issues raised in the present paper. The texts of WTO agreements mentioned in the paper as well as extensive additional information can be obtained from the WTO website (http://www.wto.org).

References

Berkowitz, D. and DeJong, D. (1998) 'Russia's internal border', Department of Economics, University of Pittsburgh, mimeo, July.

Finger, J.M., Ingco, M.D. and Reincke, U. (1996) *The Uruguay Round. Statistics on Tariff Concessions Given and Received*, Washington: World Bank.

Langhammer, R.J. and Lücke, M. (1999) 'WTO accession issues', in *The World Economy* 22(6): 837–71. Available online at http://www.uni-kiel.de/IfW/pub/kap/1999/kap905.pdf.

—— (2000) 'WTO negotiation and accession issues for vulnerable economies', conference paper, WIDER, May.

White House Office of Public Liaison (1999) 'Summary of US–China bilateral WTO agreement', mimeo. Available online at http://www.uschina.org/public/991115a.html.

WTO (1999) *Technical Note on the Accession Process*, WTO document WT/ACC/7/Rev.1. Available online from the WTO Documents Dissemination Facility at http://www.wto.org/pdf.

Yeats, A. (1990) 'Do African countries pay more for imports? Yes', *World Bank Economic Review* 4(1): 1–20.

21 Dispute settlement

A gem in need of polish and preservation

Bernhard Speyer

The WTO's dispute settlement mechanism (DSM) is widely regarded as the jewel in the crown of the Uruguay Round and the very heart of the WTO. After all, as many members repeatedly pointed out prior to the reforms agreed in the Uruguay Round, what good are multilateral rules if they cannot be enforced? Five years of experience with the new DSM have indeed documented its central role in the multilateral, rules-based international trade regime. Despite the occasional (and understandable) misgivings felt by losing parties to a dispute, the DSM enjoys widespread support and is actively used, which in itself is testimony to its attractiveness.

However, it has also been revealed that procedural weaknesses in the dispute settlement process still exist. Perhaps even more importantly, a certain disenchantment with the DSM is also discernible as governments and citizens realise that perhaps they got more than they bargained for. The WTO's dispute settlement has become the institution where the fundamental question of how to reconcile a rules-based international trade regime with the idea of sovereignty and the concerns of civil society presents itself time and again to politicians and trade negotiators and begs for answers that are not easily found.

Reform of the DSM was not at the top of any nation's negotiating agenda for the Millennium Round. This shows that, by and large, WTO member states are content with the system established in the Uruguay Round and certainly regard other issues as more pressing. Still, a review of the experience with the new DSM is of interest beyond the mechanism itself.

Experience with the new DSM

The new DSM provides WTO member states with an automatic right to lodge a complaint, entitles them to use an independent appellate review and offers them an effective enforcement mechanism. It provides a system that guarantees the framework of predictable, enforceable and generally stable rules for traders. The DSM is used actively by all member states, with the notable exception of the poorest, especially African, countries. From the birth of the WTO on 1 January 1995 up to mid-March 2000, there have been 191 requests for consultation concerning 149 distinct matters. For comparison, under the old DSM there had been only 207 cases in the entire period from 1948 to 1990. The higher number of cases also reflects the fact that member states have assumed more obligations under the Uruguay Round agreement. Countries have used the DSM responsibly: cases brought so far have merited the charge, i.e. cases have not been raised merely to harass other states.

In an earlier paper (Speyer 1998), I set out some hypotheses concerning the DSM, which can now be assessed again on a broader empirical basis. First, developing and smaller nations make more use of the new DSM than of the old. While this partly reflects the increasing role of developing countries as trading nations, it is also a sign of confidence in the system. If LDCs did not believe that the DSM would be powerful and impartial enough to guarantee their rights even against large trading powers, they would not try. Out of the 191 requests and 149 distinct matters, forty-nine and forty, respectively, have been raised by developing country members (WTO 2000). In other words, about one in four cases sees a developing country as a complainant, which is below their share in world trade but higher than their share under the old DSM.

Second, the USA has been the most active user of the DSM, having been or being the complainant in fifty-five of the 191 requests. With a share in total requests of 29 per cent, the USA is well above its share of world exports, which in 1998 amounted to 17 per cent. On top of this, the USA has reserved its third party rights in almost every other major case. In particular, there has been no case against the EU where the USA has not been the complainant or a third party. (To be fair, it should be added that the EU is catching up rapidly: forty-nine complaints were raised by the EU, which represents a share of 25 per cent. However, this is less out of line with its share in world exports, which amounted to 20.3 per cent in 1998, than is the case with the USA.)

The active role of the USA is partly explained by the fact that it is the second largest trading power and has a diverse export base; it is therefore most likely to be embroiled in numerous trade conflicts. However, of greater importance is that this active use reflects domestic politics. At the end of the Uruguay Round, the US administration found it hard to sell the results to Congress for approval. There was great scepticism on the part of Congress as to whether the obligations that trading partners had subscribed to would actually be implemented. If not, Congress would have demanded that foreign markets be prised open using unilateral measures such as 'Super 301'. The administration therefore had to demonstrate that the multilateral system, and dispute settlement in particular, works. It did so by launching a number of cases where success for the USA was most likely (e.g. India–patents, Turkey–films, Korea–shelf life).[1]

Third, a significant number of cases (forty-four) have been settled during the consultation phase or have been suspended. This is a high proportion of those cases that have moved beyond the consultation stage or have been settled (seventy-eight of the 191 requests are still in the consultation phase, which leaves 113 requests where a decision has been taken). This is easily explained by the fact that governments know that there definitely will be panel proceedings if they do not compromise. So if governments know that they are violating

WTO rules they will avoid a highly publicised case unless domestic opposition to revoking the measure is too great. Consequently, it is not surprising to find that almost all complaints that are not settled during the consultation phase have gone all the way to the appellate body. Indeed, a negligible number of panel rulings (four) have not been appealed against.

Finally, as predicted, the EU has proved to be one of the more intransigent defendants, as is particularly obvious in the EU–bananas case. The EU has used all kinds of procedural trick to avoid implementing the panel's ruling, and the case has certainly exposed a major weakness of the new DSM.

The new DSM is much quicker and has a fixed time frame; however, the whole process still takes too long. It is unattractive for commercial interests to devote resources to drawing their government's attention to a trade violation by another country unless it can be expected to realise the commercial benefits from a repeal of those violations in a reasonable period. The EU–bananas case has amply demonstrated that member states can still engage in considerable foot dragging if they want to do so. The weakness exposed by this case is that there is no mechanism that compels a losing party to implement a panel's decision properly. By doing something, but not enough, a defendant can still drag out the whole process almost indefinitely, because the complainant must challenge the new, still non-compliant measure anew. This obviously erodes trust in the system.

The EU's foot dragging is typical, and for a fundamental reason: while the new DSM automatically ensures that there is a ruling whenever a complaint is brought, the WTO has no ability to sanction offending actions directly or to compel compliance with rulings. This will remain so as long as there are nation-states. However, to deplore the lack of direct sanctioning power is to fundamentally misinterpret the nature of the DSM. It is not a strictly judicial process akin to national court proceedings. The power of the DSM rests in the fact that no country, no matter how powerful, is willing to bear the cost to its reputation of consistently standing outside the body of international trade law. As the EU has shown, it can take a very long time for countries to finally give in, but in the end, most are likely to do so. In any case, retaliation cannot be the aim of dispute settlement as it raises barriers rather than lowers them.

Besides, to regard the WTO as powerless ignores an important feature of the DSM: any country is allowed to lodge a complaint if it can demonstrate a *prima facie* violation of its legitimate export interests, even if these are only potential rather than actual. In its ruling on the EU–bananas case, the appellate body explicitly reiterated this provision (which already existed under the GATT), pointing out that the USA was entitled to act as a complaining party even though it was not an exporter of bananas itself. This provision allows for large coalitions to be built that are able to exert enormous pressure on a defendant. It is evident that this is of particular importance for smaller countries, whose sanctioning power is obviously limited because they account for only a small portion of the trade of large countries. By teaming up with other countries, considerable pressure can be generated, which in the end should discipline even the most intransigent defendant. More fundamentally, the provision underscores that WTO rules are designed to create competitive opportunities, not actual trade (Vermulst *et al.* 1999).

Diplomacy versus the rule of law

While the DSM has become more judicial, it retains important elements of diplomacy. The WTO is an intergovernmental organisation and as such the scene of diplomatic conventions. It is not without reason that the dispute settlement understanding stresses that the prior aim of the DSM is to secure a positive solution to a dispute, i.e. a mutually acceptable solution arrived at in negotiations rather than imposed by the WTO. That the DSM walks the tightrope between diplomacy and the rule of law can be seen from five features:

- It is usually not appreciated that the consultation period is extremely important. It is not only an opportunity to arrive at an amicable settlement using the good offices that the WTO Secretariat is willing to provide in this phase. It is above all a phase in which a government can signal to the other party the difficulties that domestic political conditions and concerns cause. It is also a forum where compensation and concession can be exchanged away from the eyes of the public. The confidential nature of the consultation period is therefore extremely important. Of course, this clashes with demands for more transparency in the dispute settlement process. As member states do not have a legal obligation to notify the results, let alone the circumstances of their consultations, there is also some concern on the part of the WTO that smaller countries may be bullied into agreeing to positions that are not in their interests (Hoekman and Mavroidis 1999). These concerns certainly cannot be brushed aside easily but must be weighed against the advantages of an 'out-of-court' settlement. The fact that a large number of cases are settled amicably in the consultation period attests to this.
- WTO rulings have no binding legal force beyond the issue in dispute. The intention to establish coherence in WTO rulings will establish a body of case law on which future rulings can be based. However, in the absence of binding legal powers, panels and the appellate body possess some latitude to accommodate diplomatic considerations, which, indeed, they have been willing to use (see below).
- No private party nor the WTO itself can initiate cases. It is up to member state governments to decide whether to pursue cases or not in due consideration of other political aims.
- Another instrument that the WTO uses to retain some political leeway is the doctrine of judicial restraint. When the new DSM was established, it was understood that the new body should not set law, merely interpret it. The appellate body in particular should restrict itself to ensuring the consistency of panel rulings and to rectifying legally false rulings; it should not

engage in fact finding itself. As it has turned out, the appellate body has indeed frequently found fault with the legal reasoning of the panels. It could simply have stopped there, leaving it to the disputants to lodge a new complaint. But this would certainly have been unsatisfactory; it was there-fore in the interests of member states that the appellate body engaged in some fact finding and law making. Indeed, one cannot but agree with the logic put forward by the appellate body that, in order to check whether the panel had arrived at a correct assessment of the facts, the appellate body had to assess the facts itself. What is more, some of the very broad cases brought before the DSM could not have been ruled on unless panels and the appellate body had been willing to interpret WTO regulations.

However, the appellate body has been very cautious in pushing the borders of judicial restraint. Obviously, this first responds to concerns by member states, some of which have already complained about the appellate body misusing its powers. But second, judicial restraint is also advantageous from the point of view of the appellate body itself preserving the diplomatic elements of dispute settlement. In the USA–shirts and blouses case, the appellate body explicitly endorsed the doctrine, thereby freeing itself from the obligation to rule on all legal issues raised by the disputing govern-ments. Politically, this has the advantage that both the panels and the appellate body do not necessarily have to rule on issues that might be polit-ically sensitive to either of the disputing governments.

- Another area where the WTO's dispute settlement has shown a penchant for constructive ambiguity is the question of the legal effect of a panel report. Somewhat contrary to public perception (but certainly in line with actual experience as regards implementation of panel rulings), it is ambiguous whether a losing country has the obligation to bring the violating measure into line with the panel's recommendations or whether it may choose to compensate the victorious party and leave the measure intact. Responding to concerns about the loss of sovereignty voiced in the US Congress during the ratification process of the Uruguay Round agree-ment, US government officials, among others, have maintained that there is no legal duty to perform. In contrast, Jackson (1998) points out that there is a strong propensity towards the legal obligation of countries to comply with panel rulings. However, as he rightly emphasises, focusing on compensation and/or retaliation actually misses the point. It is not the threat of retaliation that induces countries to act but the credibility of the judgement rendered, which makes it politically and diplomatically difficult to ignore even if a country could theoretically get away with it.

Involvement of the private sector

As in the area of international monetary policy, private sector involvement is a fashionable idea in international trade policy these days. However, this is where the similarities end. Whereas private sector involvement in international monetary affairs is mostly supported by the public sector and academic literature while being resented by the private sector, in dispute settlement private sector players actively seek greater influence, although the desirability of this is viewed with some apprehension by most governments and the academic literature.

Behind the idea of private sector involvement in dispute settlement is the notion that, like trade policy, dispute settlement is a two-level game (Putnam 1988). This is true in two respects: first, a government will only consider bringing a complaint to the WTO if domestic export interests draw its attention to treaty violations by nations; and, second, dispute settlement procedures must take into account that governments must be able to sell and implement the verdict domestically.

Complaints will only be lodged when domestic export interests exist and when those interests are able to exert pressure on their own government to use the DSM against another (Hoekman and Mavroidis 1999). This requires, first, that export interests are informed about the obligations other governments have taken on and, second, that they expect the return from an eventually successful verdict to exceed the cost of presenting the case to the government. The expected return in turn depends on the probability that the government pursues the case, the likelihood of winning the case and the expected pay-off when winning the case.

It follows that collective action problems may prevent cases being pursued if companies assume that the pay-off from prising export markets open would have to be shared with free riders. It also follows that the DSM will only be used to prise open large export markets. There is little incentive to sue against the violation of a WTO obligation by a small, poor country – and indeed none of the least developed countries has been involved in a DSM case. It should also be noted that the long duration of dispute settlements reduces the pay-off, which is an added disincentive. Finally, it follows that the degree of responsiveness of a government to complaints brought by the private sector will have a decisive influence.

Should one draw from this that the private sector be given the right to sue other nations in the WTO directly rather than having to go via its own government? Certainly, this would go a long way towards raising the private sector's interest in the WTO and would also greatly enhance legal security for internationally active firms. It may also prevent governments tacitly colluding at the expense of the private sector. However, as mentioned above, unfiltered access of the private sector to the DSM may not be desirable from a political point of view. Raising trade disputes inevitably causes tensions with other countries. Given the fact that trade policy is but one policy target among many, governments must retain the right to decide whether the issue at hand is important enough to be pursued at a particular point in time or, indeed, at all.

Sensitive cases: environment and food safety

Selling DSB rulings domestically has become a major issue ever since the USA–tuna case turned the attention of environmental groups to the existence and the importance of the WTO. The US government, in particular, has been under immense pressure to open the WTO to civil society. The administration has therefore proposed the enhancement of transparency of dispute settlement and giving interest groups direct access to the process. Several other governments, among them many from the developing world, have already indicated their fervent opposition to this idea.

The WTO itself has responded actively to public concerns. The appellate body has also gone out of its way to show its willingness to take into account the concerns of civil society by explicitly inviting private parties to submit their opinions: overruling the panel, the appellate body in the USA–shrimps case explicitly invited any interested party to comment on cases heard at the WTO by sending *amicus curiae* briefs. The appellate body noted that while a panel does not have to take such information into account, there was no reason not to allow the information to be sent. This statement was undoubtedly politically motivated, intended as a reaction to charges of a lack of transparency and democracy in the actions and structures of the WTO. Clearly, governments are no longer the only voices heard in WTO disputes. But to go beyond *amicus curiae* briefs and to admit private actors as parties to a case would seriously damage the DSM. Not only would it cause disputes to take longer to settle but it would also make cases more acrimonious.

No matter how skilfully the DSM walks the tightrope between diplomacy and the rule of law, the more clear-cut the case, the harder it becomes for panels and the appellate body to take the domestic political interests of the defendant into account. On the other hand, the greater the political fall-out, the more powerful the member state and the more support a defendant receives from other governments, the more likely it is that panels and the appellate body will seek a compromise. The appellate body has on several occasions accepted the overall panel ruling while substantially altering the reasoning. This was partly in order to ensure the legal consistency of WTO rulings, which is one of the tasks that the appellate body was created for; but it was also partly to enable the losing party to defuse political tensions at home by making the ruling more palatable.

The fiasco of Seattle has reinforced the impression that in the eyes of the public the DSM is not the 'jewel in the crown' that economists and lawyers tend to regard it as. Rather than seeing it as the triumph of the rule of law over power politics, the DSM is charged with undermining national sovereignty, damaging the environment, killing jobs and hurting people's health.

Exemplars of this are the EU–hormones, USA–shrimps and USA–gasoline cases (Garrett and McCall Smith 1999). In the first of these, the appellate body did not change the verdict of the panel but substantially altered the legal reasoning. In particular and most importantly, it reversed the assignment of burden of proof: governments are allowed to set safety standards higher than international standards, subject to the limitation that member states must offer some scientific justification. It is for the complainant to prove that the higher standards are unreasonable.

In the latter two cases, the appellate body addressed the sensitive issue of environmental concerns. In the USA–gasoline case, the appellate body explicitly stated that 'the ability of any WTO member to take measures ... to protect the environment is not an issue'. It fact, the appellate body goes out of its way to stress that the protection of the environment is an important issue that member states should devote some energy to. In the USA–shrimps case too, the appellate body said that the USA had a legitimate aim but pursued this aim using the wrong, *viz.* unilateral, instruments. Beyond proving the WTO's desire to display its willingness to take concerns about the transparency and accountability of the institution into account, both cases are typical examples of the appellate body's tendency to make rulings easier to swallow politically for the losing party while keeping the verdict itself intact.

It is not only the appellate body but also member states (above all, the USA and the EU) that have shown restraint and displayed an interest in preserving the integrity of the DSM. Cases that are highly politicised and that would have caused political uproar in the defending country have not been pressed hard. This is most obvious in cases such as Japan–Fuji and USA–Helms–Burton, which seem to have been dropped tacitly. Obviously, neither the EU nor the US administration (nor any other member state, for that matter) has an interest in damaging the DSM, even if they occasionally resent rulings against them (the stance of the US Congress on this is less certain, though). Governments seem to realise that while the DSM is at the heart of the WTO, it is also the potential source of conflict between member states and must therefore be handled carefully.

Recommendations

A number of recommendations can be drawn from this:

- The dispute settlement process must be speeded up. It still takes too long for rulings to be passed. In fact, some acceleration might be achieved quite quickly, e.g. by establishing panels as soon as they are requested, i.e. at the first meeting of the DSB that deals with the request rather than at the second, as is now the case. Given that there is a consultation period preceding this, where parties can make up their minds about whether to settle peacefully, there is little rationale for putting off the panel investigation if they decide not to.

- Governments should avoid disputes arising in the first place. All too often it is not protectionist intentions but simple negligence that is the reason why national laws are not in accordance with WTO commitments. (Incidentally, this may be one of the reasons why so many cases are settled quickly at the consultation stage.) When setting law, national legislators must check properly for compliance with international obligations – one would think that this was a natural thing to do in the age of globalisation, but all too often it does not seem to happen. Besides, an explicit and publicly available assessment of whether proposed legislation contradicts obligations under WTO rules would also help to make the private sector aware of WTO obligations and, therewith, export opportunities.

- The success of the DSM stretches the resources of the institution. The shortage of funds is also a problem, because almost all cases that are not settled in the consultation period are taken all the way to the appellate body. There is an urgent need for more financial support and personnel in order to ensure that all cases are adequately dealt with and that rulings are consistent.

- In order to increase the chances of the smaller and poorest states claiming their rights, special attention should be paid to their needs. Financial support given by richer nations and passed on through the WTO should ensure that the smaller and poorer nations are in a position to hire professional advice in order to be represented by private lawyers. In the EU–bananas case, the appellate body approved the use of private lawyers to represent member governments in the dispute settlement process. This is of particular importance for smaller nations, which often do not have the resources or enough trade experts to present their cases. However, it also carries the danger that proceedings acquire a more legalistic, confrontational nature, as trade lawyers may be less inclined to pay attention to diplomatic considerations and niceties than government officials.

- The consequences of China's accession for the DSM should be considered carefully in advance. Given China's size, its trade surplus with the USA and the EU and the dual nature of its economy, it is most likely that a disproportionate number of complaints could potentially be launched concerning China's trade policy regime and its social and economic system in general. This in turn would cause enormous international tensions, which could block the work of the WTO. Western governments would therefore be well advised to make up their minds which cases they really consider worth pursuing. This will be walking a tightrope between impartially preserving the integrity of WTO rules on the one hand and giving due consideration to geo-politics on the other.

- Increasing transparency and opening the WTO to civil society is the price to be paid for the political acceptance of further liberalisation. The permissive consensus that liberalisation has enjoyed for most of the postwar period is certainly gone for good, but to give private parties access to the DSM beyond the invitation to provide *amicus curiae* briefs is courting disaster. Dispute settlement must remain firmly in the hands of governments, otherwise the WTO will be paralysed.

- Governments would be well advised not to overemphasise the legal elements of WTO dispute settlement. It is not without irony that governments display a growing tendency to use the increasingly legalistic DSM, while the private sector increasingly resorts to out-of-court settlements, because court proceedings are considered too expensive, too time-consuming, too acrimonious and too damaging, both to one's own reputation and to chances for future cooperation. Legal battles always leave behind winners and losers, and sour relations. Dispute settlement must not be allowed to become the dominant feature associated with the WTO. The cause of free trade and progressive liberalisation would be lost if member states saw the organisation as little more than a courthouse. Litigation is merely about defending the *status quo* and claiming what is due; this is important, but it does not help to move forward.

Notes

This article reflects the personal opinion of the author only.
1   A brief description of these and all other cases can be found on the WTO's website at http://www.wto.org/wto/dispute/bulletin.htm.

References

Garrett, G. and McCall Smith, J. (1999) 'The politics of WTO dispute settlement', paper presented to the American Political Science Association, Atlanta, September 1–5.

Hoekman, B.M. and Mavroidis, P.C. (1999) 'Enforcing multilateral commitments: dispute settlement and developing countries', paper presented at the WTO/World Bank conference on 'Developing Countries in a Millennium Round', Geneva, September 20–21.

Jackson, J.H. (1998) 'Designing and implementing effective dispute settlement procedures: WTO dispute settlement, appraisal and prospects', in A.O. Krueger (ed.) *The WTO as an International Organization*, Chicago: University of Chicago Press, 161–80.

Putnam, R. (1988) 'Diplomacy and domestic policies: the logic of two-level games', *International Organization* 42(3): 427–60.

Speyer, B. (1998) 'The WTO dispute settlement mechanism – a new era for the world economy?', *Aussenwirtschaft* 53(1): 129–51.

Vermulst, E., Mavroidis, P.C. and Waer, P. (1999) 'The functioning of the appellate body after four years: towards rule integrity', *Journal of World Trade* 33(2): 1–50.

WTO (2000) overview of the state-of-play of WTO disputes, as of 23 March 2000; available at http://www.wto.org/wto/dispute/bulletin.htm.

22 The WTO and international governance

Sylvia Ostry

Introduction

The financial crisis in Asia in 1997 triggered a lively and sometimes raucous debate on the need to redesign the so-called architecture of the postwar Bretton Woods institutions, the International Monetary Fund and the World Bank. What has resulted thus far is most aptly described as improved plumbing and interior design. By a strange twist of events, it may be that the 'crisis' confronting the first post-Cold War institution, the World Trade Organization, could prove to be the catalyst for a serious rethink of the existing architecture. This chapter will begin with a brief account of the creation of the WTO and how it has become a magnet for dissent and policy overload, before turning to the broader question of the WTO and international governance.

The Uruguay Round

After repeated efforts by the Americans beginning in the early 1980s, the Uruguay Round was launched in Punta del Este in September 1986 and formally concluded in Marrakech, Morocco, in April 1994, several years later than the original target completion date. The extraordinary difficulty in both initiating and completing the round stemmed essentially from two fundamental factors: the nearly insuperable problem of finishing the unfinished business of past negotiations, most of all agriculture; and the equally contentious issue of introducing new agenda items, notable trade in services and intellectual property and, in a more limited way, investment. The Europeans blocked the launch to avoid coming to grips with the Common Agricultural Policy (CAP), and a number of developing countries, led by Brazil and India, were bitterly opposed to including these so-called 'new issues'. In the end, the final trade-off involved a North–South deal across the old and new issues, a deal that transformed the world trade system.

Although the 'new issues' are not identical – obviously, negotiations on telecommunications or financial services differ from intellectual property rights – they do have one common or generic characteristic. They involve not the border barriers of the original GATT but domestic regulatory and legal systems embedded in the institutional infrastructure of the economy. The Uruguay Round thus provided significant impetus to the deepening integration of the global economy or, as it is now termed, globalisation. The degree of intrusiveness into domestic sovereignty bears little resemblance to the shallow integration of the postwar years, with its focus on border barriers. The WTO has shifted trade policy from the GATT model of negative regulation – what governments must not do – to positive regulation, or what governments must do. Moreover, the WTO dispute settlement procedure – the most ambitious ever adopted in the history of international law – provides the ultimate guarantee of protection for the negotiated rules. Many legal scholars see the WTO as embedding a global constitution overseen by a supranational juridical system.

The inclusion of the new issues in the Uruguay Round was a US initiative, and this policy agenda was largely driven by American multinationals that were market leaders in the services and high-tech sectors. These corporations made it clear to the government that without a fundamental rebalancing of the GATT they would not continue to support a multilateral policy but would prefer a bilateral or regional track. But they did not just talk the talk, they also walked the walk, organising business coalitions in support of services and intellectual property in Europe and Japan as well as some smaller OECD countries. The activism paid off, and it is fair to say that American multinationals played a key – perhaps even the key – role in establishing the new global policy system.

However, it is also important to underline that by the end of the 1980s another major change in economic policy making was underway. The revolution of 'Ronald Thatcherism', which began in the OECD countries, had been adopted by many developing countries by the onset of the 1990s, and this greatly reduced the resistance to negotiations on trade in services such as financial and telecommunications services. Economic reform – deregulation, privatisation, liberalisation – in part fostered by IMF and World Bank programmes, was seen as essential to launching and sustaining higher growth. Put another way, in January 1995, at the official birth of the WTO, as a result of a favourable confluence of different forces, support by governments for domestic and international liberalisation as a dominant ideological paradigm seemed near-universal.

Because of the focus of attention on the 'new issues' and economic regulatory reform, the negotiations on social regulation concerning product standards, health and safety measures, and the environment received little publicity and little attention from the senior policy ranks. In the OECD countries, social regulation started in the late 1960s and has been accelerating since then. The OECD has called the phenomenon 'regulatory inflation', since social regulation has grown by 300 to 400 per cent in the developed countries since 1970. With a bit of a stretch perhaps, one could say that the postwar economic regulatory state of the advanced countries is withering away, while the social regulatory state is alive, well and growing. While there are a number of reasons for this development in the rich countries, a major factor has been the increasing influence of non-governmental organisations (NGOs). These advocacy coalitions are also a key element in the change in ambience of trade policy today. From the apparent 'globaphilia' of 1995, we are now witnessing a rising chorus of 'globaphobia'. But it would be unwise to evaluate the implications of these new transnational actors simply on the basis of the street theatre in Seattle, because they have and will continue to play an important role in the policy process. A brief digression on the defeat of an international negotiation, the Multilateral Agreement on Investment, or MAI, best illustrates this.

The new actors: the NGOs

In October 1997, forty-seven NGOs from twenty-three countries and five continents met at OECD headquarters in Paris. The consultation had been arranged at the request of the World Wide Fund for Nature and some national representatives, who had been lobbied by domestic advocacy organisations. The NGOs argued that the MAI would undermine sustainable development and national sovereignty. The most powerful case for this argument concerned the MAI's investor protection mechanism. This replicated the investment provisions in the North American Free Trade Agreement (NAFTA), which included procedures for resolving disputes by which private parties as well as governments could take action and adopted a very broad definition of investment expropriation, so broad that it could lead to investor claims against government regulation in, say, environmental or health areas, which negatively affect the value of investment.

After the consultation, the groups at the meeting organised an anti-MAI coalition and launched an international campaign on the Internet to stop the negotiations. Groups in Canada and the United States provided a constant flow of information to websites in many countries to coordinate the campaign. By October 1998, the negotiations had been suspended, and in December, after the official withdrawal of the French government at the request of the red–green members of the coalition, they were officially terminated.

There were a number of reasons why the MAI failed, but there seems little doubt that the NGOs played a key role. It is worth underlining the importance of the environmental issue, because it echoed earlier events in Geneva. In 1991, after a panel ruling that the USA had violated its GATT obligations by banning Mexican tuna caught by a process that killed dolphins, American environmental groups mounted a major attack on 'GATT-zilla'. The campaign in Washington raged against the cabal of faceless bureaucrats in Geneva who were undermining American sovereignty and subverting democracy. Although the GATT survived and the Uruguay Round created the WTO, many of the themes, albeit for the most part in less colourful terms, are at the core of continuing environmentalist criticism of the WTO. While the greens are not the only critics of the WTO, they have been the most effective in mobilising support among a wide range of other advocacy groups that, for different reasons, see the WTO as an institution captured by and serving only corporate interests.

As noted, the campaign against the MAI was greatly facilitated by the

Internet as use accelerated in the 1990s. However, while building on the experience of the anti-MAI campaign, the mobilisation of dissent against the WTO meeting in Seattle beginning on 30 November was far broader and deeper. A survey of a large number of websites focusing on Seattle suggests that there are two broad categories of NGO coalitions or networks – what might be termed 'mobilisation networks', whose chief objective is to rally support for a specific set of activities, and 'technical networks' designed to facilitate and provide specific information.

Two examples of mobilisation networks that organised the demonstrations in Seattle are the International Civil Society Opposing a Millennium Round (ICS) and People's Global Action (PGA). The ICS claims to represent more than 600 NGOs from over seventy-five countries. The list is attached to its statement and includes environmentalists, religious and human rights organisations, labour coalitions, student groups and others from all OECD countries and a large number of developing countries. PGA, formed in Geneva in February 1998, is an equally broad coalition solely dedicated to organising a conference in Seattle on November 30, at the start of the WTO meetings. On the Internet, the conference was termed N30. PGA organised a 'carnival against capitalism' in the city of London on 18 June 1999. The J18 carnival, as reported in the *Daily Telegraph*, deteriorated into violence, resulting in more than six hours of rioting and vandalism in the financial district. (Although both the ICS and PGA warned against violence in the weeks just before the Seattle meeting, neither seemed to be aware of the plans of the Oregon anarchist network.)

The message circulated by both these NGOs, as well as a large number of others, was very similar. They charged that the WTO is dominated by transnational corporations; that rules and procedures are undemocratic and untransparent; and that it is harming the environment and creating increasing inequality. The WTO has become a magnet for dissent and a target for the inchoate but growing backlash against globalisation, or corporate globalisation as its opponents call it. This core message is similar to that of the Council of Canadians or the US-based Preamble Center in its new publication *Globalisation: A Primer* (Weisbrot 1999) or to the book released by Ralph Nader's Public Citizen, *Whose Trade Organization: Corporate Globalisation and the Erosion of Democracy* (Wallach and Sforza 1999).

In marked contrast to the mobilisation networks are the technical networks such as the Geneva-based Centre for International Environmental Law and the Institute for Global Communications in Palo Alto, California, whose objectives include innovation in software to support NGOs' special needs. The primary purpose of these, and a number of similar networks, is to facilitate the greater participation of NGOs in the policy process by providing a continuously updated flow of strategic and technical information. Since information is a key asset in the policy process, the basic objective of these technical networks is to ensure that the market for policy ideas is contestable and no longer the sole preserve of governments and the traditional lobbies.

Another group of technical networks is dedicated to enhancing the effectiveness of developing countries in the trade policy domain. Examples include the Third World Network based in Malaysia and the International South Group Network (ISGN) centred in Africa, as well as longstanding and influential development groups such as Christian Aid and Oxfam. For the first time in the history of the postwar trading system, developing countries were provided with continually updated analytical information as well as policy options. The impact of these new networks in coordinating opposition to the inclusion of labour standards in the WTO was exemplified by the unprecedented walk-out of virtually all the developing countries from Latin America, Asia and Africa that ended the Seattle meeting.

But the new prominence of the NGOs in trade policy making should be evaluated in a broader context. Thus, the US business community – in marked contrast to their transnational activist role in the Uruguay Round – maintained a low profile with respect to the WTO negotiations. Apart from the service industries, the business community in both Europe and the United States has demonstrated little in the way of what might be termed generic or systemic interest. The current lack of activism is remarkable, and one can only speculate as to the reasons. Perhaps the Uruguay Round was truly a singular event because it involved a radical transformation of the GATT system and the stakes were very high. Moreover, the global span of many corporations today facilitates direct negotiation with host governments, so, many of them ask, why bother with lengthy and tedious intergovernmental negotiations? Privatisation of trade policy for corporations may be an attractive option but is very disturbing for the global community. Another factor in the US case was the corporate restructuring of the past decade, which has required a sharper focus on a limited number of specific objectives with shorter-term impact on the bottom line. Thus Chinese accession to the WTO was the top priority for lobbying efforts. That also seemed to be the case for the US government, whose objectives for a new round were minimal and defensive. In the absence of a multilateral option, as the 1980s so clearly demonstrated, a revival of unilateralism should not be ruled out.

To sum up, if one were asked to predict the future of the world trading system, the best single word would be 'uncertain'. But maybe that is too terse a reply. A layman's definition of Heisenberg's uncertainty principle is that we can know where we are but not where we are going, or we can know where we are going but not where we are. So, how about Heisenberg squared as a more specific response? Yet that too is inadequate. Many lessons can be learned from the Seattle experience, but the most important is the urgent need to reform the WTO, a necessary but not sufficient condition to ensure the survival of a global rules-based trading system. The postwar architecture for international cooperation also needs restructuring.

Reform of the WTO plus

The political compact that created the postwar economic architecture, the

Bretton Woods institutions and what was to have been the International Trade Organization or ITO, rested on an assurance that international rules would preserve space for domestic policy autonomy. The ITO never came into existence, but one piece of it, the GATT, survived and indeed thrived. The objectives of the GATT were liberalising trade through successive multilateral negotiations aimed at reducing border barriers and creating rules to govern and sustain the liberalising momentum. The domestic policy space, defined in terms of economic regulation and the maintenance of full employment, was safeguarded by rules to permit temporary blockage of imports under clearly specified terms (dumping, subsidies and safeguards against import surges), as well as the rarely used but very broad Article XXIII concerning 'nullification and impairment'. These rules were intended to provide a buffer or interface between the international objective of sustained liberalisation and the objectives of domestic policy, in other words sovereignty. But with the Uruguay Round, the central domain of trade policy became domestic regulation and legal systems, and the definition of domestic policy space today not only differs from that of the postwar period (with the decline in economic regulatory intervention) but also differs significantly among the members of the WTO, especially with respect to social policy. The protective buffers have become protectionist tools and in any case are largely irrelevant as a means of safeguarding the diverse and changing concept of sovereignty among the 130-plus members of the WTO.

It is not simply the move inside the border that represents the radical break between the GATT and the WTO. Of equal significance, as mentioned earlier, is the greatly strengthened dispute settlement mechanism. It is important to note that the business groups that lobbied so successfully to include intellectual property in the Uruguay Round did so because the UN agency, the World Intellectual Property Organization (WIPO), has no dispute mechanism to enforce these rights. And the same is true for labour rights in the ILO or environmental policy in UNEP, the United Nations Environment Program. That is why the WTO is not simply a magnet for discontent but also for policy overload.

Since the establishment of the WTO, the most high-profile and contentious disputes have concerned environmental or food safety issues. The WTO does not regulate environmental or social policy, but its rules, negotiated in the original GATT consensus, seek to constrain the trade-restrictive impact of domestic regulation in order to prevent such regulation being used as a disguised barrier to trade. In recent cases, dispute panels, and especially the appellate body, have been forced to interpret the WTO rules that govern domestic environmental and food safety policies. Thus, as is the case with all courts and all legal rules in such complex areas, that interpretation has essentially involved these judges in an international institution making law that defines the boundary for domestic policy space. And, not surprisingly, this has spawned the criticism, especially by the North American NGOs, that the WTO suffers a 'democratic deficit'. Here is the echo of the 1960s cry for participatory democracy.

The NGO demand for democratisation really comprises three requests: more transparency (publication of WTO documents, etc.); more access to WTO activities such as meetings of committees (this usually stops short of a request to be included in negotiations); and, for the legal advocacy NGOs, the right to observer status and to present *amicus curiae* briefs in dispute settlement panels and the appellate body. Of these three, transparency is generally agreed by most member countries, and indeed a great deal of WTO documentation is now available on its website. The right to greater participation is far more controversial and needs to be considered carefully (see below). The third request is opposed by many Southern NGOs as well as a large number of governments. This is worth spelling out.

Whatever the merits of the case for participation as *amicus curiae* in dispute settlement procedures by NGOs, it is clear that if it were granted other non-governmental actors would, in the name of fairness, demand equal treatment: for example corporations, unions and private legal firms. Furthermore, since *amicus* briefs often carry little weight in judicial decisions, it seems likely that the next step would be a demand for the right to bring cases directly. The result would be to transform the mechanism into a purely litigious and adversarial process. It is difficult to see how this would 'democratise' the WTO unless one subscribed to the view that in a 'true' democracy private litigation is preferable to government regulation. While some would argue that the United States is moving to a system where 'lawsuits make policy', this combination of *laisser-faire* and *laisser-litiger* is not a model appropriate to an international institution. Indeed, there are now a number of proposals for reform of the dispute settlement system to make it less litigious and to promote mediation and arbitration in contentious cases.

However, the NGO demand for democracy in terms of participation is perhaps the most difficult and controversial. The WTO is an intergovernmental organisation, and most member governments want to keep it that way. They argue that NGOs should deal with their own governments if they wish to play a role in the policy process. The response of the NGO advocates of participation is that only they have a truly transnational vision, which is lacking in national governments. But this is an inadequate argument. Governments are accountable to their citizens, albeit some more so than others. How would we define accountability in the case of NGOs? And what about transparency? Who and where are their members? What is their source of funding? Are they 'accountable' to their membership, or to their funders? These are simple examples of some of the questions that would have to be settled before a meaningful proposal on 'participatory democracy' in the WTO could be debated. But any such proposal would be fiercely opposed by most developing countries in the WTO – especially after their experience in Seattle.

For these countries, especially the poorest, the democratic deficit of the WTO stems from its governance structure. They feel – and are – excluded from many of the decision-making forums. The WTO is a member-driven organisation governed by a rule of consensus: there is no weighted voting, as is the case in the Bretton Woods institutions. But an organisation with over 130 members, often with widely different views on important issues, cannot function when key and contentious policy issues must be negotiated. So other decision-making processes must be and are established. And, not surprisingly, these are dominated by the so-called Quad (the USA, the EU, Japan and Canada) and the larger and more influential developing countries. This process worked in the past, but the issues today are far more divisive and likely to become even more so. Thus, the most urgent requirement for enhancing the flexibility, adaptability and legitimacy of the WTO is to establish a smaller body or executive committee.

The executive committee would be able to meet on a regular basis and, with the assistance of the director-general and the secretariat, review current and prospective policy issues in order to advise the biennial ministerial conference, which would retain full decision-making authority. With such a forum, at both ministerial conference and senior official level, the norms and principles of policy and the fundamental issue of forging a new international contract could be discussed and debated. It is essential to underline that forging a consensus in a smaller group aided by expert policy-analytical information is facilitated by peer group pressure. The executive committee can then play a role, at both the official and ministerial conference level, in promoting the extension of that consensus to the entire membership.

In establishing such a committee, the most difficult problem is membership, and the various formulas tried out in the Uruguay Round failed to secure agreement. But the establishment of the trade policy review mechanism (TPRM) created a precedent for a possible formula. Thus different countries were subject to different review schedules on the basis of the member's share of world trade. This same formula could be used to establish a committee of reasonable size and rotating membership, which would ensure that all countries and regions would be represented within a given time frame. Whether the TPRM or some other formula is chosen, the main point is that there should be a reform of the governance structure that is transparent. The present *ad hoc* 'shadow cabinet' is a legacy of the past.

Another function of the executive committee supported by a high-quality (although not necessarily large) expert secretariat would be the diffusion of knowledge in national capitals, another essential ingredient of consensus building. This would in turn facilitate a 'democratisation' of the policy-making process in member countries by making the debate more transparent and more inclusive.

In order to keep up to date and reasonably small in size, the WTO could not possibly generate all its policy analysis in-house. Like most research bodies today, the WTO Secretariat would have to establish a research network linked to other institutions such as the OECD, the Bretton Woods institutions, private think tanks, and universities and the like. Knowledge networks are key elements in promoting cooperation and coordination. This networking should also include NGOs, business groups (the International Chamber of Commerce, for example) and international labour associations.

While establishing an executive committee and improving the WTO's analytical and networking capabilities would help to entrench the legitimacy and credibility of the institution, these reforms alone would not do much to prevent further marginalisation of many developing countries, especially the least developed. Technical assistance and more effective coordination with other international institutions will be required.

The gap between rich and poor countries has been widening over the past three decades, largely due to differences in trend rates of growth of *per capita* income. The knowledge gap is far greater than the income gap, and in the absence of any change in domestic policies, as well as development policies directed at upgrading the institutional infrastructure, it is bound to widen. This growing marginalisation has little to do with trade, but that has not prevented the anti-globalisation movement blaming the WTO.

Clearly, the WTO, with very limited technical training resources (less than 1 per cent of its budget), cannot deal alone with the marginalisation problem. That may have been acceptable when trade policy was only about trade. But the much more demanding WTO agenda and the litigious and evidentiary-intensive dispute process has placed a burden on many non-OECD countries. The richer countries have access to analytical expertise at the OECD, at their home base, and also have far larger Geneva missions. So an upgrading of WTO training resources is urgently required. And this would also facilitate more effective coordination with the World Bank's efforts to improve the governance and institutional infrastructure, including legal systems and regulatory policies.

Reform of the WTO governance structure and enhanced research and training resources would help to tackle the 'democratic deficit', but the so-called 'trade and …' issues will require confronting the inadequacy of the postwar international architecture. In the absence of a stronger International Labour Organization (ILO) and a new environmental institution, the WTO will continue to be a magnet for policy overload.

If the objective of the American and other OECD unions is to improve working arrangements in developing countries, the mandate rests with the ILO. If it is not, then it is a matter for domestic policy designed to ameliorate the distributional consequences of adjustment to global forces. But the ILO has no power of enforcement. Moreover, many of its developing country members have resisted repeated attempts to improve enforcement capacity, while at the same time opposing labour standards in the WTO. This dilemma (or hypocrisy) must be resolved, and the ILO monitoring and enforcement mechanisms must be strengthened. But development institutions will also have to play their role, since labour standards are clearly linked to growth. In effect, what will be needed is reform of the ILO and more effective coordination with the WTO, the World Bank and UNCTAD, i.e. improved coherence in international policy making, which was in fact one of the objectives of the Uruguay Round, although at the time of the launch coherence was conceived in terms of coordination with only the Bretton Woods institutions.

While labour standards have no place in the WTO, the same cannot be said of environmental issues. Trade and the environment are linked in both positive and negative ways, as the recent report by the WTO has clearly demonstrated. But using trade policy as an instrument of environmental policy is both ineffective in terms of achieving environmental objection and costly in terms of growth. However, in the absence of a strong environmental institution (which the United Nations Environmental Program or UNEP is not) using the dispute settlement mechanism to define the boundary between domestic and international policies will not work, and the WTO will continue to be under attack. Only a new WEO (World Environmental Organization) with a clearly defined mission, political influence, and analytical and technical resources could launch the policy dialogue on the relationship between ecology and economy, including the role of trade. This will not be easy, because there really are significant differences between the two models – the economic and the ecological – even if we reject both utopian formulations. The economists' concepts of maximisation and trade-offs, of equilibrium and of the primacy of efficiency yield unambiguous policy statements. A defining characteristic of the ecological sciences is uncertainty, seen most vividly today in the rapid and unprecedented changes in biotechnology. If risk cannot be estimated accurately, then unambiguous assessments are precluded. What the eventual outcome of the debate will be remains to be seen. But an optimist would opine that where there is a political will there is a policy way. The best hope is that, unlike the Asian financial crisis in 1997, which led to much talk about architecture but little action, the experience in Seattle could prove to be the catalyst for a serious rethink of global policy.

References

Wallach, L. and Sforza, M. (1999) *Whose Trade Organization: Corporate Globalization and the Erosion of Democracy*, Washington: Public Citizen.
Weisbrot, M. (1999) *Globalization: A Primer*, Washington: Preamble Center.

23 Reforming WTO decision making

Lessons from Singapore and Seattle

Richard Blackhurst

A brief overview of decision making at two WTO ministerial conferences

Singapore, 12 December 1996. The first ministerial conference of the WTO was held in Singapore on 9–13 December 1996. The Singapore Ministerial Declaration issued at the end of the conference was based on a draft prepared in Geneva containing agreed text on all but some sensitive issues, including textiles and clothing, labour standards, investment, and competition policy. At the conference, an 'inner circle' composed of ministers from thirty-four of the WTO's 128 members took responsibility for arriving at an agreed text on the remaining issues.

The late evening session on 12 December was devoted to getting a consensus on the draft declaration, which had been finalised that day by the thirty-four-member inner circle. Most of the other ninety or so WTO members that had delegations in Singapore took the floor in turn, each making virtually identical interventions consisting of three points: first, they thanked the thirty-four members of the inner circle for their hard work; second, they said that although they had some reservations on certain points, they could join the consensus in favour of the draft declaration; and third, that the way in which the draft declaration had been prepared was undemocratic, unfair and disgraceful, that they were no longer willing to accept a decision-making process that always presented them with *faits accomplis*, and that they attached the highest priority to fundamentally revising the way in which important decisions are arrived at in the WTO. The conference chairman (Singapore's trade and industry minister) and the WTO's director-general solemnly assured delegates that this topic would be put at the top of the work agenda when the members resumed their work in Geneva the following month. Few people with a knowledge of the inner workings of the WTO were surprised when this experience failed to produce any improvements in WTO decision-making procedures.

Three years later, almost to the day, the venue shifts to Seattle.[1]

Seattle, 3 December 1999. Largely as a result of wide differences between WTO members concerning the desirability of including a number of complex and sensitive issues on the agenda of a new round, coupled with a preparatory process in Geneva seriously compromised by the prolonged and acrimonious process earlier in the year of selecting a new director-general, WTO ministers arrived in Seattle with little or no agreed text for a 'Seattle Ministerial Declaration' to launch a new round of multilateral negotiations. Near the end of the conference, the usual way of arriving at decisions (as exemplified by the thirty-four-member inner circle in Singapore) broke down completely. This time, comments by countries excluded from the 'green room meetings' – the name frequently given to inner circle meetings – found their way into the popular press. For example:

> 'No one combs our hair in our absence', said a furious Ugandan, as the talks lurched towards collapse.
>
> (*The Observer*, 5 December 1999)

> 'From the very beginning, we saw that the process was flawed', said Charles Norris, trade minister of the Dominican Republic. 'We want to make sure that the WTO pays attention to our needs'.
>
> (*Wall Street Journal*, European edition, 6 December 1999)

> 'Green rooms aren't in the WTO Glossary. Which clause is it in? Which article?' demanded Nicchoro Mw'wanda, a technical expert for the Kenyan delegation.
>
> (*Wall Street Journal*, European edition, 6 December 1999)

A tendency to deny the seriousness of what had happened was already evident among some delegates soon after their return to Geneva. It is helpful, therefore, to 'document' the situation further by quoting from other press reports from Seattle and the immediate post-Seattle period:

> Separate meetings of African and of Latin American and Caribbean countries Thursday night issued declarations threatening to quit the talks. 'African countries are being marginalised and generally excluded', read the African press release.
>
> (*Wall Street Journal*, European edition, 6 December 1999)

> The 'green room discussions', the next level of debate, this time mostly between the rich countries, were excluding the poor. At least one African delegate was physically barred from attending.
>
> (*The Observer*, 5 December 1999)

> The WTO's reputation for secrecy and elitism – criticised by outside protesters – was even roundly endorsed within its own ranks when many countries' delegates were excluded from the final round of talks held behind closed doors at the convention centre as leading nations tried desperately, but ultimately in vain, to hammer out a talks-saving pact.
>
> (*Financial Times*, 6 December 1999)

The 'green room' format was activated, that is, a single committee limited to 25 countries designed to make rapid progress in a short space of time. Developing country delegates, the intended beneficiaries of the new policies of transparency and inclusion, were outraged. Denouncing a return to what they charged were practices that sought to marginalise them, they pointedly warned they were ready to block consensus. Delegates contacted late Friday night after the breakdown were sharply critical of the conference and its organisers, arguing that they once again had been excluded from the real sources of power.

(Agence France-Presse, 4 December 1999)

The vast majority of developing countries were shut out of the whole green room process. They were not even informed which meetings were going on or what was being discussed. Ministers and senior officials of most developing countries were left hanging around in the corridors or the canteen, trying to catch snippets of news.

(*The Guardian*, 15 December 1999)

In the immediate aftermath of the failed ministerial conference, press reports quoted France, Japan and the WTO's director-general on the need for reform:

Tokyo – France and other nations agreed on the 'necessity of having a WTO ministerial meeting on its organization and procedures to make it more efficient, transparent and democratic', [Prime Minister Lionel Jospin] said.

(*International Herald Tribune*, 17 December 1999)

Tokyo – Japan plans to appeal to its trade partners to set up an advisory organization within the World Trade Organization aimed at ensuring greater transparency in the world trade body's decision-making process, government sources said Monday.

Tokyo expects the advisory organization to consist of representatives from some 20 to 30 nations, including both industrial and developing nations, and make proposals to reflect the interests of various WTO member countries, they said.

But any proposals put forward by the advisory organization would be nonbinding in view of the WTO's consensus-oriented decision-making rules, they said.

(Japan Economic Newswire via Dow Jones, 3 January 2000)

Auckland – 'It is evident that the way in which the WTO member governments reached decisions needs to be re-evaluated', [Director-General Mike] Moore wrote in a column in the New Zealand Herald newspaper.

'All significant decisions are made on the basis of consensus. Clearly, this principle must be retained. You cannot have a system of rules which are enforceable by a binding disputes settlement system unless everybody accepts those rules,' he said.

'Final decisions are always made in the general council or by the ministerial conference. But the deal-brokering that takes place in any negotiation is impossible in a room with 135 ministers.'

'Everybody acknowledges the need to have smaller groups thrash out the compromises, but no one wants to be excluded from those groups.'

(AFP via News EDGE, 5 January 2000)

Paris – France will propose reforms to the World Trade Organization at the start of its six-month stint as EU president beginning in July, French Trade Secretary François Huwart said Thursday.

Several ministers said [after the disastrous meeting in Seattle] that a key reason for their inability to narrow their differences was the sheer size of the organization, which made it difficult to achieve democratic discussion without the proceedings becoming too unwieldy to make any progress.

(Agence France-Presse, 13 January 2000)

Geneva – [Japan's International Trade and Industry Minister Takashi] Fukaya said Japan thinks it is useful to set up a small, informal forum in the WTO and that it is necessary to establish criteria for choosing the participants, such as trade volume, gross domestic product (GDP) and geography.

He also said it is important to ensure that the contents of its discussions are conveyed to non-participants.

(Kyodo News International Inc., 13 January 2000)

And, at the end of March in Geneva:

Geneva – [WTO] delegates on Tuesday started discussing how to improve the body's decision-making process to avoid a repetition of the collapse last December of attempts to launch a new trade round.

At an informal session of the body's General Council, envoys from the 135-member WTO also confirmed their guiding principle of making all decisions by consensus, trade sources said.

The WTO will tackle the tasks of improving the 'transparency and efficiency' of decision making simultaneously, trade sources said. Participants also suggested organizing more regular contacts through video conferencing and discussed how to make information more easily available to all members.

Japan suggested having the contents of discussions at informal meetings reported to formal meetings, thereby giving all members opportunities to express their opinions.

(Kyodo News International Inc., 29 March 2000)

The frustration and anger of countries routinely excluded from the green room meetings was not limited to their experiences in Seattle: 'Throughout the preparatory process [in Geneva] many of [the smaller countries] complained about semi-official meetings where the majority of Members could not participate' (ICTSD 2000: 4).

For the benefit of those readers who may be unfamiliar with the workings of the WTO, it is worth calling attention to three points. First, a very large proportion of the routine work takes place in committees, councils and other groups – that is, not in inner circles/green rooms.

Second, the processes by which WTO members discuss, debate and negotiate issues is distinct from the organisation's reliance on consensus to adopt decisions (the members have made it very clear that they plan to keep the emphasis on consensus decision making). Any organisation with a large membership, and in which all groups, committees and councils are open to all its members, is going to have a problem functioning, regardless of whether it takes decisions by consensus or by simple majority. It is that particular problem – the process by which WTO members arrive at the point where the entire membership is asked to adopt a particular decision – that is the subject of this paper.

Third, the question of reform of the WTO's decision-making process is not a North/South issue. Large and influential developing countries are regular participants in the green room meetings. It is, instead, a classic 'insider/outsider' issue, with the industrial countries and 'important' developing countries on the inside and all other WTO members on the outside.

The 'concentric circles' model

The inner circle/green room formula for creating discussion, consultation and negotiating groups small enough to function efficiently is known more generally as the 'concentric circles' model.[2] An issue-specific inner circle of members, varying in number (for example, from eight to thirty-four) depending on whether the topic is narrow and of interest to only a few members, or broader and of interest to a larger number of members, functions as a discussion, debating and negotiating group. It either reports the results of its efforts to a larger circle of members, which then repeats the process and sends the results of its efforts on to the next wider circle of members, or it reports directly to the entire membership. In either case, at the end of the process the entire membership is generally asked to take a consensus decision on the recommendations coming from the more restricted circle(s).

Simplifying somewhat, the evolution of the concentric circles model can be traced partly to the fact that for much of the GATT's history, most developing countries were neither interested in nor encouraged to be interested in participating actively in the 'management' of the GATT system – which meant that, for the most part, an inner circle could be constituted without excluding any (or at any rate, very many) of the members desiring to participate. When developing countries began to participate much more actively in GATT and then WTO activities, the concentric circles model became the organisation's *de facto* way of dealing with a very fundamental problem: while membership in virtu-ally every WTO body is open to all WTO members (currently 138), once the active participation in a group/committee exceeds a certain number (say twenty-five), discussion, debate and negotiation become increasingly cumber-some, inefficient and ultimately impossible. Organisations with a large membership traditionally deal with this problem by having an executive committee or board with a limited membership. As is discussed below, the IMF and the World Bank, for example, have twenty-four-member executive boards, and the UN has the Security Council. There is no corresponding *formal* body with limited membership in the WTO.

The reasons behind the growing participation of developing (and transi-tion) economies in GATT/WTO activities suggest very strongly that this trend can only intensify:

- The membership is growing. There were sixty-seven non-OECD GATT contracting parties in 1986, when the Uruguay Round was launched. At the time of the Seattle ministerial conference, the WTO had 103 non-OECD members, with thirty others at various stages in the accession process.
- Over the past fifteen years, a large number of developing countries – and virtually all the transition economies – have come to accept the view that a more liberal trade regime and fuller integration into the global economy must be a key part of their development strategies. And they understand that active participation in the WTO not only contributes importantly to both goals but also allows them to have a say in the evolution of the multilateral trading system.[3]
- In the Tokyo Round, the GATT began to write rules for policies applied 'inside the border', and that process continued in the Uruguay Round (especially services, the protection of intellectual property, and sanitary and phytosanitary measures). At Seattle, delegates were discussing invest-ment, competition policies, environment and workers' rights. Virtually all of these 'inside the border' issues are far more politically sensitive than policies applied at the border (tariffs, quotas and export subsidies), and as the GATT/WTO takes on these issues, countries are less and less willing to sit on the sidelines and let other countries do the work.
- Under the GATT, many of the rules governing trade-related policies were – officially or *de facto* – optional for developing countries. Under the WTO's 'single undertaking', every member is subject to all the rules.
- Whereas under the GATT any member had the power to block a dispute settlement case that it objected to, that option no longer exists. WTO dispute settlement progresses automatically, and a final decision by the Appellate Body is binding and cannot be appealed against.

Against this background, it is hardly surprising that the current informal (that is, opaque) and exclusionary process for deciding which WTO delegations to invite into green room meetings has come under increasing pressure.

Supporters of the concentric circles model stress that WTO members that have a strong stake in the outcome of a particular issue can gain access to the inner circle set-up to deal with that issue, and that such custom-designed, issue-specific groups are more likely to operate efficiently and effectively in the WTO context than 'fixed-membership' groups, such as the IMF and World Bank executive boards or the UN Security Council. This model is also viewed as contributing to the consensus approach to taking decisions. Members that were not in the inner circle, it is argued, will know that it was up to them to have made their claim for involvement earlier, rather than to block a consensus when the recommended decision is put to the entire membership.

The concentric circles model – heavily criticised by many WTO members in Singapore, and even more heavily criticised in the preparations for and activities in Seattle – has confronted two kinds of problem. The less serious of the two, which should not be too difficult to resolve, involves the perceived lack of transparency regarding what takes place in green room meetings (since, for the purposes of this article, 'inner circle' and 'green room meeting' are largely synonymous, I will generally use the latter term). A better-organised dissemination of information and documents to non-participants in time for them to react and have an input will be a major part of any solution (perhaps the four deputy directors-general could play more of a role here).

A much more serious problem occurs when the number of members demanding to participate in a green room meeting exceeds the limit imposed in order to ensure the group's efficiency and effectiveness. Certainly there are, and will continue to be, many issues that are of vital interest to only a limited number of WTO members. With equal certainty, we can be confident that – as in Singapore and Seattle – there will be issues of sufficiently broad interest to the membership that it will be necessary to exclude a significant number of interested members from the green room. Moreover, for the reasons noted above (the increasing membership, the WTO's growing involvement in politically sensitive policy areas), there is bound to be an increase in the number of instances in which it will be impossible to accommodate all the members desiring to participate in green room meetings.

Although the concentric circles model, in one or another of its possible versions, continues to enjoy significant support among WTO members (for reasons that are explored below), it is very difficult to avoid drawing two conclusions from the preceding discussion:

- In those instances in which interest among WTO members in the issue at hand is sufficiently narrow that a green room group can be constituted without excluding any member desiring to participate, this model functions well and should continue to be used. In other words, as a venue for special types of discussion, debate and negotiation, green room meetings – as well as bilateral meetings and all the other 'processes' that have been developed over the years in the GATT/WTO – will continue to be used.

- In those instances in which it is impossible to organise a green room meeting without excluding one or more WTO members wishing to be included, continued reliance on the concentric circles model can only progressively damage the WTO's ability to function, erode its internal and external credibility, and push the organisation even further back in the direction of more and more issues being seen – falsely and very unproductively – in North/South terms. Clearly, the WTO needs a sub-group of members of an efficient size for the purpose of discussing, debating and negotiating draft decisions that can be put to the entire membership for adoption. What needs changing is the basis for putting together such a sub-group, for deciding which delegations will be in the room and which delegations will be excluded. The new basis needs to be one that is fully transparent, predictable and equitable in the eyes of all WTO members.

One option for creating such a new sub-group of WTO members is developed below. First, however, it will be helpful to take a brief look at two types of sub-group, one from the GATT and one from the IMF and World Bank.

GATT's experience with CG.18

In 1975, the GATT's contracting parties established, on a temporary basis, a body that in a limited way resembled an executive board. Called the Consultative Group of Eighteen (CG.18), it was made a permanent body in 1979 and held its last meeting in 1987, as the Uruguay Round moved into high gear.[4] In its report to the GATT Council recommending that it become a permanent body, the CG.18 stated:

> It is strongly believed in the Group that the GATT should have at its disposal a small but representative group which would permit existing and emerging trade policy issues to be discussed in confidence among responsible officials from capitals, and thus facilitate an effective concentration of policies in the trade field.
>
> (GATT 1980: 285)

The CG.18, which met from two to four times a year, was not expected to deal with management issues ('How do you run an organisation where every committee is open to every member?') but rather to fulfil the major countries' desire for an issue-oriented consultative body of a manageable size whose participants would be senior officials from capitals.

Any thought of using the CG.18 as a rough blueprint for designing a new group that would move into action whenever a green room meeting could not accommodate all WTO members wishing to participate would have to begin by acknowledging that the CG.18 suffered – at least from today's perspective –

from a serious transparency problem. GATT contracting parties that did not have a seat on the CG.18 were barred from the meetings and did not receive CG.18 documents. A near-exclusive reliance on officials from capitals would also be unworkable, since the new group presumably would, from time to time, need to meet much more frequently than the CG.18. On the other hand, given the stated desire of WTO members to continue to rely on consensus decision making, any new group should follow the CG.18's fundamental principle of not taking any formal decisions but rather only making recommendations to the entire membership.

The 'executive director's' model

A board of twenty-four executive directors is the principal decision-making body in both the IMF and the World Bank. The IMF's Executive Board meets at least three times a week, while the bank's board of Executive Directors normally meets twice a week. Although there is provision for weighted voting in both organisations, both try as much as possible to work on the basis of consensus.

Eight executive directors represent individual countries on the IMF board (China, France, Germany, Japan, Russia, Saudi Arabia, the United Kingdom and the United States), and sixteen represent groupings of the remaining 174 members. The same eight countries have individual seats on the World Bank's board of executive directors. In the IMF, thirteen of the sixteen groups that share a board seat have between six and fourteen members, one has only four members (two of which are India and Bangladesh), and two groups of African countries have twenty and twenty-two members, respectively. The country composition of the sixteen groups of World Bank members is very similar to that of the sixteen IMF groups.[5]

Considering that the WTO is a rules-based organisation whose *raison d'être* is the provision of legally binding constraints on what countries can do in the area of trade-related policies, and that it is a one-country, one-vote organisation (in contrast to the weighted voting in the IMF and the World Bank), it is very unlikely that WTO members would be willing to create a board of executive directors that could take decisions that bind the entire membership.

A 'WTO consultative board'

The option developed in this paper for a new sub-group of WTO member countries involves creating what might be called a 'WTO consultative board'.[6] It would not be necessary to have predetermined, regularly scheduled meetings, since the board would normally meet only when a green room meeting could not accommodate all WTO members wishing to participate. The design and operating procedures of the new board would draw on the strong points of both the CG.18 and the IMF/World Bank boards while avoiding the shortcomings (from the perspective of the WTO's needs) of both.

As with the CG.18 (and the concentric circles model), the WTO consultative board would not be empowered to take decisions that bind the general membership. It would consult, discuss, debate and negotiate, but its output would be limited to recommendations put forward to the entire membership for approval/acceptance. And, as with the executive directors model, the board would be a formal part of the WTO organisation chart, and its composition – which members have a seat at the table and when – would be fixed (that is, predictable), presumably with the largest traders having individual seats and the remaining WTO members divided into groups, each with one seat that is shared between the members of the group on a rotating basis.

Minimising the exclusivity of a WTO consultative board

A major challenge would be to minimise the exclusivity of the board in the eyes of members that would have a seat at the table only on a rotating basis. The fact that the board could not take decisions would be vitally important from this perspective. Surely the other major factor would be transparency. I believe it would be crucial, as regards both substance and political acceptability, to make the work of the board fully transparent and accessible to all the members.

All WTO consultative board documents could be made available simultaneously to all WTO members. One could imagine an arrangement whereby members that were not at the table would be able to watch the deliberations of the board in their delegation offices on secure closed-circuit television. Another option, the pros and cons of which are hard for me to judge, would be to set up the meeting room with a table and chairs in the centre for the current members of the board, surrounded by seating for all the other WTO members, who would be free to observe – but not to intervene in – the proceedings. Along with increasing the political acceptability of such a board, a high degree of transparency along these lines would facilitate subsequent efforts to get a consensus because countries that were not members of the board would be aware of the nature of the 'give and take' involved in arriving at a decision to recommend to the entire membership.

Another way to minimise the exclusivity of the board, or at least the perceived down side to the exclusivity, would be to use broad similarities in interests and viewpoints on trade-related issues as the basis for composing the groups of WTO members that share seats. In this way, the members of any particular group – when it was not their turn to be at the table – would feel that at least their group's seat was occupied by a country that shared many of their concerns and priorities in the trade area. Composing the groups on this basis would not be an insurmountable task.[7]

Size of a WTO consultative board and allocation of seats

The question of how many seats the board should have would be very contentious.[8] One option for getting around this politically charged issue would be to follow the practice of the IMF and the World Bank, each of whose subgroups for discussion, debate and negotiation – that is, their respective boards – has twenty-four members.

Allocating seats would surely be the most contentious part of the task of creating a WTO consultative board. One approach would be to base seat allocation on some combination of three criteria: share of world trade and share of world GDP, 'tempered' by the fact that the WTO is a one-country/one-vote organisation (the board, of course, would never vote because it could not take formal decisions). Whatever the criteria, it is very likely that the United States, the European Union and Japan – which together account for nearly half of world merchandise trade (excluding intra-EU trade) – would have individual seats. The members of ASEAN could share a seat, as could members of other regional groupings. And so on.

As in the IMF and World Bank boards, the groupings could be self-selected and could have the option of 'self-changing' their composition, say once every two years. The countries in each group could also be given the freedom to decide how often to rotate the occupancy of the group's seat at the table. In general, the principle could be to allow as much flexibility as possible in order to accommodate a variety of situations (which can change over time).

A decision to have twenty-four seats would mean that the groups that share seats in the consultative board would have, on average, noticeably fewer members than the groups that share seats on the IMF' and World Bank boards, for two reasons: WTO membership is likely to remain below that of the IMF and the World Bank (182 and 181, respectively) for some time; and a WTO consultative board would presumably have fewer single-country seats than the eight single-country seats in the IMF and World Bank boards (for example, individual European Union member countries, three of which occupy individual country seats on the IMF and World Bank boards, would not be candidates for seats on the WTO board because the EU speaks for its fifteen members in the WTO).

The members of ASEAN share, among themselves, responsibility for covering WTO activities. In the case of the General Council, responsibility for covering the meetings and, when needed, intervening on behalf of the ASEAN group, is rotated among the members every six months. When it is the turn of one of the newer members of ASEAN, which is less experienced in WTO matters and may have fewer human resources available, the other ASEAN members help that country to carry out its responsibilities (preparation of interventions and so forth) *vis-à-vis* the General Council. Among other things, this is an important learning process for those newer and less experienced members.

There is no reason why each of the groups sharing a seat on a WTO consultative board should not function in much the same way. Cooperation between the self-selected group members to support whichever member currently occupies the seat would help to compensate for the shortage of experienced professionals – in Geneva and in support units back home – which plagues so many of the middle- and lower-income WTO members. It would be an important learning process – and morale builder – for the officials involved, both in

Geneva and in their own capitals. Domestically, the much more active involvement of these countries in important WTO activities – remember, they include the ninety or so members that have been routinely excluded from the green room meetings – would raise the profile of the WTO, and trade policy in general, in government circles and in the private sector. Governments that have been slow to recognise that commercial diplomacy has replaced political diplomacy as the critical priority for countries pursuing economic development would be encouraged to reallocate scarce human resources away from activities, abroad and at home, that contribute little or nothing to the country's economic development and put those resources to work on the WTO.[9]

The latter point calls attention to one of the most damaging aspects of the green room model, with its opaque basis for deciding which delegations are allowed into the room and its *de facto* permanent exclusion of more than three-quarters of the WTO membership. It is only human nature that if a country's senior trade officials – the Geneva ambassador and the cabinet minister responsible for trade – feel marginalised by the WTO, they will be inclined to marginalise the WTO at home. A new kind of sub-group of WTO members along the lines of a WTO consultative board could go a long way towards solving this problem.

Where will the opposition come from?

There are likely to be two overlapping sources of opposition to the proposal that a formal WTO consultative board be created to consult, discuss, debate and negotiate whenever a green room meeting cannot accommodate all WTO members that wish to participate.

First, there is very little doubt that the strongest and most vocal opposition to replacing the concentric circles model will come from a majority of the twenty to thirty members that are big enough to demand entry to any inner circle/green room they are interested in but not big enough to demand an individual seat on the new board. (A good idea of which delegations are in this category can be obtained by subtracting the United States, the European Union and Japan from the twenty-five countries reportedly invited to the green room meetings in Seattle, or from the thirty-four countries that drafted the Singapore ministerial communiqué. Bear in mind that the fifteen individual members of the European Union do not participate in the green room meetings.) Not long after their return from Seattle, at least some delegates from countries admitted to the Seattle green room meetings were privately denying that the green room model had been seriously discredited by what happened in Seattle – the same process of 'denial' that helped to torpedo the post-Singapore deliberations on decision-making reform. They argue that the press and isolated WTO delegations greatly exaggerated the extent to which the need to exclude many WTO delegations from the green room meetings had created serious problems.[10] Even worse are the frequently heard patronising remarks to the effect that the excluded delegations had nothing productive to contribute because they were unprepared and ignorant of the issues.

It is important not to underestimate the amount of hard work undertaken by the regular participants in WTO green room meetings – virtually all of whom are drawn from the same group of twenty to thirty WTO delegations – or the extent to which the individuals involved have contributed to the functioning of the WTO. At the same time, the countries excluded no doubt view the group of essentially permanent green room participants as an exclusive 'club' that has assumed responsibility for 'running the WTO'. Regular green room participants may not think of themselves as a club, but there is little doubt that many of them will exhibit a very club-like desire to protect their prerogatives against demands or proposals for reform that involve sharing those prerogatives more widely among the membership. And while it is undoubtedly true that many of the ninety-plus excluded delegations often are less well briefed on the issues, there is very much a 'chicken and egg' aspect to the situation – why should a delegation bother to use up scarce human resources to be fully prepared on the issues when it knows from experience that it will not be consulted on them?

A second source of opposition – and one that might find one or more of the United States, the European Union and Japan allied, at least to some degree, with other green room members – is the argument that it would be politically impossible to obtain a consensus on a proposal to replace the concentric circles model with a formal new body along the lines of a WTO consultative board. Without putting it to the test, there is no way of knowing whether or not this assertion is correct. What does seem clear is that if the ninety or so routinely excluded WTO members decide that they are no longer willing to be a part of the implicit consensus supporting the green room model, it will become totally unworkable.

A corollary of these observations is that, since they are the ones who are routinely excluded, it should not be difficult to convince the ninety or so medium-sized and small WTO members of the advantages of having a formal and fully representative alternative to the concentric circles model, one that can be activated whenever relying on a green room meeting would involve excluding WTO members. *Sharing a seat may not be ideal, but it is a lot better than never being allowed into the room.*

A discussion of which countries are likely to oppose or support the creation of a WTO consultative board would be incomplete without a brief mention of the response of many of the major countries to the signing, in Seattle, of the agreement establishing the new Advisory Centre on WTO Law (the only success in Seattle). The centre is a new international organisation that is completely independent of the WTO. The rationale for creating the centre is simple and compelling. While large and wealthy WTO members can afford to have experienced trade lawyers as regular full-time members of their delegations, this option is not available to most middle- and lower-income developing countries. They must turn to very expensive outside lawyers when they need qualified legal assistance. The main purpose of the new centre is to help to correct this imbalance by providing subsidised legal assistance to developing countries – in other words, to help them to defend their legal rights in the WTO.

Developed countries were asked to join the agreement and provide financial support. However, for several of them the usual keen interest in a 'level playing field' seems to evaporate when it comes to a country's ability to enforce its WTO rights. For example, the European Union (which strongly opposed the creation of the centre), the United States, Germany, France and Japan – all firm believers in the rule of law at home and in a rules-based trading system – did not sign the agreement in Seattle.[11] Although this development does not necessarily imply that the countries that failed to support the creation of the new centre would be 'unenthusiastic' about the creation of a WTO consultative board – and the more active participation of the middle- and lower-income developing countries in WTO activities that would result – the implications are not particularly encouraging.[12]

Predictability, transparency and – above all – legitimacy

Since any new sub-group of WTO members responsible for discussing, debating and negotiating an issue would be used only when a traditional inner circle/green room could not accommodate every member wishing to participate, the predictability, transparency and legitimacy of the new 'sub-group process' would be critically important. From this perspective, the IMF and World Bank boards have two very important characteristics: the board is a formal part of the organisation's structure, and every member country's 'participation rights' in the board are fully transparent and predictable. In other words, because the IMF and World Bank boards are integral parts of the organisations – each is a formal part of the organisation chart – they have predictability, transparency and, most important of all, legitimacy. This contrasts with the green room model – or for that matter, with any new informal, *ad hoc* WTO group that countries might be considering as a cosmetic response to the events in Seattle (and Singapore) – which lacks predictability, typically suffers from serious transparency problems and has none of the legitimacy that comes from being a formal part of the institution's organisational structure (witness, for example, the quote from the Kenyan delegate in Seattle).

This is why I believe it would be a very serious mistake if the perceived political difficulty of agreeing on a formal change in the WTO's structure led member countries to create yet another informal *ad hoc* 'group' or 'forum'. Any informal group or forum risks collapsing in acrimony and distrust at the first serious confrontation because it would have no 'structural strength' and would suffer from a 'deficit of legitimacy'. The new group must be a formal part of the organisation – on the WTO organisation chart and connected by a solid line, not a broken line, to the rest of the chart.[13]

A brief summing up

The risk facing the WTO is that the political challenge of obtaining a consensus on a fundamental reform of the decision-making process along the lines proposed in this paper, coupled with the GATT/WTO's traditional pragmatism, will create a nearly irresistible momentum to attempt to 'muddle through'. If the member countries and the director-general give in to this temptation, the prospects for the WTO to realise its full potential will be very bleak indeed.

As for the ninety or so WTO members that are routinely excluded from green room meetings, the choice is clear. If they want to see the creation of a formal and fully representative sub-group of WTO countries along the lines of a WTO consultative board, where each would have the opportunity to occupy a seat at the table periodically, and when they were not in the seat they would know that it is occupied by a fellow group member that shares their views on many issues and would listen to them when they want to make an input, they will have to fight for the change. The countries that have grown accustomed to 'running the show' at the GATT and now the WTO are not going to hand it to them on a silver platter.

Notes

This paper draws on work carried out during a six-week stay in 1999 as a visiting senior fellow at Stanford University's Center for Research on Economic Development and Policy Reform.

1 An intervening ministerial conference was held in Geneva in May 1998, devoted mainly to establishing the work programme for preparations for the Seattle ministerial conference and to a celebration of the fiftieth anniversary of the GATT/WTO system.
2 The discussions in the next two sections draw on Blackhurst (1998).
3 Although the vast majority of WTO members account for only a tiny proportion of world trade, a very large number of these 'tiny traders' have ratios of trade to GDP that are higher than the corresponding ratios of the big traders. For such countries, trade and the fair and efficient functioning of the multilateral trading system are crucial to their economic futures.
4 The group included nine alternative members, who were allowed to participate fully in the discussions. However, they were provided with only one seat each, in contrast to the two seats (one for an advisor) provided to each of the eighteen regular members. Membership in the CG.18 was increased to twenty-two in 1985.
5 The country composition of the sixteen 'shared seat' groups in each organisation may be found on their respective websites.
6 Obviously, there are other possible names for the new group. Including 'consultative' (or an approximate synonym, such as 'advisory') in the name would emphasise the fact – very important in dealing with the 'exclusivity' problem discussed below – that the group is not empowered to take decisions.
7 According to the World Bank website, the country groups in the board of executive directors 'more or less represent geographic regions with some political and cultural factors determining how they are constituted'.
8 Witness the current debate over proposals to expand the membership of the UN Security Council (see, for example, the *International Herald Tribune* of 5 April 2000).

9 See Blackhurst *et al.* (2000) for a specific proposal, involving the WTO's thirty-eight members from sub-Saharan Africa, along these lines.

10 Here it is important to emphasise that this paper does not argue that the Seattle ministerial conference failed because of the controversy over the exclusion of so many countries from the green room meetings. It is an open question what the impact of that controversy on the outcome of the conference would have been if there had not been such fundamental disagreements over proposals for the agenda of a new round.

11 Regarding the European Commission's position, see the *Financial Times* editorial of 18 February 1999. Nine developed countries did sign the Agreement in Seattle: Canada, Denmark, Finland, Ireland, Italy, the Netherlands, Norway, Sweden and the United Kingdom. Further details of the centre are available on the WTO website at http://www.wto.org in the section on the Trade and Development Centre.

12 The current state of the WTO's technical assistance budget is another reason to worry about the attitude of at least some of the major countries towards efforts to increase the ability of medium- and lower-income developing countries to partici-pate more fully in WTO activities (see Blackhurst *et al.* 2000).

13 An option to consider in building support for a formal consultative board would be to agree to include a 'sudden death' clause that provides for a trial period of, for example, three or four years.

References

Blackhurst, R. (1998) 'The capacity of the WTO to fulfill its mandate', in A. Krueger (ed.) *The WTO as an International Organization*, Chicago: University of Chicago Press, 31–58.

Blackhurst, R., Lyakurwa, B. and Oyejide, A. (2000), 'Options for improving Africa's participation in the WTO', *The World Economy* 23(4): 491–510.

GATT (1980) *Basic Instruments and Selected Documents*, 26th Supplement, Geneva.

International Centre for Trade and Sustainable Development (2000) *Bridges*, January–February, Geneva.

Index